A Complete Introduction to Corporate Taxation

A COMPLETE INTRODUCTION TO CORPORATE TAXATION

Reginald Mombrun

Gail Levin Richmond

CAROLINA ACADEMIC PRESS
Durham, North Carolina

ISBN 1-59460-075-9
LCCN 2006923929

CAROLINA ACADEMIC PRESS

700 Kent Street
Durham, NC 27701
Telephone (919) 489-7486
Fax (919) 493-5668
www.cap-press.com

Printed in the United States of America

This book is dedicated to my mother, Junie Mombrun. Thank you for loving us so much. We miss you, you'll always be in our thoughts, we can't wait to see you again. RM

This book is also dedicated to my wonderful daughter Bianca, my wonderful and lovely wife Orissa and my family. Thank you for all your love and support and thank you for being so proud of me. RM

TABLE OF CONTENTS

Preface   xxiii

Acknowledgments   xxv

Part One
Introduction

Chapter 1   The Tools Needed   5

Section 1.01 Coverage   5

Section 1.02 Tools Needed   5

Section 1.02(a) Internal Revenue Code   6

Section 1.02(b) Legislative History   7

Section 1.02(c) Regulations   8

Section 1.02(d) Judicial Decisions   9

Section 1.02(e) IRS Communications   9

Section 1.02(e)(1) Revenue Rulings and Revenue Procedures   9

Section 1.02(e)(2) Notices and Announcements   10

Section 1.02(e)(3) Private Letter Ruling (PLR)   10

Section 1.02(e)(4) Technical Advice Memorandum (TAM)   10

Section 1.02(e)(5) Field Service Advice (FSA) and
General Counsel Memorandum (GCM)   10

Section 1.02(e)(6) IRS Chief Counsel Advice (CCA)   11

Section 1.02(f) Other Documents   11

Chapter 2   Glossary of Terms Used   13

Document Terms   13

Government Entity Terms   13

Business Entity or Owner Terms   13

Other Terms   14

Chapter 3   Tax Policy and Tax Doctrines   15

Section 3.01 Tax Policy in General   15

Section 3.02 Economic Rationale for Tax Laws   15
Section 3.03 Tax Doctrines   16
Section 3.03(a) Substance over Form   17
Section 3.03(b) Business Purpose   18
Section 3.03(c) Step Transaction   20
Section 3.03(c)(1) End Result Test   20
Section 3.03(c)(2) Mutual Interdependence Test   20
Section 3.03(c)(3) Binding Commitment Test   21

Part Two
Taxation of C Corporations

Chapter 4   Overview of Subchapter C   25
Section 4.01 Introduction to the Double Tax Regime   25
Section 4.02 Why Do Taxpayers Accept Double Taxation?   26
Section 4.03 Differences between Corporate
and Individual Taxation   27
Section 4.03(a) Corporate Deductions versus
Individual Deductions   28
Section 4.03(b) Corporate versus Individual Tax Rates   29
Section 4.03(c) The Corporate Taxable Year
and Method of Accounting   30
Section 4.04 The LLC and the Check-the-Box Regulations   31
Section 4.05 Summary of Subchapter C   32

Chapter 5   Formation of Corporations   33
Section 5.01 Introduction   33
Section 5.02 Relevant Code Sections   33
Section 5.03 Synopsis of Section 351   34
Section 5.04 The General Rule   35
Section 5.04(a) Transfer of Property   36
Section 5.04(a)(1) Property   36
Section 5.04(a)(2) Transfer   37
Section 5.04(a)(3) Transferee   38
Section 5.04(b) Person or Persons   39
Section 5.04(c) Received Only Stock   40
Section 5.04(c)(1) General Rule   40
Section 5.04(c)(2) Preferred Stock   40
Section 5.04(c)(3) Nonqualified Preferred Stock   40
Section 5.04(d) Control   43
Section 5.04(e) Control Immediately After the Transfer   43

Section 5.04(e)(1) Disposition of Stock Acquired   43
Section 5.04(e)(2) Nonsimultaneous Transfers   44
Section 5.04(e)(3) Dispositions by Corporate Transferor   45
Section 5.04(f) Control Group Issues   45
Section 5.04(f)(1) Additional Transfers
    by Controlling Shareholder   45
Section 5.04(f)(2) Stock Received for Services   46
Section 5.05 Tax Consequences of the Transferor(s)   47
Section 5.05(a) Gain or Loss Recognition   47
Section 5.05(a)(1) General Rule   47
Section 5.05(a)(2) Receipt of Other Property   47
Section 5.05(a)(3) Assumption of Liabilities   48
Section 5.05(a)(3)(A) General Rule   48
Section 5.05(a)(3)(B) Tax Avoidance Motives   49
Section 5.05(a)(3)(C) Liabilities in Excess of Basis   50
Section 5.05(b) Basis of Stock Received   51
Section 5.05(b)(1) General Rule   51
Section 5.05(b)(2) Allocating Basis to Stock Received   52
Section 5.05(b)(2)(A) Multiple Properties Transferred   52
Section 5.05(b)(2)(B) Multiple Classes of Stock Received   52
Section 5.05(b)(3) Assumption of Liabilities   53
Section 5.05(c) Holding Period   54
Section 5.06 Tax Consequences to the Corporation   54
Section 5.06(a) Gain or Loss Recognition   54
Section 5.06(b) Basis of Property Received   55
Section 5.06(b)(1) General Rule   55
Section 5.06(b)(2) Section 362(e)   55
Section 5.06(b)(2)(A) Section 362(e)(1)   56
Section 5.06(b)(2)(B) Section 362(e)(2)   56
Section 5.06(c) Holding Period of Property Received   57
Section 5.07 Transfers That Are Ineligible for Section 351   57
Section 5.07(a) Transfers to an Investment Company   57
Section 5.07(a)(1) Transfers in a Title 11 Proceeding   59
Section 5.08 Cross References   59
Section 5.09 Overlap between Section 351 and Other Code Sections   60
Section 5.10 Miscellaneous Procedural Matters   61

Chapter 6 Capital Structure   63
Section 6.01 In General   63
Section 6.02 Relevant Code Sections   63

Section 6.03 Debt versus Equity   64
Section 6.03(a) In General   64
Section 6.03(b) Regulatory Authority   65
Section 6.03(c) Factors in Determining Debt or Equity Status   65
Section 6.03(c)(1) Section 385(b)   65
Section 6.03(c)(2) Judicial Tests   66
Section 6.04 Hybrid Instruments   67
Section 6.05 Characterization by Issuer   67

Part Three
Corporate Distributions

Chapter 7   Corporate Dividends   71
Section 7.01 Introduction   71
Section 7.02 Relevant Code Sections   71
Section 7.02(a) Section 301(a) Requirements   72
Section 7.02(b) Section 317 Requirements   72
Section 7.02(c) Section 301(c) Treatment   73
Section 7.02(d) Section 316 Current and Accumulated E&P   74
Section 7.02(d)(1) Current E&P   74
Section 7.02(d)(2) Accumulated E&P   74
Section 7.02(d)(3) Illustration of Current
    and Accumulated E&P   74
Section 7.02(e) Allocating E&P to Distributions   75
Section 7.02(e)(1) Single Distribution During Year   75
Section 7.02(e)(2) Multiple Distributions During Year   76
Section 7.02(f) Special Tax Consequences of Dividend Treatment   77
Section 7.02(f)(1) Individual Shareholders   78
Section 7.02(f)(2) Corporate Shareholders   79
Section 7.03 Distributions of Property Other Than Cash   79
Section 7.03(a) Shareholder's Tax Consequences   80
Section 7.03(b) Corporation's Tax Consequences   80
Section 7.03(c) Examples: Distributions of
    Unencumbered Property   81
Section 7.03(d) Distributions of Encumbered Property   82
Section 7.03(e) Distributions of Corporate Obligations   83
Section 7.04 Distributions of the
    Corporation's Own Stock and Rights   83
Section 7.04(a) Distributions of Stock and
    Stock Rights: General Tax Rule   84

Section 7.04(a)(1) Shareholder's Gross Income   84
Section 7.04(a)(2) Shareholder's Basis for Stock or Rights   84
    Section 7.04(a)(2)(A) General Rule   85
    Section 7.04(a)(2)(B) Special Rules for Stock Rights   85
Section 7.04(a)(3) Shareholder's Holding Period
    for Stock or Rights   86
Section 7.04(a)(4) Effect on Corporation
    Making the Distribution   87
Section 7.04(b) Distributions of Stock and Stock Rights: Exceptions 87
    Section 7.04(b)(1) Transactions Covered   88
        Section 7.04(b)(1)(A) Distributions in Lieu of Money   88
        Section 7.04(b)(1)(B) Disproportionate Distributions   88
        Section 7.04(b)(1)(C) Distributions of Common
            and Preferred Stock   89
        Section 7.04(b)(1)(D) Distributions on Preferred Stock   90
        Section 7.04(b)(1)(E) Distributions of Convertible
            Preferred Stock   90
        Section 7.04(b)(1)(F) Transactions Treated as Distributions   90
    Section 7.04(b)(2) Shareholders' Tax Consequences   91
    Section 7.04(b)(3) Corporation's Tax Consequences   91
Section 7.04(c) Eisner v. Macomber and Financial Accounting   91
Section 7.05 Computing E&P   92
Section 7.05(a) Introduction   92
Section 7.05(b) Differences in Computing Taxable
    Income and E&P   93
    Section 7.05(b)(1) Items Excluded from Gross Income   93
    Section 7.05(b)(2) Income Tax Deductible Items   93
    Section 7.05(b)(3) Income Tax Nondeductible Items   93
    Section 7.05(b)(4) Timing Items   94

Chapter 8   Redemption Distributions   95
Section 8.01 Introduction   95
Section 8.02 Relevant Code Sections   96
Section 8.03 Section 318 Attribution Rules   96
Section 8.03(a) Types of Attribution   97
    Section 8.03(a)(1) Family Attribution (Section 318(a)(1))   97
        Section 8.03(a)(1)(A) Family Dissension   97
        Section 8.03(a)(1)(B) Indirect Ownership   98
    Section 8.03(a)(2) Attribution from Entities (Section 318(a)(2))   98
        Section 8.03(a)(2)(A) Attribution from Estates   98

Section 8.03(a)(2)(B) Attribution from Partnerships
and S Corporations   99
Section 8.03(a)(2)(C) Attribution from Trusts   99
Section 8.03(a)(2)(D) Attribution from C Corporations   100
Section 8.03(a)(3) Attribution to Entities (Section 318(a)(3))   101
Section 8.03(a)(3)(A) Attribution to Estates   101
Section 8.03(a)(3)(B) Attribution to Partnerships
and S Corporations   101
Section 8.03(a)(3)(C) Attribution to Trusts   102
Section 8.03(a)(3)(D) Attribution to C Corporations   102
Section 8.03(a)(4) Option Attribution   103
Section 8.03(a)(5) Operating Rules   103
Section 8.03(a)(5)(A) General Rule   103
Section 8.03(a)(5)(B) Exceptions   104
Section 8.03(a)(5)(C) Option Attribution   105
Section 8.04 Section 302   105
Section 8.04(a) Redemptions Covered by Section 302   105
Section 8.04(b) Substantially Disproportionate
Redemptions (Section 302(b)(2))   105
Section 8.04(b)(1) Ownership Percentage After
the Redemption   106
Section 8.04(b)(2) Reduction in Voting Stock After
the Redemption   106
Section 8.04(b)(3) Reduction in Common Stock
After the Redemption   107
Section 8.04(b)(4) Special Rules   107
Section 8.04(b)(4)(A) Redemption of Preferred Stock   107
Section 8.04(b)(4)(B) Series of Redemptions   108
Section 8.04(b)(4)(C) Multiple Redemptions   108
Section 8.04(b)(5) Constructive Ownership   109
Section 8.04(c) Complete Terminations (Section 302(b)(3))   109
Section 8.04(c)(1) Avoiding Attribution   109
Section 8.04(c)(1)(A) Family Attribution   110
Section 8.04(c)(1)(B) Entity Attribution   112
Section 8.04(d) Partial Liquidation (Section 302(b)(4))   113
Section 8.04(d)(1) Qualified Recipient   114
Section 8.04(d)(2) Qualified Distribution   114
Section 8.04(e) Not Essentially Equivalent to a Dividend   115
Section 8.05 Section 303   116

Section 8.05(a) Introduction   116
Section 8.05(b) Requirements   116
Section 8.05(b)(1) Inclusion of Shares in Decedent's Estate   117
Section 8.05(b)(2) Portion of Estate Represented by Stock   117
Section 8.05(b)(3) Limitation on
    Qualifying Redemption Amount   118
Section 8.05(b)(4) Redemptions from Other Shareholders   119
Section 8.05(b)(5) Time Limit for Completing Redemption   119
Section 8.06 Redemptions Using Related Corporations Section 304   119
Section 8.06(a) Brother-Sister (Sibling) Redemptions   120
Section 8.06(a)(1) Control—General Rule   120
Section 8.06(a)(1)(A) Control—Constructive Ownership   121
Section 8.06(a)(1)(B) Control—Stock Acquired
    in Transaction   122
Section 8.06(a)(1)(C) Control—Ownership Chains   122
Section 8.06(a)(2) Testing the Redemption   123
Section 8.06(b) Parent-Subsidiary Redemptions   123
Section 8.06(c) Interrelationship of Sections 304 and 351   124
Section 8.06(d) E&P Computations   124
Section 8.07 Dispositions of Certain Preferred Stock Section 306   124
Section 8.07(a) Definition of Section 306 Stock   125
Section 8.07(b) Transactions Covered by Section 306   126
Section 8.07(b)(1) Redemptions of Section 306 Stock   126
Section 8.07(b)(2) Other Dispositions of Section 306 Stock   127
Section 8.07(b)(3) Avoiding Dividend Treatment   128
Section 8.07(b)(3)(A) Redemptions   128
Section 8.07(b)(3)(B) Non-Redemption Dispositions   128
Section 8.07(b)(3)(C) All Dispositions   129
Section 8.08 Tax Consequences of Redemptions   129
Section 8.08(a) Redeeming Corporation   130
Section 8.08(a)(1) Gain or Loss   130
Section 8.08(a)(2) Incidental Outlays   130
Section 8.08(a)(3) E&P   130
Section 8.08(b) Redeemed Shareholders   131
Section 8.08(b)(1) Gain or Loss   131
Section 8.08(b)(2) Dividend Income   132
Section 8.08(b)(3) Basis   132
Section 8.08(c) Other Shareholders   133
Section 8.09 Determining the Appropriate Taxpayer   134

Section 8.09(a) Transfer of Control Using Corporate Funds   134
Section 8.09(b) Transfer of Stock in Marital Dissolution   135

Part Four
Corporate Fissions, Fusions, and Liquidations

Chapter 9   Corporate Fissions: Section 355   **139**
Section 9.01 Introduction   139
Section 9.01(a) Overview   139
Section 9.01(b) Types of Section 355 Transactions   140
Section 9.02 Relevant Code Sections   142
Section 9.03 Basic Requirements   143
Section 9.03(a) Distribution of Stock or Securities   143
Section 9.03(b) Distribution of Controlled Corporation   144
Section 9.03(b)(1) In General   144
Section 9.03(b)(2) Control Immediately before the Distribution 145
Section 9.03(b)(3) Impact of Warrants and Options   147
Section 9.03(c) The Anti-Device Requirement   147
Section 9.03(c)(1) Device Factors   148
Section 9.03(c)(1)(A) Pro Rata Distribution   148
Section 9.03(c)(1)(B) Subsequent Sale or Exchange of Stock   149
Section 9.03(c)(1)(C) Nature and Use of Assets   151
Section 9.03(c)(2) Non-Device Factors   152
Section 9.03(c)(2)(A) Corporate Business Purpose   152
Section 9.03(c)(2)(B) Distributing Corporation is
    Publicly Traded and Widely Held   153
Section 9.03(c)(2)(C) Distribution to Domestic
    Corporate Shareholder   153
Section 9.03(c)(3) Transactions Not Ordinarily
    Considered Devices   153
Section 9.03(c)(3)(A) No E&P or Gain Potential   153
Section 9.03(c)(3)(B) Qualified Redemption   155
Section 9.03(c)(4) Section 355 PLRs   155
Section 9.03(d) The Active Trade or Business Requirement   156
Section 9.03(d)(1) In General   156
Section 9.03(d)(2) Definition of Trade or Business   156
Section 9.03(d)(3) What Constitutes "Active"?   157
Section 9.03(d)(4) Ownership of Real Property   159
Section 9.03(d)(5) Activities of Independent Contractors   159
Section 9.03(d)(6) Employees of Related Entities   160

Section 9.03(d)(7) Active Trade or Business in a Partnership   160
Section 9.03(d)(8) Attribution of Active Trade
  or Business from a Corporation   161
Section 9.03(d)(9) The Five-year Requirement   162
Section 9.03(d)(10) Expansion of a Business   164
Section 9.03(e) The Continuity of Interest Requirement   164
Section 9.03(f) The Business Purpose Requirement   165
Section 9.03(f)(1) Criteria for Business Purpose   166
Section 9.03(f)(2) Deciphering the Business Purpose   166
Section 9.04 Transactions Kicked out of Section 355   168
Section 9.04(a) In General   168
Section 9.04(b) Section 355(d)—In General   170
Section 9.04(b)(1) Disqualified Distribution   171
Section 9.04(c) Section 355(e)   172
Section 9.04(c)(1) Plan   173
Section 9.04(d) Section 355(f)   174
Section 9.05 Tax Consequences of Distributing Corporation   177
Section 9.05(a) Gain or Loss   177
Section 9.05(b) Liabilities Transfer—General Rule   177
Section 9.05(b)(1) Section 357(b) Exception   178
Section 9.05(b)(2) Section 357(c) Exception   178
Section 9.05(b)(3) Changes to Section 357(c) Made in 2004   179
Section 9.05(c) Gain or Loss in D/355 Transactions   179
Section 9.05(d) Other Tax Consequences   179
Section 9.06 Shareholders' Tax Consequences   180
Section 9.06(a) Gain or Loss   180
Section 9.06(a)(1) Section 355(a)   181
Section 9.06(a)(1)(A) Definition of Stock   181
Section 9.06(a)(1)(B) Receipt of Boot   182
Section 9.06(a)(1)(C) Retained Stock   182
Section 9.06(a)(2) Receipt of Securities   183
Section 9.06(a)(3) Receipt of Property Attributable
  to Accrued Interest   183
Section 9.06(a)(4) Characterization of Boot Received   183
Section 9.06(b) Basis of Stock or Securities   184
Section 9.06(b)(1) Basis of Stock   184
Section 9.06(b)(2) Basis of Securities and Other Boot Received   185
Section 9.06(c) Holding Period   185
Section 9.07 Distributing Corporation's Tax Attributes   186

Section 9.08 Controlled Corporation's Tax Consequences   187
Section 9.08(a) In General   187
Section 9.08(b) Recognition of Gain or Loss   187
Section 9.08(c) Basis of Controlled Corporation's Assets   188
Section 9.08(d) Transfer of Tax Attributes   188
Section 9.09 Tax Consequences of
Taxable Spin-off   189
Section 9.09(a) Recognition of Gain or Loss   189
Section 9.09(b) Basis of Stock   190
Section 9.09(c) Transfer of Tax Attributes   190
Section 9.10 Review   190
Section 9.11 Conclusion   192

Chapter 10   Corporate Reorganizations   195
Section 10.01 Introduction   195
Section 10.01(a) Origin of Reorganization Provisions   195
Section 10.01(b) Defining Reorganization   195
Section 10.01(c) Significance of Attaining Reorganization Status   196
Section 10.02 What Is a Reorganization?   196
Section 10.03 Reorganization Terminology   201
Section 10.04 General Reorganization Requirements   201
Section 10.04(a) Business Purpose   201
Section 10.04(b) Continuity of Interest (COI)   202
Section 10.04(c) Continuity of Business Enterprise (COBE)   203
Section 10.04(d) Step Transaction Doctrine   203
Section 10.05 Technical Reorganization Requirements   205
Section 10.05(a) In General   205
Section 10.05(b) Technical Requirements of A Reorganizations   205
Section 10.05(b)(1) The Temporary Regulations   206
Section 10.05(b)(2) The Triangular A Reorganizations   207
Section 10.05(b)(2)(A) The Forward Triangular Merger   208
Section 10.05(b)(2)(B) Liabilities of Disregarded Entities   209
Section 10.05(b)(2)(C) Basis in Triangular Reorganizations   210
Section 10.05(b)(2)(D) The Reverse Triangular Merger   212
Section 10.05(c) Technical Requirements of the B Reorganization   214
Section 10.05(c)(1) Creeping B Reorganizations   214
Section 10.05(c)(2) IRS Concerns   216
Section 10.05(d) Technical Requirements of the C Reorganization   216
Section 10.05(d)(1) The Solely for Voting Stock Requirement   217
Section 10.05(d)(2) Creeping C Reorganizations   218

Section 10.05(d)(3) The Liquidation Requirement   219
Section 10.05(d)(4) The Substantially All Requirement   219
Section 10.05(d)(5) Final Concerns   220
Section 10.05(e) Technical Requirements of the D Reorganization 222
Section 10.05(e)(1) Transfer of Assets   222
Section 10.05(e)(2) The Control Requirement   223
Section 10.05(e)(3) The Distribution Requirement   224
Section 10.05(f) Technical Requirements of the E Reorganization 225
Section 10.05(f)(1) Boot Concerns   227
Section 10.05(f)(2) COI and COBE in Recapitalizations   227
Section 10.05(g) Technical Requirements of the F Reorganization 229
Section 10.05(g)(1) Change of Tax Status   229
Section 10.05(g)(2) Identification of Shareholders   230
Section 10.05(g)(3) Benefits of the F Reorganization   231
Section 10.05(h) G Reorganizations   231
Section 10.05(i) Drop Downs of Assets and Push Ups   232
Section 10.05(i)(1) Push Ups of Assets   233
Section 10.06 Reorganizations Involving Investment Companies 234
Section 10.07 Tax Consequences to Shareholders   236
Section 10.07(a) In General   236
Section 10.07(b) Party to a Reorganization   236
Section 10.07(c) Gain or Loss to Acquiring Shareholders 238
Section 10.07(d) Gain or Loss to Target Shareholders   238
Section 10.07(d)(1) Nonqualified Preferred Stock   240
Section 10.07(d)(2) Transaction Involving Railroads   241
Section 10.07(d)(3) Warrants   241
Section 10.07(e) Treatment of Boot   241
Section 10.07(f) Basis Consequences to
    Target Shareholders   243
Section 10.07(f)(1) Rationale of Section 358   244
Section 10.07(f)(2) Assumption of Liability   246
Section 10.07(g) Holding Period of Acquiring Stock
    in the Hands of Target Shareholders   246
Section 10.08 Tax Consequences to
    the Acquiring Corporation   246
Section 10.08(a) Gain/Loss   247
Section 10.08(b) Basis Consequences to
    the Acquiring Corporation   247
Section 10.08(c) Holding Period   248

Section 10.08(d) Carryover of Tax Items   248
Section 10.09 Tax Consequences to the Target Corporation   249
Section 10.09(a) Gain or Loss   249
Section 10.09(b) Basis and Holding Period of Property Received   249
Section 10.10 Reporting Requirements for Taxable Reorganizations Imposed by The American Jobs Creation Act of 2004   250

Chapter 11   Corporate Liquidations   **251**
Section 11.01 Introduction   251
Section 11.02 Relevant Code Sections   251
Section 11.02(a) Liquidations   251
Section 11.02(b) Section 338 Deemed Asset Purchases   252
Section 11.03 Liquidations of Corporations
other than Subsidiaries   252
Section 11.03(a) Introduction   252
Section 11.03(b) Liquidating Corporation's Tax Consequences   252
Section 11.03(b)(1) General Rule   252
Section 11.03(b)(2) Loss Disallowance Rules   253
Section 11.03(b)(2)(A) Capital Losses   253
Section 11.03(b)(2)(B) Related Parties   253
Section 11.03(b)(2)(C) Property Received
in Nonrecognition Transactions   255
Section 11.03(b)(3) Effect of Liabilities   256
Section 11.03(b)(4) Earnings & Profits Account   256
Section 11.03(c) Recipient Shareholder's Tax Consequences   256
Section 11.03(c)(1) Gains and Losses   256
Section 11.03(c)(2) Basis for Property Received   257
Section 11.03(c)(3) Holding Period for Property Received   257
Section 11.04 Liquidations of Corporate Subsidiaries   257
Section 11.04(a) Introduction   257
Section 11.04(a)(1) Ownership Requirement   258
Section 11.04(a)(2) Liquidation Completion Requirement   258
Section 11.04(a)(3) Plan of Liquidation   259
Section 11.04(b) Liquidating Corporation's Tax Consequences   260
Section 11.04(b)(1) General Rule   260
Section 11.04(b)(2) Distributions to Minority Shareholders   260
Section 11.04(b)(3) Earnings & Profits Account
and Other Tax Attributes   261
Section 11.04(c) Recipient Shareholders' Tax Consequences   261

Section 11.04(c)(1) Gains and Losses   261
Section 11.04(c)(2) Basis for Property Received   262
Section 11.04(c)(3) Holding Period for Property Received   264
Section 11.04(c)(4) Earnings & Profits and Other Attributes   264

Chapter 12   Section 338   **265**
Section 12.01 Introduction   265
Section 12.01(a) Significance of Section 338   265
Section 12.01(b) Origins of Section 338   266
Section 12.02 Section 338 Terminology   267
Section 12.03 Qualifying for Section 338   267
Section 12.03(a) Required Amount of Stock   268
Section 12.03(b) Purchase   268
Section 12.03(c) Acquisition Period   268
Section 12.03(d) The Section 338 Election   269
Section 12.04 Effect of Section 338 Election   269
Section 12.05 Target Corporation's Tax Consequences   270
Section 12.05(a) Gain or Loss on Deemed Sale   270
Section 12.05(a)(1) 100 percent of Target's Stock Acquired   270
Section 12.05(a)(2) Less Than 100 percent of
Target's Stock Acquired   271
Section 12.05(b) Basis for Assets Deemed Purchased   271
Section 12.05(b)(1) Total Basis   272
Section 12.05(b)(1)(A) Basis Attributable to Stock   272
Section 12.05(b)(1)(B) Election for
Nonrecently Purchased Stock   273
Section 12.05(c) Allocation Rules   273
Section 12.05(d) Holding Period   274
Section 12.06 Asset and Stock Consistency Rules   274
Section 12.06(a) Statutory Provisions   274
Section 12.06(b) Regulations   275
Section 12.07 Section 338(h)(10) Election   276
Section 12.07(a) In General   276
Section 12.07(b) Step Transaction Issues   276
Section 12.08 Section 1060   277
Section 12.08(a) Introduction   277
Section 12.08(b) Applicable Asset Acquisition   277
Section 12.08(c) Asset Allocation Rules   278
Section 12.08(d) Holding Period   278

Chapter 13   Carryover of Tax Attributes   279
Section 13.01 Introduction   279
Section 13.02 Relevant Code Sections   279
Section 13.03 Section 381   279
    Section 13.03(a) Scope   279
    Section 13.03(b) Acquisitions Covered   280
    Section 13.03(c) Acquiring Corporation   280
    Section 13.03(d) Attributes   281
Section 13.04 Section 381(b) Operating Rules   282
    Section 13.04(a) End of Taxable Year   282
    Section 13.04(b) Date of Distribution or Transfer   282
    Section 13.04(c) NOL and Capital Loss Carryovers   283
Section 13.05 Tax Attributes Governed by Section 381   284
    Section 13.05(a) Overview   284
    Section 13.05(b) NOL Carryovers   284
    Section 13.05(c) Capital Loss Carryovers   285
    Section 13.05(d) E&P Carryovers   285
    Section 13.05(e) Accounting Methods   286
Section 13.06 Section 382   286
    Section 13.06(a) Comparison to Section 381   286
    Section 13.06(b) Section 382 Loss Limitation   286
    Section 13.06(c) Section 382 Definitions   287
        Section 13.06(c)(1) Loss Corporation   287
        Section 13.06(c)(2) Ownership Change   287
    Section 13.06(d) Operation of Section 382   288
Section 13.07 Section 383   289
Section 13.08 Section 384   289

Part Five
Controlled Corporations, Affiliated Corporations, and Consolidated Returns

Chapter 14   Controlled Corporations and Affiliated Corporations   293
Section 14.01 Introduction   293
Section 14.02 Controlled Corporations   293
    Section 14.02(a) In General   293
        Section 14.02(a)(1) Parent-Subsidiary Controlled Group   294
        Section 14.02(a)(2) Brother-Sister Controlled Group   294
        Section 14.02(a)(3) Combined Group   296
        Section 14.02(a)(4) Insurance Group   297

Section 14.03 Restrictions Applied to a Controlled Group   297
Section 14.04 Affiliated Groups   298
   Section 14.04(a) In General   298
   Section 14.04(b) Definition of Affiliated Group   298
   Section 14.04(c) The 80 percent Test   299
   Section 14.04(d) Reconsolidation Following Disaffiliation   299
   Section 14.04(e) Definition of Stock   300
      Section 14.04(e)(1) Statutory Definition   300
      Section 14.04(e)(2) Regulations   301
      Section 14.04(e)(3) Notice 2004-37   302
   Section 14.04(f) Ineligible Corporations   302
      Section 14.04(f)(1) General Rule   302
      Section 14.04(f)(2) Exceptions   303

Chapter 15   Consolidated Returns   307
Section 15.01 Introduction   307
Section 15.02 Consolidated Return Issues   308
   Section 15.02(a) In General   308
   Section 15.02(b) Deciding to File Consolidated Returns   308
Section 15.03 Consent to File Consolidated Returns   309
Section 15.04 Difficulty in Deconsolidating   309
Section 15.05 Group Remaining in Existence   311
Section 15.06 Computation of Income
   and Liability for Tax   312
Section 15.07 Intercompany Transaction Rules   313
   Section 15.07(a) In General   313
   Section 15.07(b) What Is an Intercompany Transaction?   313
   Section 15.07(c) Matching and Acceleration Rules   314
Section 15.08 The Basis Investment Adjustment Rules   315
   Section 15.08(a) Introduction   315
   Section 15.08(b) Adjustments to Basis   315
Section 15.09 Loss Disallowance Regulations   316

Table of Cases   319

Table of Revenue Rulings   321

Table of Revenue Procedures   323

Index   325

PREFACE

Welcome to A Complete Introduction to Corporate Taxation. This book reflects the co-authors' experiences over several years of teaching and practice. One author has taught individual and corporate taxation for many years and has written several books and articles. The other practiced tax law for more than fourteen years in the IRS National Office, drafted numerous regulations, revenue rulings, revenue procedures, and articles in the corporate tax area, and has been responsible for countless private letter rulings on corporate tax. The knowledge each of us has gained should provide the reader a sound understanding of corporate taxation.

Although this book provides in-depth explanations, it cannot substitute for up-to-date research. As you learned in the individual tax course, tax laws are complex and in constant flux.

Acknowledgments

This book would not have been possible without the financial help provided by the FAMU College of Law through summer grants and research assistants. I am also greatly indebted to the College of Law's Library for their support and the faculty at the College of Law for having given me this wonderful opportunity. I also thank my research assistants Yolanda Washington and Joshua Meyer for their help. RM

A COMPLETE INTRODUCTION TO
CORPORATE TAXATION

PART ONE

INTRODUCTION

Chapter 1

The Tools Needed

Section 1.01 Coverage

This book is written to help you understand fundamental corporate tax concepts. The fundamental concepts have survived many congressional amendments precisely because they are generally sound. In covering the fundamentals, this book indicates those provisions that have received significant attention from the IRS.

This book primarily focuses on the rules contained in Subchapter C of Chapter 1 of Subtitle A of the Internal Revenue Code (commonly referred to as Subchapter C or as Sub C). Because Code sections that appear elsewhere in the Code also affect a corporation's tax liability, this book also addresses those provisions.

Some topics are covered in greater depth than others. A few, such as tax-exempt organizations and foreign corporations, are discussed only tangentially. Taken as a whole, however, this book provides a sound understanding of Subchapter C and the taxation of corporations.

This book covers Code sections enacted through June 2005. That includes those sections added or amended by the H.R. 4520, which became the American Jobs Creation Act of 2004.

Section 1.02 Tools Needed

As you likely learned in the introductory income tax class, judicial decisions are important but they are only a small part of the authorities that a tax lawyer must consult. While the IRS is bound by Supreme Court decisions, it must follow lower court opinions only when litigating in the jurisdiction covered by the particular court.[1] More importantly, most tax transactions never

---

1. The IRS carefully analyzes a judicial decision before it decides not to follow it. If the IRS disagrees with a court decision, it may publish its nonacquiesence in the Internal Rev-

involve litigation. They are concluded based on administrative pronounce-ments, including regulations, revenue rulings, and private letter rulings. Need-less to say, a good understanding of the many documents encountered in tax research is necessary for the successful practice of tax.

The list below will always need updating because the IRS may produce new documents that are disclosed to the public. In researching a corporate tax question, you should ask two questions about any document you find: (1) Can it help in my understanding of my tax problem; and (2) Can I cite it as prece-dent? Even if a document cannot be cited as a precedent, it may still be use-ful in persuading the IRS to accept a particular position.

Section 1.02(a) Internal Revenue Code

Tax lawyers often refer to the Internal Revenue Code as the Code, and this book follows that tradition. Problem-solving begins, and often ends, with the Code because it is the ultimate authority.[2] The Code is Title 26 of the United States Code. In this book, we will be focusing almost exclusively on Subtitle A, which covers the federal income tax. Within Subtitle A, we will primarily concern ourselves with the taxation of corporations and their shareholders.

At first glance, the Code may appear disjointed. For example, section 368 defines the transactions that qualify as reorganizations. Once you determine that your transaction qualifies as a reorganization, you go backwards to sec-tion 354 or section 356 to determine whether gain will be recognized. For basis consequences, you must look at section 358 or section 362 (depend-ing on whether you are a shareholder or a corporation involved in the reor-ganization). Nothing in section 368 alerted you to look at those other Code sections.

Once you understand its structure, you will find that the Code is not that hard to navigate. It is divided into subdivisions: Title; Subtitle; Chapter; Sub-chapter; Part; and Subpart. Related Code sections are often found in close proximity, frequently within a single subdivision.

---

enue Bulletin (IRB), an official IRS publication. If it agrees with the decision, it may pub-lish its acquiescence. The impact of these pronouncements is unclear, because they cannot be used as precedents. Sometimes acquiescences languish in the IRB long after the views of the IRS or the underlying law has changed. It is important not to rely heavily on such a notice.

2. Because so few judicial decisions consider constitutional questions involving federal taxation, this text ignores the Constitution as an authority.

When the term Title is used, it refers to the entire Code. For example, section 7701 contains a number of definitions that apply to "this Title." Those definitions apply to the entire Code. If, instead, a rule applies for purposes of Subtitle A, it applies only to the income tax provisions.

When studying a particular Code section, you will find it useful to survey the landscape. For example, section 368 is contained in Part III of Subchapter C of Chapter I of Subtitle A. If you look at section 368 in this fashion, it becomes less daunting. You will see that the effect of a reorganization on the shareholders is covered by Subpart B of Part III; the effect on the corporations engaged in the reorganization is covered by Subpart C; etc. Reviewing a group of sections can be extremely valuable because Code sections often do not refer to each other.

One last advice to follow in reading the Code: Do not be satisfied that a particular provision in a particular section provides the answer. The rule you found may be negated elsewhere in the Code. The typical Code section provides a general rule, clarifications of that general rule, exceptions that negate the general rule, and, sometimes, exceptions to those exceptions.[3]

Another problem relates to terminology. The Code is often very cryptic. For example, section 368(a)(1)(A) defines a reorganization as a "statutory merger or consolidation" but does not elaborate on what those terms mean. If no Code section defines those terms, taxpayers can look to other sources, including the legislative history, regulations, and other sources discussed in this chapter.

Section 1.02(b) Legislative History

Most Code sections originated in bills introduced in the House of Representatives and that were later considered by the Senate and by a Senate/House conference committee. After the conference resolves differences and the two chambers pass the final bill, it goes to the President for action. A researcher who studies committee reports and other aspects of a Code section's history may learn what Congress was thinking when it enacted a particular provision. That history may even include language indicating how Congress expects the IRS and Treasury to administer a particular provision. Although many courts prefer to focus on a statute's "plain meaning," citations to appropriate legislative history may persuade the IRS or a court that the taxpayer's position is correct.

After major legislation is enacted, the staff of the Congressional Joint Committee on Taxation publishes an explanatory document, which is referred

---

3. *See* Chapter 5, which covers section 351, for an example of Code section structure.

to as the Blue Book. Although that document cannot be used as precedent, it is generally quite helpful in the understanding of new Code sections.

Section 1.02(c) Regulations

Treasury regulations are promulgated by the IRS and Treasury. The authority for a particular body depends on the statutory language used to authorize the regulations. Section 7701(a)(11) indicates that the term "Secretary" means the Secretary of the Treasury or his designee whereas the term "Secretary of the Treasury" means the Secretary of the Treasury personally and shall not include any delegate of his. Reference to the Secretary in the context of regulations is generally taken as a reference to the National Office of the Chief Counsel of the IRS.

Section 7805(a) gives the Secretary a broad mandate to publish regulations to implement tax legislation. It specifically provides that "the Secretary shall prescribe all needful rules and regulations for the enforcement of [Title A of the Code]" unless that authority was expressly granted by Congress to another person. Normally, the regulations drafters work at the IRS, but Treasury plays a very pivotal role in the drafting process. Unless a court invalidates them, or the government withdraws or amends them, regulations are binding authority. Regulations are seldom invalidated.

Regulations can be proposed, which means that they are not yet effective; temporary, which means that they are effective for three years from the date of promulgation; or final, which means that they are effective unless invalidated, withdrawn, or amended.

Generally, regulations start at the proposed stage. In many cases, the IRS will issue a regulation as both a temporary and proposed regulation. Tax professionals have a chance to comment on the proposed regulations. Once comments are reviewed, the regulations may be adopted (with or without change) as final or temporary regulations.

Regulations can either be interpretative or legislative. Interpretative regulations are regulations promulgated under the general authority given the IRS and Treasury by section 7805. Legislative regulations are promulgated under the express authority of a particular Code section. Legislative regulations are generally given greater deference than interpretative regulations. Assuming the IRS has acted within the authority granted by Congress, legislative regulations are invalidated only if they are arbitrary and capricious.[4] Because the IRS fol-

---

4. The numbering system used for regulations is based on a combination of the Code of Federal regulations part and the underlying Code section. Because the income tax regulations are in Part 1, the first number of income tax regulations is 1. For example, the

lows the requirements of the Administrative Procedure Act in issuing regulations, courts recognize that taxpayers have had adequate opportunities to comment on these pronouncements.[5]

Section 1.02(d) Judicial Decisions

Both taxpayers and the IRS must follow decisions of the Supreme Court. The IRS is bound by lower court decisions only in that particular court. If Congress disagrees with a decision of the Supreme Court, or of any other federal court, it can legislate around it.[6] Courts rarely overturn a Code provision on constitutional grounds, so most decisions involve interpreting Code language. Courts generally opine in situations where there is a gap or uncertainty in legislation.

Section 1.02(e) IRS Communications

Section 1.02(e)(1) Revenue Rulings and Revenue Procedures

Revenue rulings represent the IRS' litigating position about a particular substantive law question. Because they bind only the IRS, taxpayers can ignore revenue rulings if they are willing to litigate.

Although revenue rulings are not subject to the Administrative Procedure Act, they are well-thought-out positions of the IRS and often benefit from outside influence. Revenue rulings derive from several sources: issues encountered in the PLR process; questions raised by taxpayers; or documents produced by tax professors or tax sections of bar associations.

Revenue procedures normally discuss the way the IRS will administer one of its functions. For example, the IRS' administration of its PLR program is found in the first revenue procedure published for the year. For the year 2005 this revenue procedure was Rev. Proc. 2005-1; for the year 2006, it will be Rev. Proc. 2006-1.

---

regulations under Code section 355 are numbered section 1.355-1 *et seq*. Regulations so numbered can be either interpretative or legislative regulations. Temporary regulations have a "T" at the end. For example, see §1.368-2T of the income tax regulations.

5. *See* 5 U.S.C. §1 *et seq*.

6. *See Rite Aid Corp. v. United States*, 255 F.3d 1357 (Fed. Cir. 2001). Congress changed the result of that decision by inserting a sentence at the end of section 1502 permitting the IRS and Treasury to create rules for taxpayers filing consolidated returns that would not be applicable if the taxpayer were filing a separate return.

Section 1.02(e)(2) Notices and Announcements

Notices and Announcements generally signal a change in IRS policies or procedures. They have the flavor of revenue procedures, but they are not as formal. They can be relied on by taxpayers unless revoked.

Section 1.02(e)(3) Private Letter Ruling (PLR)

A PLR arises out of a taxpayer request for a ruling on the tax consequences of a proposed transaction. A PLR has no precedential value. It binds the IRS only vis-à-vis the particular taxpayer that received it, and does so only if the transaction is consummated as described in the PLR. If the transaction is not consummated, or if the taxpayer significantly changes its terms, then the PLR becomes invalid and may be revoked by the IRS.[7] See Rev. Proc. 2005-1 for the process of obtaining a PLR and Rev. Proc. 2005-3 for areas in which PLRs will not be issued.[8] Although other taxpayers cannot rely on them, PLRs provide insight into IRS national office's thinking on a particular issue.

Section 1.02(e)(4) Technical Advice Memorandum (TAM)

TAMs are produced by the IRS' national office in response to disagreements between taxpayers and the IRS' Examination Division. They have no precedential value but are binding on the Examination Division. See Rev. Proc. 2005-2 (or the current year's rev. proc.) for explanations on how to get a TAM. Every TAM includes the heading "Technical Advice Memorandum."

Section 1.02(e)(5) Field Service Advice (FSA) and General Counsel Memorandum (GCM)

An FSA is written advice given to the Examinations Division by the IRS' National Office. The advice is not binding on the Examinations Division and has no precedential authority. A GCM usually precedes a revenue ruling and explains the legal basis of the revenue ruling. The National Office no longer publishes GCMs, but you may still encounter them in research. A GCM may be helpful in understanding the law but has no precedential value.

---

7. The IRS seldom revokes PLRs because under a cost/benefit analysis, it may not be worth it to revoke a piece of paper that has limited application.

8. *See* Rev. Proc. 2005-1, 2005-1 I.R.B. 1; Rev. Proc. 2005-3, 2005-1 I.R.B. 118.

Section 1.02(e)(6) IRS Chief Counsel Advice (CCA)

Like PLRs, Chief Counsel Advices (CCAs) have no precedential value and cannot be relied on by taxpayers. They generally provide the National Office's opinion to an office in the "Field" (non-national office). An example is CCA 200518079, which concluded that a consent to extend the time to assess tax can be accepted by a field office by fax. As is true for many IRS documents, sometimes CCAs provide valuable insights. Taxpayers may use them to persuade the field office that a particular position is correct.

The above list is not exhaustive because the IRS and Treasury often communicate with the public through other documents.[9] In looking at any document published by the IRS or Treasury, always try to determine (1) whether the document is binding on the IRS and (2) whether it is binding on taxpayers. Generally, unless a document is part of a closing agreement, only documents that have met the requirements of the Administrative Procedure Act (such as regulations) can bind taxpayers. Nevertheless, other documents should not be lightly rejected because they often represent the IRS' litigating position.

Section 1.02(f) Other Documents

Treatises and articles may lead to greater comprehension, but they represent only the writer's perspective. Although they have no precedential value, courts sometimes cite to them.

---

9. The IRS may also provide oral advice. Although oral advice does not bind the IRS, carefully documented oral advice can be helpful if the attorney needs to show that she used due diligence.

Chapter 2

Glossary of Terms Used

Tax lawyers use a number of terms that make talking about tax easier. For example, each Internal Revenue Bulletin, an official IRS publication, includes several terms and abbreviations. These terms signal changes made to IRS documents (particularly revenue rulings), and the abbreviations are designed to be acceptable conventions. For example, "superseded" means that a document has been replaced by another document. We will use the following terms throughout this book:

Document Terms

Code   =   Internal Revenue Code (1986 Code, as amended)
Regulations =   Treasury Regulations

Government Entity Terms

IRS   =   Internal Revenue Service
Treasury =   Department of the Treasury

Business Entity or Owner Terms

A, B, C =   Individuals and noncorporate entities (letters other than N–Z)
LLC   =   Limited Liability Company
Newco   =   Newly-created corporation (usually wholly-owned)
P   =   Parent Corporation
S   =   Subsidiary Corporation
SH   =   Shareholder
T   =   Target Corporation
X, Y, Z =   Corporation X, Corporation Y, or Corporation Z

Other Terms

Basis	=	Taxpayer's investment, generally cost
Boot	=	Property that does not qualify for nonrecognition
COI	=	Continuity of interest
COBE	=	Continuity of business enterprise
E&P	=	Earnings and Profits
FMV	=	Fair market value
PLR	=	Private Letter Ruling
CCA	=	Chief Counsel Advice
Rev. Rul.	=	Revenue Ruling
Rev. Proc.	=	Revenue Procedure

Chapter 3

Tax Policy and Tax Doctrines

Section 3.01 Tax Policy in General

While a good understanding of tax policy helps in deciphering the Code, it is not always necessary. Regardless of the policy underlying a particular Code provision, both taxpayers and the government are bound by the statutory language. If that language does not achieve its purpose, Congress may ultimately choose to amend the Code. Whether or not they formally studied tax policy in law school, most tax lawyers have encountered it when they read legislative history documents or discuss the rationale for a provision.

Tax policy has been defined simply as congressional intent.[1] Because Congress enacts all tax legislation, its intent in enacting such provisions reflects various policy goals. Tax policy discussions involve two broad categories: (1) the broad economic reasons justifying a particular tax provision; and (2) how Congress intends the section to be read and implemented. Lawyers are likely to be more familiar with the latter category.

Section 3.02 Economic Rationale for Tax Laws

The main purpose of taxation is to raise funds for the government to operate. Why then is the Code so complicated? If the government wants to raise $1 trillion for its needs, would it not be much simpler to simply impose $1 trillion in taxes on the citizenry? Proponents of such alternate systems as the

---

1. *See* Reginald Mombrun, E&P As We Know It (Or Should Know It), 75 Tax Notes 1659 (June 23, 1997).

flat tax and value added tax certainly think so. However, tax policy involves more than just raising revenues.

Congress realized long ago that taxes can be used to stimulate the economy and for social engineering. Special interest groups also seek particular deductions and other tax benefits. The net result is a system that purports to tax all income (section 61) but provides business and investment incentives through deductions (e.g., section 162) and nonrecognition provisions (e.g., section 351). The system also redistributes wealth through transfer taxes and the earned income tax credit.

Each Code section represents an attempt to tax an economic transaction or to exempt it from taxation. The current income tax system is so complicated because it deals with thousands of economic transactions and attempts to categorize them for tax purposes. Despite its complexity, many analysts believe the income tax will survive.[2]

Section 3.03 Tax Doctrines

The courts have long recognized that strict application of the tax laws sometimes produces results not intended by Congress. To remedy this situation, judges have devised several doctrines that, when applied, prevent unwarranted tax benefits. In their attempts at reining in aggressive taxpayers, the courts have used such doctrines as substance over form, business purpose, and step transaction.

After constructing a transaction and determining that it reaches a particular tax result, the prudent tax lawyer should step back and consider if the transaction violates the spirit of the relevant Code provision. If the lawyer thinks that the spirit is violated, chances are good that the IRS will feel the same way and will attack the transaction. Do not be surprised to encounter one or more of these doctrines in your study of corporate tax.

As will be discussed later, taxpayers are not obliged to pay the highest tax possible on their transactions. But reducing one's tax burden should not involve violating the language and spirit of the law. The IRS can deal with technical violations relatively easily. If the taxpayer does not follow the letter of the law, as stated in the Code, the taxpayer loses. If, instead, the taxpayer violates the spirit of the law, substance over form and other judicial doctrines may come into play.

---

2. *See* Halperin, Saving the Income Tax: An Agenda for Research, Tax Policy Readings, Tax Analysts (November 24, 1997), http://www.taxanalysts.com/.

An example of good tax planning involves the decision to incorporate. Assume that Taxpayer A wants to incorporate a business, which includes a particular piece of property. A would also like to cash out some of his equity by selling some rights in the property for cash. If A incorporates the property using section 351[3] and, as part of the same transaction, sells rights in the property to B, the IRS might argue that, because the corporation did not receive all rights in the property, the transaction does not meet section 351's property transfer requirement. If A instead sells the rights to the property to B first and then both A and B transfer all rights to that property to the corporation in exchange for 80 percent or more of the stock of the corporation, the transaction should satisfy section 351. That change in structure represents good tax planning.[4]

There is often a fine line between tax evasion and tax planning. If tax planning is too aggressive, it can become tax evasion. Good tax planning involves deciding on a course of action (a business transaction) and, being mindful of the Code, attempting to do the transaction in the most tax efficient manner. The planner will take potential statutory "traps" into account in planning the transaction. For example, if the corporation's board of directors has decided that it would be beneficial if the corporation's two businesses are held independently of each other, attempting to achieve this separation in a tax-free manner by using section 355 of the Code is good tax planning. But what if their ultimate plan is to put cash in the hands of the corporation's shareholders by allowing them, instead of the corporation, to sell the business (thereby avoiding the double tax regime)? If the IRS considers this to be tax evasion, it will rely on Code language and anti-tax avoidance doctrines in challenging the reported tax consequences.

Section 3.03(a) Substance over Form

The substance over form doctrine generally stands for the proposition that, although the form of a transaction may follow what Congress prescribed, if the substance of the transaction does violence to congressional intent, the transaction will be taxed according to its substance. The IRS may assert this doctrine when it objects to a transaction a taxpayer has constructed.

---

3. Generally I.R.C. section 351 provides that no gain or loss is recognized on the transfer of property to a corporation if the transferor is in control (owns 80 percent or more of the stock) of the transferee corporation. We study section 351 in Chapter 5.

4. This restructuring works only if B is willing to own those rights indirectly, through the corporation, rather than outright. The tax planner must study potential options and explain them to the client before a transaction closes.

Unlike the IRS, taxpayers are generally locked into the form they choose and cannot ignore it in order to get a better tax result. There are rare exceptions. For example, using the regulations under section 482, related taxpayers can attempt to reallocate items of income and deductions among themselves. Under limited circumstances, taxpayers can request in a private letter ruling that the IRS restructure a transaction entered into for foreign law purposes.[5]

The substance over form doctrine resembles the other doctrines discussed below. Indeed, it has been said that the other doctrines are really subsets of the substance over form doctrine. Those doctrines appear to be more precise formulations of the substance over form doctrine. Generally, the IRS will assert several doctrines to attack a transaction. Thus, substance over form may be asserted along with lack of business purpose, step transaction, or some other doctrine.

Section 3.03(b) Business Purpose

As early as *Gregory v. Helvering*,[6] courts have understood that strict application of a tax statute may not result in what was intended by Congress. In the case, the taxpayer (A) owned all the stock of one corporation (X). X's assets included 1,000 shares of another corporation (Y). X transferred the Y shares to a new corporation (Z), which issued all its shares to A. Z liquidated soon thereafter. As its sole shareholder, A received the Y stock, which she sold. No other business was conducted. If the initial transaction qualified as a reorganization, A's taxes would be lower than if she received the Y shares as a dividend.

The Supreme Court collapsed the transaction. The Court held that it did not qualify as a reorganization because when the statute speaks of a transfer in a reorganization, "it means a transfer made 'in pursuance of a plan of reorganization'... of corporate business; and not a transfer of assets by one corporation to another in pursuance of a plan having no relation to the business of either, as plainly is the case here."[7]

The case can be illustrated as follows:

---

5. One such example is the so called "Butterfly" transaction, which is governed by Canadian law. This reorganization transaction allows holding companies to divide assets of an operating company. To preserve both Canadian and United States tax benefits, the parties would request a ruling from the Canadian authorities and a private letter ruling that the transaction qualified under Code section 355.

6. 293 U.S. 465 (1935).

7. *Id.* at 469.

Gregory v. Helvering

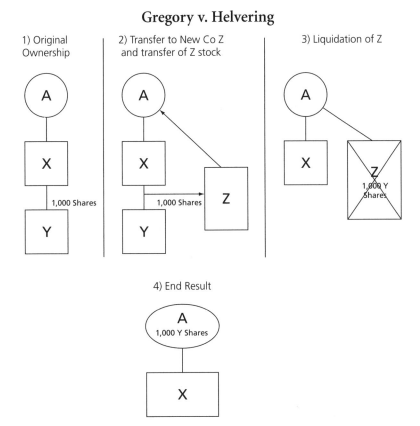

This case supports the notion that, in order to receive tax-free treatment, transactions must be entered into for valid business reasons and not merely to let taxpayers reap tax benefits that otherwise would not be available. The business purpose doctrine has been integrated into many Treasury regulations and now is a recognized part of the Subchapter C landscape. The requirement applies to reorganizations and various other corporate transactions. It is particularly important for transactions involving section 355 distributions.

As the Supreme Court has recognized, taxpayers have the legal right to decrease, or altogether avoid their taxes so long as they do so by means permitted under the law.[8] Both the statutory language and congressional intent may be relevant in this context. The prudent tax lawyer must be aware of this doc-

---

8. *See Superior Oil Co. v. Mississippi*, 280 U.S. 390 (1930), *cited in Gregory v. Helvering*, 293 U.S. 465, 469 (1935).

trine (especially if engaging in a section 355 transaction) and must investigate the business reasons behind a proposed transaction. If the business purpose of a transaction is carefully documented, and the transaction is not an obvious tax avoidance scheme, the transaction should survive IRS scrutiny.

Section 3.03(c) Step Transaction

The step transaction doctrine is pervasive in the area of corporate tax, particularly in reorganization transactions. Many consider it a subset of the substance over form doctrine. However, because it has been formulated specifically by the courts, it deserves its own consideration. As you will see, the step transaction doctrine is somewhat more mechanical in its approach.

Generally, there are three tests used in applying the step transaction doctrine: end result; mutual interdependence; and binding commitment.

Section 3.03(c)(1) End Result Test

The end result test is both controversial and widely used. Simply put, this test amalgamates separate transactions when it appears that they were really component steps of a single transaction and that each step was taken for the purpose of reaching a specific result.[9]

Example: Corporation X acquires all the stock of Corporation Y in exchange for its own stock. After this acquisition and as part of the same plan, Y merges into X. Is the transaction treated as a stock acquisition followed by a merger? Or is it a direct acquisition of the Y assets by X? The end result of the transaction appears to be the acquisition of the Y assets by X in exchange for X stock. Because the two acquisitions were made pursuant to the same plan, the end result test treats the transaction as a direct acquisition of Y assets by X for X stock. As we will see later, this may have important tax implications.

Section 3.03(c)(2) Mutual Interdependence Test

The mutual interdependence test is slightly more mechanical than the end result test. It applies if steps are so interdependent that the first step would not be taken unless the subsequent steps of the transaction (through to its completion) would also be taken. This test focuses on the interdependency of the steps, not merely on the end result.[10]

---

9. *See King Enterprises, Inc. v. United States,* 418 F.2d 511 (Ct. Cl. 1969).

10. *See American Bantam Car Co. v. Commissioner,* 11 T.C. 397 (1948), *aff'd per curiam,* 177 F.2d 513 (3rd Cir. 1949), *cert denied,* 339 U.S. 920 (1950).

Section 3.03(c)(3) Binding Commitment Test

The binding commitment test is the least used and most mechanical of the tests. Under this test, a transaction will be aggregated with other transactions if there is a binding commitment to do the other transactions.[11] This is the most restrictive of the tests and the one that taxpayers try to force the IRS into using. Obviously, finding a binding commitment is not easy unless such a commitment is reduced to writing or can be proven by clear evidence.

---

11. *See Intermountain Lumber Co. v. Commissioner*, 65 T.C. 1025 (1976).

Part Two

Taxation of C Corporations

CHAPTER 4

OVERVIEW OF SUBCHAPTER C

Section 4.01 Introduction to the Double Tax Regime

By now you should be familiar with the notion of Subchapter C, which includes Code sections 301-385. You may also have heard that corporations covered by Subchapter C are subject to double taxation or that there is a "double tax" regime in Subchapter C.

The double tax regime simply means that income earned by C corporations is subject to two levels of tax. Income is first taxed at the corporate level. When the corporation distributes its earnings to its shareholders, that income is again taxed at the shareholder level. Commentators have debated whether the double tax regime hinders the economy and should be eliminated.[1] Congress has softened its bite in various ways. These include providing lower tax rates for dividends and capital gains, expanding Subchapter S eligibility, and increasing other devices. Because it appears the double tax regime will be here for the foreseeable future, you should understand how it operates. The example below is designed as an illustration and does not reflect actual tax rates.

Example: Corporation X has $100 of taxable income and pays $30 in tax. X then distributes the remaining $70 to its shareholders (Individuals A and B). Assuming that X has sufficient E&P (discussed in Chapter 7), A and B will report gross income of $70 and be taxed at the appropriate rate. If that rate is 15 percent, they will pay $10.50. The combined corporate and individual taxes of $40.50 will exceed 40 percent of the corporation's taxable income.

---

1. *See* Michael J. Graetz and Alvin C. Warren Jr., Integration of Corporations and Individual Income Taxation: An Introduction, Tax Analysts, Tax Policy Readings (September 27, 1999), http://www.taxanalysts.com/.

Section 4.02 Why Do Taxpayers Accept Double Taxation?

Although the example above provides for a large tax liability, the actual tax bite is likely to be much smaller. A significant number of individuals invest in corporations for the potential stock appreciation, not necessarily in order to receive dividends.[2] Others invest only indirectly, through pension funds, and defer any tax liability until retirement. It is important to remember that the double corporate tax regime is not the only situation in which two taxpayers are taxed on the same income.

Example: Individual A earns $100 and pays $30 in tax. A then pays his plumber and roofer $35 each for repairs. Assuming both the plumber and the roofer are each subject to a 15 percent tax rate, they would pay combined taxes of $10.50. The combined taxes paid on the original $100 are $40.50, or more than 40 percent of A's original income.

The transactions above give the correct result, because these are separate economic transactions involving different taxpayers. Because a corporation and its shareholders are also different taxpayers, that rationale also applies to the corporation and its shareholders. Nevertheless, the double tax applicable to corporations can impose a significant tax bite.

There are important reasons why taxpayers select corporate status. Some businesses have no choice but to be taxed as corporations. These are called per se corporations. For example, an entity that is taxed as a corporation in certain foreign jurisdictions must be taxed as a corporation in the United States.[3] Certain publicly traded partnerships are treated as corporations.[4] Banks and other lending institutions may require a business to incorporate because the usury laws generally do not apply to corporations. Therefore, banks can impose a higher rate of interest on an incorporated business than they could on an unincorporated business.

Incorporating may also make it easier for an entity to raise capital. An investor buying stock of a corporation is only at risk to the extent of his investment. In addition, there may be statutory pressures to incorporate. Finally, as

---

2. For example, Berkshire Hathaway, the large conglomerate headed by Warren Buffett, has not paid dividends since 1967. *See* Washington Post, April 20, 2004 (Business Section).

3. *See* Treas. Reg. §301.7701-2(b)(8).

4. *See* I.R.C. §7704.

we will see later, only corporations can elect to file consolidated returns. In some instances, filing such returns may be advantageous.

There are ways to lessen, or even avoid, the double tax. For, example, electing S corporation status generally avoids the double tax.[5] A small C corporation managed by its shareholders may have relatively little earnings to distribute. Salaries paid to shareholder-employees may eliminate most corporate earnings. Corporations needing capital for expansion are likely to retain their earnings and not pay dividends.

Electing to incorporate is a very important decision. The tax consequences of corporate status are among the considerations to be studied. But nontax advantages, including the limitation on personal liability generally afforded shareholders, cannot be ignored. For many entities, the nontax advantages of incorporating outweigh the burden of double taxation.

Section 4.03 Differences between Corporate and Individual Taxation

Often, a primary reason for investors to incorporate their business is to shelter their personal wealth from the risks and vicissitudes of the business. As is widely known, if the rules of incorporation are followed and the corporate veil is not pierced[6], the investor's only risk is the investment she has made in the corporation. Protection from personal risks may be the main driving force of incorporating businesses. Another driving force is the relative ease of attracting investors and borrowing money. As we saw earlier, banks sometimes require businesses to incorporate in order to avoid usury laws which are generally not applicable to corporations. Hence, banks can charge corporations a higher interest rate for their loans and, thus, reap more profits.

The taxation of the business is usually a secondary concern of the would-be entrepreneur. If the issue of taxation is brought up (particularly, double taxation of corporate income), the investor's advisers dismiss this concern by explaining that electing S corporation status for Federal income tax purposes will get rid of this double tax. There are, however, restrictions to electing S corporation status, namely the restriction on the number of shareholders, the

---

5. *But see* I.R.C. § 1374, which applies to built-in-gains. Generally, section 1374 applies if the corporation was a C corporation prior to electing S status.

6. You will recall from your business law class that piercing the corporate veil is a drastic measure that courts undertake only in extreme circumstances.

type of shareholders and the number of classes of stock that the corporation can have.[7]

If a tax advisor is brought in at the stage where a decision is being made whether to incorporate or not, the tax advisor needs to be aware of the major tax consequences of electing to incorporate versus conducting the business as a proprietorship or other form of business. In addition to the potential double taxation of corporate income, there are a number of important distinctions between filing a corporate income tax return versus filing an individual tax return. The corporate taxpayer is subject to different exclusions and deductions rules, different rate structures, different accounting methods and different accounting period rules.

Section 4.03(a) Corporate Deductions versus Individual Deductions

The Code allows individuals to take a number of deductions that are not allowed to corporations, including the standard deduction, the deduction for personal exemptions, the additional itemized deductions for such items as medical expenses, alimony, moving expenses, retirement savings and a 2 percent floor on miscellaneous itemized deductions applied only to individuals.[8] Some statutory provisions do not distinguish between individuals and corporations as such, but instead draw a line separating individuals and closely held corporations from other corporations in order to prevent restrictions aimed primarily at individuals from being sidestepped by a transfer of the restricted activities to a closely held corporation.[9]

With regard to corporations, the following deductions or restrictions on deductibility are generally applicable: (1) the deductibility of business expenses and losses (NOLs), (2) charitable contributions, (3) limitations on capital losses, (4)deductions for net operating losses, (5) certain shareholder taxes paid by the corporation, (6) the at-risk rules and passive rules of sec-

---

7. Section 1361(b)(1) provides restrictions on the number of shareholders an S corporation can have and also states that an S corporation cannot have as a shareholder a person other than an estate, a trust described in section 1361(c)(2) or an organization described in section 1361(c)(6) who is not an individual. The section also provides that an S corporation cannot have a nonresident alien as a shareholder and cannot have more than one class of stock.

8. *See* Bittker & Eustice, Federal Income Taxation of Corporation & Shareholders, ¶ 5.03.

9. *Id.*

tion 465 and section 469, (7) percentage cut-backs under section 291, (8) corporate deductions under section 243 for dividends received, and (9) as recently enacted by the American Jobs Creation Act of 2004,[10] the deduction provided under section 199 relating to income attributable to domestic production activities. Some of the deductions allowed to corporations are also available to individuals because the language of the Code is broad enough to include both corporate and individual businesses. For example, the deduction allowed by section 162 applies to both corporations and individuals so long as they are engaged in the conduct of a trade or business. Although corporations are not allowed to deduct net capital losses, they are eligible to carry capital losses both back and forward.[11] Carryback and carryforward of NOLs are some of the main tax advantages granted the corporation. The corporation is also granted a deduction for dividends received from another corporation.

Section 4.03(b) Corporate versus Individual Tax Rates

The determination of corporate income is computed generally in the same manner as the computation of individual income. Gross income of the corporation, just like that of the individual, is defined under section 61 of the Code as income from whatever source derived. Net income is then computed by subtracting allowable deductions. The tax rate structure applicable to corporations is more simplistic than the rate structure applicable to the individual. Section 11(a) provides that a tax is hereby imposed on the taxable income of every corporation. Section 11(b) provides that the tax imposed on such corporation shall be as follows: (1) 15 percent on taxable income of $50,000 or less; (2) 25 percent on taxable income that exceeds $50,000 but does not exceed $75,000; (3) 34 percent on income that exceeds $75,000 but does not exceed $10,000,000; and (4) 35 percent on income that exceeds $10,000,000.

The rates provided by the first two brackets are phased out by a surtax in the case of a corporation which has taxable income in excess of $100,000. In such case, the corporation has to pay a surtax of the lesser of (i) five percent of such excess or (ii) $11,750. A similar surtax is imposed on corporate taxable income that exceeds $15,000,000. In case of such income, a surtax equal to the

---

10. Pub. L. No. 108-357, 108th Cong., 2d Sess. § 102 (2004).

11. I.R.C. §§ 1211 (a) & 1212 (a) (corporations); cf. I.R.C. §§ 1211(b) & 1212(b) (invididuals).

lesser of (i) three percent or (ii) $100,000 is added to the tax of the corporation. Thus, the effective tax rates applicable to the corporation are as follows:

Taxable Income	Rate
Up to $50,000	15%
Over $50,000 but not over $75,000	25
Over $75,000 but not over $100,000	34
Over $100,000 but not over $335,000	39
Over $335,000 but not over $10,000,000	34
Over $10,000,000 but not over $15,000,000	35
Over $15,000,000 but not over $18,333,333	38
Over $18,333,333	35[12]

In the case of a "qualified personal service corporation,"[13] section 11 provides no tax rate preference. Such a corporation is taxed at the flat 35 percent rate on all of its taxable income. In the case of corporations, Congress has eliminated the rate preference that was provided for capital gains. Note, however, that section 1201 of the Code provides that if the corporate tax rate exceeds 35 percent, the rate on capital gains will remain at 35 percent. Finally, the corporation, just like the individual, may be subject to the alternative minimum tax.

The tax rates for individuals are provided by section 1 of the Code. These rates apply to taxable income and range from a low of 10 percent to a high of 35 percent. The complexity of these rates derives from the application of the rates to different types of individuals. Generally, they apply to different income levels of (i) married individuals filing joint returns and surviving spouses; (ii) heads of households; (iii) unmarried individuals (other than surviving spouses and heads of households); and (iv) married individuals filing separate returns.

Section 4.03(c) The Corporate Taxable Year and Method of Accounting

Under section 441, a corporation must adopt an accounting method to clearly reflect its income. Generally, a corporation elects its taxable year and

---

12. *See* Bittker & Eustice, Federal Income Taxation of Corporations & Shareholders, Corporate Tax Rates, ¶ 5.03.

13. A personal service company is defined under section 269A as a corporation the principal activity of which is the performance of personal services and such services are performed by employee-owners. Section 269A(b)(2) defines an employee-owner as any employee who owns, on any day during the taxable year, more than 10 percent of the outstanding stock of the personal service corporation.

its accounting method shortly after its incorporation, in any case prior to filing its return. The corporation can choose to file its return on a calendar year basis or on a fiscal year basis.[14] A personal service corporation, however, has to file its tax returns based on the calendar year, unless such corporation can convince the IRS that filing its return using a fiscal year is appropriate.[15] Individual taxpayers cannot file their returns on a fiscal year basis but must use the calendar year basis. Under section 448, a C corporation cannot use the cash receipts and disbursements method of accounting, but must use the accrual method of accounting. An exception applies to farming businesses, qualified personal service corporations and entities with gross receipts of not more than $5,000,000.[16]

Section 4.04 The LLC and the Check-the-Box Regulations

Limited liability company (LLC) statutes generally provide the limited liability protection afforded corporations without the additional burdens imposed on corporations. Keep in mind, however, that the LLC is a state law creation. For federal tax purposes, the LLC is treated either as a corporation, a partnership, or a sole proprietorship. In addition, many states require that the LLC's federal tax classification correspond to its state tax classification.

The real flexibility in the federal income tax laws with respect to tax classification has been provided by the check-the-box regulations.[17] These regulations were promulgated after years of controversy between the IRS and taxpayers regarding the proper classification of entities. These regulations allow an unincorporated business entity to elect to be taxed as a corporation, a partnership, or a proprietorship. A wholly-owned entity can elect to be treated as a disregarded entity, which means that it will be treated as if it does not exist for federal income tax purposes. The check-the-box regulations provide ad-

---

14. *See* Treas. Reg. § 1.441-1(c), which provides that a new taxpayer can elect to file its return using any method permitted by section 441.

15. *See* I.R.C. § 441(i)(1).

16. See I.R.C. § 448(b).

17. *See* Treas. Reg. § 301.7701.

ditional flexibility. A taxpayer is not bound by its initial election and can change its classification as business needs dictate.[18]

Section 4.05 Summary of Subchapter C

What tax lawyers refer to as Subchapter C is actually Subchapter C of Chapter 1 of Subtitle A of Title 26. Title 26 is the Internal Revenue Code. Subtitle A, entitled "Income Taxes," contains the bulk of our income tax laws. Subtitle A is the largest Internal Revenue Code subtitle, but Subchapter C, in and of itself, is not the largest subchapter of Subtitle A. However, because transactions described in Subchapter C are affected by and also affect other subchapters, its impact is far-reaching.

Subchapter C contains seven parts, Parts 1–7. Of these parts, only five are active. Part 4 (Insolvency Reorganizations) and Part 7 (Miscellaneous Corporate Provisions) have been repealed for some time and will not be discussed in this book.

We will, of course, discuss the remaining parts of Subchapter C at length and we will make sure that we apprise you of the most important parts of the Subchapter (the moving parts). Our coverage of corporate spin-offs (section 355) and reorganizations (section 368) is the most extensive. This is because these two sections are the most important sections in Subchapter C. They may not be the most complex but because the application of many other sections in Subchapter C depends on these two sections, a corporate tax lawyer has to have a sound understanding of these areas. They are the heart of Subchapter C.

Subchapter C contains the sections that affect the taxable corporation the most. Although it does not follow that order, it provides rules governing the corporation's tax consequences from its birth (organization), through dealings with its shareholders (dividend distributions and redemptions), non-taxable dealings with other parties (reorganizations), taxable dealings with other parties (section 338 elections), and, finally, its "death" (liquidations). This book addresses those transactions and also covers rules for affiliated and consolidated corporations (Chapters 14 and 15). That coverage differentiates this book from many other texts on corporate taxation. The corporate tax lawyer must understand consolidated return issues in order to spot such issues and properly advise clients.

---

18. Some restrictions apply. For example, under Treas. Reg. § 301.7701-3(c)(1)(iv), an election is generally effective for five years unless more than fifty percent of the ownership of the business entity has changed and the permission of the IRS Commissioner is granted.

CHAPTER 5

FORMATION OF CORPORATIONS

Section 5.01 Introduction

Although Subchapter C begins with section 301, we chose not to begin our discussion of corporate tax with that section. Instead, we begin with section 351 because, arguably, it is the first instance where a corporation encounters the federal income tax system. While technically this has some appeal, it is also true that very few taxpayers engage in section 351 transactions. The typical corporation is created with little investment from its incorporators. Following incorporation, it seeks capital from investors who usually buy corporate stock with cash. Such transactions are not taxable to either the corporation or its investor(s). The corporation is protected from tax by section 1032. The investor who pays cash for stock has no gain or loss to report on the transaction.

Although most investors will never encounter section 351, a tax attorney must understand its effect on corporate formations. If an investor transfers appreciated assets instead of cash, section 351 may protect that investor from recognizing gain on the transfer. Not surprisingly, this situation is likely to occur as a sole proprietorship or partnership expands and seeks the benefits of incorporation. In this case, section 351 will be the parties' first journey into corporate taxation.

Section 5.02 Relevant Code Sections

In this chapter, we will, of course, study section 351, which generally provides that no gain or loss is recognized on the transfer of property to a corporation if the transferor (or transferors) controls the corporation following the transfer. In addition to section 351, we will study several other Code sections that apply once we meet the section 351 qualifications. Section 358 governs the shareholders' basis for the stock received in a section 351 transaction.

33

Section 1223 provides the holding period rules for that stock. With respect to the corporation receiving the property, section 1032 prevents gain recognition. Section 362 provides the basis for the property received, and section 1223 provides the corporation's holding period. If the corporation assumes shareholder liabilities as part of the transfer, section 357 may provide adverse tax consequences.

Section 5.03 Synopsis of Section 351

Section 351 is a nonrecognition provision. It protects taxpayers from taxation in situations where they would otherwise recognize gain. It also prevents them from currently deducting a potential loss. As you will recall from the introductory income tax course, section 1001(a) provides that gain or loss from the sale or other disposition of property is computed by comparing the amount realized to the adjusted basis of the property. Section 1001(c) provides a general rule—unless there is an exception in Subtitle A, all realized gain or loss is recognized. Section 351 is such an exception.

Section 351 prevents adverse tax consequences that might otherwise discourage businesses from incorporating. Although taxpayers may desire such corporate attributes as limited personal liability or easy transferability of ownership interests, adverse tax consequences might discourage them from transferring appreciated assets into corporate form. An unincorporated business that has prospered is likely to have such assets. Although Congress has amended section 351 many times, reflecting "holes" that needed to be patched, its basic goal remains unchanged.

The diagram below illustrates a typical section 351 transaction. Two persons (Individual A and Corporation X) transfer property to new Corporation Y in exchange for its stock. Immediately after the transfer, Corporation Y owns that property and A and X own stock issued by Y.

In studying section 351, keep in mind our promise and premise in section 1.02 about the structure of most Code sections. There will be a general rule, refinements of the general rule, exceptions, and exceptions to the exceptions. Section 351's general rule is found in section 351(a), while refinements appear in section 351(c), (d), (f), and (g). Exceptions to the general rule are contained in section 351(b), (e) (which is actually labeled exceptions), (f), and (g). Within section 351(g), there is an exception to the section, which means that the general rule of section 351(a) applies.

In this chapter, we will investigate the various parts of section 351. As with any other Code section, it is important that we know which parties are

351 Transaction

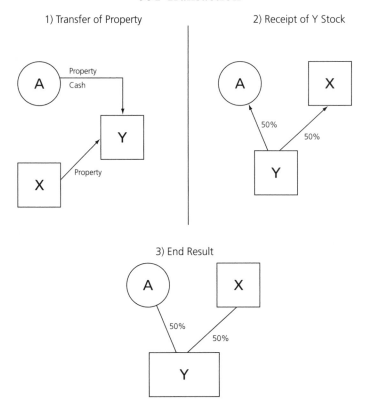

1) Transfer of Property

2) Receipt of Y Stock

3) End Result

affected. In section 351, we will study the tax consequences of the trans-feror(s) of property and of the corporation exchanging its stock for that property.

Keep two limitations in mind. First, unless both parties follow the mandate of the section, partial or full taxation may ensue. Second, section 351 is really a tax deferral provision. Any gain that would have been recognized if the section did not apply is still there—waiting for the right triggering event.[1]

Section 5.04 The General Rule

Section 351(a) provides that no gain or loss shall be recognized if **property** is **transferred** to a corporation by **one or more persons solely** in **exchange for**

---

1. This tax deferral is contained in the basis rules which we will study later.

stock in such corporation and immediately after the exchange such person or persons are in **control** (as defined in section 368(c)) of the corporation. As you can see, we have highlighted certain key terms that are critical to your understanding of section 351 transactions.

Caveat: As will be true throughout this book, keep in mind an important rule about definitions. Never assume that a term used in a tax section has its "natural" meaning. The Code often provides a different or additional meaning for purposes of the particular tax provision.

From the terms highlighted above, we can see that section 351 has four requirements:

(a) There must be a transfer of property;
(b) The transfer must be by a person or persons;
(c) Such person or persons must receive only stock in the exchange; and
(d) Such person or persons must control the corporation immediately after the transfer.

Consider a situation in which A and B acquire all the stock of Corporation X for cash. Will this transfer of cash in exchange for 100 percent of the corporation's stock be covered by section 351? To answer that question, we must ascertain the identity of the seller.

If A and B acquire the stock from X shareholders who are selling their investment, the transaction would not qualify under section 351. In that situation, the cash is transferred to the former shareholders and not to the corporation. Because the former shareholders are not covered by section 351, they do not qualify for nonrecognition. Only the transferor(s) of property to the corporation and the corporation receiving such property are protected.

If A and B purchased the stock from Corporation X itself, the corporation is protected from tax by section 1032. As we saw earlier, the cash purchasers have no gain to recognize. As we will see shortly, although a transfer of cash is really a purchase of stock, it may be become part of a section 351 transaction.

Section 5.04(a) Transfer of Property

Section 5.04(a)(1) Property

What constitutes property for purposes of section 351? Because section 351 does not define property, we briefly look elsewhere in the Code. Section 7701, which provides definitions that apply throughout the Code, also fails to define property. Although section 317, which we will encounter in Chapter 7, does define the term, that section does not apply for section 351 purposes.

Section 351(d) sheds some light by providing some restrictions on the type of qualifying consideration that can be exchanged in a section 351 transaction. Stock that is received in exchange for services, certain indebtedness, and accrued interest will not be treated as received for property for section 351 purposes. Besides these exceptions, we are left with the natural meaning of the word property, and, as you can imagine, it is expansive. The lack of a definition has apparently not deterred taxpayers from entering into section 351 transactions.[2]

Example: A and B established Corporation X. A transferred cash to X in exchange for 50 percent of the stock, and B transferred appreciated land in exchange for the remaining 50 percent. Clearly A and X are not worried about the transfers because neither is subject to tax. What about B? B transferred appreciated property but is not in control of X. B can postpone recognizing gain if the transaction qualifies as a section 351 transaction. If A's cash qualifies as property, then the two transferors together are in control of X. In that case B avoids gain recognition on the land. Fortunately for B, U.S. currency is property for purposes of section 351.[3]

Generally, anything of value can be transferred to a corporation and qualify as property for section 351 purposes. Real property, computers, intellectual property such as copyrights, and other types of assets can be part of a section 351 transaction.

Section 5.04(a)(2) Transfer

There are different views regarding whether a transfer has actually occurred. These may be particularly important when transfers of intellectual property are involved. The IRS has ruled that a property transfer cannot qualify for section 351 purposes unless all the substantial rights to the property are transferred.[4] If less than all substantial rights are transferred, the transfer will not qualify for section 351 treatment and will be taxable. For purposes of section 351, the IRS considers that substantial rights have been transferred only if the transferor transfers an unqualified, exclusive right in perpetuity, to use a prod-

---

2. *See* Rothman, Capps, Herzog and Brady, 758-2nd T.M., Transfers to controlled corporations: In General, for an exhaustive review of section 351.

3. *Id.*, citing *Halliburton v. Commissioner*, 78 F.2d 265 (9th Cir. 1935); *Portland Oil Co. v. Commissioner*, 109 F.2d 479 (1st Cir.), *cert. denied*, 310 U.S. 650 (1940); *Holstein v. Commissioner*, 23 T.C. 923 (1955); *Dillard v. Commissioner*, 20 T.C.M. (CCH) 137 (1961); Rev. Rul. 69-357, 1969-1 C.B. 101.

4. Rev. Rul. 64-56, 1964-1 C.B. 133.

uct. For example, it has ruled that a license to use a patent will not qualify as a transfer for section 351 purposes.[5]

As we explained in Chapter 1, a revenue ruling only represents the IRS' views on a particular transaction. Courts have taken a more lenient approach to this question, choosing to focus instead on whether something of value has been transferred. For example, in *E.I. Dupont de Nemours and Co. v. United States*,[6] the Court of Claims held that a non-exclusive transfer of a patent qualified for section 351 purposes even though the transferor did not transfer all the rights under the patent.

From an administrative point, the IRS' views have merit. Requiring that all rights must be transferred for section 351 purposes makes the transfer issue easier to administer. If, instead, only substantial rights must be transferred, litigation may ensue over what is a substantial transfer. Perhaps a better standard should be whether the transferee has received a property interest. Whether that property interest represents "substantial rights" in the property should arguably be the transferor's and transferee's decision, but that viewpoint may lead to abuse. In any event, you should be aware of this potential problem.

Section 5.04(a)(3) Transferee

To what entity must the transfer be made? Although one might think that the transfer must be to the corporation that will be controlled following the transfer, that is not always required. As you may have noticed by now, there are few obvious answers in the tax world.

Example: Corporation X merges into Corporation S, a subsidiary of Corporation P. Individual A, the sole shareholder of X, receives 50 percent of the P stock. As part of the same transaction, Individual B transfers land to P in exchange for 30 percent of the P stock. This transaction does not qualify under section 351.

Example: Corporation X merges into Corporation P. Individual A, the sole shareholder of X, receives 50 percent of the P stock. As part of the same transaction, Individual B transfers land to P in exchange for 30 percent of the P stock. P then transferred the X assets to Corporation S, a subsidiary of P. This transaction qualifies under section 351.

Although the two examples appear to have the same end result, they are treated differently for purposes of section 351. Rev. Rul. 84-44[7] holds that the

---

5. Rev. Rul. 69-156, 1969-1 C.B. 101.
6. 471 F.2d 1211 (Ct. Cl. 1973).
7. 1984-1 C.B. 105.

first transaction cannot qualify for section 351 treatment because the X assets were transferred to S instead of to P. Although A and B obtained control of P, they did not do so in exchange for a transfer of property to P, a requirement of section 351. Section 368(a)(2)(C) permits the second transaction to qualify. Section 368(a)(2)(C) would permit a transfer of the assets of X down to S. We will revisit section 368(a)(2)(C) in Chapter 10, which covers reorganizations.

Section 5.04(b) Person or Persons

Section 7701(a)(1) broadly defines a person as either an individual, a trust, estate, partnership, association, company or corporation. Because section 351 permits a person *or* persons to be transferors for section 351 purposes, two or more persons can join together to make a section 351 transfer. Their respective ownership will be aggregated to determine whether they meet the control requirement.

Example: Corporation X merges into Corporation Y. A, who was X's sole shareholder, receives 50 percent of the Y stock in the merger. As part of the same transaction, Corporation Z transfers appreciated land to Y in exchange for the remaining Y stock. This transaction qualifies under section 351 because the two transferors (A and Z) have transferred property (assets of X and land) to Y in exchange for control of Y.

Caveat: When a transaction involves multiple transferors and the planner wants the IRS to issue a private letter ruling providing for section 351 qualification, the ruling request must include a statement that the transfers and exchanges will occur pursuant to an agreement.[8]

What if the two transfers were unrelated? If the transfers were truly unrelated, the parties would not be looking for section 351 protection. A would be able to avoid gain recognition if the merger of X into Y qualified as a reorganization (discussed in Chapter 10). And as we have seen earlier, X would be protected from tax by section 1032.

Although Z would have a taxable transaction, that may have been Z's goal. A taxable transaction may be advantageous. First, it gives the taxpayer a higher basis for the property received. Second, if the taxpayer has losses from other transactions, those losses may offset the gain recognized on this transaction.

---

8. *See* Rev. Proc. 83-59, 1983-2 C.B. 575.

Section 5.04(c) Received Only Stock

Section 5.04(c)(1) General Rule

The transferor(s) in a section 351 transaction must receive only stock in exchange for property. Section 7701(a)(7) defines stock as including "shares in an association, joint-stock company or insurance company." Based on that definition, common or preferred stock should qualify. The discussion below discusses situations in which preferred stock is disqualified. The discussion in section 5.05 covers the tax consequences of receiving consideration other than stock.

Section 5.04(c)(2) Preferred Stock

For purposes of section 351, stock is divided into two categories, common stock and preferred stock. Until the American Jobs Creation Act of 2004, section 351(g)(3)(A) treated stock as preferred if it "is limited and preferred as to dividends and does not participate in corporate growth to any significant extent." Stock with a fixed dividend and redemption price clearly satisfies that definition. In the 2004 Act, Congress added the following sentence at the end of section 351(g)(3): "Stock shall not be treated as participating in corporate growth to any significant extent unless there is a real and meaningful likelihood of the shareholder actually participating in the earnings and growth of the corporation."

The legislative history provides two examples of stock covered by the revision. The first example is stock that has preference on liquidation and is entitled to the same dividends as those declared on common stock if the corporation does not pay dividends on any of its stock. The second example is stock that is entitled to a dividend that is the greater of seven percent or the dividends distributed to common shareholders if the common shareholders are not expected to receive dividends greater than seven percent.[9] Until the IRS issues guidance on this change, you should keep this legislative history in mind.

Section 5.04(c)(3) Nonqualified Preferred Stock

A corporation may transfer both common and preferred stock in exchange for property. If a shareholder receives only common stock, such stock will always qualify for section 351 purposes. But if the shareholder receives preferred stock, we must first determine whether that preferred stock is nonqualified

---

9. *See* H.R. Conf. Rep. No. 108-755, 108th Cong., 2d Sess. 771 (2004).

preferred stock as defined in section 351(g). If it is nonqualified preferred stock, that part of the transfer will not qualify under section 351. It will be a taxable transaction unless the recipient shareholder qualifies for the benefits of another nonrecognition provision.

The House committee report on the original iteration of section 351(g) states that when certain preferred stock instruments are received in an exchange purported to qualify under section 351, it is appropriate to view such instruments as taxable consideration since the investor has often obtained a more secure form of investment.[10]

Although common shareholders are subordinated to preferred shareholders for purposes of dividends and liquidation distributions, they are not necessarily disadvantaged by a corporation's decision to issue preferred stock. Because preferred shareholders generally have limited rights, they provide an infusion of capital (which the corporation may really need) but do not share future corporate growth with the common shareholders. In many ways, preferred shareholders resemble creditors more than they do shareholders.

Even though preferred stock does not share in corporate growth, it is not automatically disqualified from use in a section 351 transaction. Only so-called nonqualified preferred stock is prohibited. That stock is defined in section 351(g)(2).

Preferred stock is nonqualified if it has any of the four characteristics listed below:

(i)   the holder of such stock has the right to require the issuer or a related person to redeem or purchase the stock;
(ii) the issuer or a related person is required to redeem or purchase such stock;
(iii) the issuer or a related person has the right to redeem or purchase the stock and, as of the issue date, it is more likely than not that such right will be exercised; or
(iv) the dividend rate on such stock varies in whole or in part (directly or indirectly) with reference to interest rates, commodity prices, or other similar indices.

By enacting section 351(g), Congress clearly intended to restrict section 351 to situations in which the transferor is making a permanent type of investment in the corporation. The preferred stock described in section 351(g)(2) has qualities that are simply too much like debt.

Example: Individual A transfers property to Corporation X in exchange for X preferred stock. A is granted the right to require a repurchase at any time,

---

10. H.R. Rep. No. 105-148, 105th Cong., 1st Sess. 472 (1997).

subject to A's giving thirty days notice. The preferred stock is nonqualified preferred stock and cannot qualify for section 351 treatment.

Stock that might be treated as nonqualified preferred stock can qualify for section 351 treatment if it meets the tests described in section 351(g)(2)(B). The stock can qualify if none of the redemption or purchase features can be exercised within twenty years of its issue date. Second, even if they can be exercised within that period, the stock will qualify if these features are subject to a contingency that makes the likelihood of redemption or purchase remote.

Example: Individual A transfers property to Corporation X in exchange for X preferred stock. A is granted the right to require a repurchase after forty years have elapsed, subject to A's giving thirty days notice. In the absence of any other facts, the preferred stock is not nonqualified preferred stock and can qualify for section 351 treatment.

Section 351(g)(2)(C) provides additional exceptions. Preferred stock that would otherwise be disqualified can qualify for section 351 exchange treatment if a redemption or purchase feature is exercisable only upon the holder's death, disability or mental incompetency.[11] Congress recognizes that those situations are so unpredictable that they may, in fact, never occur (or at least are not expected to occur within a reasonable time), thus making the shareholder's investment sufficiently "permanent." In addition, stock will qualify if the redemption or purchase feature can be exercised only when the holder separates from the service of the issuing corporation or a related person.[12] This exception requires that the stock have been issued in connection with the performance of services and represents reasonable compensation.

Example: Individual A transfers property to Corporation X in exchange for preferred stock in X. A insists on a clause that the stock can be redeemed upon his death. In the absence of any other facts, the preferred stock is not nonqualified preferred stock and can qualify for section 351 treatment.

Not surprisingly, there are exceptions to the exceptions. Section 351(g)(2)(C)(ii) provides an exception to the death, disability, or mental incompetency exception. The safe harbor will not apply to stock received or exchanged in the transaction if any class of that corporation's stock is readily tradable. It also does not apply if the exchange is part of a transaction or series of transactions in which the issuer is to become a corporation whose stock is readily tradable.[13] Congress has determined that if there is a ready market for a stock,

---

11. I.R.C. §351(g)(2)(C)(i)(I).

12. I.R.C. §351(g)(2)(C)(i)(II).

13. The section 351(g)(2)(C)(ii) limitations are broadly written. Stock can be "readily tradable" even if it does not trade on an established securities market.

there is no need to provide a special death or disability exception. Upon death or disability, the stock can be readily sold to comply with the owner's death wishes or to provide for the needs of a disabled or mentally incompetent owner.

Example: Individual A transfers property to Corporation X in exchange for preferred stock in X. A insists on a clause that the stock can be redeemed upon his death. The common stock of Corporation X stock is readily tradable. The preferred stock received by A will be nonqualified preferred stock and the transfer will not qualify for tax-free treatment under section 351. A's preferred stock is disqualified if any class of X stock is readily tradable.

Section 5.04(d) Control

Control is defined by reference to section 368(c), a section we discuss at greater length in Chapter 10. Control has two aspects. First, there must be ownership of stock possessing at least 80 percent of the corporation's total combined voting power. For this purpose, all shares with the right to vote are aggregated rather than judged on a per-class basis. Second, there must be ownership of at least 80 percent of the total number of shares of all other classes of stock. The IRS applies the second test on a class by class basis.[14]

Section 5.04(e) Control Immediately After the Transfer

Section 5.04(e)(1) Disposition of Stock Acquired

Section 351(a) provides that the transferor(s) in a section 351 transaction must control the corporation to which the property is transferred immediately after the exchange. In using the word "immediately," did Congress restrict application of the step transaction doctrine and provide taxpayers some leeway in financing a corporation? Even if the transferors later lose control, the "immediately" requirement would still be met. Unfortunately, the legislative history provides no answer.

So must the word immediately be taken at its literal meaning? If a transferor sells stock acquired in a section 351 transaction two to three days following the section 351 transaction, would the "immediately after" requirement be met? It depends.

As we have seen earlier, application of the step transaction doctrine is always a possibility you should consider. If a transferor had entered into a con-

---

14. Rev. Rul. 59-259, 1959-2 C.B. 115.

tract to sell stock acquired in a section 351 transaction, would this sale be subject to the step transaction doctrine? Arguably, that doctrine would not apply because its aim is to eliminate steps that are unnecessary to a transaction, not to add steps.[15] If A transfers property to X in exchange for X stock, and then A sells the stock received to B, no step can be eliminated. If step (1) is eliminated (transfer of property by A to X in exchange for X stock), the transaction will not be completed.

The step transaction doctrine is normally applied using the end result test, the mutual interdependence test, or the binding commitment test. Arguably, none of these tests applies because application of the tests will result in a changed transaction. However, some courts would apply the step transaction doctrine regardless of whether any steps are eliminated. In *Culligan Water Conditioning of Tri-Cities v. United States*,[16] the court did not apply the step transaction doctrine to the incorporation of a sole proprietorship followed six months later by a sale of the corporation's stock. The court held that there had been no plan to obtain control of the corporation and then dispose of it. Although the court's discussion of how to apply the step transaction doctrine was dictum, if there had been such a plan, it would have been interesting to see how the court would apply the doctrine. Which step would have been eliminated?

Note that in *Culligan*, the corporation was arguing for application of the step transaction doctrine so that the sole proprietor would not have control and the transaction would not qualify for section 351 treatment. If the transaction did not qualify under section 351, the corporation would not have to calculate its basis in the property received under section 362 (generally, basis of the transferor). Because it would receive a fair market value basis in the property received, its depreciation deductions would be higher and it would report less gain on selling the property.

Section 5.04(e)(2) Nonsimultaneous Transfers

Section 351 does not require that the transferors in a section 351 transaction transfer property simultaneously. Nevertheless, the prudent attorney would ensure that a transfer by multiple transferors be reduced to writing so as to eliminate or reduce concerns about the make-up of the control group. In drafting the agreement, the attorney should be guided by the regulations.

---

15. *See Esmark, Inc. v. Commissioner*, 90 T.C. 171 (1988). It is not clear that the IRS has totally accepted the *Esmark* decision.

16. 567 F.2d 867 (9th Cir. 1978).

They provide that the parties' rights will be defined and the execution occurs in a manner consistent with "orderly procedure."[17]

Section 5.04(e)(3) Dispositions by Corporate Transferor

Can the control requirement be met if a corporate transferor that receives stock in a section 351 transaction transfers that stock to its own shareholders? The parties do not have to worry about the step transaction doctrine in this context. Section 351(c) permits a corporate shareholder to distribute stock received in a section 351 transaction to its shareholders and still meet the control requirement. The nexus between a corporate shareholder and its shareholders is deemed close enough that ownership by the corporation's shareholders is equated to ownership by the corporation itself.

Caveat: Section 351(c) illustrates the importance of carefully reading the Code rather than hoping that a court will apply common sense in categorizing a transaction. If no Code provision specifically supports an interpretation, the taxpayer may be forced into costly litigation.

Section 5.04(f) Control Group Issues

Section 5.04(f)(1) Additional Transfers by Controlling Shareholder

Section 351 does not require that control be acquired in exchange for the property transferred. It requires only that the transferor(s) have control of the corporation. A shareholder who already has control can later transfer additional property to the corporation and qualify this transfer for nonrecognition under section 351. Even though control is not "obtained" in the second transaction, it still qualifies for section 351 treatment.

Example: A owns 80 percent or more of the stock of Corporation X and transfers additional property to X in exchange for additional shares. That transaction qualifies under section 351.

What if another person wants to transfer appreciated property to an existing corporation? If not part of the existing control group, that person may not be able to acquire enough stock to independently gain control. In that case, the transfer may not qualify even if the existing shareholders transfer additional property at the same time. The regulations apply a substance over form analysis in this situation. An existing shareholder will not be included as part

---

17. *See* Treas. Reg. § 1.351-1(a)(1).

of the transferor group if the property transferred is of relatively small value in comparison to the stock that shareholder already owns, and the primary purpose of the transfer is to qualify exchanges by other persons for section 351 treatment.[18]

Example: A owns 80 percent or more of the stock of Corporation X. B transfers property worth $100,000 to X in exchange for 10 percent of the X stock. At the same time, A transfers $100 to X in exchange for one additional X share. B's transfer does not qualify for section 351 treatment.

Section 5.04(f)(2) Stock Received for Services

If stock is received in exchange for services, the recipient cannot use section 351 to postpone reporting the value of those shares. In addition, if the value of the services is too high, other transferors may also be unable to qualify for section 351 treatment.

Example: Individual A transferred property worth $70,000 to Corporation X in exchange for 70 percent of its stock. As part of the same transaction, Individual B rendered services worth $30,000 to X and received 30 percent of the X stock. Because transferors of property did not acquire control, A will not be able to qualify for section 351 nonrecognition.

What if the person rendering services also transfers property? The outcome will depend on the relative values of the services and the property. If the value of the stock issued to that person for property is relatively small when compared to the value of the stock issued for services, and the primary purpose is to qualify other transferors for section 351 treatment, the stock issued for property will be disregarded.[19]

Example: Individual A transferred property worth $70,000 to Corporation X in exchange for 70 percent of its stock. As part of the same transaction, Individual B transferred property worth $20,000 and rendered services worth $10,000 to X and received 30 percent of the X stock. The transferors of property acquired control. A and B will qualify for section 351 nonrecognition for any gains on the property transferred to X.

Example: Individual A transferred property worth $70,000 to Corporation X in exchange for 70 percent of its stock. As part of the same transaction, Individual B transferred property worth $1,000 and rendered services worth $29,000 to X and received 30 percent of the X stock. B will not be treated as

---

18. Treas. Reg. § 1.351-1(a)(1)(ii).
19. Treas. Reg. § 1.351-1(a)(1)(i).

transferring property for stock. As a result, neither A nor B will qualify for section 351 nonrecognition.

Section 5.05 Tax Consequences of the Transferor(s)

Section 5.05(a) Gain or Loss Recognition

Section 5.05(a)(1) General Rule

If the transferors who are part of the control group receive only qualifying stock, they recognize no gain or loss on the transaction. If they receive any additional consideration, their tax consequences depend on what they receive and on whether they realize a gain or a loss on the transfer.

Section 5.05(a)(2) Receipt of Other Property

If a transferor receives qualifying stock and also receives other property or money, then the transaction may still qualify for section 351 purposes. The transferor, however, will recognize some or all of any realized gain. The amount of gain recognized cannot exceed the amount of money received plus the fair market value of any property received. If the transferor had a realized loss, the loss will not be recognized. This is an instance where section 351 is punitive to taxpayers.

Example: Individual A transfers appreciated property to Corporation X in exchange for all the X common stock. A also receives preferred stock valued at $100, which is redeemable on demand by A. The transaction will qualify under section 351, and A recognizes no gain or loss on the receipt of the common stock. Because the preferred stock is nonqualified preferred stock, A has received other property for section 351 purposes. A will recognize the lesser of the gain realized on the property transferred to X or $100. As we will see later, that gain will affect A's basis for the X stock.

With some planning, taxpayers can avoid the "boot" problem or use it to their benefit. For example, assume that an individual wants to incorporate an existing sole proprietorship. The proprietorship owns gain property (basis of $10 and value of $20) and loss property (basis of $20 and value of $10). The individual wants to receive common stock plus $10 cash as part of the incorporation transfers. If he transfers both properties to the new corporation in exchange for stock and $10 in cash, he must recognize $10 in gain because the cash received did not exceed the gain realized on the gain property.

The individual might be able to avoid this result if he transfers only the gain property solely in exchange for control of the corporation. Because this transaction qualifies under section 351, he recognizes none of his gain. He can sell the loss property to a third party and transfers one-half of the cash to the corporation. That will allow him to deduct his loss and retain $10.[20]

Section 5.05(a)(3) Assumption of Liabilities

A taxpayer who incorporates an existing business is likely to owe debts in addition to owning assets. Not surprisingly, the taxpayer may want the corporation to take responsibility for those debts. After all, it is receiving the business assets. But, because debt assumption is consideration other than stock, a transaction that makes economic sense could trigger gain recognition. The tax consequences associated with debt assumption are governed by the section 357 recognition rules, discussed below, and the section 358 basis rules, discussed in **section 5.06.**

Section 5.05(a)(3)(A) General Rule

As is true for other exchanges, the transferor computes gain or loss realized using section 1001 and includes a reduction in liabilities as part of the amount realized and the gain or loss realized.[21] Section 357(a) allows the taxpayer to avoid recognizing gain in this situation. It provides that debt assumption will not be treated as money or other property when used as consideration in an exchange that would otherwise qualify under section 351.

Example: Individual A transferred property worth $500,000 to Corporation X in exchange for all of the X stock. X also assumed a $100,000 debt. A's basis for the property transferred is $320,000. A realizes a gain of $180,000 but does not recognize any of that gain.

Although section 357(a) uses the term "assumes a liability," you should not assume that the transferee must formally assume the transferor's debt. Section 357(d)(1) provides rules for determining whether a debt is deemed assumed for purposes of section 357. That provision divides debts into two categories: recourse and nonrecourse.

If a recourse debt is involved, the creditor can satisfy the obligation by retaking the property and can also proceed against the debtor's other assets. For

---

20. If the corporation needs that particular item of property, this strategy will not work. The shareholder cannot deduct a loss on selling the property to the corporation if he owns more than 50 percent of its stock value. I.R.C. §§ 267(a)(1) & (b)(2).

21. Treas. Reg. § 1.1001-2. This rule applies to debt assumed by the transferee and to debt that encumbers property even though not formally assumed by the transferee.

purposes of section 357, the corporation is treated as assuming any portion of a recourse debt if the facts and circumstances indicate it has agreed to satisfy the debt and is expected to do so. It does not matter whether the original transferor has been relieved of liability by the creditor.

If a nonrecourse liability is involved, the creditor can satisfy the obligation only by retaking the property. For purposes of section 357, the corporation is generally treated as assuming any nonrecourse liability if it has received the asset subject to that liability. The amount treated as assumed will be reduced if the transferor owns other assets that are subject to the liability. The reduction will be the lesser of the amount of liability that the transferor has agreed to pay (and is expected to pay) or the value of the other assets.[22]

Section 5.05(a)(3)(B) Tax Avoidance Motives

The transferor may be forced to recognize gain if the principal purpose behind the debt assumption was to avoid income tax on the exchange.[23] Even if the taxpayer's principal purpose is not tax avoidance, the transaction is tainted if the taxpayer's principal purpose for the assumption was not a bona fide business purpose. The transaction is judged based on the nature of the liability and the circumstances surrounding the arrangements for its assumption. The taxpayer bears the burden of proving the debt assumption should not be treated as money.[24] Thus, a taxpayer who borrows money against equity in a piece of property shortly before transferring it to a corporation is likely to run afoul of section 357(b). Because he receives cash and the corporation will repay the debt, that taxpayer will find it difficult to establish "good" motives for the debt assumption.

If section 357(b) applies, it taints not only debt assumed for a "bad" purpose. The section treats all debt assumed for that transferor as money or other property.

Example: Individual A owned property worth $500,000 and subject to a $100,000 mortgage that financed its purchase. Three weeks before transferring the property to Corporation X in exchange for all of the X stock, A borrowed an additional $50,000 and used the property as security. X took the property subject to the $150,000 debt. A's basis for the property transferred is $320,000. A realizes a gain of $180,000. Because all $150,000 of debt as-

---

22. I.R.C. §357(d)(2).

23. I.R.C. §357(b).

24. I.R.C. §357(b)(2). The taxpayer must sustain its burden by the clear preponderance of the evidence.

sumption is treated as cash, A will recognize $150,000 of gain. The tax avoidance purpose associated with the $50,000 debt resulted in the entire debt being treated as cash.

Section 5.05(a)(3)(C) Liabilities in Excess of Basis

Section 357(c) applies if the liabilities assumed by the transferee corporation exceed the transferor's basis for the assets transferred.[25] It states a general rule that the amount by which liabilities assumed exceed adjusted basis is treated as gain from the sale or exchange of those assets. The character of the gain (e.g., capital or ordinary) will depend on the character of the underlying assets.

Section 357(c) applies only if the total liabilities exceed the total basis. Fortunately for taxpayers, it is not applied on an asset by asset basis. A taxpayer can increase the basis of property being transferred by adding an item of property or by transferring additional money. Some courts have also allowed taxpayers basis for transferring their own IOUs to the corporation.[26]

Example: Individual A transferred two pieces of property to Corporation X. Property 1 had a basis of $100,000 and a value of $500,000. It was subject to a $120,000 mortgage associated with its original purchase. Property 2 had a basis of $250,000 and a value of $300,000. A received all of the X stock. In addition, X assumed the mortgage. Individual A recognizes no gain. Although the mortgage exceeds A's basis for Property 1, it does not exceed the combined bases of Properties 1 and 2.

Section 357(c)(3) ignores some liabilities for purposes of section 357(c). If paying the liability would give rise to a deduction, that liability is not included in the section 357(c) computation.[27] One exception to this exception applies. A liability cannot be ignored if it resulted in the creation of basis, or increase in basis, in any property.

Example: Individual A transferred property with a basis of $100,000 and a value of $160,000 to Corporation X. X transferred all its stock to A and also agreed to pay A's liabilities. These include the $95,000 mortgage that was given when the property was purchased and $8,000 in property taxes due with respect to the property. Although liabilities exceed basis, the property tax is ignored because it is deductible. As a result, A recognizes no gain on this transfer.

---

25. We will revisit section 357(c), including changes made by the American Jobs Creation Act of 2004, in Chapter 10, which deals with reorganizations.

26. *See Lessinger v. Commissioner*, 872 F.2d 519 (2d Cir. 1989); *Peracchi v. Commissioner*, 143 F.3d 487 (9th Cir. 1998); *cf.* Rev. Rul. 68-629, 1968-2 C.B. 154.

27. Section 357(c)(3)(A)(ii) also ignores liabilities described in section 736(a), which deals with payments in liquidation of the share of a retiring or deceased partner.

If both sections 357(b) and 357(c) apply, you should not be surprised that section 357(b) governs.[28] When that happens, taxpayers have the most onerous result. Instead of recognizing gain only to the extent liabilities exceed basis, they must treat all liabilities assumed in the transaction as money. If liabilities will be assumed in a section 351 transaction, the prudent lawyer must consider section 357(b) & (c).

Section 5.05(b) Basis of Stock Received

Section 5.05(b)(1) General Rule

Section 358(a)(1) provides that the starting point for determining a transferor's basis in the stock received is the transferor's basis for the property exchanged. That basis is decreased by the value of nonqualifying property or money received. It is also decreased by any loss that the transferor recognized in the transaction.[29] The basis is increased by any dividend received in the transaction and by any non-dividend gain that the taxpayer recognized.[30]

Section 358(a)(2) provides that the transferor's basis for any other property received is its fair market value. If the transferor receives nonqualified preferred stock, it is treated as "other property" for basis purposes.

The examples below illustrate these rules. Each example is based on an exchange that qualifies under section 351 and in which the only stock issued is common stock.

Example: Individual A transfers a single piece of property to Corporation X and receives all its stock. A's basis for the X stock is that same as the basis A had for the property transferred.

Example: Individual A transfers a single piece of property to Corporation X and receives all its stock and $5,000. A's basis for the property transferred was $80,000. The property was worth $100,000. A's basis for the X stock is $80,000. A's basis for the property transferred ($80,000) is reduced by the $5,000 money received and increased by the $5,000 gain recognized.

---

28. I.R.C. § 357(c)(2).

29. If the shareholder transfers only items that qualify as "property," section 351(a) provides that no loss is recognized. If the shareholder also transfers indebtedness of the transferee corporation that is not evidenced by a security, that item is not covered by the nonrecognition rules. I.R.C. § 351(d)(2).

30. If a shareholder receives money or other property in an exchange that otherwise qualifies under section 351, gain recognition is the most likely outcome. However, if the transfer is to an existing, closely held corporation that has E&P, money or other property may be treated as a distribution of a dividend. Dividends are discussed in Chapter 7.

Example: Individual A transfers a single piece of property to Corporation X and receives all its stock and $5,000. A's basis for the property transferred was $120,000. The property was worth $100,000. A's basis for the X stock is $115,000. A's basis for the property transferred ($120,000) is reduced by the $5,000 money received.

Section 5.05(b)(2) Allocating Basis to Stock Received

Section 5.05(b)(2)(A) Multiple Properties Transferred

How does the transferor determine the basis for stock if he transfers more than one piece of property to the corporation? The section 358 regulations provide that "the basis of all the stock and securities received in the exchange shall be the same as the basis of all property exchanged therefor."[31] Does this language require that basis be determined by aggregating all transferred property and allocating the total basis pro rata to the shares received? If not, can the shareholders apply a specific identification method and allocate the basis of individual properties transferred to separate shares of stock?

The latter method would allow shareholders to select which stock they later sell, thus allowing them to choose between short and long term holdings and between gain and loss holdings. Not surprisingly, the IRS has ruled that the aggregate method must be used when a taxpayer transfers different assets in exchange for stock in a section 351 exchange.[32]

Section 5.05(b)(2)(B) Multiple Classes of Stock Received

The transferors may receive more than one class of stock in exchange for their property. Possibilities include voting common stock, nonvoting common, and various types of preferred stock. With the exception of the non-qualified preferred stock discussed in section 5.04(c)(3), these shares can be received without gain recognition and will have received the substituted basis described in section 5.05(b)(1). That substituted basis is allocated among all shares received based on their relative fair market value.[33]

---

31. Treas. Reg. §1.358-1(a). This rule is not affected by the proposed section 358 regulations. *See* REG 116564-03, 69 Fed. Reg. 24107 (2004).

32. Rev. Rul. 85-164, 1985-2 C.B. 117. The language in the ruling that applied to securities other than stock is no longer relevant. Although the IRS provides that basis is determined on an aggregate basis, it requires transferors to determine gains and losses on a per-item basis. Rev. Rul. 68-55, 1968-1 C.B. 140.

33. Treas. Reg. §1.358-2(b)(2).

Section 5.05(b)(3) Assumption of Liabilities

While an assumption of liability will not prevent a transaction from qualifying under section 351, the liability assumption does affect the basis of the stock received. Section 358(d) generally provides that the liability assumption will be treated as money received by the transferor. If the taxpayer's basis does not fall below zero as a result of the liabilities, the taxpayer suffers only a reduction in basis. The taxpayer will realize a larger gain (or smaller loss) when the stock received is sold.

Example: Individual A transfers a single piece of property to Corporation X and receives all its stock. A's basis for the property was $100,000. The property was worth $180,000 and was encumbered by a $25,000 purchase money mortgage, which X will pay. A's basis for the X stock is $75,000. A's $100,000 basis for the original property is reduced by the $25,000 debt assumption.

Example: Individual A transfers a single piece of property to Corporation X and receives all its stock. A's basis for the property was $100,000. The property was worth $85,000 and was encumbered by a $25,000 purchase money mortgage, which X will pay. A's basis for the X stock is $75,000. A's $100,000 basis for the original property is reduced by the $25,000 debt assumption.

A transferor that does not have enough basis must recognize gain, thus preventing the stock basis from falling below zero.[34]

Example: Individual A transfers a single piece of property to Corporation X and receives all its stock. A's basis for the property was $100,000. The property was worth $180,000 and was encumbered by a $125,000 purchase money mortgage, which X will pay. A's basis for the X stock is zero. A's $100,000 basis for the original property is reduced by the $125,000 debt assumption. It is also increased by the $25,000 gain that A recognizes.

Section 358(d) contains an exception for liabilities excluded under section 357(c)(3) because they would give rise to a deduction or described under section 736(a). The transferor received no tax benefit from such liabilities, as any deduction will be taken by the corporation that assumed them.

Example: Individual A transferred property with a basis of $100,000 and a value of $160,000 to Corporation X. X transferred all its stock to A and also agreed to pay the $8,000 in property taxes due with respect to the property. A's basis for the X stock is $100,000. The property tax liability is not treated as cash because it is deductible.

---

34. A zero basis is almost never permitted. We will encounter a rare occurrence of this phenomenon when we study consolidated returns in Part Five.

Section 5.05(c) Holding Period

While the holding period of property is less important than the basis of such property, it does have tax consequences. The holding period determines whether the sale of the property will result in long term or short term capital gain or loss. As you learned in basic income tax class, the tax rate applied to long term capital gains is lower than that applied to short term capital gains.[35]

Although the normal holding period for property begins with its acquisition, section 1223 provides different rules for a number of acquisition methods, including acquiring property in a section 351 exchange. If property acquired in exchange for a capital asset has a basis computed with reference to that asset, its holding period includes the transferred asset's holding period.[36] This rule also applies to property received in exchange for section 1231 property.

Example: Individual A exchanged a capital asset for stock of Corporation X in a section 351 transaction. A had held the asset for the two years preceding the exchange. A's holding period for the X stock includes the two years he held the asset transferred to X.

If a taxpayer transfers several assets in a section 351 transaction, each share of stock received may have multiple holding periods.

Section 5.06 Tax Consequences to the Corporation

Section 5.06(a) Gain or Loss Recognition

Section 1032 provides that a corporation recognizes no gain or loss on the receipt of property in exchange for its stock. Section 1032 applies to the corporation whether or not the shareholder qualifies to use section 351 or another nonrecognition section.

On the other hand, if a corporation transfers property other than its own stock in a section 351 transaction, part of the property it receives is for consideration other than its own stock. If that other property is cash, the corporation has made a purchase and does not realize a gain or loss. But if that other

---

35. *See* I.R.C. § 1(h).
36. I.R.C. § 1223(1).

property is another type of asset, section 351(f) applies. That provision requires the corporation to recognize gain on such transfer but does not allow it to recognize loss.

Example: Individual A transfers land to Corporation X in exchange for 80 percent of X's stock and equipment valued at $100 and in which X had a basis of $80. X recognizes a gain of $20 on the transfer of the equipment.

Example: Individual A transfers land to Corporation X in exchange for 80 percent of X's stock and equipment valued at $100 and in which X had a basis of $110. X does not recognize its $10 loss on the transfer of the equipment.

Section 5.06(b) Basis of Property Received

Section 5.06(b)(1) General Rule

Section 362 generally provides that the corporation's basis for property received in a section 351 transaction is the same as the transferor's basis, increased by gain recognized by the transferor.[37]

Example: Individual A transfers property to Corporation X in a section 351 transaction. The property had a basis of $100 and FMV of $150. A received only X common stock and recognized no gain. X's basis for the property will be $100.

Example: Individual A transfers property to Corporation X in a section 351 transaction. The property had a basis of $100 and FMV of $150. A received X common stock and $5 and recognized gain of $5. X's basis for the property will be $105.

Section 362(d) limits the corporation's basis increase for gain recognized. If the gain recognized is attributable to the corporation's assumption of a liability, the basis cannot exceed the property's value.

Example: Individual A transfers property to Corporation X in a section 351 transaction. The property had a basis of $100 and FMV of $150. A received X common stock worth $150. Because X also assumed a $52 liability, A recognized gain of $52. X's basis for the property will be $150.

Section 5.06(b)(2) Section 362(e)

The American Jobs Creation Act of 2004 added section 362(e), which applies to two types of transactions that Congress decided offered excessive tax benefits.

---

37. If the transferor depreciated the property, as would be likely if the transferor was incorporating an existing business, the corporation is likely to be treated as the transferor's alter ego for purposes of depreciating the property received. *See* I.R.C. § 168(i)(7).

As we discussed earlier in this chapter, the shareholder's basis for stock received is computed based on his basis for the property transferred. The corporation generally takes the same basis for that property. If the property is appreciated, the shareholder's stock and the corporation's property both have unrealized gain potential. If the property is worth less than the shareholder's basis, both parties have unrealized loss potential. Section 362(e) seeks to limit the benefits associated with the unrealized losses.

Section 5.06(b)(2)(A) Section 362(e)(1)

Section 362(e)(1) applies to acquisitions made from foreign transferors. This provision, which covers importations of so-called net built-in losses, will affect domestic corporations with foreign investors.

A loss importation occurs if the aggregate bases of property covered by this provision exceeds the aggregate value of such property. Property transferred in a section 351 transaction is covered by section 362(e)(1) if gains or losses on such property are not subject to federal income tax in the hands of the transferor immediately before the transfer but are subject to such tax in the hands of the transferee immediately after such transfer.[38]

Example: In a section 351 transaction, Corporation X, a domestic corporation acquires property assets from Corporation Y, a foreign corporation not subject to United States income tax. Y's aggregate basis for those assets is $100 and their value is $80. This property has a built-in net loss that is covered by section 362(e)(1).

When section 362(e)(1) applies, the corporation's basis for the covered property is its fair market value and not the transferor's basis.

Section 5.06(b)(2)(B) Section 362(e)(2)

Section 362(e)(2) applies even though the shareholder and the corporation are both subject to federal income tax. It alters the normal section 362 basis rules to prevent the parties from deducting built-in losses at both the shareholder and corporate level.

Section 362(e)(2) provides that if the aggregate adjusted basis of property transferred to the corporation exceeds its value, the corporation's basis cannot exceed the property's value. The corporation applies this rule to each property by allocating the reduction to each property based on its share of the built-in loss.[39]

---

38. I.R.C. §362(e)(1)(B).
39. I.R.C. §362(e)(2)(B).

Instead of reducing the corporation's basis for the property, the transferor shareholder and transferee corporation can instead elect to reduce the transferor's stock basis.[40] This election may benefit taxpayers who do not intend to sell the stock in the near future. Depending on the nature of the assets transferred, it may allow the acquired corporation to take advantage of higher depreciation deductions or to recognize a loss on selling property.

Section 5.06(c) Holding Period of Property Received

The holding period of property received by a corporation in a section 351 transaction is determined under section 1223(2). Section 1223(2) provides that the transferee's holding period of property includes the period during which the property was held by the transferor if the transferee's basis for the property is determined in whole or in part by reference to the transferee's basis.

Section 5.07 Transfers That Are Ineligible for Section 351

Section 5.07(a) Transfers to an Investment Company

We now know that a transaction qualifies for section 351 if one or more persons transfer property to a corporation solely in exchange for its stock and are in control of the corporation immediately after the exchange. Certain transfers that seemingly meet this requirement are ineligible for section 351 under section 351(e) because they confer an inappropriate benefit on the transferor.

In your initial income tax course, you encountered the "realization principle." Generally, any property disposition gives rise to a realized gain or loss. If a gain is realized, the taxpayer is subject to tax unless an exclusion or a nonrecognition section applies. If a taxpayer incorporates its business, there is a mere change of form and not an actual disposition of the business assets. For that reason, section 351 allows nonrecognition treatment.

The transaction's substance is different if several taxpayers transfer property to a corporation and end up owning a less risky investment. Going from a risky investment to a less risky investment may reflect financially sound planning. But should taxpayers be allowed to use section 351 to diversify their fi-

---

40. *See* I.R.C. §362(e)(2)(C).

nancial assets? Congress uses section 351(e) to prevent that from happening. That provision provides that a transfer to an investment company (which results in diversification of the taxpayer's interest) will not qualify for nonrecognition under section 351.

Example: Individual A has owned Corporation X stock for twenty years. The stock is highly appreciated but subject to value fluctuations. A's investment in X constitutes 60 percent of her retirement investments. In order to balance her portfolio, A organizes a swap fund. She and several other individuals transfer their stock holdings in different companies to Newco in exchange for all of Newco's stock. Prior to the enactment of section 351(e), such a transaction would qualify under section 351. Under current law, the transfers would be considered transfers to an investment company and, therefore, would not qualify for nonrecognition.

Although it lists assets that are considered in determining investment company status, section 351(e) does not define the term "investment company." The regulations provide the details. Treasury regulations section 1.351-1(c)(1) states that a transfer will be treated as a transfer to an investment company if (i) the transfer results, directly or indirectly, in diversification of the transferors' interests and (ii) the transferee is (a) a regulated investment company (RIC), (b) a real estate investment trust (REIT), or (c) a corporation more than 80 percent of the value of whose assets (excluding cash and nonconvertible debt obligations) are held for investment and are readily marketable stocks or securities, or interests in RICs or REITs. The determination of whether a corporation is a RIC or a REIT is usually done by the corporation. Thus, the typical investor only needs to inquire from the corporation whether it is a RIC or a REIT. Because there are important tax advantages to being a RIC or a REIT, these entities are very careful that they meet and continue to meet the requirements for RIC and REIT status.[41]

Because the determination of whether a corporation is an investment company is somewhat complicated, it requires a certain level of sophistication.[42] The investor should not count on getting significant assistance from the corporation in making such a determination. As noted earlier in this chapter, whether or not a transfer to it qualifies under section 351, the corporation is protected from gain recognition by section 1032. Consequently, it behooves

---

41. RICs and REITs, and their owners, are generally subject to one level of tax even though RICs and REITS are corporations. This tax regime is accomplished by allowing deductions for distributions made to their shareholders.

42. Section 351(e) provides an extensive list of property taken into account in determining whether an entity is an investment company.

the planner to be familiar with the diversification rules and to help clients avoid losing section 351 qualification unnecessarily.

Diversification requires that two or more persons transfer nonidentical assets to a corporation.[43] Obviously, if there is only one transferor, or if the transferors transfer the same type of property, diversification does not occur. There is also no diversification for section 351 purposes, if a transferor or transferors transfer assets that are already diversified, for example a diversified portfolio of stocks.[44] Even if transfers result in diversifying the transferors' assets, section 351 may still be satisfied if the transferee corporation is not a RIC, REIT, or investment company as defined above. The point of section 351(e) is to attack swap funds. Transferors that make transfers to an operating company and do not use such transfers as a ruse to diversify their investments are unlikely to run afoul of section 351(e).

Section 5.07(a)(1) Transfers in a Title 11 Proceeding

If a corporation is involved in a proceeding governed by the bankruptcy laws, a taxpayer may transfer property to satisfy the corporation's debts. Because a transfer directly to the creditor is a realization event, the transferor would recognize gain or loss. Section 351(e)(2) prevents the transferor from using the corporation as a conduit to section 351 status. If the transferor uses any of the stock received to pay corporate debt, that portion of the transfer cannot qualify for section 351 treatment.

Section 5.08 Cross References

As we indicated in section 1.02(a), Code sections generally do not refer to each other. It is a good idea to look at the Code section's "neighborhood" to determine what other Code sections may be applicable. Section 351(h), which provides several cross references, is an exception to our general statement. It provides cross references to sections 61, 304, 357, 358, 362, and 2501.

Notwithstanding section 351(h), our advice still stands for three reasons: (1) other Code sections may not be that user-friendly; (2) it is a good habit to look beyond the Code section that you are currently perusing; and (3) igno-

---

43. Treas. Reg. § 1.351-1(c)(5).

44. Treas. Reg. § 1.351-1(c)(6). The determination of whether a portfolio is diversified is made with reference to certain tests contained in section 368(a)(2)(F). In this context, both corporate and non-corporate transferors are included.

rance of the law is never an excuse—even if cross references are incomplete, you will still be charged with knowing the law. For example, section 351(h) does not mention the interaction between section 351(b) and section 1239 (gain from sale of depreciable property between certain related taxpayers) or the section 1245 and 1250 depreciation recapture rules.

Section 5.09 Overlap between Section 351 and Other Code Sections

It is not unusual for two or more Code sections to apply to a transaction. For example, a transaction may qualify both as a section 351 transfer and as a reorganization.[45] When this occurs, the taxpayers may be subject to tax consequences under both Code sections. This may benefit any transferor who is trying to qualify under section 351 because he cannot take advantage of the reorganization provision.

A transaction can qualify under more than one Code section only if the requirements of each Code section are met. How do we know that more than one Code section applies to a transaction? First, the transaction must be described in more than one Code section. Second, Congress must not have indicated that one Code section takes priority in such a case.

One Code section may have more rigorous requirements than the other. For example, the regulations under the reorganization provisions clearly provide business purpose, continuity of interest, and continuity of business purpose requirements. Those requirements don't appear to clearly apply to section 351 transactions.

With respect to business purpose, the IRS has attempted to impose such a requirement in the section 351 context, and some courts have been receptive to that position.[46] Nevertheless, it is not clear whether a business purpose in addition to merely wanting to incorporate is needed. If the transfer is made to a corporation, and there is no tax abuse involved, the IRS will be hard pressed to impose a business purpose requirement. With respect to the continuity of interest and continuity of business requirements, the section 351

---

45. If Corporation X merges into Corporation Y and one or more other persons also transfer property to Y, the ownership of Y stock will be aggregated to determine whether the transaction qualifies under section 351.

46. *See* Rev. Rul. 55-36, 1955-1 C.B. 340; *West Coast Marketing Corp. v. Commissioner,* 46 T.C. 32 (1966).

regulations do not impose such requirements. This is not surprising, given that section 351 generally requires only that the transferor(s) of property control the corporation immediately following the transfer(s).

If Congress decides that one Code section takes precedence over another, it is likely to favor the section that grants fewer benefits. For example, if a transaction is described under both sections 351 and 304, section 304(b) provides that section 304 takes priority. Instead of enjoying section 351 nonrecognition, the taxpayers involved in the transaction, may be treated as receiving a dividend taxable under section 301.[47]

Section 5.10 Miscellaneous Procedural Matters

Although less interesting than the substantive law, certain procedural matters are nevertheless important. The regulations under section 351 impose certain reporting requirements on the transferor(s) and the transferee corporation.[48] The new corporation may also qualify for several elections. These include selecting an accounting method and electing S Corporation status. Finally, if the transaction qualifies under both section 351 and a reorganization provision, section 381 determines whether the transferee corporation inherits certain tax attributes (such as E&P). Some of the matters discussed above would normally be handled by an accountant, but the tax lawyer must be aware of the issues and understand their significance.[49]

---

47. Similarly, transactions described in both section 368(a)(1)(C) and section 368(a)(1)(D) are treated as described in the latter Code section. Until the American Jobs Creation Act of 2004 made section 357(c) inapplicable to acquisitive D reorganizations, that meant that section 357(c) (generally taxing liabilities assumed in excess of basis) applied to these transactions. Reorganizations are discussed more fully in Chapter 10.

48. Treas. Reg. § 1.351-3.

49. For a more complete discussion of these issues, see Rothman, Ehrenkranz, and Settineri, 759 T.M., Transfers to controlled corporations: Related Problems.

Chapter 6

Capital Structure

Section 6.01 In General

The average corporate tax lawyer is normally not concerned with the corporation's capital structure. The appropriate debt/equity ratio depends on the particular industry and the sensibilities of the corporation's managers. Tax consequences should not override sound business judgment.

Nevertheless, debt and equity do have different tax consequences. When a corporation pays interest on debt, it receives a deduction and the payee reports gross income. When it pays a dividend with respect to stock, the corporation receives no deduction but the payee reports gross income. Because of these and other differences, it is important for the taxpayer to know which financial instruments are debt and which are equity.

Taxpayers that are raising capital often want flexibility in deciding whether to issue debt or equity. They may also want the ability to change their mind at a later date. For example, it may be more advantageous to call an instrument debt sometime after its issuance even though it was advantageous to call it equity at the time of issuance.

If the corporation that issued the "debt" has suffered losses, canceling the debt instrument will cause it to recognize gain that may be offset by those losses. The creditor may be entitled to a bad debt deduction under section 166. If, on the other hand, the instrument was equity, no favorable tax benefits would ensue until the stock is deemed to be worthless and subject to a worthless securities deduction under section 165(g).

Section 6.02 Relevant Code Sections

This is the only chapter of this book in which we discuss just one Code section, section 385. Although that section stands on its own, once a determination is made under section 385, other Code sections come into play. For example, if a determination is made that a taxpayer's interest in the corporation is equity as opposed to debt, transfers of money from the corporation to the taxpayer may be treated as dividends under section 301 (assuming the corporation has E&P as determined under section 312). If the taxpayer's interest is determined to be debt, transfers of money will be treated as interest received or as repayment of the debt itself. As we will see later, judicial decisions interpreting section 385 are extremely important.

Section 6.03 Debt versus Equity

Section 6.03(a) In General

At first glance, the difference between debt and equity appears to follow your common sense. If you loan money and expect repayment, the transaction will typically be a loan. If you receive more than you loaned, the additional amount is interest and is includible in your gross income. Assuming a deduction section applies, the payor can deduct the interest paid.

If you do not expect to be repaid for money transferred to another person, the transfer will be treated as a gift if made to a friend or relative. If the transfer is made to a corporation, it will probably be treated as an equity contribution if you were a shareholder or as a non-shareholder capital contribution if you were not.[1] Distributions, to the extent the corporation has E&P, are likely to be included in your gross income as dividends.[2]

Although the classification of an instrument as debt or equity is partly determined by the intent of the parties, an objective observer may question their categorization. Section 385 was enacted to assist parties in determining an instrument's classification. Unfortunately, as discussed below, it has not provided certainty.

---

1. *See* I.R.C. § 118. The tax consequences may be affected by the relationship between two parties. For example, a transfer of money from an employer to an employee is likely to be treated under sections 61(a)(1) and 162(a)(1) as payment for services rendered (past, present or future).

2. In most instances, dividends received by an individual will qualify for the reduced section 1(h) tax rate. Dividends received by a corporation will qualify for the section 243 dividends received deduction.

Section 6.03(b) Regulatory Authority

Section 385(a) authorizes the Secretary "to prescribe such regulations as may be necessary or appropriate to determine whether an interest in a corporation is to be treated ... as stock or indebtedness" or in part as each.[3] Delegation at the beginning of the section implies that Congress has decided debt-equity classification issues are too complex for it to resolve by statute.[4] Although section 385(b) lists factors that the regulations could consider, the list is neither mandatory nor exclusive.

Section 385(c)(3) provides additional regulatory authority. It allows the IRS to require taxpayers to submit the information necessary for carrying out subsection 385(c).

Although section 385 was enacted in 1969, final regulations that classify instruments as debt or equity do not exist. In the early 1980's, the IRS tried to provide regulatory guidance. Although it promulgated final regulations in 1980, it delayed their effective date several times and ultimately withdrew them.[5]

Section 6.03(c) Factors in Determining Debt or Equity Status

Section 6.03(c)(1) Section 385(b)

Section 385(b) lists factors that the IRS can take into consideration in promulgating classification regulations. The five factors listed are:

(1) whether there is a written unconditional promise to pay on demand or on a specified date a sum certain in money in return for an adequate consideration in money or money's worth, and to pay a fixed rate of interest;

---

3. Section 7701(a)(11) of the Code defines the term "Secretary of the Treasury" as the Secretary of the Treasury personally and does not include any delegate. The term "Secretary" means the Secretary of the Treasury or his delegate. Section 7701(a)(12) defines "or his delegate" as any "officer, employee, or agency of the Treasury Department duly authorized by the Secretary of the Treasury directly, or indirectly by one or more redelegations of authority, to perform the function mentioned or described in the context." The authority to publish regulations is usually delegated to the IRS.

4. *See also* I.R.C. §§ 337(d) & 384(f).

5. *See* T.D. 7747, 45 Fed. Reg. 86438 (1980), *delayed by* T.D. 7774, 46 Fed. Reg. 24945 (1981), T.D. 7801, 47 Fed. Reg. 147 (1982), and T.D. 7822, 47 Fed. Reg. 28915 (1982). *See also* Notice of Proposed Rulemaking, 47 Fed. Reg. 164 (1982). The withdrawal was announced in T.D. 7920, 48 Fed. Reg. 50711 (1983).

(2) whether there is subordination to or preference over any indebtedness of the corporation;

(3) the ratio of debt to equity of the corporation;

(4) whether there is convertibility into the stock of the corporation; and

(5) the relationship between holdings of stock in the corporation and holdings of the interest in question.

Because there are no regulations, taxpayers and the IRS must rely on authorities such as revenue rulings and lower court opinions; the Supreme Court has not yet decided a case involving section 385. In a pre-section 385 decision, the Court indicated that the determination of whether an instrument is debt or equity is generally a factual question to be determined by an appropriate lower court.[6]

Section 6.03(c)(2) Judicial Tests

Courts have used a number of tests to help in classifying an instrument as debt or equity. These tests include the following:

(1) Is there a pro-rata holding of debt and equity?

(2) Is the corporation thinly capitalized?

(3) Is the instrument called debt or stock?

(4) Does the instrument have a fixed maturity date?

(5) Is the interest at a fixed rate and is payment unconditionally required?

(6) Is the instrument subordinated to the claims of other creditors?

(7) Did the parties treat the instrument as debt or equity on their books?

(8) Did the parties intend to create debt or equity?

(9) Was the instrument issued to acquire the essential operational assets of the business enterprise?

(10) Are the usual creditor rights available to the holder?

(11) Is repayment possible only out of corporate earnings?

(12) Has the holder enforced his rights?

(13) Did the holder gain the right to participate in management as a result of the advances?

(14) Were there alternative financing sources available at the debt's issuance?

(15) Was the issuer in default on other loans when the instrument was issued?

(16) Is repayment secured with liens on property or with guarantees?[7]

---

6. *See John Kelley Co. v. Commissioner*, 326 U.S. 521 (1946).

7. Bittker & Eustice, Federal Income Taxation of Corporation & Shareholders, ¶4.03 Classifying Hybrid Securities, cites to numerous cases, including what is probably the best-known decision of *Fin Hay Realty Co. v. United States*, 398 F.2d 694 (3d Cir. 1968).

It is not clear if any of the 16 criteria have priority over the others. Certainly, the name by which the instrument is called will not be outcome determinative. For example, if an instrument is called debt but calls for no interest payments (or interest is payable only if the corporation has earnings), such instrument will not be considered to be true debt.

In order to avoid recharacterization, a prudent tax lawyer must understand these criteria and draft an instrument that has as many of the characteristics of the desired category as possible. Even a carefully crafted instrument can be recharacterized if the facts show that the instrument was actually used for a different purpose. For example, an instrument initially characterized as debt might later be recharacterized as equity if interest was never collected and is not expected to be collected.

Section 6.04 Hybrid Instruments

Section 385(a) provides that an instrument can be treated as in part debt and in part equity. Although Congress included this language in section 385, it provided no guidance beyond the five factors listed in section 6.03(c)(1). In the absence of statutory or regulatory guidance, aggressive taxpayers have used hybrid instruments in a variety of tax sheltered investments.

Section 6.05 Characterization by Issuer

Section 385(c) provides that the characterization of an instrument as debt or equity by its issuer at the time of the issuance is binding on the issuer and on holders of the instrument. That characterization is not binding on the IRS.[8]

---

8. A holder may be able to avoid being bound by the issuer's classification. The holder's tax return must disclose the inconsistent treatment. I.R.C. §385(c)(2).

PART THREE

CORPORATE DISTRIBUTIONS

Chapter 7

Corporate Dividends

Section 7.01 Introduction

Taxpayers do not invest in corporations to build a collection of decorative stock certificates. They invest because they expect a financial profit. If the corporation is profitable, shareholders may receive some of that profit as dividend distributions. They may also profit by selling their shares for an amount that exceeds their adjusted basis. In addition to selling their shares, they may dispose of them in a redemption (Chapter 8), reorganization (Chapter 10), or liquidation (Chapter 11). As you learned in the basic income tax course, there are tax advantages to donating appreciated shares to charity instead of selling the shares and donating cash.

This chapter focuses on the tax consequences of dividend distributions. Those consequences depend on several factors, which include the corporation's earnings and profits (E&P), the type of property distributed, the shareholder's basis for the stock, and the shareholder's holding period. As the discussion in this chapter indicates, both the corporation and its shareholders have tax consequences.

Section 7.02 Relevant Code Sections

Section 61(a)(4) includes dividends as a component of gross income. But, as is true for much of section 61, the important rules appear in other Code sections. The relevant provisions depend on the nature of the distribution. If the corporation distributes cash, the most important provisions are sections 301, 312, 316, and 317. If it distributes property other than cash, section 311 also applies. If it distributes its own stock, section 305 is also relevant.

Because distributions in cash are the norm, this section focuses on sections 301, 316, and 317. The discussion of property distributions in **section 7.03** adds section 311, and the discussion of stock distributions in **section 7.04** covers section 305. Section 312 E&P computations are introduced in **section 7.05**.

The discussion below is based on some general rules. First, a shareholder receives a taxable dividend if there is a distribution of "property" and the corporation has sufficient E&P. Second, distributions that exceed E&P are treated as a tax-free return of capital or gain from the sale of the stock.

Section 7.02(a) Section 301(a) Requirements

Section 301(a) provides: " … a distribution of property (as defined in section 317(a)) made by a corporation to a shareholder with respect to its stock shall be treated in the manner provided in subsection (c)." That sentence establishes three requirements. First, there must be a distribution of property. Second, that distribution must be made by a corporation to a shareholder. Third, the distribution must be made with respect to the shareholder's stock. Unless all three requirements are met, section 301 does not apply.

Example: Corporation X borrowed money from Shareholder A. The debt instrument requires that X pay 8 percent interest until the debt is repaid. If the transaction creates a bona fide debt, section 301 does not apply to the interest payments. The interest payments X will make to A are not distributions "with respect to the corporation's stock."[1]

Section 7.02(b) Section 317 Requirements

The distribution must be in property. Section 317(a) defines property as "money, securities, and any other property; except that such term does not include stock in the corporation making the distribution (or rights to acquire such stock)."

Although section 317(a) appears to exclude the distributing corporation's own stock from that definition, we will cover exceptions to that rule in **section 7.04** in the context of so-called "stock dividends." At this point, we will consider only cash, securities in other corporations, and other property. The other property could be land, buildings, machinery, copyrights, collectibles, or any other item the corporation chooses to distribute to a shareholder with respect to his or her stock.

---

1. The differences between debt and equity investments are important in a variety of corporate tax contexts.

Distributions of property other than cash are more complicated than distributions of cash. The property must be valued, and the corporation must ascertain its holding period. Property distributions will affect the E&P computation differently from cash distributions.

Caveat: Remember that cash is property for purposes of computing the tax consequences of a distribution under section 301.

Section 7.02(c) Section 301(c) Treatment

If the corporation distributed property, section 301(c) provides the general tax treatment. It categorizes distributions as follows:

The amount that is treated as a dividend is included in the shareholder's gross income. The term dividend is defined in section 316, discussed in **section 7.02(d)**.

Any additional amount received, up to the amount of the shareholder's basis for the stock, is a tax-free return of capital and reduces the shareholder's stock basis.

If the distribution exceeds the shareholder's basis, the excess is treated as gain from the sale or exchange of stock.[2] The fact that the shareholder did not actually sell the stock is irrelevant.

Example: Corporation X distributes $75,000 in cash to Individual A, its sole shareholder. Immediately before the distribution, X had $90,000 in E&P and A had an adjusted basis for her X stock of $52,000. A treats the entire $75,000 as a dividend and includes it in her gross income. Her basis is not affected.

Example: Assume instead that X had only $71,000 in E&P. A treats $71,000 as a dividend. She treats $4,000 as a tax-free return of her investment and reduces her stock basis by $4,000. Her adjusted basis is now $48,000

Example: Assume instead that X had only $7,000 in E&P. A treats $7,000 as a dividend. She treats $52,000 as a tax-free return of her investment and reduces her stock basis by $52,000. Her adjusted basis is now $0. She treats the remaining $16,000 as a gain from the sale or exchange of her stock. That gain will probably be capital gain. Its status as short-term or long-term depends on A's holding period for the stock.[3]

---

2. If any of the distribution represents an increase in value accrued before March 1, 1913, that portion will be tax exempt. I.R.C. § 301(c)(3)(B).

3. As you learned in Chapter 5, if A acquired her shares by transferring a capital asset or section 1231 property to X in a section 351 transaction, her holding period for the stock will include her holding period for that other property. I.R.C. § 1223(1).

Section 7.02(d) Section 316 Current and Accumulated E&P

Section 316 treats distributions of property as dividends if they are made out of (1) E&P accumulated since March 1, 1913 or (2) E&P of the taxable year in which the distribution is made. Depending on its operating results and the prior distributions it has made, a corporation may have both current and accumulated E&P, one but not the other, or neither.

E&P is the tax counterpart to the corporate law concept of earned surplus. E&P represents the corporation's dividend-paying ability for tax purposes. Although a distribution may be called a "dividend" for state law purposes, because the corporation has earned surplus, it cannot be a dividend for tax law purposes unless the corporation has E&P.

Example: Corporation X distributes $100,000 to its shareholders. If X's E&P is at least $100,000, the entire distribution is a taxable dividend. If its E&P is only $90,000, only $90,000 is a dividend. The remaining $10,000 will generally be a tax-free return of basis. If the shareholders' basis is less than $10,000, part of the distribution will be treated as a gain from the sale or exchange of the stock.

Section 7.02(d)(1) Current E&P

Current E&P is determined based on events that occur in the current year. It is not affected by balances in the corporation's accumulated E&P account. As noted in section 7.05, current E&P will be similar to current taxable income, but there are differences in the two computations.

Section 7.02(d)(2) Accumulated E&P

Accumulated E&P is the sum of current E&P for the corporation's prior years minus reductions for distributions that "used up" E&P. Those distributions include the dividend distributions discussed in this chapter, redemption distributions (Chapter 8), and distributions reflecting changes in corporate structure (Chapters 9–11). Accumulated E&P is affected by current year distributions if current E&P is insufficient.

Caveat: Distributions can reduce E&P to zero but they cannot reduce it below zero.

Section 7.02(d)(3) Illustration of Current and Accumulated E&P

Example: Corporation X began operations in 2000 and has never made a distribution to its shareholders. The table below illustrates its current and accumulated E&P for 2000 through 2004.

Year	2000	2001	2002	2003	2004
Current E&P for year	22,000	(40,000)	(32,000)	60,000	8,000
Accumulated E&P, beginning of year	0	22,000	(18,000)	(50,000)	10,000

A distribution can be a dividend if the corporation has sufficient current or accumulated E&P. It does not need to have both. See section 7.02(e) for a discussion of how to determine whether E&P are sufficient.

Section 7.02(e) Allocating E&P to Distributions

Distributions are treated as coming from the most recently accumulated E&P and then going backward. Current year E&P count even if the corporation has no accumulated E&P or has an accumulated E&P deficit. No matter when the distribution is made, the corporation does not compute current E&P until year-end.

Regulations section 1.316-2(b) provides different rules for computing and applying accumulated E&P to distributions. If the corporation that has a current E&P deficit can determine when that deficit occurred, accumulated E&P will be reduced on that date. If it cannot be so precise, accumulated E&P will be reduced ratably throughout the year.

Section 7.02(e)(1) Single Distribution During Year

The examples in this section are based on the table below and assume that the distribution discussed is the only distribution X makes. As they illustrate, the computation is relatively simple if distributions for the year do not exceed (a) current E&P or (b) current and accumulated E&P. They are also relatively simple if both current and accumulated E&P are negative. The computations are more complicated if the distributions exceed both current and accumulated E&P.

Year	2000	2001	2002	2003	2004
Current E&P for year	15,000	24,000	(17,000)	(44,000)	8,000

Example: X distributes $3,000 in 2000. All of it is a dividend because X has at least $3,000 in current E&P. X will begin 2001 with accumulated E&P of $12,000 (its current E&P for 2000 reduced by the dividend).

Example: X instead distributes $19,000 in 2000. Only $15,000 is a dividend because X has only $15,000 of current E&P and no accumulated E&P. The remaining $4,000 reduces the shareholder's basis; if it exceeds basis, the shareholder realizes gain. X begins 2001 with accumulated E&P of zero, not negative $4,000. Distributions cannot reduce E&P below zero.

Example: X instead distributes nothing in 2000 and $28,500 in 2001. All of it is a dividend. The first $24,000 comes from current E&P; the remaining $4,500 comes from E&P accumulated from 2000. X begins 2002 with $10,500 of accumulated E&P.

Example: X instead distributes nothing in 2000–2003 and distributes $5,000 in 2004. All of it is a dividend because X has at least $5,000 in current E&P. X begins 2005 with an accumulated E&P deficit of $19,000 ($15,000 + $24,000 − $17,000 − $44,000 + $3,000).

Example: X instead distributes nothing in 2000–2001 and distributes $30,000 on December 31, 2002. Because its current E&P are negative, accumulated E&P must be determined. Because X distributed the $30,000 at year-end, 100 percent of the $17,000 current E&P deficit offsets the $39,000 accumulated E&P. As a result, only $22,000 is a dividend out of accumulated E&P. The remaining $8,000 reduces the shareholder's basis; if it exceeds basis, the shareholder realizes gain. X begins 2003 with accumulated E&P of zero.

Example: The facts are the same as in the prior example, except that X instead distributes $30,000 on September 30, 2002. X is unable to determine a precise date for when its 2002 deficit occurred. Because X distributed the $30,000 three-quarters of the way through the year, 75 percent of the $17,000 current E&P deficit offsets the $39,000 accumulated E&P; that amount is $12,750. As a result, $26,250 is a dividend out of accumulated E&P. The remaining $3,750 reduces the shareholder's basis; if it exceeds basis, the shareholder realizes gain. X begins 2003 with accumulated E&P of zero.

Section 7.02(e)(2) Multiple Distributions During Year

The examples in section 7.02(e)(1) are based on a single distribution date. If the corporation distributes more frequently (for example, semiannually or quarterly), it must allocate available E&P to each distribution. If a shareholder sold stock during the year, two owners who received distributions of identical amounts may have quite different tax consequences.

The examples in this section are based on the table below and assume that X makes two identical distributions during the year, one at mid-year and one at year-end. For purposes of applying accumulated E&P, assume that X cannot pinpoint exact dates for its current E&P.

Year	2000	2001	2002	2003	2004
Current E&P for year	15,000	24,000	(17,000)	(44,000)	8,000

Example: X distributes $26,000 at mid-year 2001 and another $26,000 at year-end 2001. Because the distributions are equal, the $24,000 of current E&P are allocated equally to each of them. The $15,000 of accumulated E&P is applied first to the mid-year distribution and then to the year-end distribution. The distributions are categorized as follows:

Tax Treatment	Mid-Year	Year-End
Dividend from current E&P	12,000	12,000
Dividend from accumulated E&P	14,000	1,000
Reduction in basis	0	13,000
Total distribution	26,000	26,000

Example: X instead distributes $26,000 at mid-year 2002 and another $26,000 at year-end 2002. Because the 2002 E&P deficit is deemed to occur ratably, the $39,000 of accumulated E&P is reduced at mid-year by $8,500 of the current deficit before being applied to that distribution. Only $4,500 of accumulated E&P remains after the reduction for the mid-year loss and the mid-year distribution. That amount offsets the year-end loss, leaving no E&P to cover the year-end distribution.

Tax Treatment	Mid-Year	Year-End
Dividend from current E&P	0	0
Dividend from accumulated E&P	26,000	0
Reduction in basis	0	26,000
Total distribution	26,000	26,000

Section 7.02(f) Special Tax Consequences of Dividend Treatment

Corporations cannot deduct the amount they distribute to their shareholders as dividends. Dividends are a distribution of after-tax profits; they are not an expense to create profits. If a distribution is treated as a dividend, the

shareholder reports it as gross income. As a result, both the distributing corporation and the recipient shareholder pay tax on the amount distributed.[4]
Two Code provisions reduce the effect of double taxation. Individual shareholders are eligible for a reduced tax rate on dividends included in gross income. Corporate shareholders may qualify for a dividends received deduction.
These relief provisions also apply to property dividends discussed in section
7.03, and to those stock dividends treated as distributions of property that are
discussed in section 7.04.

Section 7.02(f)(1) Individual Shareholders

Section 1(h), which originally applied only to net capital gain income, has applied to dividend income since 2003. Section 1(h)(11) adds qualified dividends
to net capital gains in determining taxable income.[5] As a general rule, the maximum tax rate on qualified dividends will be 15 percent instead of the 35 percent
maximum for ordinary income. A 5 percent rate will apply to dividends received
by shareholders whose highest tax bracket is less than 25 percent. The 5 percent
rate declines to zero for dividends received in taxable years beginning after 2007.

The reduced rates are available only for so-called qualified dividends. Distributions from domestic corporations that are not tax-exempt entities are
qualified dividends. Distributions from foreign corporations can also qualify
if the corporation is incorporated in a United States possession, if the dividend qualifies under an income tax treaty, or if the corporation's stock trades
on a United States stock exchange.[6]

Although the tax rate for qualified dividends is lower than that for other
types of ordinary income, shareholders must understand that this is a rate reduction, not an exclusion provision. Because the dividend is fully included in
the shareholder's gross income, it increases adjusted gross income and makes
it more likely that AGI-based phase-outs will apply.[7]

Shareholders who take advantage of the reduced rate cannot treat those dividends as investment income.[8] Shareholders whose investment interest expense
exceeds their other investment income will be affected by the decision to take
the lower tax rate on dividends. Although they will lose some of their current
year interest deduction, they can carry that excess to future years. The deci-

---

4. The so-called "double tax" regime is discussed in Chapter 4.
5. Section 1(h)(11)(B)(iii) imposes a minimum holding period for eligibility.
6. I.R.C. §1(h)(11)(C).
7. *See, e.g.,* I.R.C. §67.
8. I.R.C. §163(d)(4)(B).

sion between the current interest deduction and the reduced tax rate for dividends varies based on each taxpayer's individual circumstances.

Section 7.02(f)(2) Corporate Shareholders

Section 243 gives corporate shareholders a dividends received deduction equal to 70 percent of the dividend. The percentage is increased to 80 percent if the recipient corporation owns at least 20 percent of the distributing corporation's stock.[9] The percentage is increased to 100 percent if the distributing corporation is a small business investment company. The percentage is also 100 percent for certain dividends paid within an affiliated group.

To qualify for the dividends received deduction, the corporate shareholder must have held the stock for a minimum time period. Code section 246(c)(1) requires that the corporation must have held the stock for more than 45 days "during the 91-day period beginning on the date which is 45 days before the date on which such share becomes ex-dividend."[10] Special rules also apply to corporate shareholders that receive preferred dividends from public utility companies,[11] dividends from foreign corporations,[12] and debt-financed portfolio stock.[13]

If the corporation has not held the stock for at least two years and receives an "extraordinary" dividend, it reduces its basis by the nontaxed portion of the dividend.[14] It reports gain if the untaxed portion exceeds its basis.

Section 7.03 Distributions of Property Other Than Cash

The previous discussion focused on cash distributions. If the corporation distributes property other than cash, the computation is more complicated. In addition to the consequences that flow from a cash distribution, the shareholder must also determine basis and holding period for the non-cash item

---

9. I.R.C. §243(c). The shareholder must own the 20 percent based on both vote and value.

10. I.R.C. §246(c)(2) provides slightly different rules for certain preferred shares.

11. I.R.C. §244 & 247.

12. I.R.C. §245.

13. I.R.C. §246A.

14. I.R.C. §1059. The determination of whether a dividend is "extraordinary" is made by comparing the dividend to a threshold percentage of the corporation's basis for the stock. The percentage is 5 percent for preferred stock and 10 percent for other stock. Section 1059 aggregates dividends paid within certain prescribed time periods.

received. The corporation must determine gain or loss for the property it distributes. Because that computation affects the corporation's E&P, it might also affect the amount the shareholder treats as a dividend.

Section 7.03(a) Shareholder's Tax Consequences

As a general rule, a shareholder who receives a non-cash distribution reports dividend income to the extent of available E&P (and reduces stock basis by any excess). Section 301(b) provides that the amount distributed is the property's fair market value at the time of the distribution. As provided in section 301(d), that amount becomes the shareholder's original basis for the property. The shareholder's holding period does not include the corporation's holding period for the property.

Section 7.03(b) Corporation's Tax Consequences

If a corporation distributes property, the property's value is treated as a substitute for the amount realized. As a result, the corporation realizes gain or loss, depending on whether the property had increased or declined in value.

Although gains and losses are generally recognized in the year they are realized, these gains and losses are governed by section 311 instead of section 1001(c). The section 311 rules depend on whether there is gain or loss. Section 311(a) applies to distributions of loss property and to distributions of the corporation's own obligations.[15] When it applies, the corporation does not recognize gain or loss on distributing property to a shareholder with respect to the shareholder's stock. Section 311(b) applies to all other property and requires that gain be recognized on distributions of appreciated property.

If the corporation recognizes gain, its E&P account is increased accordingly. Because the gain increased E&P, the E&P reduction on account of the dividend is the property's fair market value rather than its lower basis.

If the corporation distributes loss property, it does not recognize the loss. Although the shareholder reports the value of the property as a distribution, the corporation reduces its E&P account by its basis for the property. That amount is higher than the property's value.

Example: Corporation X distributes property with a basis of $100 and a fair market value of $95. X does not recognize its loss, but does reduce its E&P by $100. The shareholder is treated as receiving a distribution of $95.

---

15. These obligations include bonds and notes but not mere promises to pay dividends in the future.

Section 7.03(c) Examples: Distributions of Unencumbered Property

Example: Corporation X has $41,000 of current and accumulated E&P. It distributes a vacant lot to A, its only shareholder. X purchased the lot five years ago for $23,000 and used it for customer parking. It recently built a parking garage and no longer needs the vacant lot, which is now worth $83,000. X recognizes gain of $60,000. Because the gain increases X's taxable income by $60,000, it also increases its E&P by that amount (offset by the additional income tax on that gain).[16] A purchased the X stock 10 years ago for $190,000.

Example: Assume instead that X paid $85,000 for the lot five years ago.

Example: Assume instead that X distributed only its promise to pay $83,000.

In each example above, A receives property worth $83,000. Because the rules are different for gain and loss property, A's dividend consequences vary considerably. Those consequences are summarized in the table below, which ignores the reduction in E&P attributable to the tax on X's recognized gain.

Tax Information	Received by A		
	Vacant Lot	Vacant Lot	X's Obligation
FMV	83,000	83,000	83,000
X's basis	23,000	85,000	0
X's recognized gain/loss	60,000	0	0
Effect on X's E&P	60,000	0	0
X's revised E&P (pretax)	101,000	41,000	41,000
A's dividend income	83,000	41,000	41,000
A's original stock basis	190,000	190,000	190,000
Reduction in A's stock basis	0	42,000	42,000
A's adjusted stock basis	190,000	148,000	148,000
A's basis for distributed property	83,000	83,000	83,000

Distributing the $85,000 basis lot may have been an income tax mistake. If X had instead sold that lot, and distributed the cash proceeds, it could have

---

16. The income tax liability may reduce current E&P, even though paid in a later year, if X is an accrual method taxpayer. *James Armour, Inc. v. Commissioner*, 43 T.C. 295, 310 (1964).

deducted its $2,000 loss.[17] Because this is a closely held corporation, it is possible that the shareholder wanted this particular piece of property.[18]

Section 7.03(d) Distributions of Encumbered Property

The corporation may distribute property that is encumbered by a mortgage, or shareholders may assume (or take property subject to) some other corporate debt as part of the non-cash distribution. If the shareholder agrees to pay a corporate liability, that agreement reduces the value of the distribution. It also benefits the corporation. Not surprisingly, this reduces the amount treated as a distribution and affects the computation of corporate taxable income and E&P.

Section 301(b)(2) reduces the amount treated as a distribution by any corporate liability that the shareholder assumes in connection with the distribution. It also reduces the amount of the distribution by any liability to which the property is subject immediately before and after the distribution. If, for example, the shareholder assumed a $14,000 mortgage on the vacant lot described in section 7.03(c), the distribution is actually worth $69,000 instead of $83,000. Although the shareholder received a distribution of only $69,000, he takes a basis of $83,000. The additional basis reflects the shareholder's future outlay to pay the liability.

One limitation applies to the section 301(b)(2) reduction. The amount of the distribution cannot be reduced below zero even if the shareholder takes on corporate debts that exceed the property's value.

In determining whether it has a gain or loss on the distribution, the corporation generally uses the property's value as a deemed amount realized. By its reference to section 336(b), section 311(b)(2) slightly alters this rule. The deemed amount realized cannot be less than the amount of liabilities taken on by the shareholder.

---

17. Unless X had a net gain from section 1231 transactions, the loss would have been ordinary and not subject to the section 1211(a) capital loss limitations.

18. If X had sold the property to its sole shareholder, section 267 would have disallowed its loss deduction. Although the shareholder's basis would be the $83,000 paid, he would be entitled to reduce any gain from any subsequent sale by the previously disallowed $2,000 loss. I.R.C. §267(d). In addition, although the corporation could not deduct that loss for income tax purposes, it could take a $2,000 deduction in computing E&P. See the discussion of differences between taxable income and E&P in section 7.05.

Section 7.03(e) Distributions of Corporate Obligations

As discussed in Chapter 6, corporations may issue both debt and equity to their shareholders. They may do so in exchange for shareholder investments as part of the initial incorporation or at a later date. Corporations may also issue obligations to shareholders in lieu of cash dividend payments. This section summarizes the shareholder and corporate tax consequences of such distributions.

The obligation's value is treated as the amount of the distribution. Assuming the corporation has sufficient E&P, the shareholder reports that value as gross income. If E&P aren't sufficient, the shareholder reduces basis. The obligation's value becomes the shareholder's basis for it. At the shareholder level, the distribution is essentially the same as any distribution of property.

The corporation reduces its E&P to reflect the distribution. Section 312(a)(2) provides that the reduction is generally the obligation's principal amount. If the obligation has original issue discount, the reduction is for the aggregate issue price. Neither of these amounts is necessarily the same as the obligation's fair market value.[19]

Section 7.04 Distributions of the Corporation's Own Stock and Rights

In addition to distributing money or other property to its shareholders, a corporation might distribute additional shares of its stock or rights to acquire additional shares. Although such distributions are frequently referred to as stock dividends, you must be careful to ascertain exactly what occurred. First, the accounting rules for distributions of a corporation's stock differ from the tax rules. Second, some distributions of a corporation's stock are initially tax-free to the recipient, but others are not. This section discusses distributions of a corporation's stock that are not associated with a corporate restructuring. Those actions are discussed in Part Four.

---

19. Because bonds are payable in the future, their value fluctuates along with changes in the prevailing market rate of interest. As a result, the principal amount to be paid in the future may be higher or lower than the obligation's current value.

Section 7.04(a) Distributions of Stock and Stock Rights: General Tax Rule

As noted earlier in this chapter, if a corporation distributes its own stock or rights to acquire its stock, its shareholders generally do not have dividend income because they have not received "property." Although section 317, which defines property, indicates that these items are not property, it is not an absolute rule. If one of the exceptions set forth in section 305 applies, the distribution will be treated as property. This section considers the general rule, and section 7.04(b) discusses the exceptions. The accounting rules are briefly discussed in section 7.04(c).

Section 7.04(a)(1) Shareholder's Gross Income

If a corporation distributes money to its shareholders, it has changed the nature of their investment. Before, each shareholder owned a certain percentage of the corporation's stock. After, each shareholder still owns the same percentage of the corporation's stock, but each shareholder also has money. If the corporation's E&P are adequate, the distribution is a dividend and is included in each shareholder's gross income.

If a corporation instead distributes more shares of its own stock, it has not changed the nature of its shareholders' investment. When the distribution is pro rata based on prior stock ownership, each shareholder still owns the same percentage of the corporation's stock. Because there has been no relative change in a shareholder's interest, the fact that each owns more shares of stock is irrelevant.

In the situation described above, section 305(a) provides a general rule: "gross income does not include the amount of any distribution of the stock of a corporation made by such corporation to its shareholders with respect to its stock." Section 305(d)(1) defines stock to include rights to acquire stock.

Example: Corporation X distributes to its shareholders 10 shares of X common stock for each 100 common shares they already own. Shareholder A, who owned 200 shares, receives 20 more shares. A does not have gross income.

Example: Corporation X distributes to its shareholders the right to purchase 1 share of Y common stock for each Y common share they already own. Shareholder B, who owned 500 shares, receives the right to purchase 500 more shares. B does not have gross income.

Section 7.04(a)(2) Shareholder's Basis for Stock or Rights

Although the shareholders described in section 7.04(a)(1) report no gross income, they cannot avoid computing a basis for the stock or rights they received.

Unless they know their basis, they cannot determine gain or loss on a later sale or provide accurate information to a donee if they transfer the shares by gift.

Section 7.04(a)(2)(A) General Rule

Section 307(a) provides rules for allocating part of the shareholders' basis to the stock or stock rights received in the distribution. Regulation section 1.307-1 provides rules for allocating the basis between the original stock and the new stock or rights based on their respective fair market values on the date of distribution.

Example: Corporation X distributes to its shareholders 10 shares of X common stock for each 100 X common shares they already own. Shareholder A, who owned 200 shares, receives 20 more shares. A does not have gross income. A paid $110 per share ($22,000) for the original shares. If the new shares are in all respects identical to the original shares, A's $22,000 basis is allocated equally among the 220 shares A owns after the distribution. A now has a basis of $22,000/220 ($100) per share. Because all the shares are identical, Shareholder A did not have to separately value the old and the new shares.

Example: Assume that A's original common shares are voting shares but the newly distributed shares are not. Immediately after the distribution, the old shares are worth $125 per share and the new shares are worth $90 per share. A's 200 old shares are worth a total of $25,000. A's 20 new shares are worth a total of $1,800. The combined value is $26,800. A's basis will be allocated between the two blocks of stock based on their value:

200 original shares $25,000/$26,800 * $22,000 = $20,522.39 ($102.61 each)
20 new shares $ 1,800/$26,800 * $22,000 = $1,477.61 ($ 73.88 each)

Section 7.04(a)(2)(B) Special Rules for Stock Rights

Rights That Are Exercised or Sold. If a shareholder receives rights instead of actual shares, the section 307(b) basis rules take the value of the rights into account. If the value of the rights is at least 15 percent of the value of the old shares, the rights are treated in the manner described in section 7.04(a)(2)(A). If the rights have a lower value, they take a zero basis unless the shareholder elects to apply the basis rules described in section 7.04(a)(2)(A).

Example: Corporation X distributes to its shareholders the right to purchase 1 share of X common stock for each XYZ common share they already own. Shareholder B, who owned 500 shares, receives the right to purchase 500 more shares for $20 each. B does not have gross income. B paid $30 per share ($15,000) for the original shares. Immediately after the distribution, the original shares are worth $60 each and the rights are worth $40 each. The combined value is $30,000 (shares) plus $20,000 (rights), or $50,000. Because the rights are worth at least 15 percent of the value of the old shares, B's original $15,000 basis is allocated among the shares and the rights:

500 original shares $30,000/$50,000 * $15,000 = $9,000.00 ($18.00 each)
500 stock rights $20,000/$50,000 * $15,000 = $6,000.00 ($12.00 each)

Example: Assume instead that the rights entitle the holder to purchase X shares for $55 each. Immediately after the distribution, the original shares are worth $60 each ($30,000) and the rights are worth $5 each ($2,500). The rights are worth only $2,500/$30,000 (8.33 percent) of the original shares. If B does not elect to assign basis to the rights, they take a basis of zero; the original shares retain their full $15,000 basis. If B elects to assign basis to the rights, B's original $15,000 basis is allocated among the shares and the rights:

500 original shares $30,000/$32,500 * $15,000 = $13,846.15 ($27.69 each)
500 stock rights $ 2,500/$32,500 * $15,000 = $ 1,153.85 ($ 2.31 each)

Caveat: In determining whether the value of the rights is at least 15 percent, the rights are compared only to the original stock, NOT to the combined value of the stock and the rights.

If the shareholder later exercises the rights, their basis is added to the basis of the newly acquired stock. If the shareholder instead sells the rights, their basis is used in determining if the shareholder realizes a gain or loss on the sale.

Rights That Are Allowed to Lapse. Regulation section 1.307-1 provides that rights receive a basis only if they are exercised or sold. Because rights that are allowed to lapse receive no basis, the rights holder cannot deduct a loss on the lapse. In this situation, no basis is transferred from the original shares to the rights.

Section 7.04(a)(3) Shareholder's Holding Period for Stock or Rights

If a shareholder reports no gross income on receiving stock or rights because they are not treated as property, the holding period for the stock or rights received is governed by section 1223(5). That holding period includes the shareholder's holding period for the original stock.

Caveat: If the shareholder receives and exercises rights to acquire stock, the holding period for the newly purchased stock begins with its purchase. It does not relate back to either the date the rights were received or to the date on which the original shares were acquired.

Section 7.04(a)(4) Effect on Corporation Making the Distribution

If the corporation makes a distribution of stock or rights that is not considered a distribution of property, there are no tax consequences. Section 311(a)(1) provides that the corporation recognizes no gain or loss. It does not matter whether the distributed stock was newly issued or whether the corporation had previously repurchased it from other shareholders. Section 312(d) provides that that distribution has no effect on the corporation's E&P.

Section 7.04(b) Distributions of Stock and Stock Rights: Exceptions

If section 305 had no exceptions, shareholders in closely held corporations could use it to convert dividend income to capital gain without giving up control or a significant share of future corporate income. Although none of the examples below involves an exception to section 305, they illustrate the trade-offs between immediate cash dividends and receipt of marketable corporate shares.[20]

Example: A is the only shareholder of Corporation X. A has complete control whether she owns one share or one million shares of the X voting common stock. Assuming X has sufficient E&P and distributes a cash dividend, A has gross income equal to the full distribution. A has no gross income if she receives more voting common X stock.

A may want cash but may prefer not to report the full amount as gross income. That would be the result if she received a dividend. She could sell some of her shares to a third party, and be taxed only on her gain. That option requires her to give up some of her control.

Example: X distributes one nonvoting common share to A for every voting common share she owns. A has no gross income and allocates her basis between the two types of stock.

A can sell her nonvoting shares and pay tax only on the difference between the amount realized and her adjusted basis. She gives up no control, because the new shares are nonvoting. She does give up a share of the corporation's future growth unless the nonvoting shares also have lesser rights to dividends and liquidation proceeds.

Example: X distributes one nonvoting, nonparticipating preferred share to A for every voting common share she owns. The preferred shares are en-

---

20. To some extent this discussion is hypothetical. Unless A can induce a third party to buy shares in her closely held corporation, selling dividend stock may not prove feasible.

titled to receive only a fixed dividend. They do not share in future corporate profitability.

A can sell her preferred shares and pay tax only on the difference between the amount realized and her adjusted basis. She gives up no control, because the new shares are nonvoting. She gives up only a fixed dividend because the preferred shares are nonparticipating. They do not share in the corporation's future growth. This series of events may trigger the anti-abuse provisions of section 306. Those provisions are covered in Chapter 8.

Section 7.04(b)(1) Transactions Covered

Section 305(b) lists five exceptions to the general rule. Each covers a transaction that shareholders might otherwise use to avoid dividend consequences for stock distributions that share at least some characteristics of property dividends.

Section 7.04(b)(1)(A) Distributions in Lieu of Money

Section 305(b)(1) applies if a shareholder can elect between distributions of shares or of money or other property. Shareholders who elect property suffer a decrease in ownership percentage. Shareholders who elect to receive shares increase their ownership percentage.

Example: Corporation X has four equal shareholders, A, B, C, and D. Each owns 100 shares of X common stock. X offers its shareholders the option to receive either 1 X share for each 10 they own or the equivalent value in cash. A and B elect to receive shares; C and D elect to receive cash. After the distribution, A and B each own 110 shares; C and D each own 100 shares. A and B each own 110 of the 420 outstanding shares. Each has increased his ownership from 25 percent to 26.2 percent. Together, they now own a majority of the X shares.

Section 305(b)(1) applies even if some shareholders are not offered an election. It also applies even if no shareholder makes the election. The opportunity alone is sufficient to trigger this provision.

Section 7.04(b)(1)(B) Disproportionate Distributions

Section 305(b)(2) applies if a distribution or a series of distributions results in some shareholders receiving money or other property and other shareholders receiving an increase in their ownership interest. The examples below illustrate both the general rule and a safe harbor.[21]

---

21. *See* Treas. Reg. §1.305-3(e) for additional examples of how section 305(b)(2) operates.

Example: Corporation X has four equal shareholders, A, B, C, and D. Although each owns 100 shares of X common stock, there are four identical classes. A owns class A shares; B, class B; C, class C; and D, class D. X declares a dividend of 1 class A share for each 10 class A shares owned. X declares a cash dividend on classes B, C, and D. After these distributions A owns 110 shares; B, C, and D each own 100 shares. A has increased his ownership from 25 percent to 26.8 percent.

Section 305(b)(2) applies to both a single distribution and to a series of distributions if the net result is that some shareholders receive property and others receive an increased ownership interest. Regulation section 1.305-3(b)(4) provides a safe harbor for distributions that occur more than 36 months apart unless the distributions are made pursuant to a plan.

Regulation section 1.305-3(c) provides a safe harbor rule for corporations that pay cash in lieu of fractional shares to shareholders who do not fully qualify for a stock dividend. This non-abusive situation technically meets the section 305(b)(2) definition.

Example: Corporation X has 100,000 shares outstanding. It declares a dividend of 1 X share for each 10 already owned and provides cash in lieu of issuing fractional shares to holders of fewer than 10 shares. Many X shareholders receive only stock, others receive stock and cash, and a few receive only cash. In this situation, some shareholders receive property and others increase their ownership percentage. So long as the corporation did not choose this distribution for the purpose of achieving that outcome, section 305(b)(2) will not apply.

Section 7.04(b)(1)(C) Distributions of Common and Preferred Stock

Section 305(b)(3) applies to distributions or series of distributions that result in some common shareholders receiving common stock and other common shareholders receiving preferred stock. Because common shares generally have the residual rights to earnings and assets, their owners are likely to share in future corporate profits at a greater rate than do the owners of preferred shares.

Section 305 does not define "preferred stock." Regulation section 1.305-5(a) applies the term to "stock which, in relation to other classes of stock outstanding, enjoys certain limited rights and privileges ... but does not participate in corporate growth to any significant extent."

Example: Corporation X has four equal shareholders, A, B, C, and D. Although each owns 100 shares of X common stock, there are four identical classes. A owns class A shares; B, class B; C, class C; and D, class D. X declares a dividend of 1 class A common share for each 10 class A shares owned. It declares a dividend of 1 class E preferred for each 10 class B, C, and D shares.

After these distributions A owns 110 common shares; B, C, and D each own 100 common shares and 10 preferred shares. Unless the preferred shares have dividend and liquidation rights that are the same as those of the common shares, this distribution is covered by section 305(b)(3).

Section 7.04(b)(1)(D) Distributions on Preferred Stock

Preferred stock, as defined in section 7.04(b)(1)(C), has limited rights to participate in corporate growth. If preferred shareholders receive a distribution of the corporation's common stock, they increase their participation in future growth. Even a distribution of additional preferred stock may trigger the application of section 305(b)(4), which covers distributions on preferred stock.

Example: Corporation X has 100 shares of common stock and 50 shares of preferred stock outstanding. It distributes 1 common share for every 10 preferred shares owned. This distribution is covered by section 305(b)(4).

Example: Corporation X has 100 shares of common stock and 50 shares of preferred stock outstanding. It distributes 1 preferred share for every 10 preferred shares owned. This distribution is covered by section 305(b)(4).

Section 7.04(b)(1)(E) Distributions of Convertible Preferred Stock

Section 305(b)(5) applies to distributions of preferred stock that can be converted into common stock. If every common share received the same distribution, shareholders might argue that no shareholder's proportionate interest increased. Regulation section 1.305-6(a) accepts this reasoning in situations that are unlikely to result in a disproportionate distribution. If the conversion terms make it likely that some shareholders will convert and others won't, the distribution is disproportionate. If the terms make this disparity unlikely, the distribution avoids section 305(b) treatment.

In determining whether the distribution is tainted, we look to the regulations. Factors that indicate the distribution is disproportionate are a relatively short period for exercising the conversion right and dividend rates, redemption provisions, marketability, or conversion price factors that make it likely that only some shareholders will exercise their conversion rights.

Section 7.04(b)(1)(F) Transactions Treated as Distributions

Section 305(b) is supplemented by section 305(c). The latter provision authorizes regulations to apply similar rules to other situations. These include changes in a conversion ratio or redemption price, differences between redemption and issue price, certain redemptions governed by section 301, and other transactions that result in a shareholder's proportionate interest in corporate earnings or assets increasing.[22]

Example: Several years ago, Corporation X issued preferred stock that could be converted into common stock at the rate of 1 common share for each 10 preferred shares. Because the common stock's price has declined, X changed the conversion rate to offer 2 common shares for each 10 preferred shares.

Example: Several years ago, Corporation X issued preferred stock that could be converted into common stock at the rate of 1 common share for each 10 preferred shares. X recently split its common stock; each common shareholder received an additional common share for each share already owned. To recognize the effect of the stock split, X changed the conversion rate to offer 2 common shares for each 10 preferred shares.

The preferred shareholders in the first example received an increase in their interest in the corporation. Those in the second example did not. The change in the conversion ratio reflected the split in the underlying common shares. One old common share was equivalent to two new common shares.

Section 7.04(b)(2) Shareholders' Tax Consequences

If a distribution is governed by section 305(b), the shareholder treats the stock or rights received as property. The tax consequences mirror those discussed in section 7.03. Assuming adequate E&P, the value of the shares received is a taxable dividend. The dividend shares take a basis equal to their fair market value. Their holding period begins when they are received.

Section 7.04(b)(3) Corporation's Tax Consequences

Regulation section 1.312-1(d) reduces the corporation's E&P by the value of the distribution included in the shareholder's income.

Section 7.04(c) *Eisner v. Macomber* and Financial Accounting

The general rule of section 305(a) can be traced back to the Supreme Court's decision in *Eisner v. Macomber*.[23] That case involved the Revenue Act of 1916, which provided that a stock dividend was income. Mrs. Macomber, who owned stock in Standard Oil Company of California, received a distri-

---

22. *See* Treas. Reg. §1.305-7.
23. 252 U.S. 189 (1920).

bution of one share for every two shares she owned. Standard Oil reduced its surplus account and increased its capital stock account to reflect the distribution. Because the surplus account was reduced, the distribution bore some resemblance to a cash distribution.[24]

The Supreme Court held the distribution was no more than a reconfiguration of the shareholder's existing investment. She did not receive any corporate assets for her separate use.

As illustrated in section 7.04(b), section 305 now has many exceptions. But the general rule continues to reflect the holding in *Eisner v. Macomber*—a distribution in the corporation's own stock is not a distribution of property and is therefore not subject to section 301. For financial accounting purposes, corporations still reduce their surplus account to reflect a stock dividend.

Section 7.05 Computing E&P

Section 7.05(a) Introduction

How do we determine whether a corporation has E&P? As noted in section 7.02(d), E&P is the tax law analog to corporate earned surplus. Earned surplus is thus one potential starting point. In addition, the corporation computes its taxable income each year. The corporation's cumulative taxable income and loss over time is another potential starting point. Because they are based on different rules, earned surplus and cumulative taxable income differ from each other. Neither of them is a perfect surrogate for E&P.

Congress and the Treasury Department have issued guidance designed to standardize the E&P computation as much as possible. Section 312(k)–(n) applies to such transactions as depreciation, debt discharge income, construction period carrying charges, and particular accounting methods.

Regulation section 1.312-6 is particularly instructive. It provides that "while mere bookkeeping entries increasing or decreasing surplus will not be conclusive, the amount of the earnings and profits in any case will be dependent upon the method of accounting properly employed in computing taxable income (or net income, as the case may be)." Although that clause refers to taxable income, E&P includes many items that are not part of taxable income. For example, Regulation section 1.312-6(b) includes both items that are section 61 gross income and items exempted from tax by statute or the Constitution.

---

24. If the corporation distributed cash, it would reduce its cash account instead of increasing its capital stock account.

Section 7.05(b) Differences in Computing Taxable Income and E&P

As a general rule, taxpayers use the same accounting methods and gross income and deduction rules in computing taxable income and E&P. But, because they have different purposes, the two computations differ. Taxable income is a measure of ability to pay tax; E&P is a measure of ability to pay dividends. The E&P computation adds back tax-free items and subtracts out nondeductible items, such as the federal income tax itself, that affect dividend-paying ability.

Section 7.05(b)(1) Items Excluded from Gross Income

Items are included in E&P because they increase the corporation's financial ability to pay dividends. As a result, the income tax exclusions for life insurance proceeds (section 101) and for interest on state and local government obligations (section 103) do not apply in computing E&P.

Caveat: Although section 103 excludes municipal bond interest from a corporation's gross income, it does not exclude it from the E&P computation. Even if the corporation's E&P account is attributable only to municipal bond interest, shareholders will have gross income from dividends if they receive a distribution from current or accumulated E&P.

Some items are excluded from both gross income and E&P because they result in basis adjustments. Income from discharge of indebtedness is one such example. A taxpayer that qualifies for the section 108 exclusion reduces one or more tax attributes. These include net operating loss carryovers, business tax credits, and property basis. Section 312(l) excludes debt discharge from E&P if the corporation reduces basis under section 1017.

Section 7.05(b)(2) Income Tax Deductible Items

A taxpayer cannot reduce its E&P by income tax deductions that don't affect financial ability to pay dividends. The section 243 dividends received deduction is an example of this type of item.

Section 7.05(b)(3) Income Tax Nondeductible Items

Outlays that do not give rise to tax deductions may nevertheless affect a corporation's financial ability to pay dividends. Items that are deductible for E&P purposes, but not for income tax, include dividends paid to shareholders and federal income tax payments.

Section 7.05(b)(4) Timing Items

Some items affect taxable income and E&P in different years. For example, the income tax depreciation deduction is likely to be an accelerated deduction; section 312(k) limits the E&P deduction for certain items to the straight-line method. If the corporation takes a section 179 deduction for income tax purposes, it must spread the deduction over five years for E&P purposes. Timing items are likely to result in a corporation having one adjusted basis for income tax purposes and another for E&P purposes.

Example: ABC Corporation purchased new office furniture for $10,000. For income tax purposes, it elected to use section 179 and deduct all $10,000 that year. For E&P purposes, its deduction is limited to $2,000 per year. At the end of the first year, ABC's income tax basis is zero; its E&P basis is $8,000.

CHAPTER 8

REDEMPTION DISTRIBUTIONS

Section 8.01 Introduction

Shareholders whose stock is redeemed are selling some (or all) of their stock. Because the buyer is the issuing corporation or a related entity, the transaction's substance may differ from its form.[1] If it does, the transaction is not treated as a sale for tax purposes. Instead, it is governed by the rules applied to distributions of property discussed in Chapter 7.

In some cases, a transaction could be structured as a purchase by a surviving shareholder or as a redemption. Examples include transfers made pursuant to buy-sell agreements and transfers during marital dissolutions. The potential tax consequences of these transactions are addressed in section 8.09.

Because a market exists for stock of publicly traded companies, a shareholder can easily ascertain a fair price and sell shares to third parties. Neither buyer nor seller is likely to own enough stock to have any influence on the corporation's activities (or on its share price). Shareholders in closely held corporations have a much different relationship to their corporations. The examples below illustrate two quite different types of corporate-shareholder relationships.

Example: The stock of Corporation X is publicly traded on the New York Stock Exchange. X has several million shareholders, none of whom owns more than two percent of its stock. Individual A owns 100 shares of X stock.

Example: B is the only shareholder of Corporation Y. She owns all 1,000 shares of Y's stock.

In the first example, A has no special relationship to Corporation X and no ability to influence its policies. The X shares are merely an asset in which he has invested. If A sells any of his X shares, the buyer's identity is irrelevant. In

---

1. This section covers redemptions by the corporation that issued the stock. Section 8.06 covers the tax consequences when a related corporation purchases the stock.

the second example, B controls Corporation Y. If Y purchased one-half of her shares, B would still own all of the remaining outstanding stock. Because B owns all the shares, the actual number of shares she owns is irrelevant.

This chapter will illustrate that A and B will have quite different tax consequences.

Section 8.02 Relevant Code Sections

Section 317(b) defines redemption: "[S]tock shall be treated as redeemed by a corporation if the corporation acquires its stock from a shareholder in exchange for property, whether or not the stock so acquired is cancelled, retired, or held as treasury stock." As we learned in section 7.02(b), property includes cash and other assets but generally does not include stock in the particular corporation or rights to acquire such stock.

Depending on factors discussed in this chapter, redemptions are treated either as sales or exchanges or as dividends. In determining the appropriate treatment, we focus on four redemption provisions: sections 302, 303, 304, and 306. In deciding whether these sections apply, we also study the section 318 attribution rules. The Code sections discussed in Chapter 7, particularly section 312, are also relevant.

Caveat: If a redemption fails to qualify for sale or exchange treatment, the shareholder being redeemed will report dividend treatment. Other shareholders may also have dividend treatment. Section 305, discussed in section 7.04, can be applied to a shareholder whose interest in the corporation is increased when the redemption of another shareholder is treated as a section 301 distribution.[2]

Section 8.03 Section 318 Attribution Rules

Because closely held corporations are frequently owned by family members, a redemption that appears to change a shareholder's relationship with the corporation may be merely a ruse to avoid dividend treatment. Rather than judging each redemption by facts and circumstances, we apply several bright-line tests for judging whether a shareholder's position has changed vis-à-vis the corporation. One set of tests is represented by the attribution rules, which are covered in this section. When those rules apply, a shareholder's ownership

---

2. I.R.C. § 305(c).

percentage includes not only shares she actually owns but also shares she is deemed to own by attribution from others. When the attribution rules apply, the shareholder is said to have constructive ownership of those shares.

The other set of bright-line tests appears in the specific redemption sections. These sections provide their own requirements for sale or exchange treatment. In addition, they provide rules for applying or not applying the attribution rules. If a shareholder fails the bright-line tests, section 302(b)(1) applies a facts and circumstances final test.

The discussion in this section introduces the attribution rules. We will cover exceptions to those rules when we discuss the specific redemption provisions.

Section 8.03(a) Types of Attribution

Attribution rules are based on relationships between people, between entities, or between people and entities. They cover actual ownership of shares and the ability to obtain ownership. Ownership may be attributed from an owner to an entity or from an entity to an owner. The paragraphs that follow discuss how attribution rules work to make a person a constructive owner.

Caveat: When discussing attribution rules, the term person is used generically. It covers both human beings and entities.

Section 8.03(a)(1) Family Attribution (Section 318(a)(1))

A shareholder constructively owns stock owned by family members. Family is defined for this purpose as the shareholder's spouse, children, grandchildren, and parents. It does not include brothers and sisters, grandparents, or great-grandchildren. Legal adoption is treated the same as blood relationship.

Caveat: The Code provides different definitions of family members for different purposes. The definition in section 318 differs from that used in section 267 for disallowing losses between related parties and from that used in section 152 for treating a relative as a dependent. Make sure you use the correct definition.

Section 8.03(a)(1)(A) Family Dissension

A spouse is not considered a family member if the couple is legally separated under a decree of divorce or separate maintenance.[3] No other family dis-

---

3. *See* section 8.09(b) for a discussion of redemptions in the context of a divorce settlement.

sension is taken into account. For example, in *Cerone v. Commissioner*, the Tax Court refused to read a family hostility exception into the section 318 rules.[4]

Section 8.03(a)(1)(B) Indirect Ownership

In determining constructive ownership, the shareholder is deemed to own stock that is directly or indirectly owned by the listed relatives. The family cannot avoid attribution by transferring stock to in-laws in a transaction that lacks substance. The shareholder is also deemed to own shares owned "for" the listed relative. This includes both trust and nominee ownership arrangements.

Example: The stock of Corporation X is owned equally by A and A's two children, B and C. A is treated as owning 100 percent of the X shares, one-third actually and two-thirds constructively.

Example: Assume the same facts but B and C each transfer their shares to their respective spouses. The deeds of transfer provide that B and C will continue to vote the shares and have an absolute right to demand return of the shares at any time. Because B and C own the transferred shares at least indirectly, A is still treated as owning 100 percent of the X shares.

Section 8.03(a)(2) Attribution from Entities (Section 318(a)(2))

Stock owned by entities may be treated as constructively owned by persons that have a beneficial interest in the entity. For example, if a partnership owns stock in a corporation, each partner is treated as owning a pro rata share of that stock. Attribution from an entity to its beneficial owners occurs in four contexts, ownership by an estate, a partnership, a trust, or another corporation. As was true for ownership by family members, the attribution rules apply to stock owned directly or indirectly, and by or for, the entity.

Section 8.03(a)(2)(A) Attribution from Estates

Section 318(a)(2)(A) provides that each beneficiary of an estate owns his or her proportionate share of the stock owned by the estate. The regulations expand on this statement by indicating when an estate is deemed to own stock and when an individual is treated as a beneficiary.[5]

---

4. 87 T.C. 1 (1986). *See also Metzger Trust v. Commissioner*, 76 T.C. 42 (1981), *aff'd*, 693 F.2d 459 (5th Cir. 1982), *cert. denied*, 463 U.S. 1207 (1983).

5. Treas. Reg. § 1.318-3(a).

The estate is treated as owning stock even if title passes directly to a third party if the stock is subject to administration by the personal representative for the purposes of paying claims against the estate and expenses of administration.

Example: A owned 100 shares of Corporation X stock in a payable on death (POD) account. B was the POD payee. A also owned land and other non-stock assets. A bequeathed those assets by will to C. At A's death, title to the X stock passed directly to B as payee. Only the land and other non-stock assets were part of A's probate estate. The laws of A's state of residence provide that the personal representative of A's estate can subject the non-probate assets (in this case the X stock) to claims against the estate unless the decedent's will provides otherwise. If A's will failed to provide otherwise, the estate is deemed to own the X stock, and C is treated as owning a portion of it constructively.

Section 8.03(a)(2)(B) Attribution from Partnerships and S Corporations

Each partner owns his or her proportionate share of the stock owned by the partnership.[6] S corporations are treated as partnerships for this purpose.[7]

Example: A, B, and C are each 30 percent partners in ABCDE Partnership. D and E are each 5 percent partners. ABCDE owns 100 shares of Corporation X. A, B, and C each constructively own 30 shares of X; D and E each constructively own 5 shares of X.

Example: F, G, and H each own 30 percent of the shares of Corporation FGHIJ, which is an S corporation. I and J each own 5 percent of the FGHIJ shares. FGHIJ owns 100 shares of Corporation X. F, G, and H each constructively own 30 shares of X; I and J each constructively own 5 shares of X.

Partnership interests take a variety of forms. A partner may have an interest in capital, in profits, or in both. A partner may be a general partner with management rights and unlimited liability for partnership debts or a limited partner with no management rights and limited liability.

Section 8.03(a)(2)(C) Attribution from Trusts

The extent to which stock is attributed from trusts depends on the trust's status. If it is a "grantor" trust, stock that it owns is attributed to the grantor

---

6. I.R.C. §318(a)(2)(A).
7. I.R.C. §318(a)(5)(E).

or other deemed owner. If it is not a grantor trust, stock that it owns is attributed to the beneficiaries based on their actuarial interests in the trust.[8]

Example: The DEF Trust owns 100 shares of Corporation X. Individual D established this trust. While D is alive, income is paid to his three children in the proportions that D decides each year. After D's death, each child will receive 1/3 of the income. The corpus will be paid to whichever of D's children survives the other two. If all die simultaneously, the corpus will be paid to charity. Because D has the power to allocate income, this is a grantor trust.[9] D constructively owns all of the trust's 100 shares of X stock.

Example: If D's wife W had the same powers as D, DEF would still be a grantor trust. The grantor is deemed to have any power that his spouse has.[10]

Example: After D's death, each child has a one-third interest in the trust's income and a contingent interest in the corpus. Both interests can be actuarially valued to determine the amount of X stock each child constructively owns.

Section 8.03(a)(2)(D) Attribution from C Corporations

The rules in section 318(a)(2)(C) relate to stock owned by C corporations. If a shareholder owns at least 50 percent of the value of a C corporation's stock, that shareholder is treated as owning a proportionate share of any stock owned by that corporation. The proportionate share reflects the relative value of the shareholder's ownership.

Example: Corporation X owns 900 shares of Corporation Y. A and B each own 50 percent of the X voting common stock but are otherwise unrelated to each other. A and B each constructively own 450 of the Y shares owned by X.

Example: Corporation X owns 900 shares of Corporation Y. A owns 70 percent of the X voting common stock. B, who is not related to A, owns the other 30 percent. A constructively owns 630 of the Y shares owned by X. B does not constructively own any of those Y shares.

Example: Corporation X owns 900 shares of Corporation Y. A owns all of the X voting common stock. B, who is not related to A, owns all of the X nonvoting common stock. Unless we know the total value of the voting and nonvoting shares, we cannot ascertain whether only one shareholder owns at least

---

8. Beneficiaries of tax-exempt trusts that fund employee pension benefits do not constructively own stock owned by those trusts. I.R.C. § 318(a)(2)(B)(i).

9. I.R.C. § 674(a). Subject to certain statutory exceptions, grantor trust rules apply if prohibited powers are exercisable by the grantor or by any nonadverse party without the approval or consent of an adverse party.

10. I.R.C. § 672(e).

50 percent of the value of X stock or whether both do.[11] We need that information to determine if either A or B constructively owns stock in Y.

Section 8.03(a)(3) Attribution to Entities (Section 318(a)(3))

Entity attribution goes in both directions. An entity may be the constructive owner of stock owned by persons that have a beneficial interest in that entity. For example, if a trust beneficiary owns stock, the trust may be treated as constructively owning that stock. Attribution from owners to the entity occurs in four contexts, attribution to an estate, a partnership, a trust, or another corporation.[12] The attribution rules apply to stock owned directly or indirectly, and by or for, the owner.

Caveat: Attribution *to* an entity is an all or nothing proposition. The entity is treated as owning all the stock owned by its owners. Attribution *to* entities differs in this regard from the rules applied in section 8.03(a)(2), which covered attribution *from* entities.

Section 8.03(a)(3)(A) Attribution to Estates

Section 318(a)(3)(A) provides that an estate constructively owns 100 percent of the stock owned by each beneficiary. The regulations define beneficiary in the same way for attribution to estates as for attribution from estates.

Section 8.03(a)(3)(B) Attribution to Partnerships and S Corporations

Section 318(a)(3)(A) treats partnerships as owning stock owned by their partners and treats S corporations as owning stock owned by their shareholders.[13]

Example: A, B, and C are each 30 percent partners in ABCDE Partnership. D and E are each 5 percent partners. E owns 100 shares of Corporation X. ABCDE Partnership constructively owns E's 100 X shares.

Example: F, G, and H each own 30 percent of the shares of Corporation FGHIJ, which is an S corporation. I and J each own 5 percent of the FGHIJ

---

11. Because there are only two shareholders in this example, at least one of them must own 50 percent of the stock value. It is possible that each does. In a corporation with more than two shareholders and multiple classes of stock, it is possible that none of them will own at least 50 percent of the value.

12. As discussed in section 8.03(a)(2)(B), S corporations are treated as partnerships for this purpose.

13. S Corporations are treated as partnerships for this purpose. I.R.C. §318(a)(5)(E).

shares. J owns 100 shares of X Corporation. FGHIJ constructively owns J's 100 X shares.

Section 8.03(a)(3)(C) Attribution to Trusts

Whether stock is attributed to trusts depends on the trust's status.[14] If it is a "grantor" trust, it constructively owns stock owned by anyone treated as the owner of a trust interest. If it is not a grantor trust, it constructively owns stock owned by beneficiaries in two categories. The trust constructively owns stock owned by a beneficiary with a vested interest. It also constructively owns stock owned by a beneficiary with a contingent interest unless that interest is remote.

Example: D established the DEF Trust. While D is alive, income is paid to his three children in the proportions that D decides each year. After D's death, each child will receive 1/3 of the income. The corpus will be paid to whichever of D's children survives the other two. If all die simultaneously, the corpus will be paid to charity. Because D has the power to allocate income, this is a grantor trust.[15] DEF Trust constructively owns any corporate stock owned by D.

Contingent interests are valued actuarially to determine if they are remote. The valuation is based on the assumption that the trustee will exercise its maximum discretion in favor of that beneficiary.

Example: The GHI trust was established at G's death. The trustee is to accumulate income until G's oldest child dies and then distribute corpus to G's grandchildren equally (with an alternate remainder to charity). The trustee has the authority to distribute up to $4,000 income per year to each of G's children. Each child's interest is contingent on the trustee exercising its discretion. Its present value depends on the oldest child's life expectancy. If the present value of $4,000 per year for that life expectancy exceeds 5 percent of the trust's value, the trust constructively owns any corporate stock owned by the income beneficiary. If the value is 5 percent or less, the trust does not constructively own stock owned by the income beneficiary.[16]

Section 8.03(a)(3)(D) Attribution to C Corporations

The rules in section 318(a)(3)(C) relate to stock owned by C corporations. If the shareholder owns at least 50 percent of the value of a C corporation's

---

14. Tax-exempt trusts that fund employee pension benefits do not constructively own stock owned by their beneficiaries. I.R.C. §318(a)(3)(B)(i).

15. I.R.C. §674(a). Subject to certain statutory exceptions, grantor trust rules apply if prohibited powers are exercisable by the grantor or by any nonadverse party without the approval or consent of an adverse party.

16. I.R.C. §318(a)(3)(B)(i).

stock, that C corporation constructively owns all corporate stock owned by the shareholder.

Example: A owns 900 shares of Corporation X. A and B also own 50 percent of the Corporation Y voting common stock but are otherwise unrelated to each other. Y constructively owns the 900 X shares owned by A.

Example: A owns 900 shares of Corporation X. A also owns 30 percent of the Corporation Y voting common stock. B, who is not related to A, owns the other 70 percent of Y Corporation. Y does not constructively own any of the X shares owned by A. If B happened to own stock in another corporation, Y would constructively own 100 percent of whatever B owned.

Section 8.03(a)(4) Option Attribution

If stock is subject to a purchase option, the option holder constructively owns that stock.[17]

Example: A owns 500 shares of Corporation X. B, who is unrelated to A, has an option to purchase 125 of A's shares. B constructively owns those 125 shares.

Section 8.03(a)(5) Operating Rules

Multiple attribution rules might apply to a particular situation. For example, what if B had an option on 125 of A's 500 shares but also was A's son? Do the family rules treat B as owning all 500 shares, or do the option rules treat B as owning only 125 shares?[18] And, if B constructively owns A's shares, does B's daughter C also constructively own those shares?[19] Section 318(a)(5) provides rules that answer these questions.

Section 8.03(a)(5)(A) General Rule

If a person owns stock constructively, that person is generally treated as the actual owner for purposes of treating yet another person as constructive owner. This general rule is subject to exceptions discussed in section 8.03(a)(5)(B).

Example: A is the only beneficiary of ABC Trust. The trust was established by A's ex-husband. B, who is A's mother, owns stock in Corporation X. Be-

---

17. I.R.C. §318(a)(4). An option to acquire an option is also treated as an option to acquire stock.

18. Because B can't constructively own the same shares twice, B cannot constructively own 625 shares based on A's ownership of 500 shares.

19. C cannot constructively own through A, because section 318(a)(1) applies only to stock owned by an individual's spouse, parents, children, and grandchildren. A does not have any of those relationships to C.

cause of family attribution, A constructively owns the X stock owned by her mother. Because of attribution to an entity, ABC Trust also constructively owns the X stock. A was treated as the actual owner for purposes of making ABC the constructive owner.

Section 8.03(a)(5)(B) Exceptions

The first exception to reattribution involves family attribution. If an individual constructively owns stock because of family attribution, that stock will not be attributed from the constructive owner to yet another family member.[20] Put another way, if there would not be family attribution from the actual owner to the second individual, there can't be attribution through an intermediate family member.

Example: A owns 400 shares of Corporation X. A's son P constructively owns those shares. P's wife Q does not constructively own those shares. Because Q is not A's child, grandchild, or parent, or spouse, A's shares would not be directly attributed to Q. As a result, they cannot be attributed from A to P and from P to Q.

Example: E and F are brother and sister. F owns 500 shares of Corporation X. A, who is E and F's mother, constructively owns F's shares. Because siblings are not family members for purposes of section 318(a)(1), F's shares would not be attributed directly to E. As a result, they cannot be attributed from F to A and then from A to E.

The second exception to reattribution involves attribution from an owner to an entity followed by attribution from that entity to another owner. As with family attribution, if direct attribution from the first to the second owner is not possible, reattribution through an entity is also forbidden.[21]

Example: M and N are equal partners in the MN Partnership but are otherwise unrelated. M owns 1000 shares of Corporation X. MN constructively owns the X shares by attribution from M. Because the shares could not be attributed directly from M to N, they cannot be reattributed from MN to N.

Caveat: The rules discussed above do not prevent reattribution of constructively owned shares. They merely prevent using family attribution twice or using owner to entity attribution followed by entity to owner attribution. The general rule that reattribution of constructively owned shares is allowed applies in all other situations. An example of reattribution appears in section 8.03(a)(5)(A).

---

20. I.R.C. §318(a)(5)(B).
21. I.R.C. §318(a)(5)(C).

Section 8.03(a)(5)(C) Option Attribution

Any individual who would constructively own stock because of both family and option attribution is treated as owning it by option attribution.[22] Because the option rules trump the family rules, it is possible to reattribute this stock to another family member.

Example: E and F are brother and sister. F owns 500 shares of Corporation X. A, who is E and F's mother, has an option to purchase 100 of F's shares. A constructively owns 100 shares through option attribution and the other 400 through family attribution. Only the 100 shares owned through option attribution can be reattributed from A to E.

Section 8.04 Section 302

Section 8.04(a) Redemptions Covered by Section 302

Sale or exchange treatment is appropriate if the redemption significantly changes the shareholder's relationship with the corporation. Section 302(b)(1)–(4) lists four redemption categories that satisfy that criterion:

(1) The redemption is not essentially equivalent to a dividend;

(2) The redemption is substantially disproportionate;

(3) The redemption terminates the shareholder's interest; or

(4) The redemption occurs in a partial liquidation.

The last three categories rely on objective criteria. Because a redemption that does not satisfy any of those criteria may still qualify as "not essentially equivalent to a dividend," that category operates as a fall-back. Because it is a fall-back, the discussion below covers it last rather than first.

Section 8.04(b) Substantially Disproportionate Redemptions (Section 302(b)(2))

A redemption is substantially disproportionate only if the shareholder's actual and constructive ownership satisfies three numerical tests. The first test is based on absolute ownership; the other two are based on ownership ratios.

---

22. I.R.C. §318(a)(5)(D).

Caveat: In determining whether a shareholder meets these tests, remember to reduce the total number of outstanding shares in doing the "after" computation. After the redemption, the redeemed shares are no longer outstanding.

Section 8.04(b)(1) Ownership Percentage After the Redemption

The absolute test requires that actual and constructive ownership immediately after the redemption be less than 50 percent of the corporation's total combined voting power. All classes of voting stock are considered in making this determination.

Example: Corporation X has only one class of stock, voting common. To be substantially disproportionate, a redemption must leave the redeemed shareholder with actual and constructive ownership of less than 50 percent of the shares outstanding immediately after the redemption.

Example: Corporation X has two classes of stock, voting common and non-voting preferred. To be substantially disproportionate, a redemption must leave the redeemed shareholder with actual and constructive ownership of less than 50 percent of the voting common shares outstanding immediately after the redemption. The nonvoting preferred shares are not a factor in meeting this test.

Section 8.04(b)(2) Reduction in Voting Stock After the Redemption

The first ratio test compares the shareholder's actual and constructive ownership of voting stock before and after the redemption. To make this comparison, we make three computations:

(1) Compute the shareholder's voting percentage before the redemption;
(2) Compute the shareholder's voting percentage after the redemption; and
(3) Compute a ratio by dividing the second percentage by the first percentage.

To satisfy the ratio test, the second percentage must be less than 80 percent of the first ratio.

Example: Corporation X has only one class of stock, voting common. Shareholder A, who is unrelated to any other X shareholder, owns 600 of the 1,000 X shares. If X redeems 551 of A's shares, A will own 49 of the 449 shares that remain outstanding. A owned 60 percent of the voting power before the redemption and 10.9 percent after the redemption. That reduction qualifies because 10.9 percent is less than 80 percent of 60 percent.

Example: Corporation X has two classes of stock, voting common and voting preferred. Shareholder A, who is unrelated to any other X shareholder, owns 600 of the 1,000 X common shares and 300 of the 1,000 X preferred shares. If X redeems 550 of A's common shares, A will own 50 of the 450 common shares (and 300 of the 1,000 preferred shares) that remain outstanding. A owned 45 percent of the voting power before the redemption and 24.1 percent after the redemption. That reduction qualifies because 24.1 percent is less than 80 percent of 45 percent.

Section 8.04(b)(3) Reduction in Common Stock After the Redemption

The second ratio test compares the shareholder's actual and constructive ownership of common stock before and after the redemption. This test covers both voting and nonvoting common stock. Because common stock participates in corporate success, this ratio test complements the voting power reduction test described in section 8.04(b)(2). Taken together, they prevent shareholders who retain "too much" voting power or equity rights from qualifying a redemption as substantially disproportionate.

Example: Corporation X has two classes of stock, voting common and voting preferred. Shareholder A, who is unrelated to any other X shareholder, owns 300 of the 1,000 X common shares and 600 of the 1,000 X preferred shares. If X redeems 550 of A's preferred shares, A will own 50 of the 450 preferred shares (and 300 of the 1,000 common shares) that remain outstanding. Although A owned 45 percent of the voting power before the redemption and 24.1 percent after, A owned 30 percent of the common shares both before and after the redemption. As a result, the redemption is not substantially disproportionate.

Section 8.04(b)(4) Special Rules

Section 8.04(b)(4)(A) Redemption of Preferred Stock

Redemptions of stock from shareholders who own only *nonvoting* preferred stock cannot satisfy any of the mathematical tests.[23] Redemptions from shareholders who own only *voting* preferred stock may satisfy the voting power tests, but they still cannot satisfy the common stock reduction test. Redemptions from either group will not qualify for the section 302(b)(2) safe harbor.

A shareholder who owns voting common stock in addition to his preferred shares may have a better outcome. Redemptions of nonvoting preferred stock will qualify if they occur simultaneously with a qualifying redemption of vot-

---

23. For purposes of section 302(b)(2), preferred stock is considered voting preferred only if it actually has voting rights. If voting rights are contingent on an event, the stock is not voting until the event occurs. Treas. Reg. § 1.302-3(a)(flush language).

ing common stock.[24] This relief does not apply if the preferred shares are so-called section 306 stock, discussed in section 8.07.

Section 8.04(b)(4)(B) Series of Redemptions

Because the tests for substantially disproportionate status apply to ownership "immediately after" the redemption, Congress was concerned that closely held corporations might schedule transactions that appeared disproportionate but really weren't. Section 302(b)(2)(D) covers redemptions that are pursuant to a plan whose purpose or effect is a series of redemptions. The testing for substantially disproportionate status occurs after the series has ended. The regulations provide that the existence of a plan will be based on a facts and circumstances test.[25]

Example: Corporation X has only one class of stock, voting common. Shareholder A, who is unrelated to any other X shareholder, owns 600 of the 1,000 X shares. Two weeks after X redeemed 551 of A's shares, it redeemed 349 of the 400 shares owned by the other shareholders. Immediately after the first redemption, A's voting power had dropped from 60 percent to 10.9 percent. But after the second redemption, A's voting power was 49 percent. If the two redemptions were pursuant to a plan, the redemption from A does not qualify as substantially disproportionate.

Section 8.04(b)(4)(C) Multiple Redemptions

As the example in section 8.04(b)(4)(B) indicated, stock may be redeemed from more than one shareholder. Although that example looked at a series of redemptions, similar computations are made for a single redemption event. When stock is redeemed from more than one shareholder, each shareholder's qualification is tested separately.

Example: Corporation X has one class of stock, voting common. Its 1,000 shares are owned by four unrelated shareholders: A (200), B (400), C (280), and D (120). X plans to redeem 100 shares each from A and B. After the redemption, the remaining 800 X shares will be owned by A (100), B (300), C (280), and D (120). A's ownership declines from 20 percent to 12.5 percent. B's declines from 40 percent to 37.5 percent. The redemption from A qualifies under section 302(b)(2).The redemption from B does not qualify because 37.5 percent is not less than 80 percent of 40 percent.[26]

---

24. Treas. Reg. § 1.302-3(a)(flush language).
25. Treas. Reg. § 1.302-3(a)(flush language).
26. The redemption from B may ultimately qualify under another section 302(b) rule. If it does not, C and D may also have adverse tax consequences. Because their ownership

Section 8.04(b)(5) Constructive Ownership

All of the examples above involved unrelated shareholders. Don't forget that the section 318 constructive ownership rules apply if shareholders have any of the relationships discussed in section 8.03.

Example: Corporation X has only one class of stock, voting common. Shareholder A owns 500 of the 1,000 X shares. LMN Trust, of which A is a 10 percent beneficiary, owns 400 of the shares. The other 100 shares are owned by unrelated persons. Immediately before any redemption, A actually owns 500 shares and constructively owns 40 of the shares owned by LMN Trust; that is 54 percent of X. (LMN actually owns 400 shares and constructively owns all 500 of A's shares; that is 90 percent of X.)

If X redeems 300 of A's shares, there will be 700 A shares outstanding. A will actually own 200 shares and will constructively own 40. That is 240/700, or 34.3 percent. That redemption would qualify for section 302(b)(2) treatment because it meets all the numerical ownership tests.

What if X *instead* redeems 300 of LMN Trust's shares. Of the 700 X shares outstanding, LMN will actually own 100 and will constructively own all 500 of A's shares. That is 600/700, or 85.7 percent of the shares. That redemption would not qualify, as it fails all of the section 302(b)(2) numerical ownership requirements. Failing even one test prevents qualifying for section 302(b)(2).

Section 8.04(c) Complete Terminations (Section 302(b)(3))

If a redemption completely terminates a shareholder's interest in the corporation, Section 302(b)(3) treats it as a sale or exchange. In determining whether a shareholder's interest has been completely terminated, we look at actual stock ownership. In addition, we must consider constructive ownership and other relationships the shareholder has with the corporation.

Section 8.04(c)(1) Avoiding Attribution

In a partial redemption, the shareholder retains an ownership interest. This is not the case for a complete termination. But if constructive ownership rules

---

percentages increase, section 305(c) may treat them as having received a dividend distribution.

automatically applied to complete terminations, they would disqualify many of these transactions. To preserve a shareholder's ability to qualify, we ignore family or entity attribution if the redemption satisfies the termination requirements discussed below.[27]

Section 8.04(c)(1)(A) Family Attribution

Family attribution is ignored if the redeemed shareholder meets tests involving interests in the corporation immediately after the redemption, interests acquired in the ten years following the redemption, and shares acquired in the ten years preceding the redemption.

The first test requires that, immediately after the redemption, the shareholder being redeemed have no interest in the corporation other than as a creditor. Prohibited interests include serving as an officer, director, or employee.

To qualify as a permitted creditor interest, the former shareholder's interest must not be subordinated to the interest of general creditors. Subordination makes it a residual interest, which would be more akin to equity. The debt instrument must not provide that repayment is dependent on corporate earnings, have an interest rate that fluctuates with corporate earnings, or be convertible into a stock interest. All these are indicia of an equity interest.[28]

The prohibition against being an officer, director, or employee does not extend to other relationships between the corporation and its former shareholder. Permitted interests include those of customer/vendor and landlord/tenant. In *Hurst v. Commissioner*,[29] the Tax Court applied section 302(b)(3) even though the former shareholder's wife continued as an employee. She had never owned stock in the corporation.

Caveat: The prohibition against retaining or acquiring a prohibited interest applies only if the redeemed shareholder is trying to waive attribution. If no related person owns stock, the redeemed shareholder may continue as an officer, director, or employee.

---

27. I.R.C. §302(c).

28. Treas. Reg. §1.302-4(d). *See* Chapter 6 for a general discussion of debt and equity classifications.

29. 124 T.C. 16 (2005). *Hurst* involved several redemption issues. The shareholders retained a security interest in corporate stock acquired by the new owners, one of the new owners was the couple's son, the corporation was an S Corporation, so certain fringe benefits were affected by attribution rules, and the section 304 rules discussed in section 8.06 might have applied but were raised too late.

The second test requires that the former shareholder not acquire a prohibited interest during the ten years following the redemption distribution. The shareholder must file an agreement to notify the government if any interest is acquired during that period.[30] Acquisition by bequest or inheritance is permissible; acquisition by inter vivos gift is not.

The third test involves stock acquisitions that occurred within the ten-year period that ended with the redemption distribution. If either type of acquisition occurred, the redeemed shareholder must establish that the event did not have avoidance of income tax as one of its principal purposes. The first situation applies if the shareholder acquired any portion of the redeemed stock from a related person.

Example: Mom was the sole shareholder of Corporation X until Year 4. In Year 4, she gave 25 percent of her shares to Son and 25 percent to Daughter. Three years later, in Year 7, X redeemed all of Son and Daughter's shares. Because they received those shares from a related person within the ten-year period preceding the redemption, they can waive attribution from Mom only if the acquisition and disposition of the X shares were not part of a plan that had avoidance of income tax as one of its principal purposes. Because Mom was originally the sole shareholder, and became the sole shareholder after the redemption, the IRS would argue that Mom used X to transfer funds to Son and Daughter. But if it could be shown that Son and Daughter worked in the business but later lost interest, the family might prevail on the "plan" issue.

The second situation applies if any related person acquired stock from the redeemed shareholder and continues to hold the stock after the redemption. Waiver is allowed in this situation if the related acquirer's shares were redeemed in the same transaction.

Example: Assume the same initial facts as in the preceding example, but the Year 7 redemption was of Mom's stock. Son and Daughter will remain as shareholders. This fact pattern illustrates the second questionable acquisition/redemption scenario.

Example: Dad was the sole shareholder in Corporation X until Year 4. In Year 4, he gave 25 percent of his shares to Son and 25 percent to Key Employee. Three years later, X redeemed the shares owned by Dad and Son. In this case, Dad can waive attribution from Son because Son's shares were redeemed in the same transaction.

---

30. The statute of limitations is also extended for taxes and interest arising from a shareholder's acquiring a prohibited interest in the ten-year period. I.R.C. § 302(c)(2) (flush language).

Section 8.04(c)(1)(B) Entity Attribution

If a shareholder's estate includes stock in a closely held corporation, redemptions from that estate are likely. You may also encounter situations in which the corporation's stock is owned by another corporation, a partnership, or a trust. As you trace the ownership of these entities, you will eventually reach individuals who are related to other shareholders.

Example: Corporation X has the following ownership for its one class of stock. A owns 50 percent; LMN Trust owns 10 percent; and unrelated third parties own 40 percent. LMN Trust has one beneficiary. That beneficiary is A's daughter. As a result of family attribution, Beneficiary constructively owns A's 50 percent of X stock. As a result of owner to entity attribution, LMN Trust constructively owns that 50 percent in addition to the 10 percent it actually owns. If X redeemed LMN Trust's shares, LMN would still constructively own X stock because A's stock is attributed to Beneficiary and then to LMN.

Section 302(c)(2)(C) allows an entity to waive family attribution in this situation. If this section's requirements are met, LMN can waive family attribution from A to Beneficiary and qualify the redemption as a complete termination of its interest.

The requirements for waiver follow those discussed in section 8.04(c)(1)(A). Both the entity and the individual whose family member owns the stock must agree not to acquire a prohibited interest in the ten-year period. In addition, they must accept joint and several liability for any tax liability if either acquires a prohibited interest.

Caveat: If Beneficiary also owned an option to acquire any of A's shares, LMN could not waive attribution from A to Beneficiary. As noted in section 8.03(a)(5)(C), if both option and family attribution apply, the shares are deemed owned by option attribution. Section 302(c)(2)(C) does not provide for waiver of option attribution.

Caveat: Because corporate ownership structures can be quite convoluted, it is important to work through the attribution rules. The two examples that follow appear similar but the results are quite different.

Example: Corporation X has the following ownership for its one class of stock. Corporation Y owns 50 percent; LMN Trust owns 10 percent; and unrelated third parties own 40 percent. LMN Trust has one beneficiary. That beneficiary is T's daughter. T owns 90 percent of Y's stock. As a result of entity attribution, T constructively owns 90 percent of the X shares that Y owns. Because Y owns 50 percent of the X shares, T constructively owns 90 percent of 50 percent—45 percent of the X shares. Beneficiary constructively owns T's 45 percent of X. As a result of owner to entity attribution, LMN Trust constructively owns that 45 percent in addition to the 10 percent it actually owns. If X redeemed LMN Trust's shares, LMN would still constructively own X stock because T's stock is attributed to Beneficiary and then to LMN. The redemption can qualify only if both LMN and Beneficiary waive attribution from T to Beneficiary.

The pre-redemption ownership in the example above is illustrated as follows:

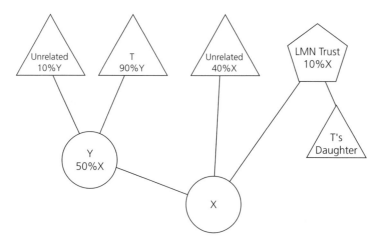

Example: Assume the same facts as in the preceding example, except that T owns only 30 percent of Y's stock. Because T does not own at least 50 percent of the Y stock value, there is no attribution to T of the X stock owned by Y.[31] Because T doesn't actually or constructively own any X stock, there is no family attribution to Beneficiary. In that case, X can redeem LMN Trust's shares. No attribution waivers are needed.

Section 8.04(d) Partial Liquidation (Section 302(b)(4))

A redemption qualifies as a partial liquidation if it meets two tests. First, the shareholder being redeemed can not be a corporation. Second, the redemption must be in partial liquidation of the distributing corporation. These tests are discussed further in this section.

---

31. The result would be different if Y was an S corporation instead of a C corporation. Because the attribution rules treat S corporations as partnerships, any S corporation shareholder will constructively own a portion of the stock owned by the corporation. I.R.C. §318(a)(5)(E).

Section 8.04(d)(1) Qualified Recipient

If the shareholder is an individual, the redemption passes the first test. But what if the shareholder is a partnership, estate, or trust? In those situations, we treat the entity's stock as owned proportionately by its partners or beneficiaries.[32] If one of them is a corporation, its portion of the redemption fails the first test.

Section 8.04(d)(2) Qualified Distribution

The second test looks to the corporation making the distribution.[33] The distribution must not be essentially equivalent to a dividend, a determination made at the corporation level.[34] In addition, the distribution must be pursuant to a plan and must be completed in the same taxable year as the plan's adoption or the next taxable year.

The Code provides one safe harbor for establishing the distribution is not essentially equivalent to a dividend.[35] Distributions qualify if the corporation ceases to conduct a "qualified" business, distributes the assets of that business (or the sales proceeds), and is engaged in the active conduct of another "qualified" business immediately after the liquidation. A business is "qualified" if the corporation has actively conducted it during the five-year period ending on the date of the redemption. A business is also qualified if another person actively conducted it during part of the five-year period so long as the distributing corporation did not acquire it in a taxable transaction.

Example: Corporation X has actively conducted a newspaper distribution business and a dental supplies business for the past ten years. Both are qualified businesses.

Example: Corporation Y has actively conducted a newspaper distribution business for the past ten years. Four years ago, Y purchased a dental supply business from its prior owner, who had actively conducted it for more than a year. The dental supply is not a qualified business. Y acquired it in a taxable transaction (by purchase). The dental supply business would qualify if Y had acquired it in a nontaxable transaction.

---

32. I.R.C. § 302(e)(5).
33. I.R.C. § 302 (e)(1).
34. See section 8.04(e) for the rules governing distributions that are not essentially equivalent to a dividend judged at the shareholder level.
35. I.R.C. § 302(e)(2)–(3).

Example: Z Corporation has actively conducted a newspaper distribution business the past ten years. Three years ago, Z was the surviving entity in a tax-free merger in which it acquired the assets of a four-year-old dental supply business. The dental supply business is a qualified business. It was acquired within the past five years in a reorganization (Chapter 10), which is a nonrecognition transaction.

One might think that a pro rata redemption is a dividend equivalent because the shareholders' ownership percentage does not change. Nevertheless, even a pro rata distribution is acceptable if it meets the safe harbor.[36]

Distributions outside the safe harbor definition may still qualify as not essentially equivalent to a dividend. The regulations give as one example a genuine corporate contraction occasioned by a fire. Distribution of insurance proceeds attributable to the fire can qualify as not essentially equivalent to a dividend.[37]

Section 8.04(e) Not Essentially Equivalent to a Dividend

A redemption that fails to meet one of the section 302(b)(2)–(4) safe harbors may still qualify for sale or exchange treatment.[38] Section 302(b)(1) allows sale or exchange treatment if the distribution is not essentially equivalent to a dividend. Unlike the partial redemptions discussed in the previous section, this status is tested at the shareholder level. It is based on a facts and circumstances test.

The regulations indicate some of the factors considered in determining whether a redemption is essentially equivalent to a dividend.[39] Pro rata redemptions of the only class of stock will not qualify because they do not change the shareholders' relationship. If the corporation has several classes of stock outstanding, a pro rata redemption of one class may qualify if the other classes are held by other shareholders (or by the shareholders being redeemed but in significantly different proportions). The most important consideration is whether there is a meaningful reduction in the shareholder's interest.[40]

Attribution rules, which indicate the extent to which the redeemed shareholder constructively owns stock, are also relevant. They are much less important, however, if the corporation is publicly held.

---

36. I.R.C. § 302(e)(4).

37. Treas. Reg. § 1.346-1. The Tax Equity and Fiscal Responsibility Act of 1982 repealed former section 346. Its regulations apply in interpreting section 302(b)(4).

38. I.R.C. § 302(b)(5).

39. Treas. Reg. § 1.302-2(a)–(b).

40. *United States v. Davis*, 397 U.S. 301 (1970).

Shareholders in publicly traded companies encounter qualifying redemptions in at least two situations. First, the corporation may offer to redeem shareholders who hold very small blocks of stock, say fewer than 100 shares, or may issue a tender offer to bolster its stock price or meet some other business need.[41] Some of these shareholders may still constructively own shares because a family member is also a shareholder. Second, the corporation may pay cash in lieu of fractional shares as part of a so-called stock dividend.[42] Shareholders in this situation will continue as owners of their pre-dividend shares.

Section 8.05 Section 303

Section 8.05(a) Introduction

As we illustrated in sections 8.03 and 8.04, the relationship between a closely held corporation and its controlling shareholder may not be affected by a redemption that leaves that shareholder in actual or constructive control. As a result, such transactions are likely to be treated as dividends rather than as redemptions.

That rule could cause hardships if stock in a closely held corporation comprises a significant portion of a decedent's estate. The corporation may have more liquid assets than does the estate, but attribution rules may prevent the estate from qualifying under section 302.

Section 303 provides another means of qualifying a redemption as a sale. If it applies, the shareholder being redeemed can ignore the section 318 attribution rules.

Section 8.05(b) Requirements

To take advantage of section 303, a redemption must meet several requirements.[43] The paragraphs below discuss the required relationship of the shares to the decedent's estate, limitations on the amount that can qualify, and time periods for completing the redemption. These requirements are designed to limit section 303 to the situations that would otherwise be hardships.

---

41. *See, e.g.*, Rev. Rul. 76-385, 1976-2 C.B. 92 (applying section 302(b)(1) to a redemption that reduced the shareholder's ownership from .0001118 percent to .0001081 percent).

42. Distributions of cash in lieu of fractional shares are discussed in section 7.04(b)(1)(B) as part of the explanation of section 305.

43. Additional rules apply to make section 303 available if the generation-skipping tax applies. *See* I.R.C. §303(d).

Section 8.05(b)(1) Inclusion of Shares in Decedent's Estate

Section 303(a) requires that the stock being redeemed be included in the decedent's gross estate for federal estate tax purposes.[44] It does not require that it be included in the decedent's probate estate or taxable estate.

Example: A and her son B own all of the stock in Corporation X as joint tenants with right of survivorship. At A's death, B takes title to the stock by operation of law as surviving tenant. The stock is not subject to probate. If A provided 100 percent of the consideration for the stock, all of its value is included in her gross estate even though none of it is in her probate estate.[45]

Example: Assume instead that A provided 84 percent of the consideration and B provided 16 percent. A's gross estate includes 84 percent of the stock's value; none of it is in her probate estate.[46]

Example: C and her husband D own all of the stock in Corporation X as joint tenants with right of survivorship. At C's death, D takes title to the stock by operation of law as surviving tenant. The stock is not subject to probate. Because C and D are married to each other, only 50 percent of the stock's value is included in C's gross estate. Because the transfer qualifies for the estate tax marital deduction, none of the stock's value is included in her taxable estate.[47]

Caveat: The future of the federal estate tax is unclear. It is currently scheduled for repeal in 2010 and reinstatement in 2011. If Congress permanently repeals the federal estate tax, section 303 as currently written will have much less significance.

Section 8.05(b)(2) Portion of Estate Represented by Stock

It is not sufficient to establish that the stock is included in the gross estate. To qualify for section 303 relief, the stock's value must generally exceed 35 percent of the excess of the total gross estate over the deductions allowed by sections 2053 and 2054.[48]

---

44. Alternatively, stock can qualify if it is acquired after the decedent's death but takes its basis from stock included in the decedent's gross estate. If, for example, the decedent owned qualifying stock in Corporation X, which merged with Corporation Y, shares of Corporation Y can qualify for section 303.

45. I.R.C. § 2040(a).

46. I.R.C. § 2040(a).

47. I.R.C. §§ 2040(b) & 2056.

48. I.R.C. § 303(b)(2)(A). These sections cover funeral and administrative expenses, claims against the estate, mortgages, certain taxes, and casualty and theft losses.

Example: When A died, he owned shares of Corporation X and a variety of other assets. A's gross estate was $7,000,000. The estate had deductible section 2053 and 2054 expenses of $800,000. The estate can qualify for section 303 relief for a portion of the X shares if the total value of its X shares exceeds $2,170,000 (35 percent of $6,200,000).

If a decedent owned stock in more than one corporation, the estate can aggregate the decedent's holdings to meet the more than 35 percent test. Shares qualify for aggregation if the amounts included in the gross estate are at least 20 percent of the value of that corporation's outstanding stock.[49]

Example: When A died, he owned shares of Corporation X, Corporation Y, and Corporation Z. It is impossible for each of these holdings to exceed 35 percent of A's gross estate minus section 2053 and 2054 deductions, as 3 times 35 percent would equal 105 percent of that amount. If A happened to own at least 20 percent of the value of each corporation's stock, the estate could aggregate the holdings to meet the 35 percent of gross estate test.

Caveat: Don't confuse these tests. The 35 percent test looks to the value of the stock as compared to the value of the gross estate minus funeral and administrative expenses. The 20 percent test looks to the value of the stock as a percentage of the outstanding shares of a particular corporation. A decedent who owns stock in many corporations may satisfy the 20 percent test for none, some, or all of them. Unless he satisfies them for at least two corporations, the estate cannot aggregate their stock to satisfy the 35 percent test.

Example: When A died, he owned 10 percent of the shares of Corporation X, 25 percent of the shares of Corporation Y, and a variety of other assets. E's gross estate minus section 2053 and 2054 deductions was $6,000,000. The X shares were worth $2,500,000. The Y shares were worth $1,000,000. The X shares qualify for section 303 relief because they meet the 35 percent test. The Y shares do not qualify. Although A owned at least 20 percent of the Y stock, he did not own at least 20 percent of the X stock. To aggregate stock, the decedent must own at least 20 percent of each corporation's stock value.

Section 8.05(b)(3) Limitation on Qualifying Redemption Amount

Section 303(a) limits the value of the qualifying stock to the sum of (a) estate, inheritance, legacy, and succession taxes imposed by reason of the death;

---

49. I.R.C. §303(b)(2)(B). If spouses own stock in a survivorship tenancy, as community property, or as tenants in common, and only one-half is included in the decedent's gross estate, the estate can count both spouses' stock in testing whether the 20 percent test is met. *Id.*

and (b) the funeral and administration expenses allowable as deductions in computing the taxable estate. In computing this limitation, we take into account state and foreign taxes in addition to any federal estate tax.

Example: When A died, he owned 500 shares of Corporation X, valued at $5,000,000, and a variety of other assets. The estate's federal and state estate taxes, and deductible funeral and administrative expenses, totaled $2,000,000. Assuming A's holdings of X meet the 35 percent test described in section 8.05(b)(2), X can redeem up to $2,000,000 of the estate's stock in a section 303 redemption.

Section 8.05(b)(4) Redemptions from Other Shareholders

The corporation may redeem stock from a beneficiary who inherited the stock from the decedent instead of directly from the estate. In that situation, section 303 applies only to the extent that shareholder's interest in the estate is reduced by, or is subject to a binding obligation to contribute to, the items discussed in section 8.05(b)(3).[50]

Section 8.05(b)(5) Time Limit for Completing Redemption

Even if all other tests are met, a redemption will not qualify under section 303 unless it is completed within the authorized time limits. The permitted time period begins with the decedent's death and ends no more than 90 days after the expiration of the period for assessing the federal estate tax.[51] A longer period may apply if a Tax Court petition has been filed or the estate is paying taxes in installments pursuant to section 6166. The qualifying redemption amount may be reduced if distributions occur more than four years after the decedent's death.[52]

Section 8.06 Redemptions Using Related Corporations Section 304

In sections 8.04 and 8.05, we discussed situations in which a corporation redeems its own stock. Another possibility, discussed in this section, involves a redemption by a related corporation. The relationship could be direct, as in the case of a parent-subsidiary structure. It could also be indirect; two corporations could have related owners. Redemptions in the latter situation are

---

50. I.R.C. §303(b)(3).
51. I.R.C. §303(b)(1). Only section 6501(a) applies in determining this period.
52. I.R.C. §303(b)(4).

referred to as brother-sister redemptions. Section 304 provides the rules for determining if redemptions by related corporations are treated as sales or exchanges for purposes of both sections 302 and 303.

Section 8.06(a) Brother-Sister (Sibling) Redemptions

Section 304(a)(1) applies if one corporation acquires the stock of a sibling corporation in exchange for property.[53] Corporations are siblings if they (1) have a common shareholder control group and (2) are not in a parent-subsidiary relationship.[54]

Section 8.06(a)(1) Control—General Rule

Control is defined as ownership of at least 50 percent of the corporation's voting power *or* at least 50 percent of the total value of all classes of stock.[55] The control group does not have to satisfy the same test for each corporation. It can satisfy the voting power test for one corporation and the value test for the other.

Example: Corporation X and Corporation Y each have only one class of stock, voting common. X's shares are owned equally by three unrelated individuals A, B, and C. The Y shares are owned equally by A and B. Because A and B are in control of both X and Y, the two corporations are related. If A and B sell X stock to Y, the transaction is a brother-sister redemption. If A and C make the sale, the transaction is not a brother-sister redemption.[56] The example above is illustrated below:

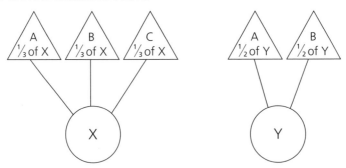

---

53. Property is defined in section 317(a), discussed in Chapter 7.
54. I.R.C. §304(a)(1) (flush language) (" ... then (unless paragraph (2) applies....").
55. I.R.C. §304(c)(1). The 50 percent test is based on aggregate value; the shareholders do not have to own 50 percent of the value of each class of stock. Rev. Rul. 89-57, 1989-1 C.B. 90.
56. If A and C received DEF stock instead of cash, the transaction could be a brother-sister redemption. See the discussion in section 8.06(a)(1)(B).

Example: Corporation X has two classes of stock, voting common and non-voting preferred. Corporation Y has only one class of stock, voting common. A owns all of the X voting common stock; B owns all of its nonvoting preferred. If A owns all of the Y stock, the two corporations are related, because A owns at least 50 percent of the voting power of each. If, instead B owns all of the Y stock, the two corporations are related only if the X nonvoting preferred stock is worth at least 50 percent of the total value of all X stock.

Section 8.06(a)(1)(A) Control—Constructive Ownership

Although the attribution rules discussed in section 8.03 apply in determining control, the rules used for attributing ownership from and to a corporation are modified. Instead of the 50 percent of value threshold normally needed to trigger attribution, section 304(c)(3) applies a 5 percent of value threshold.[57] For purposes of section 304, stock will be attributed *from* a corporation to any person owning at least 5 percent of the value of that corporation's stock. It will also be attributed *to* a corporation from a shareholder owning at least 5 percent of the value of that corporation's stock.

The rules for attribution *to* a corporation have a slight twist. If the shareholder owns at least 50 percent of the value of the corporation's stock, the corporation constructively owns all of that shareholder's stock. If the shareholder owns at least 5 percent but less than 50 percent, the corporation constructively owns only part of the shareholder's stock. The percentage deemed owned reflects the percentage of the other corporation's stock value owned by that shareholder.[58]

Example: Corporations X and Y each have one class of stock outstanding. The X shares are owned by individuals A (42 percent), B (7 percent), and C (6 percent) and by Corporation Z (45 percent). A owns 30 percent of the Z stock. A also owns 60 percent of the Y stock. The remaining Y and Z shares are owned by unrelated parties. If the normal section 318 rules applied, X and Y would not be related corporations. Because A does not own at least 50 percent of Z, we would not normally attribute A's X shares to Z or Z's X shares to A. But, for purposes of section 304 control, we attribute ownership when a shareholder owns at least 5 percent of a corporation's stock. As a result, A constructively owns 30 percent of the X shares owned by Z. A thus constructively owns 30 percent of 45 percent, or 13.5 percent. When those 13.5 per-

---

57. I.R.C. §304(c)(3)(B).

58. I.R.C. §304(c)(3)(B)(ii)(II). Pro rata rather than full attribution is the rule for attribution *from* a corporation to a shareholder. I.R.C. §318(a)(2)(C).

cent are added to the 42 percent that A actually owns, A is in control of X. A is also in control of Y because of her 60 percent ownership.[59]

The ownership structure described above is illustrated below:

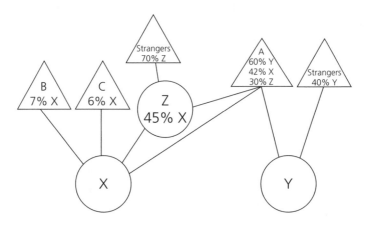

Section 8.06(a)(1)(B) Control—Stock Acquired in Transaction

If a corporation uses cash or other property to acquire the stock of a related corporation, we determine control using the rules discussed earlier in this section. If the corporation instead uses its own stock, the computation of control includes the stock received from the acquiring corporation.[60] In other words, the transaction itself can give the transferors control of the acquiring corporation.

Example: Corporation X and Y Corporation each have 1,000 shares of stock outstanding. A and B own all of the X shares but do not own any of the Y shares. Y issues 2,000 new shares to A and B in exchange for all of their X shares. Immediately before the exchange, A and B owned 100 percent of the X shares and 0 percent of the Y shares. Immediately after the exchange, A and B owned 0 percent of the X shares and 66.7 percent of the Y shares. A and B control both corporations for purposes of section 304.

Section 8.06(a)(1)(C) Control—Ownership Chains

If one or more persons control a corporation, which itself controls another corporation, the persons in control of the first corporation are treated as being in control of the second corporation.[61]

---

59. We will return to this example when we discuss parent-subsidiary corporations.
60. I.R.C. §304(c)(2)(A).
61. I.R.C. §304(c)(1).

Example: The shares of Corporations X and Y are owned equally by A and B. X owns 60 percent of the shares of Corporation Z; unrelated persons own the remaining Z shares. X and Y are brother-sister corporations. Because A and B control X, and X controls Z, A and B are treated as in control of Z. As a result, Y and Z are brother-sister corporations.

Section 8.06(a)(2) Testing the Redemption

If a sibling corporation acquires stock from a controlling shareholder, the transaction is tested with reference to the issuing corporation.

Example: Corporations X and Y each have 1,000 shares outstanding. A owns 100 percent of these shares. If X purchases 100 of A's Y shares, A still owns 100 percent of Y. He owns 900 shares actually and 100 constructively by attribution from X. This redemption fails to qualify as a section 302(b) sale or exchange.[62]

Example: Corporations X and Y each have 1,000 shares outstanding, and there is only one class of stock. B owns 520 shares (52 percent) of each corporation. Unrelated parties own the other shares. If X purchases 100 of B's Y shares, her ownership of Y is 420 shares actually owned and 52 shares constructively owned, a total of 472 shares. B now owns less than 50 percent of the voting power of Y. But her ownership percentage of both common stock and voting stock after the sale (47.2 percent) is not less than 80 percent of her 52 percent voting power before the sale. The redemption will not qualify under section 302(b)(2) as substantially disproportionate. Without additional facts, it is unlikely it will qualify under section 302(b)(1) as not essentially equivalent to a dividend.

In testing redemptions, remember to differentiate the attribution rules used to determine if corporations are related from those used to determine if the transaction meets the section 302(b) tests. Section 304(c)(3) uses a 5 percent ownership test to trigger attribution, it applies only for purposes of determining if the shareholders are a control group. Section 304(b)(1) provides that in determining if the redemption qualifies for section 302(b) treatment, the 50 percent ownership requirement is completely ignored.

Section 8.06(b) Parent-Subsidiary Redemptions

Section 304(a)(2) applies if a subsidiary corporation acquires the stock of its parent corporation in exchange for property. Corporations have a parent-

---

62. The examples in this chapter assume that none of the redemptions qualifies as a partial liquidation described in section 8.04(d).

subsidiary relationship if one of them is in control of the other. Control is tested using the rules discussed in section 8.06(a). The tests to determine if the redemption satisfies section 302(b) are based on ownership of the parent corporation's stock.[63]

Section 8.06(c) Interrelationship of Sections 304 and 351

If the acquiring corporation issues stock instead of acquiring the other corporation's stock with property, the shareholders may qualify as a section 351 control group.[64] When a transaction qualifies under both section 304 and section 351, the section 304 rules generally apply to property received by the transferor.[65] If the acquiring corporation assumes a debt, or takes the acquired stock subject to a debt, section 351 applies to the debt. In that situation, the transaction is governed partly by section 304 and partly by section 351.

Caveat: Section 304 applies only if the stock is acquired for property. If a corporation acquires stock in a related corporation solely in exchange for its own stock, section 304 does not apply.

Section 8.06(d) E&P Computations

If a section 304 redemption fails to qualify as a section 302 or 303 redemption, it will be treated as a section 301 distribution. As discussed in Chapter 7, section 301 provides for dividend treatment only to the extent of E&P. Section 304(b)(2) provides that we look first to the acquiring corporation's E&P. If those are insufficient, we look to the issuing corporation's E&P. Additional tax consequences are addressed in section 8.08.

Section 8.07 Dispositions of Certain Preferred Stock Section 306

A shareholder may acquire preferred stock in a variety of situations. It might be received as consideration in exchange for property transferred to the corpo-

---

63. *See* example in Treas. Reg. §1.304-3(b).

64. As discussed in Chapter 5, section 351 control requires ownership of at least 80 percent of the combined voting power and ownership of at least 80 percent of the shares of all other classes of stock.

65. I.R.C. §304(b)(3).

ration. It might be received from a third party in a gratuitous transaction or in payment for goods or services. Or it might be received as a stock dividend.

If a corporation distributes preferred stock to its shareholders, the initial tax consequences depend on how section 305 characterizes the distribution.[66] One possibility is that the distribution will be a nontaxable stock dividend. The other possibility is that the preferred stock will be treated as property. In that situation, section 301 will govern the shareholder's tax consequences.

Because preferred stock generally provides limited ownership rights, shareholders can dispose of their holdings without significantly reducing their share of corporate growth or voting rights. As a result, a tax-free preferred stock dividend followed by a sale for the stock's value could provide better tax consequences than a taxable cash dividend of the same amount. Section 306 limits the earnings "bail-out" potential for both redemptions and sales of so-called section 306 stock.

Section 8.07(a) Definition of Section 306 Stock

There are four categories of section 306 stock, the first three of which are covered by a general rule.[67] The first category covers preferred stock distributed to the shareholder and excluded from gross income by section 305(a).[68] The second category covers preferred stock received in a reorganization or section 355 transaction if the shareholder did not fully recognize gain or loss on the transaction.[69] The third category covers stock that does not fall into the first two categories but which has its basis determined with reference to section 306 stock. Stock could fall into that category because its current owner received section 306 stock by gift from the original owner. It could also fall into that category because it was received in a tax-free reorganization in which the shareholder exchanged section 306 stock.

Note that the third category includes "stock," while the first two categories include "stock (other than common stock)." If a shareholder exchanges preferred stock for common stock in a nonrecognition transaction, that common stock might be treated as section 306 stock. If that common stock has no con-

---

66. *See* section 7.04 for a discussion of stock dividends.

67. I.R.C. § 306(c)(1).

68. Preferred stock covered by section 305(b) is not in this category even if insufficient E&P resulted in the distribution being a tax-free return of basis.

69. The effect of the transaction must have been substantially the same as a stock dividend, or the stock must have been received in exchange for section 306 stock. I.R.C. § 306(c)(1)(B).

version privileges or can be converted only into common stock, it will not be treated as section 306 stock even though it was received in exchange for section 306 stock. If it can be converted into preferred stock or into property, the common stock will be section 306 stock.[70]

The fourth category of section 306 stock is preferred stock received in a section 351 exchange if a cash payment would have been treated as a dividend. Stock falls into this category even if only part of a cash payment would have been a dividend.

Stock that otherwise meets one of the definitions will not be section 306 stock if an equal cash distribution would not have been a dividend.[71] Because a corporation with no E&P could have issued a cash dividend tax-free, a dividend in preferred stock would not be treated as a potential earnings bail-out device.

Additional rules apply to stock rights. If the shareholder owns rights instead of stock, those rights will be treated as stock in applying section 306. If the stock was acquired through the exercise of rights, the stock is treated as having been distributed when the rights were distributed. However, only the rights' original value is treated as section 306 stock. Any additional funds paid to exercise the rights are not treated as section 306 stock.

Section 8.07(b) Transactions Covered by Section 306

Section 306 applies to both redemptions and other dispositions of section 306 stock. A shareholder cannot escape section 306 by selling shares to an unrelated person. Because the tax consequences of redemptions and sales differ slightly, the discussion below covers them separately.

Section 8.07(b)(1) Redemptions of Section 306 Stock

If the issuing corporation redeems section 306 stock, the general rule provides that the full redemption proceeds will be treated as an amount covered by section 301. As a result, the full redemption proceeds may be a dividend. This is true even if a lesser amount would have been a dividend when the section 306 stock was first issued.

Example: Corporation X made only one distribution in Year 1. It distributed preferred stock to its common shareholders. At that time X had E&P of

---

70. I.R.C. § 306(e).

71. I.R.C. § 306(c)(2). If the corporation changes the terms and conditions applicable to any of its stock, it must have no E&P at the distribution date and when the change occurs. I.R.C. § 306(g)(3).

$100,000. The preferred shares distributed had a total value of $120,000 in Year 1. In Year 5, when those shares had a total value of $300,000, X redeemed one-half of them. X's Year 5 E&P account was $800,000. If X had distributed cash in Year 1 instead of the preferred stock, its shareholders would have reported a $100,000 dividend and a $20,000 basis reduction for their common shares. Instead, they reported no gross income in Year 1 because they received a tax-free stock dividend. In Year 5, because X's E&P covers the cash paid to redeem the preferred stock, they report a $150,000 taxable dividend.

Section 8.07(b)(2) Other Dispositions of Section 306 Stock

If the acquisition is by a person other than the issuing corporation, section 306(a)(1) applies. As a general rule, the shareholder treats the amount realized as ordinary income.[72] If the amount realized exceeds the amount that would have been a dividend when the section 306 stock was distributed, only that lesser amount is treated as ordinary income. This determination is based on the value of the section 306 stock at the time of the distribution.

Example: Instead of a cash distribution in Year 1, Corporation X distributes section 306 stock to its shareholders. At that time, X had E&P of $100,000 and the preferred stock was worth $40,000. The shareholder allocated some of its common stock basis to the preferred stock, resulting in a basis for the preferred stock of $7,000.[73] If the preferred stock is later sold for $52,000, the amount treated as ordinary income is $40,000. The shareholder reports a gain of $5,000 ($52,000 amount realized minus the $40,000 treated as ordinary income minus the $7,000 basis).

If the proceeds exceed both the amount treated as ordinary income and the stock's basis, the excess is treated as gain from the sale of the stock. If the proceeds are less than the stock's basis, the shareholder cannot recognize loss.

Example: Instead of a cash distribution in Year 1, Corporation X distributes section 306 stock to its shareholders. At that time, X had E&P of $100,000 and the preferred stock was worth $40,000. The shareholder allocated some of its common stock basis to the preferred stock, resulting in a basis for the preferred stock of $7,000.[74] If the preferred stock is later sold for $32,000, the amount treated as ordinary income is $32,000. The shareholder

---

72. The amount so treated can qualify for the reduced tax rates applied to dividend income. I.R.C. §306(a)(1)(D).
73. I.R.C. §307, discussed in Chapter 7.
74. I.R.C. §307, discussed in Chapter 7.

cannot deduct a loss on the unrecovered $7,000 basis. Instead, that basis is added back to the shareholder's basis for the common stock that gave rise to the stock dividend.[75]

Additional rules apply if the corporation changed the terms and conditions that apply to any of its stock.[76] In that case, the amount potentially treated as ordinary income may be increased. Instead of using the fair market value of the stock when it is distributed, we use the greater of that value or the value when the change occurred. Instead of using the stock's share of E&P at the distribution date, we use the greater of that amount or the share when the change occurred.

Section 8.07(b)(3) Avoiding Dividend Treatment

There are several exceptions to the treatment described in sections 8.07(b)(1)–(2). Some of these exceptions apply to redemptions, some to non-redemption dispositions, and some to all dispositions.

Section 8.07(b)(3)(A) Redemptions

If a redemption qualifies under section 302(b)(3) (complete termination of shareholder's interest) or section 302(b)(4) (partial liquidation), the shareholder treats the redemption as a sale or exchange.[77] Note that this exception does not apply if the transaction qualifies only under section 302(b)(1) or (2). If a redemption occurs as part of the complete liquidation, the tax consequences follow the liquidation rules discussed in Chapter 11.[78]

Section 8.07(b)(3)(B) Non-Redemption Dispositions

A taxpayer who disposes of section 306 stock in a non-redemption transaction can treat the disposition as a sale or exchange by meeting two conditions.[79] First, the person acquiring the stock, directly or indirectly, cannot be a related person. Second, the disposition must terminate the shareholder's entire stock interest. The section 318 rules define which persons are related and whether the shareholder's interest has been terminated.

---

75. Treas. Reg. § 1.306-1(b)(2) (Examples (2) & (3)). A shareholder who no longer owns that common stock may be able to qualify the disposition under section 302(b)(3).

76. I.R.C. § 306(g).

77. I.R.C. § 306(b)(1)(B).

78. I.R.C. § 306(b)(2).

79. I.R.C. § 306(b)(1)(A).

Example: A owns section 306 stock but does not own any other stock in Corporation X. A sells that stock to unrelated person B. The transaction is treated as a sale. If A sold only one-half of his stock, he could not qualify for this safe harbor but might still qualify for one of the exceptions discussed below.

Section 8.07(b)(3)(C) All Dispositions

If a redemption or other disposition is covered by a nonrecognition section, the shareholder avoids dividend treatment. For example, if the corporation exchanges a new class of preferred stock for the old class of preferred stock, section 1036(b) provides for nonrecognition. The new preferred stock will assume the section 306 status of the old stock.[80] Stock transferred from one spouse to another is another example. Because section 1041 provides for nonrecognition and carryover basis, the recipient spouse takes the stock as section 306 stock.

The final exception looks to the purpose behind the events.[81] The taxpayer must satisfy the IRS that that the distribution and the subsequent redemption or other disposition was not in pursuance of a plan having avoidance of the income tax as one of its principal purposes.

Section 306(b)(4)(B) appears to apply this requirement to dispositions of section 306 stock if there has been a prior or simultaneous disposition of the stock with respect to which it was issued. However, the regulations indicate that the subsequent disposition of the section 306 stock in these circumstances "would not ordinarily be considered a disposition one of the principal purposes of which is [tax avoidance]."[82]

Section 8.08 Tax Consequences of Redemptions

The tax consequences of redemptions affect the corporation that redeems the shares and the shareholder being redeemed. Corporations that are related to the redeeming corporation, and shareholders whose interest in the corporation changes because of the redemption, may also have tax consequences. Tax consequences include those that are immediate, such as computation of gain or loss or dividend treatment. Other consequences include the effect on E&P available for future dividends and reduction in stock basis.

---

80. I.R.C. § 306(c)(1)(C). Section 1036(b) does not apply to so-called nonqualified stock described in section 351(g)(2).

81. I.R.C. § 306(b)(4)(A).

82. Treas. Reg. § 1.306-2(b)(3).

The paragraphs below set forth both general rules and rules whose application is limited to specific redemption types. The final topic in this section discusses the interaction of dividend and redemption treatment in marital dissolution and change of corporate ownership situations.

Section 8.08(a) Redeeming Corporation

Section 8.08(a)(1) Gain or Loss

The corporation's tax consequences are not affected by whether the redemption qualifies as a sale or exchange or is treated as a dividend. A corporation that uses cash to redeem its own stock has no gain or loss to report. If it uses property other than cash, the corporation recognizes no loss even if the property is worth less than its adjusted basis.[83] The corporation recognizes gain if the property is appreciated.[84]

If the corporation uses its own stock as the redemption consideration, it does not recognize gain or loss even if the stock is treated as property.[85]

Section 8.08(a)(2) Incidental Outlays

The corporation cannot deduct expenditures associated with the redemption, such as legal fees. If it borrows the funds needed to pay for the redemption, it can deduct the interest expense.[86]

Section 8.08(a)(3) E&P

The corporation's E&P account is increased if it recognizes gain on using appreciated property to make a redemption.[87] The account is also reduced to reflect the redemption. The amount of the reduction depends on whether the redemption is treated as a dividend or as a sale.

If the redemption is treated as a dividend, the E&P reduction is governed by section 312(a) and (b). The corporation reduces its E&P by the amount of money distributed. If it instead distributes a corporate obligation, it reduces

---

83. I.R.C. §311(a).

84. I.R.C. §311(b). The only exception to gain recognition involves use of corporate obligations.

85. I.R.C. §1032.

86. I.R.C. §162(k).

87. I.R.C. §312(b). If the property has two bases—one for income tax and one for E&P—E&P is increased by the gain computed for E&P purposes. See section 7.05 for a review of E&P computations.

E&P by the principal amount of the obligation. If the corporation uses any other property, it reduces E&P by the property's E&P basis (loss property) or fair market value (gain property).[88]

If the redemption is not treated as a dividend, section 312(n)(7) limits the E&P reduction to the redeemed stock's ratable share of E&P. In this regard, the redemption that is treated as a sale differs from a redemption that is treated as a dividend. The dividend could theoretically use up the entire E&P account.[89]

Example: Corporation X has 1,000 shares outstanding. There are four equal shareholders—A, B, C, and D. It has E&P of $8,000. X redeemed A's shares this year for their fair market value of $11,000. It made no other distributions this year. If the redemption is treated as a section 301 distribution, X's E&P are reduced to zero. If the redemption is instead treated as a sale or exchange, its E&P are reduced by $2,000 (the amount attributable to the redeemed shares).

If section 304 or section 306 applies, there are additional rules to remember. In section 304 brother-sister and parent-subsidiary redemptions, the amounts paid are first charged against the E&P of the acquiring corporation. If that account is insufficient, the payments are charged against the E&P of the issuing corporation.[90] If a shareholder sells section 306 stock rather than having it redeemed, the shareholder may qualify for the reduced section 1(h) tax rate. Because the corporation made no distribution to the shareholder, it does not reduce its E&P account.

Section 8.08(b) Redeemed Shareholders

Section 8.08(b)(1) Gain or Loss

If the redemption qualifies as a sale or exchange, the shareholder realizes gain or loss. The gain is gross income, and usually is capital gain. The loss will generally be deductible because the stock was acquired with a profit motive. If the shareholder and the corporation are related parties, the shareholder will be unable to deduct the loss.[91]

Caveat: Two sets of attribution rules may be relevant in the loss context. Section 318 attribution rules apply in determining whether a redemption is

---

88. Although section 312(a)(3) indicates that basis will be used, section 312(b)(2) substitutes fair market value for basis for distributions of appreciated property.

89. Remember that a distribution cannot reduce E&P below zero.

90. Section 312(n)(7) does not specify how to allocate E&P when a section 304 redemption is treated as a sale or exchange.

91. I.R.C. §267(a)(1).

treated as a section 302 sale or exchange. Section 267 attribution rules determine whether the shareholder and corporation are related parties for loss deduction purposes.

Section 8.08(b)(2) Dividend Income

If the redemption is treated as a section 301 distribution, and is fully covered by corporate E&P, the shareholder reports the amount received as dividend income. If the value of the consideration received exceeds E&P, the excess is applied against basis and could even result in gain realized if basis is insufficient.

If the shareholder is an individual, the amount treated as a dividend can qualify for the reduced rate of taxation on dividends and net capital gain income.[92] If the shareholder is itself a corporation, it may qualify for the dividends received deduction discussed in section 7.02.

If the extraordinary dividend rules of section 1059 apply, the corporate shareholder must reduce its stock basis and will report gain if the "nontaxed amount" exceeds basis. These rules apply to redemptions that are not pro rata, that are treated as section 302(e) partial liquidations, or that are treated as dividends because of either section 318 option attribution or section 304 related corporation redemption rules.[93]

As discussed in section 8.07(b)(2), a shareholder who sells section 306 stock reports at least part of the sales proceeds as ordinary income. Although these sales proceeds are not dividends, section 306(a)(1)(D) makes them eligible for the reduced rate of tax on dividends.

Section 8.08(b)(3) Basis

The shareholder has two concerns. The first is the basis of any property received from the corporation. The shareholder takes a fair market value basis for that property.[94]

The shareholder must also ascertain the basis of the shares that were redeemed and of any shares that were retained. That determination will depend on how the redemption is categorized and on whether the shareholder is a corporation.

---

92. I.R.C. § 1(h).

93. *See generally* I.R.C. § 1059(e).

94. Section 301(d) provides this treatment if the redemption is subject to the dividend rules. If the redemption is treated as a sale or exchange, the "tax cost" doctrine provides the same outcome.

If the redemption is categorized as a sale or exchange, the shareholder compares the basis of the redeemed stock to the amount realized for purposes of computing gain or loss. The basis of any remaining shares is unchanged.

If the redemption is categorized as a dividend, the distribution is governed by section 301. A noncorporate shareholder treats amounts received as a dividend if the corporation's E&P cover the distribution. Redemption proceeds that exceed E&P are treated as a return of basis. Any unrecovered basis is transferred to the redeemed shareholder's remaining stock. If the shareholder has not retained any shares, and is subject to dividend treatment because of attribution rules, the basis will be transferred to the related parties.[95]

Although corporate shareholders are treated similarly, it is important to keep in mind the possible basis reduction required if the dividend is treated as extraordinary, as discussed in Chapter 7.

If the transaction described in section 304 is treated as a dividend, the shareholder is concerned with basis for his holdings in each corporation. For section 304(a)(1) brother-sister relationships, the shareholder follows a multi-step hypothetical format. First, the shareholder is treated as transferring the issuing corporation's stock to the acquiring corporation in a transaction described in section 351(a). The fact that the shareholder does not meet the section 368(c) control definition is irrelevant. The shareholder is deemed to have received back stock of the acquiring corporation. The acquiring corporation is then deemed to have redeemed its own stock from the shareholder in exchange for the consideration it actually used to acquire the stock of the related corporation.

The first step in this transaction results in the acquiring corporation taking the shareholder's basis for the issuing corporation's stock.[96] The shareholder's basis for the acquiring corporation's stock equals his basis for the issuing corporation's stock.[97] That basis then disappears because the shareholder did not really receive stock in the acquiring corporation; he received other property. The basis is assigned to the stock in the acquiring corporation that the shareholder actually owned.

Section 8.08(c) Other Shareholders

Unless a redemption is pro rata, shareholders whose stock is not being redeemed have their ownership percentage increased. If the redemption did not

---

95. Treas. Reg. § 1.302-2(c).

96. I.R.C. § 362(a).

97. I.R.C. § 358(a). *See also* Treas. Reg. § 1.304-2(c).

qualify as a sale or exchange, the remaining shareholders may have dividend treatment. Section 305(c), discussed in section 7.04(b), authorizes regulations to treat an increase in a shareholder's proportionate interest in earnings or assets as a dividend. One of the triggering events listed in section 305(c) is a redemption that is itself treated as a dividend.

The other tax consequence remaining shareholders may have relates to basis. As noted in section 8.08(b)(3), a redeemed shareholder may be unable to use his basis because the redemption is treated as a dividend. If attribution rules are responsible, the related continuing shareholders may acquire the redeemed shareholder's basis.

Section 8.09 Determining the Appropriate Taxpayer

Section 8.09(a) Transfer of Control Using Corporate Funds

If a shareholder has his stock redeemed by the corporation or sells it to the continuing shareholders, he has severed his ownership relationship. The continuing shareholders now own all the remaining stock. But, as the examples below illustrate, the tax consequences can be quite different.

Example: Corporation X has two equal shareholders, A and B. X has E&P of $500,000. Each shareholder's stock is worth $2,000,000. Each shareholder has a basis of $100,000 for that stock. If A purchased B's stock, A would have to pay $2,000,000. A would then have a basis of $2,100,000 for his X stock. B would report a gain of $1,900,000, which would probably be long-term capital gain. X reports no gain or loss; its E&P account is unaffected. If X distributed $300,000 to A the following year, A would report a $300,000 dividend.

Example: Corporation Y has two equal shareholders, P and Q. Y has E&P of $500,000. Each shareholder's stock is worth $2,000,000. Each shareholder has a basis of $100,000 for that stock. If Y purchased Q's stock, Y would have to pay $2,000,000. P would still have a basis of $100,000 for his Y stock. Q would report a gain of $1,900,000, which would probably be long-term capital gain. Y reports no gain or loss; its E&P account would be reduced to $250,000 to reflect the redemption. If Y distributed $300,000 to P the next year, P would report only $250,000 as a dividend.

The examples above have quite different tax consequences. Yet the operative facts are quite similar. Each corporation began with two shareholders and ended with one. Would our analysis of the second transaction change if we knew that P was obligated to purchase Q's stock? In other words, by having Y discharge her liability, did P constructively receive a dividend from Y? This sort of question arises when there is a transfer of corporate control using corporate rather than shareholder funds. If the corporation satisfied a purchase obligation for which the shareholder was "primarily and unconditionally liable," the IRS can recast the transaction and treat the surviving shareholder as if she received a dividend.[98]

Section 8.09(b) Transfer of Stock in Marital Dissolution

A similar situation occurs during a marital dissolution if the spouses own shares in a closely held corporation. Because section 1041 provides nonrecognition for transfers to the other spouse, the spouse being bought out wants the benefit of that treatment. If the redeemed shareholder succeeds in treating the redemption as an indirect sale to the continuing shareholder, the redeemed shareholder reports no gain or loss. If the redeemed shareholder fails and is subject to normal redemption rules, she is taxed on her gain. Even though she would be eligible for long-term capital gain rates, nonrecognition is clearly a better outcome.

If the IRS established that the redemption satisfied the continuing owner's property settlement obligation, he would have to report a dividend up to the amount of the available corporate E&P. If the IRS failed, he would have no tax consequences from the redemption.

The Service litigated many of these cases, trying to establish that at least one of the shareholders had gross income. Ultimately, it issued Regulation section 1.1041-2. That regulation provides that if the continuing spouse has dividend treatment, the redeemed spouse qualifies for section 1041 nonrecognition. The IRS will treat the redeemed spouse as if she sold her stock to the other spouse. It will treat the continuing spouse as if he received a distribution from the corporation to redeem that stock. Because he owns all the stock, the redemption would be treated as a dividend.[99]

If the continuing spouse does not have dividend treatment, the regulation states that the redeemed shareholder will have redemption treatment and will not qualify for section 1041 nonrecognition. While redemption treatment is preferable to dividend treatment, it is not as beneficial as section 1041 treatment.

---

98. *See* Rev. Rul. 69-608, 1969-2 C.B. 42, for examples of this test.
99. Similar results would apply even if the corporation also had minority shareholders.

PART FOUR

CORPORATE FISSIONS, FUSIONS, AND LIQUIDATIONS

CHAPTER 9

CORPORATE FISSIONS: SECTION 355

Section 9.01 Introduction

Section 9.01(a) Overview

Section 355, which applies to many corporate fission transactions, is an extremely important provision. Since the repeal of the *General Utilities*[1] doctrine, it is one of the few Code sections that permit the transfer of corporate property to shareholders without the recognition of gain—thus avoiding a double tax on that gain.

The *General Utilities* doctrine allowed a corporation to distribute property to its shareholders without corporate-level gain recognition. The doctrine went beyond the actual *General Utilities* holding, which involved only a liquidation distribution. That decision in effect mirrored the results on incorporation. If, as we saw in Chapter 5, incorporation can be accomplished without recognition, shouldn't "unincorporating" receive the same nonrecognition treatment? Nonrecognition is not the general rule. As we will discuss in Chapter 11, nonrecognition treatment for liquidations is limited to liquidations of a subsidiary into a corporate parent.

Although section 243, which we discussed in Chapter 7, allows generous deductions for dividends received, it applies only to corporate shareholders. Following a distribution to a corporate shareholder, the money distributed remains within corporate form. So unlike section 355, section 243 does not really avoid the double tax.

---

1. *See General Utilities & Operating Co. v. Helvering*, 296 U.S. 200 (1935). The doctrine was codified in the 1954 Code but repealed by the Tax Reform Act of 1986, which enacted the 1986 Code.

In section 4.01, we provided an example of a corporation that had taxable income of $100, paid tax of $30, and distributed its $70 after-tax income to its shareholders. Would the results be different if, instead of transferring cash to its shareholders, the corporation transferred stock (valued at $70) in a subsidiary? If the transaction meets the requirements of section 355, both the distributing corporation and its shareholders may avoid gain recognition.

Because section 355 provides significant tax benefits, you should not be surprised that the parties must clear several hurdles to qualify for its use. As we will see, sections 355(d), 355(e), and 355(f) are significant restrictions, which the IRS actively enforces through regulations and other rulings.

Section 355 applies to distributions of stock of one corporation (the controlled corporation) made by another corporation (the distributing corporation) to its shareholders. Unlike section 301 distributions of money, which have no negative tax consequences for the distributing corporation (other than its inability to deduct paying dividends), defective section 355 distributions involve adverse tax consequences. Because these distributions often are made using appreciated stock, failure to qualify under section 355 results in gain being recognized by the distributing corporation.

It is important that you not confuse section 355 with section 305. Section 355 involves distributing stock of a subsidiary corporation; section 305 involves distributing the corporation's own stock. As we saw in Chapter 7, a distribution of a corporation's own stock is generally not treated as distribution of property under section 317. A distribution of stock of a corporation's subsidiary is considered a distribution of property.

Section 9.01(b) Types of Section 355 Transactions

There are three basic section 355 transactions, the spin-off, the split-off, and the split-up. Each is illustrated below:

Spin-Off

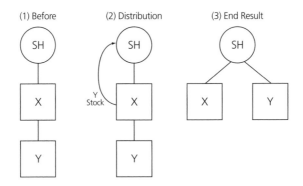

(1) Before   (2) Distribution   (3) End Result

Split-Off

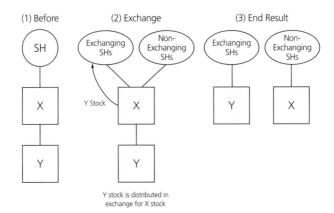

(1) Before   (2) Exchange   (3) End Result

Y stock is distributed in
exchange for X stock

Split-Up

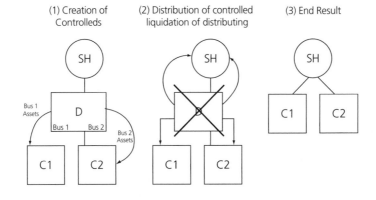

(1) Creation of Controlleds   (2) Distribution of controlled liquidation of distributing   (3) End Result

One of the transactions illustrated above may be preceded by a reorganization under section 368(a)(1)(D). Such a transaction is common and is illustrated as follows:

D/355 Transaction

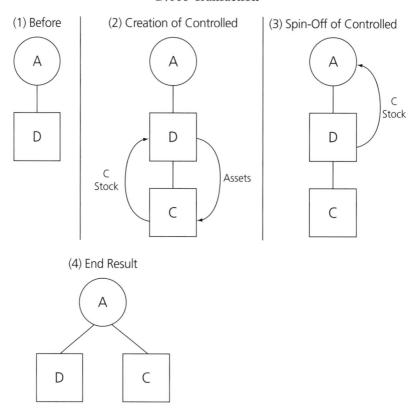

(1) Before   (2) Creation of Controlled   (3) Spin-Off of Controlled

(4) End Result

Section 9.02 Relevant Code Sections

Several other Code sections are involved in determining the tax consequences of a section 355 distribution. Because some section 355 transactions take place in the context of section 368(a)(1)(D) (the "D reorganization"), this chapter provides a brief introduction to the section 368 reorganization provisions (discussed in greater detail in Chapter 10). Other tax consequences are governed by sections 358 and 362 (basis) and by section 1223 (holding period). Section 357 must be consulted if liabilities are assumed.

Section 9.03 Basic Requirements

The general rule of section 355 is contained in section 355(a). Shareholders and security holders of the distributing corporation qualify for nonrecognition if the distribution meets these requirements:

(a) a distribution of stock/securities of the controlled corporation to the stockholders/securities holders of the distributing corporation;
(b) control must be distributed;
(c) the transaction must not be a device; and
(d) both distributing and controlled corporations must meet the active business requirement.

Each of these basic requirements is subject to additional requirements, which are explained below. This chapter also discusses the continuity of interest and business purpose requirements, which are included in the regulations.

Section 9.03(a) Distribution of Stock or Securities

Section 355(a)(1) provides for distributions to two groups, shareholders and security holders. The distribution requirements vary for the two groups.

Section 355(a)(1) requires that the corporation distribute to its shareholders solely stock or securities of a controlled corporation. The distribution must be made to the shareholders in their capacity as shareholders and not as payment for services rendered or for some other reason. Section 355 applies whether or not the distribution is pro rata and whether or not the shareholders exchange stock of the distributing corporation for the stock or securities that they receive.[2]

Section 355(a)(1) requires that distributions to security holders must be in exchange for securities in the distributing corporation.

If either shareholders or security holders receive securities, two further limitations apply. The principal amount of securities distributed cannot exceed the principal amount surrendered. If securities are distributed, securities must be surrendered in exchange. These rules apply on an owner by owner basis. They are not measured in the aggregate. If a shareholder or security holder runs afoul of either requirement, some—possibly all—of that person's gain will be recognized.[3]

---

2. I.R.C. §355(a)(2).
3. I.R.C. §355(a)(3).

The treatment of stockholders differs from the treatment of security holders because distributions of stock necessarily dilute the ownership of a corporation. Distribution of securities may not involve any ownership dilution. Although it is assumed that the economic position of stockholders will not significantly change following a section 355 transaction, the transaction will be recast to reflect the economics of the transaction if it results in a significant economic disparity.[4]

As we saw in Chapter 5, certain stock lacks the equity characteristics to qualify for nonrecognition treatment. With one exception, section 355(a)(3)(D) provides that certain nonqualified preferred stock will not be treated as stock or securities. It can qualify if distributed with respect to nonqualified preferred stock of the distributing corporation.

Section 9.03(b) Distribution of Controlled Corporation

Section 9.03(b)(1) In General

Section 355 does not apply unless the distribution is of stock or securities in a controlled corporation. Section 355(a)(1)(A)(flush language) defines controlled corporation as a corporation which is controlled by the distributing corporation. Control requires ownership of 80 percent of the voting power and 80 percent of the nonvoting shares.[5]

Section 355(a)(1)(D) requires the distributing corporation to distribute (1) all of the stock and securities it holds in the controlled corporation or (2) an amount of such stock constituting control within the meaning of section 368(c). If the distributing corporation retains any stock or securities in the controlled corporation, the retention must not further a tax avoidance plan. For example, retaining stock of the controlled corporation

---

4. For example, if prior to a spin-off, A and B were equal shareholders in the distributing corporation, they will be expected to retain their prior economic positions following the spin-off. If, instead, A receives a larger portion of the economic pie (*i.e.*, receives more stock in the controlled corporation), the transaction may be recast using a substance versus form analysis as a stock distribution of that larger portion from the distributing corporation to B and then from B to A. If B is related to A, such transfer will be treated as a gift. If B is A's employer, it will be treated as payment for services rendered. Recasting this distribution will not affect qualification under section 355.

5. Section 368(c) makes its rules applicable to Parts I, II, and III of Subchapter C. Part III includes section 355.

because the distributing corporation will pay the controlled corporation's liabilities is acceptable.

Caveat: If the distributing corporation does not control the other corporation, section 355 cannot apply to the distribution. The amount of stock that must be distributed and the requirement that the corporation be controlled are separate requirements. The distributing corporation must meet each requirement.

Example: Corporation X distributed to its shareholders all of its shares in Corporation Y. The distributed stock represented 85 percent of Y's only class of stock. This transaction can qualify under section 355(a). X distributed all of the stock it owned in a controlled corporation.

Example: If X owned only 70 percent of Y's stock, the transaction cannot qualify under section 355(a). Although X distributed all its Y stock, it did not distribute stock of a "controlled" corporation.

Section 9.03(b)(2) Control Immediately before the Distribution

Section 355(a) requires that the distributing corporation be in control "immediately" before the distribution. Will section 355 apply if a corporation purchases control shortly before the distribution? Section 355(a)(3)(B) applies in this situation. If the distributing corporation acquires stock in the controlled corporation within five years of the distribution and gain or loss was recognized in that transaction, the stock acquired during that period is treated as other property and not as stock. This rule applies whether or not the distributing corporation attained control through that acquisition.

The stock acquired during the five year period is counted toward determining whether the corporation is a controlled corporation. It is counted toward the requirement that the distributing corporation distribute at least a controlling interest in the controlled corporation. But it is not counted as stock for purposes of nonrecognition by the shareholders.

Example: Corporation X has owned 90 percent of the stock of Corporation Y for ten years. Y has been a controlled corporation throughout the past ten years. Two years ago, X purchased 5 percent more of the Y stock in a taxable transaction. Section 355(a) may apply in part if X distributes its Y stock to the X shareholders. X must distribute at least 80 percent of the Y stock and may have to distribute all 95 percent. X's shareholders treat shares representing 90 percent of Y as qualifying property. Because the remaining shares they receive are boot, they will have at least partial gain recognition.

X may be able to qualify for section 355 treatment without waiting five years. If Y recapitalizes its stock so that X obtains control of Y, control will have been acquired in a nonrecognition transaction. The recapitalization may occur immediately prior to the spin-off and still satisfy the control requirement so long as X's acquisition of control involves a permanent shift of control.[6] If the realignment of interests was done solely to meet section 355, and a readjustment establishes the prior ownership after the spin-off, the IRS could assert substance over form, collapse the transaction, and argue that the control requirement was not met.

Example: Corporation X owns 70 percent of the stock of Corporation Y. B, the sole shareholder of X, owns the remaining Y stock. If B contributes his Y stock to X, and X distributes its now 100 percent of the Y stock to B, the transaction does not qualify. The control requirement is not met because X's control of Y was transitory.[7]

At first glance, it may be argued that control is also transitory in any recapitalization followed by a distribution. After all, the distributing corporation does not retain control of the controlled corporation. The difference is that in the example immediately above, B owned 100 percent of the stock of Y, the controlled corporation (30 percent directly and 70 percent indirectly through X) before the recapitalization. Following the distribution, B directly owned 100 percent of Y. Because no change has really occurred, there has not been a permanent realignment of interests.

At one time, the IRS argued that post-distribution transactions affected meeting the control requirement. For example, if following the distribution of a controlled corporation, the shareholders of the distributing corporation disposed of the stock of the controlled corporation, the IRS could invoke the step transaction doctrine and argue that control was not met. Currently, the IRS will not consider post-distribution transactions in determining whether control is met. Nevertheless, taxpayers are not completely free to do as they please following a section 355 transaction. Sections 355(d) and 355(e) may make certain dispositions taxable.[8]

---

6. *See* Rev. Rul. 56-117, 1956-1 C.B. 180. In the ruling, X owned all the Y common stock and 12 percent of the preferred stock. In a section 368(a)(2)(E) recapitalization, Y issued common stock in exchange for preferred stock to all the preferred stock holders except X. As a result, X held 93 percent of the only class of stock. The IRS held the transaction met the control requirement. *See also* Rev. Rul. 71-593, 1971-2 C.B. 181; Rev. Rul. 70-18, 1970-1 C.B. 74.

7. *See* Rev. Rul. 63-260, 1963-2 C.B. 147.

8. Taxpayers may find the section 355(e) regulations relatively easy to avoid. The regulations only generally require that taxpayers not enter into negotiating sales prior to the section 355 disposition.

Section 9.03(b)(3) Impact of Warrants and Options

In addition to common and preferred stock, ownership in a corporation is sometimes reflected by warrants and options to acquire stock. If a warrant or option is very likely to be exercised ("deep in the money"), it will be treated as stock for most purposes.

The IRS once argued that rights to acquire stock were not treated as stock or securities for purposes of section 355.[9] The regulations now provide that stock rights and warrants are treated as securities for purposes of section 355, and they have no principal amount for purposes of that section.[10] Hence, receipt of stock rights or warrants will not automatically trigger gain recognition.

Section 9.03(c) The Anti-Device Requirement

Although section 355(a) allows taxpayers to avoid gain recognition, you must not forget that it is designed to eliminate tax advantages for certain transactions. The predecessor of section 355 was codified in 1951 following the trial court decision in *Gregory v. Helvering*,[11] which had permitted the taxpayer to bail out her corporation's E&P at capital gains rates while maintaining her equity interest in the enterprise.[12] The anti-device language of section 355 is designed to prevent taxpayers from receiving disguised dividend distributions.

Section 355(a)(1)(B) prevents a transaction from qualifying for non-recognition treatment if the transaction was used principally as a device for the distribution of the E&P of the distributing corporation, the controlled corporation, or both. What if some of the shareholders sell shares in either corporation shortly after the transaction occurs? Section 355(a)(1)(B) provides that a subsequent sale or exchange does not automatically mean that the transaction fails the device test. A sale or exchange fails the device test if

---

9. *See Commissioner v. Gordon*, 391 U.S. 83 (1968), *rev'g* 382 F.2d 499 (2d Cir. 1967); *Baan v. Commissioner*, 45 T.C. 71 (1965), *aff'd*, *Commissioner v. Baan*, 382 F.2d 485 (9th Cir. 1967).

10. *See* Treas. Reg. § 1.355-1(c). If Regulations § 1.355-6 provides a contrary rule, it will override § 1.355-1(c). These regulations are discussed later in the context of section 355(d).

11. 27 B.T.A. 223 (1932), *rev'd*, 69 F.2d 809 (2d Cir. 1934), *aff'd*, 293 U.S. 465 (1935). Section 112(b)(11) of the 1939 Code covered both failure to continue the active conduct of a business or using a distribution principally as a device for distributing E&P.

12. *Gregory v. Helvering* is described in section 3.03(b). The E&P computation is discussed further in Chapter 7.

made pursuant to an arrangement "negotiated or agreed upon" before the distribution.

Although neither the Code nor the regulations define E&P, we know that E&P is generally an attempt to measure a corporation's realized accretion of wealth.[13] By including an anti-device requirement, Congress protects the double tax regime of corporate taxation by limiting the parties' ability to manipulate E&P. The typical transaction that Congress was concerned with is described in the example below.

Example: Corporation X is owned by Individuals A and B. Corporation X has accumulated liquid assets of $100,000 attributable to its earnings. If X transfers these assets to A and B as dividends, A and B will report gross income. What if X, instead, transfers the liquid assets to a wholly-owned subsidiary, Y, and then transfers the Y stock to A and B? If A and B sell the Y stock, part of their amount realized will reflect the value of those liquid assets. If this transaction is not treated as a device, A and B will have converted dividend income into capital gain.[14]

The regulations provide that the determination of whether a device exists will be made from all the facts and circumstances.[15] The regulations list several device factors and non-device factors and also list transactions that are ordinarily not considered to have been used principally as a device. These factors and transactions are discussed below.

Section 9.03(c)(1) Device Factors

Section 9.03(c)(1)(A) Pro Rata Distribution

The first device factor is a pro rata distribution to all the corporation's shareholders.[16] At first glance, this rule appears to conflict with the language

---

13. *See* Mombrun, *E&P As We Know It (Or Should Know It)*, 75 Tax Notes 1659 (June 23, 1997).

14. Even if the tax rates on dividend income and long-term capital gains are equal, capital gains provide advantages. First, the tax rate is applied to gain, not to the full amount received. Second, if the taxpayer has a large capital loss, the gain can be offset by a larger loss deduction than might otherwise be allowed. I.R.C. § 1211. The IRS has traditionally viewed converting ordinary income into capital gain as a device. *See* Rev. Rul. 71-383, 1971-2 C.B. 180. The substantial capital contribution by distributing corporation to controlled corporation prior to the distribution of the controlled corporation (in exchange for 85 percent of the stock in the distributing corporation) was not treated as a device. That particular transaction would have qualified as a disproportionate redemption under section 302(b)(2).

15. Treas. Reg. § 1.355-2(d).

16. Treas. Reg. § 1.355-2(d)(2)(ii).

of section 355. Section 355(a)(2) provides that section 355(a) can apply whether or not the distribution is pro rata with respect to all of the shareholders of the distributing corporation. In actuality, the two provisions are not really in conflict. The Code provides that a distribution can qualify for tax-free treatment even if it is pro rata. The regulations, which provide for considering the facts and circumstances, indicate that pro rata distributions are a potentially negative factor. The mere fact that a distribution is pro rata does not automatically make it a prohibited device.

Why do the regulations look less favorably on pro rata, as opposed to non-pro rata, distributions? As we discussed in Chapter 3, tax rules are generally based on the assumption that taxpayers enter into transactions that make economic sense. Therefore, if a distribution is non-pro rata, it is likely that shareholders who received more shares of the controlled corporation exchanged more of their stock in the distributing corporation. Otherwise, the parties would not have maintained their original economic positions, albeit in different ownership form. A non-pro rata transaction generally looks more like a corporate reorganization and generally carries out a corporate business purpose. A pro rata distribution, on the other hand, keeps the shareholders in the same economic position. They will benefit on a pro rata basis if the controlled corporation is sold following the spin-off. Hence, pro rata transactions have strong dividend features. If the controlled corporation is sold following the spin-off, the shareholders may be able to transform a potential dividend distribution into a capital gain.

Section 9.03(c)(1)(B) Subsequent Sale or Exchange of Stock

The second device factor is a sale or exchange of stock in either the distributing or controlled corporation following the distribution.[17] The regulations divide this category into subcategories, which have different weights. For example, a prearranged sale or exchange is considered "substantial" evidence of device. A sale or exchange that is not negotiated or agreed upon in advance is merely evidence of device.[18] The regulations indicate the evidence of device

---

17. Treas. Reg. § 1.355-2(d)(2)(iii). Applying this device factor is now somewhat complicated by the enactment of section 355(e). A transaction may fall under section 355(e) and at the same time be a device for the distribution of the corporation's E&P. Obviously the device regulations will provide the worst results for the taxpayer since the whole transaction will be taxable whereas if section 355(e) applies, only part of the transaction will be taxed.

18. *Compare* Treas. Reg. § 1.355-2(d)(2)(iii)(B) *with* Treas. Reg. § 1.355-2(d)(2)(iii)(C).

increases if a greater percentage of stock is disposed of or if the dispositions occur relatively soon after the distribution.[19]

In applying this device factor, we look at whether there is a connection between the distribution and the subsequent disposition. If the disposition of either the distributing or controlled corporation's stock was prearranged, then that subsequent disposition will be treated as substantial evidence of device. Although the taxpayer has a high hurdle to clear, the transaction may still qualify under section 355. For example in Revenue Ruling 59-197,[20] the IRS held that the sale of distributing corporation stock by one of its shareholders followed by the spin-off of a controlled corporation in exchange for the shares just purchased qualified for section 355 tax-free treatment. The two transactions had a business purpose—to enable a key employee to acquire an interest in the controlled corporation.

The IRS subsequently challenged a similar transaction in *Pulliam v. Commissioner*.[21] In *Pulliam*, a controlled corporation was spun off and 49 percent of its stock was sold by a shareholder to a key employee of the business. Although the IRS asserted that the pre-arranged sale was substantial evidence of device, the Tax Court found that the transaction was motivated by the key employee business purpose. In situations like *Pulliam*, the prudent tax lawyer is likely to recommend that the controlled corporation itself sell shares to the employee in order to avoid a challenge by the IRS.

What if either the distributing or controlled corporation engages in a transaction in which gain or loss is not recognized (for example, a reorganization)? Would this be a device?

Example: A and B each owned 50 percent of the stock of Corporation X, which owned all the stock of Corporation Y. X distributed all of its Y stock to A in exchange for A's shares in X. X then merged into Corporation Z, and B received Z stock in the merger.

In judging whether this series of transactions are a device, we should consider whether the double tax regime was violated. Arguably, it was not. The assets of X remained in corporate solution and therefore subject to double tax. For purposes of the device regulations, the transaction should not be treated as a device for the distribution of the corporations' E&P.

---

19. Treas. Reg. §1.355-2(d)(2)(iii)(A).

20. 1959-1 C.B. 77. The device regulations generally speak of sales or exchanges following the distribution, but the sale described in the ruling occurred prior to the distribution. As the ruling indicated, "Obviously, such a sale has exactly the same effect as a binding contract to sell some of the stock after the transaction."

21. T. C. Memo 1997-274, 73 T.C.M. (CCH) 3052 (1997), *nonacq.*, 1998-47 I.R.B. 4.

Caveat: Notwithstanding that the double tax regime is not violated, section 355(e) might apply to reduce the benefits associated with a section 355 transaction. That possibility is discussed in section 9.04(c).

The situation described above involved an exchange of stock. The same rationale applies if the stock of the controlled corporation is transferred by gift. There may also be situations in which a spin-off is followed by another spin-off. Generally, the IRS will not treat the second spin-off as a device so long as there are valid reasons for the second or subsequent spin-offs.

Section 9.03(c)(1)(C) Nature and Use of Assets

As we saw above, the classic device example involves the transfer of liquid assets by one corporation to another, followed by the spin-off and eventual sale of the second corporation. The classic device example is fairly easy to spot and easy to attack. In other situations, the regulations provide that the IRS will scrutinize the division of assets between the distributing and controlled corporation to determine whether a device is present. Thus there is evidence of device if assets that are not used in an active trade or business are transferred to the controlled corporation or retained by the distributing corporation (to an extent that there is an unbalance). The regulations provide that such assets include cash and liquid assets that are not related to the reasonable needs of the business.[22] Again, a determination of the strength of this device factor, if present, will be made from all the facts and circumstances.

For example, in one ruling, the IRS ruled that a small shift in investment assets will be taken into account in determining whether device is present.[23] In the ruling, a corporation engaged in the active conduct of two businesses was required to separate those businesses. It transferred one business to a new corporation, along with investment assets not related to the new corporation's business. Although the investment assets represented less than 20 percent of the new corporation's total assets, the IRS held that such shift in assets should be taken into account in determining whether device is present.

These rulings are very fact-specific. In another ruling, the IRS permitted a transfer of liquid and movable assets because the taxpayer was under imminent threat of nationalization in a foreign country.[24]

---

22. Treas. Reg. § 1.355-2(d)(2)(iv)(B). The regulations indicate that the inquiry will not be limited to cash and liquid assets.

23. Rev. Rul. 86-4, 1986-1 C.B. 174.

24. Rev. Rul. 78-383, 1978-2 C.B. 142.

Implicit in section 355 transactions is the notion that the two businesses may be somehow incompatible and require separating. If, prior to the separation, one business was functionally related to the other business and the relationship continues following the separation, the transaction may be considered to be a device. Regulations section 1.355-2(d)(2)(iv)(C) provides that such a situation will be evidence of device especially if one business can be sold without adversely affecting the other.

Example: Corporation X is engaged in the manufacturing of widgets. X owned all the stock of Corporation Y, which is engaged solely in selling the widgets produced by X. X distributed all the Y stock to its shareholders. Following the transaction, Y continued to be engaged in the sale of X's widgets. If Y were sold, X's business would not be adversely affected. Because Y continued to engage in the same business, these facts do not provide a good business reason for the spin-off. Under the regulations this would be evidence of device.

Section 9.03(c)(2) Non-Device Factors

As stated above, the regulations provide certain factors that will be treated as evidence of non-device. If one of these factors is present, this would be treated as evidence that the transaction was not entered into as a device for distributing the E&P of either the distributing or controlled corporation.

Section 9.03(c)(2)(A) Corporate Business Purpose

If the transaction is undertaken for a valid corporate business purpose, the taxpayers would have support for their argument that the transaction was not a device. The regulations provide that the business purpose requirement is independent of the other requirements under section 355. Even transactions with little or no device potential must still have a business purpose to satisfy section 355.[25] Although not specifically mentioned in section 355 itself, the business purpose requirement is a natural extension of the anti-device requirement.

In weighing device and non-device factors, you should consider the importance of achieving the purpose to the success of the business, the extent to which the transaction is prompted by outside factors beyond the control of the distributing corporation, and the immediacy of the conditions prompting the transaction. These factors go to the heart of the business purpose re-

---

25. *See* Treas. Reg. § 1.355-2(b).

quirement. We will return to the business purpose requirement later in this chapter.

Section 9.03(c)(2)(B) Distributing Corporation is Publicly Traded and Widely Held

If the distributing corporation is publicly traded and widely held, and no shareholder beneficially owns more than 5 percent of any class of its stock, this will be evidence of non-device.[26] Not surprising, the IRS readily accepts section 355 distributions involving publicly traded corporations because the potential for device is very low. It is very hard for a corporation with a large number of shareholders to be in collusion with the shareholders.

Section 9.03(c)(2)(C) Distribution to Domestic Corporate Shareholder

The regulations provide that a distribution to a domestic corporate shareholder entitled to a deduction under section 243 is evidence of non-device.[27] As we discussed in Chapter 7, corporate shareholders are entitled to a dividends received deduction for 70 percent or more of their dividend income. Hence, in such a distribution, the potential for device is quite low.

Section 9.03(c)(3) Transactions Not Ordinarily Considered Devices

The regulations also list three situations that ordinarily do not present the potential for tax avoidance. As the regulations indicate, "such distributions are ordinarily considered not to have been used principally as a device, notwithstanding the presence of any of the device factors ...."[28]

Section 9.03(c)(3)(A) No E&P or Gain Potential

The first situation described is a distribution of a controlled corporation if three requirements are met: Neither the distributing nor controlled corporation can have accumulated E&P on the first day of the taxable year. Neither corporation can have current E&P on the date of the distribution. No distri-

---

26. Treas. Reg. § 1.355-2(d)(3)(iii).
27. Treas. Reg. § 1.355-2(d)(3)(iv). The regulation does not provide the same evidence of non-device treatment for distributions to foreign corporations, because corporate earnings could be potentially transferred to a jurisdiction beyond the reach of the United States. *See* Ridgway, 776-2nd T.M., Corporate Separations, section V(F).
28. Treas. Reg. § 1.355-2(d)(5).

bution of property by the distributing corporation immediately before the separation would require recognition of gain resulting in current E&P for the taxable year of the distribution.

As we saw in Chapter 7, positive E&P results if a corporation distributes appreciated property to its shareholders. The distribution would be treated as a sale of that property for fair market value. To meet this factor's requirements, the distributing corporation must either have no appreciated asset or must have a current E&P loss that exceeds the aggregate appreciation in all its assets. It has been said that if this was the case, the regulation would be useless because it would be too restrictive.[29] The regulations provide no examples illustrating this rule.

Example: Corporation X has no E&P and conducts two businesses. X transfers one of the businesses to new Corporation Y. The assets transferred to Y have a fair market value that exceeds their basis. X then transfers the stock of Y to its shareholders. The transaction would not be covered by Regulations section 1.355-2(d)(5)(ii) because a distribution of the property by X would have caused X to recognize gain under section 311 and increase its E&P.

The transaction above does not really involve a bail-out of corporate earnings. Following the distribution, Y would have X's basis for the property, so the built-in gain would remain in corporate form. Remember that the IRS is very cautious about unequivocally stating that a distribution is protected from taxation under section 355. Although this distribution is not treated as "ordinarily" not being device, it may yet qualify under section 355.

The existence of a strong business purpose would have been helpful in the above example. In the past, if taxpayers were unsure about their business purposes or whether a device was present in their cases, they could apply for a PLR. The PLR would provide some assurance that the transaction would be respected unless there was a material difference between the facts presented to the IRS and the actual transaction. Such assurances are becoming rare since the publication of Revenue Procedure 2003-48,[30] a pilot program under which the IRS will not issue rulings on whether the transaction meets the business purpose requirement, is not a device, or is not part of a plan under section 355(e). Taxpayers seeking section 355 rulings are required to submit representations on these issues.

Caveat: Even before issuing to Revenue Procedure 2003-48, the IRS did not issue specific rulings regarding device or business purpose. Implied in its rulings granting nonrecognition treatment under section 355 were findings of

---

29. Ridgway, 776-2nd T.M., Corporate Separations, section V(G), at A-24.

30. 2003-29 I.R.B. 86. As it promised in the revenue procedure, the IRS issued more published guidance, regulations, revenue rulings, and other materials on which taxpayers can rely and that have precedential value.

non-device and an acceptance of the taxpayer's business purpose. The rulings granted following Revenue Procedure 2003-48 will specifically state that the IRS has not looked beyond the taxpayer's representations regarding device.

Section 9.03(c)(3)(B) Qualified Redemption

The second and third situations involve transactions covered by provisions we discussed in Chapter 8. If the transaction would have qualified under section 302 (redemptions not treated as dividends) or section 303 (redemptions to pay estate taxes and related expenses), it will not ordinarily be considered a device. To take advantage of this presumption, the distribution must qualify as to each shareholder receiving a distribution.

Section 9.03(c)(4) Section 355 PLRs

Because the IRS no longer issues PLRs on device, rulings involving that issue take on a greater instructional role even though, as we saw earlier, they cannot be cited as precedent. These PLRs, which reflect IRS thinking at the time they were issued, help in identifying issues taxpayers might otherwise miss. The paragraphs below provide a representative sample of such rulings.

A 2002 ruling held that the sale of a distributing corporation's stock in anticipation of a section 355 transaction was not evidence of device.[31] This ruling makes sense, because the stock sold represents an interest in both the distributing and the controlled corporations. Such sales do not bail out E&P. Following the section 355 distribution, the distributing corporation's E&P account will be divided between it and the controlled corporation. More importantly, the position of the distributing corporation's shareholders is unchanged.

In another PLR, the IRS held that proportionate sales of both distributing and controlled corporations' stock following a section 355 transaction are permitted.[32]

The IRS has also held that boot received in a section 355 transaction is not treated as device.[33] In that PLR, a shareholder received stock of a controlled corporation in exchange for part of his shares in the distributing corporation. The shareholder's remaining distributing stock was redeemed for a note.

---

31. PLR 200223007 (issued Mar. 6, 2002).

32. PLR 200324039 (issued Mar. 4, 2003).

33. PLR 200211032 (issued Dec. 17, 2001). PLR 200145029 (issued Aug. 9, 2001) has a similar holding. Even though the IRS did not specifically rule that there was no device in the transactions, such holding is implied because had the IRS found a device it would have never issued the rulings.

Often, in section 355 transactions and in reorganizations, cash is transferred to the shareholders in lieu of fractional shares, thereby avoiding unnecessary administrative expense. A 1999 PLR held that such transfers of cash will not cause disqualification under section 355.[34]

Section 9.03(d) The Active Trade or Business Requirement

Section 9.03(d)(1) In General

One of the major requirements of section 355 relates to "active trade or business."[35] Section 355 allows nonrecognition treatment only if the distributing and controlled corporations are each engaged in an active trade or business following the distribution. If either corporation is an investment company, the distribution will receive no protection from section 355 and may be subject to taxation.

The active trade or business requirement is an independent requirement. Even if there is no device or little device potential, the transaction must satisfy the active trade or business requirement.

In reading section 355(b), you should focus on two major requirements: (1) the corporations must engage in an "active" trade or business; and (2) the active trade or business must be conducted for at least five years prior to the distribution date. The legislative history sheds no light on the purpose behind either rule. Nevertheless, it is reasonable to infer that these requirements support the congressional purpose of preventing devices to bail out the E&P of the distributing and/or controlled corporations. Active assets are less likely than investment assets to be used as devices because moving active assets to a different ownership structure has a greater potential to disrupt the corporation's business activities.

Section 9.03(d)(2) Definition of Trade or Business

Although section 355(b) does not define what constitutes an active trade or business, the regulations do provide a definition. Regulations section 1.355-3(b)(2)(i) provides that a corporation will be treated as engaged in an active

---

34. PLR 199923027 (issued Mar. 11, 1999). See also Rev. Rul. 66-365, 1966-2 C.B. 116 (a ruling involving B and C reorganizations), holding that such transfer of cash will not violate the solely for voting stock requirement.

35. Although lower tax rates apply to net capital gains and qualified dividends, many Code sections illustrate congressional antipathy toward passive activities. *See, e.g.,* I.R.C. §469, which limits passive activity losses.

trade or business if it meets the requirements and limitations contained in section 1.355-3(b)(ii)–(iv). Section 1.355-3(b)(2)(ii) defines a trade or business as a specific group of activities being carried out by the corporation for the purpose of earning income or profit and the activities included in such group include every operation that forms a part of, or a step in, the process of earning income or profit. The group of activities must include the collection of income and the payment of expenses.

Example: Corporation X, a not-for-profit corporation, owns Corporation Y, also a not-for-profit corporation. Both corporations operate homeless shelters. Each corporation has more than 100 employees and has actively operated shelters for longer than five years. For valid business reasons, X distributes Y to its members. This transaction cannot qualify under section 355. Although there might be a business purpose for the transaction, the distribution will not qualify for section 355 treatment. Non-profit corporations cannot engage in activities for profit and, thus, are not engaged in an active trade or business for purposes of section 355.[36]

What if the non-profit corporation is engaged in a significant for-profit activity taxable under the unrelated business income tax rules? That activity arguably should qualify as a trade or business because the regulations only require that the corporation conduct a group of activities for the purpose of earning a profit. Although it is clear that the regulations were intended to apply to for-profit corporations, they do not limit their application only to such corporations. Because the law is unclear in this area, requesting a PLR may be a wise investment in this situation.

Section 9.03(d)(3) What Constitutes "Active"?

The regulations next address the heart of the active trade or business requirement—which activities will be considered active. For purposes of section 355(b), the determination of what qualifies as an active trade or business will be made from all the facts and circumstances of a particular case.

The regulations impose some general requirements. First, a corporation will be required itself to perform active and substantial management and operational functions of the business. Activities performed by persons outside the corporation, including independent contractors, generally will not be treated as activities performed by the corporation itself. The regulations also provide

---

36. *See also* Rev. Rul. 57-492, 1957-2 C.B. 247 (exploring for oil is not a trade or business because no income is produced); Rev. Rul. 57-464, 1957-2 C.B. 244 (the described rental operation is not a trade or business because net rental income is incidental).

that the corporation can satisfy the active trade or business requirements through the activities it performs even though some of its activities are performed by others.

For PLR purposes, the IRS normally will require a breakdown of the activities or the steps in which the corporation normally engages in its trade or business. The corporation will be required to list its management activities and its operational activities. Although most corporations that are engaged in a business can easily meet this requirement, some corporations will have a more difficult time. Corporations engaged in farming may be scrutinized because farming corporations often hire a large number of farm laborers as independent contractors, especially during planting and harvest time. Corporations that have employees who are engaged full-time in the enterprise and who are engaged in substantial managerial and operational activities will be able to meet the requirement. Even one full-time employee may be sufficient.[37]

The regulations provide that the active conduct of a trade or business does not include: (1) the holding, for investment purposes, of stock, securities, land or other property or (2) the ownership and operation (including leasing) of real or personal property used in a trade or a business, unless the owner performs significant services with respect to the operation and management of the property.[38]

The exclusion of investment companies from being engaged in an active trade or business for purposes of section 355 stems from the main purpose of section 355 to prevent taxpayers from bailing out E&P. An investment company by design is much more closely monitored by its investor shareholders because its only goal is to provide earnings to its shareholders. Therefore, the device potential in an investment company setting is inherently present. The restriction on investment companies applies even if the company has a sizable staff of full-time employees to conduct its business.[39] A dealer in securities may, however, be engaged in an active trade or business. The reason for this distinction is that the dealer in securities does not necessarily hold the stock and securities for investment purposes. The dealer is engaged in the business of buying and selling stock and securities. A closely related case is the finance business. A corporation engaged in a finance business and a retail business could easily spin off its finance business without affecting the retail business. In addition to being vulnerable to attack as not meeting the active trade or business

---

37. *See* Rev. Rul. 73-234, 1973-1 C.B. 180 (farming corporation is engaged in an active trade or business even though it only has one full-time employee and uses independent contractors for a large amount of its activities).

38. Treas. Reg. § 1.355-3(b)(2)(iv).

39. *See* Rev. Rul. 66-204, 1966-2 C.B. 113.

requirement, this type of transaction would appear to be a classic case of device. Courts, however, have blessed such transactions.[40]

Section 9.03(d)(4) Ownership of Real Property

Ownership of real property is given more latitude under the regulations than holding investment property. If the owner of real property rents the property but provides significant services with respect to the property, the activities of the owner may rise to the level of an active trade or business. For example, in Rev. Rul. 79-394,[41] the IRS held that a corporation leasing real property was engaged in an active trade or business because the owner of the property engaged in a number of activities including providing maintenance and repairs, made payment for gas, water, electricity, taxes and insurance, advertised for tenants and negotiated leases. A triple-net lease under which the tenant is responsible for all the maintenance of the property and the owner provides little services will not qualify as an active trade or business.

Section 9.03(d)(5) Activities of Independent Contractors

We have seen earlier that activities of independent contractors will not be attributed to the corporation. We have also seen that just the mere fact that the corporation employs independent contractors will not necessarily doom the transaction. As required by the regulations, the "facts and circumstances" of each case will be determinative. In addition to this broad statement in the regulations, the IRS has provided several revenue rulings to help taxpayers. Although the revenue rulings only apply to their respective facts, they can be useful to taxpayers with analogous facts. In Rev. Rul. 73-237,[42] the Service held that a construction company with several salaried employees who, among other things, supervised the work of the subcontractors, was engaged in an active trade or business. In Rev. Rul. 89-27,[43] the IRS ruled that a corporation that was a non-operator of working interests in oil and gas properties was engaged in an active trade or business because its employees were engaged in significant activities. The corporations employed geologists, petroleum engineers and accountants on full-time basis. On the other hand, the IRS held in Rev. Rul. 86-126[44] that a corporation that operated a farm through independent

---

40. *See, e.g., Hanson v. U.S.*, 338 F. Supp. 602 (D. Mont. 1971).
41. 1979-2 C.B. 141, *amplified by* Rev. Rul. 80-181, 1980-2 C.B. 121.
42. 1973-1 C.B. 184.
43. 1989-1 C.B. 106.
44. 1986-2 C.B. 58.

contractors (tenant-farmers) was not engaged in an active trade or business because its employees only provided occasional consultation and their main activities consisted of leasing the land. From these rulings, the prudent tax lawyer engaged in a section 355 transaction should ensure that both the distributing corporation and the controlled corporation have employees engaged in significant management and operational activities of the corporation. Depending on the facts of the case, the amount of exposure and the potential gain involved, a PLR request may be appropriate. The costs of a PLR normally include a substantial user fee to the IRS ($6,000 or more in 2005), in addition to time preparing the PLR request and follow up on IRS questions.

Section 9.03(d)(6) Employees of Related Entities

There are instances in which employees of a related entity can help a taxpayer meet the active trade or business requirement. For example in Rev. Rul. 79-394,[45] a spin-off was held to meet the requirements of section 355 even though the business activities of the controlled corporation were conducted by the distributing corporation (the parent of the controlled corporation). In the ruling, the controlled corporation reimbursed the distributing corporation employees but such reimbursement was not controlling as clarified in Rev. Rul. 80-181.[46] The active trade or business requirements may also be met through the use of the employees of a sister corporation. Following such transactions, however, the controlled corporation must retain its own employees to conduct its business activities. As required in Rev. Proc. 96-30[47] and Rev. Proc. 2003-48,[48] for advance ruling purposes, the taxpayer is required to make a representation that the distributing and controlled corporation will each be engaged in an active trade or business using their own separate employees.

Section 9.03(d)(7) Active Trade or Business in a Partnership

A more interesting scenario involves the conduct of an active trade or business in a partnership. Can a corporation be treated as engaged in an active trade or business through ownership of a general partnership interest in a partnership? Rev. Rul. 92-17[49] answers this question in the affirmative. In the revenue ruling, the distributing corporation distributes the stock of its only

---

45. 1979-2 C.B. 141.
46. 1980-2 C.B. 121.
47. 1996-1 C.B. 696
48. 2003-29 I.R.B. 86.
49. 1992-1 C.B. 142.

subsidiary corporation, Controlled, that has been engaged in an active trade or business. Following the distribution, the only remaining asset of the distributing corporation is a 20 percent interest as a general partner in a partnership. For more than five years, the distributing corporation's officers have performed active and substantial management functions with respect to the partnership. In addition, they regularly participate in the overall supervision, direction and control of the partnership's employees in their performance of the partnership's operational functions. The IRS held that the distributing corporation was engaged in an active trade or business immediately following the distribution. Rev. Rul. 92-17 has been extended to the LLC arena by Rev. Rul. 2002-49.[50] In Rev. Rul. 2002-49, the distributing corporation owns a 20 percent interest in a LLC, taxed as a partnership for federal income tax purposes. The LLC owns several commercial properties which it periodically refurbishes and makes alterations as necessary. The distributing corporation, through its officers, performs active and substantial management functions with respect to the LLC's activities and also participates in the supervision of the LLC's employees in their performance of the LLC's operational functions. The revenue ruling held that the distributing corporation met the active trade or business requirement.

It is interesting to note that both revenue rulings posited a 20 percent interest in the partnership. What if the interest in the partnership was only 1 percent? It is not clear what the answer would be in that situation. The premise of the regulations is that the properties involved in the conduct of the active trade or business of the distributing and controlled corporation are owned by the corporations. The revenue rulings approve a 20 percent ownership in the underlying assets of a partnership. If the ownership interest is insignificant, arguably, this may not be enough to support a finding of active trade or business.

Section 9.03(d)(8) Attribution of Active Trade or Business from a Corporation

There are instances where the active trade or business of a corporation can be attributed to another corporation. As we have seen above, section 355(b)(1)(B) provides that a distributing corporation can be engaged in an active trade or business if immediately before the distribution, it had no assets other than stock or securities of the controlled corporation and the controlled corporation is engaged in an active trade or business. Section 355(b)(2)(A) softens the blow of the previous section by stating that a corpo-

---

50. 2002-2 C.B. 288

ration is engaged in an active trade or business if it is directly engaged in an active trade or business or substantially all of its assets consist of stock or securities of a controlled corporation which is engaged in an active trade or business. This rule benefits holding companies that are not directly engaged in an active trade or business. Without this rule, a holding company not directly engaged in an active trade or business would never be able to engage in a section 355 distribution.

Example: Corporation X, a holding company not directly engaged in an active trade or business, owns the stock of two corporations, Corporation Y and Corporation Z, both actively engaged in a trade or business. X's assets consist only of the stock of Y and Z. For valid business reasons, X distributes the stock of Z to its shareholders. Is the active trade or business requirement met?

Yes. Following the distribution, 100 percent of X's assets will consist of stock of Y, a corporation engaged in an active trade or business. The active trade or business of Y will be attributed to X.

Note that this attribution rule only applies to corporations. In the partnership and LLC examples above, the active trades or businesses of these entities were not attributed to the corporation. The corporation, through the management of the partnership or the LLC, was held to be conducting its own active trade or business. What if the management of the LLC was conducted by two or more of its members? Would each of these members be treated as engaged in an active trade or business? This is not clear. Under the facts of the revenue rulings, the corporation was the sole entity engaged in the active management of the partnership or LLC. If one or more members of an LLC are actively engaged in the management function of the LLC, and, like the corporation in the revenue rulings, supervise the operational activities of the LLC, the prudent tax lawyer should seek a PLR. At the very least, the views of the national office of the IRS should be sought in a phone call.[51]

Section 9.03(d)(9) The Five-year Requirement

It is not sufficient that both the distributing and controlled corporations are immediately engaged in an active trade or business following the distribution. Under section 355(b)(2)(B), both corporations must have con-

---

51. The IRS' national office gives oral guidance with regard to transactions. Before seeking the views of the IRS, you should ensure that you have done as much research as possible. This will ensure a more dynamic conversation with the IRS. Also, the views expressed by the IRS over the phone are not binding on the IRS.

ducted the active trade or business for five or more years prior to the distribution. What if the controlled corporation is newly formed? Will it have been engaged in an active trade or business for five years? The answer is: it depends. The statute looks to the business being conducted or to be conducted by the controlled corporation and whether that business has been conducted for five or more years. If that business has been conducted for five or more years and the controlled corporation acquired the business in a non-taxable transaction (say a section 351 transfer), then the controlled corporation will be deemed to have satisfied the five-year active business requirement.

The five-year requirement is a bit arbitrary. Why not four years or three or six? Throughout the Code there are limitations imposed on tax benefits based on holding property for a certain amount of time. The rationale behind these time limitations is that if a taxpayer holds property for a certain length of time, the taxpayer must be engaged in a real economic transaction, not a transaction solely driven by tax avoidance.

As with almost any tax concept, there is more than meets the eye. Questions regarding the computation of the five-year requirement abound, such as when does a business commence or when does it end for purposes of the five-year requirement, or does a break in business toll the five-year period? The IRS has been somewhat flexible in this area because section 355 is really an anti-abuse provision. If a taxpayer is of pure heart, he should not be unduly penalized. Thus, in Rev. Rul. 57-126,[52] the IRS held that a business that was inactive from 1951 to 1956 still met the active trade or business requirement. This should not be confused as a concession that inactive businesses can qualify for section 355 treatment. The business in Rev. Rul. 57-126 would be fully active if it had been conducted during those years and was active when it resumed full scale activity by the time of the spin-off. Similarly in Rev. Rul. 82-219,[53] the IRS ruled that the five-year active trade or business requirement was met even though Controlled collected no income during one year and virtually shut down for that year because its sole customer went bankrupt. Again, as in Rev. Rul. 57-126, in Rev. Rul. 82-219 Controlled was active at the time of the spin-off. If Controlled is not engaged in an active trade or business at the time of the spin-off, the IRS would likely challenge the transaction as not meeting the active trade or business requirement.

---

52. 1957-1 C.B. 123.
53. 1982-2 C.B. 82.

Section 9.03(d)(10) Expansion of a Business

We already learned that the five-year active trade or business requirement will be met if the business was acquired in a tax-free transaction and had been conducted for five or more years prior to the acquisition. In such a case, the taxpayer is not seen as gaming the tax system. But what if the business being transferred was an expansion of a five-year business that was achieved by a taxable purchase? Clearly a factory that has been operating for five years will not lose its five-year status because the owner purchases new machinery. What if the owner of the factory purchased a new factory that produces metal products instead of paper products like his old factory? Would the new metal products factory benefit from the five-year history of the paper product factory? The answer is no! Section 1.355-3(b)(3)(ii) provides that a business is treated as actively conducted during the five years preceding a spin-off even though the business undergoes changes unless the changes are so extensive as to constitute the acquisition of a new or different business. The examples interpreting this regulation allow for benign changes such as the relocation of a business or the opening of a new factory producing the same products as the old factory.

Section 9.03(e) The Continuity of Interest Requirement

In addition to meeting the technical requirements of a particular Code section, taxpayers must often meet the spirit of the Code section. In other words, just meeting the technical requirements of a Code section may not be enough if the transaction goes against the intent of the Code section. Who are the guardians of this intent test? The IRS, of course, and the courts. As we have seen before, the courts use numerous tools to protect the integrity of the Code. In the reorganization area (including section 355), the courts have used the continuity of interest and the continuity of business enterprise requirements to ensure that reorganizations are undertaken for appropriate purposes.

Generally, in a reorganization continuity of interest is met if the shareholders of the acquired corporation maintain an interest in the acquiring corporation that reflects their prior ownership in the acquired corporation. For advance ruling purposes, the retained interest must reflect at least 50 percent of the prior interest.[54] The same rules apply for section 355 transactions. The only minor twist is that the regulations under section 355 rec-

---

54. *See* Rev. Proc. 96-30, 1996-1 C.B. 696.

ognize that due to the divisive nature of section 355, one or more share-holders may lose their interest in either the distributing or controlled corporation. Accordingly, the regulations only require that one or more original shareholders continue to hold an adequate interest in either the distributing or controlled corporation.

Section 9.03(f) The Business Purpose Requirement

We have alluded to the business purpose requirement several times above. It is time to investigate this requirement in detail. The business purpose requirement generally applies to most reorganizations, but because of the potential device inherent in section 355 transactions, there is a heightened standard for these situations. In other words, not strictly meeting the business purpose requirements in a section 355 transaction can get you into a lot of trouble really fast—or at least trigger many questions from the IRS auditor. In the past, business purpose issues could be resolved by seeking a PLR from the IRS, but the IRS has severely curtailed the use of the PLR with respect to business purpose issues. It is now very hard to get the IRS to issue a ruling on this issue because under Rev. Proc. 2003-48, the IRS says it will no longer issue rulings on device or business purpose.

The IRS stated in the revenue procedure that it is curtailing issuing rulings on business purpose in order to conserve resources and focus more on published guidance. Following publication of the revenue procedure, there was a sharp increase in guidance on section 355.[55] It is not clear whether the IRS will continue with this increase in section 355 guidance. Also note that Rev. Proc. 2003-48 is supposed to be a one-year pilot program. Presumably, after that one year, the IRS will revisit the revenue procedure and decide whether to pursue its mandate on a permanent basis or revert back to issuing PLRs on section 355.

If you look at the statute (section 355), you will not find mention of a business purpose requirement. This requirement comes from the regulations. The Code applies to complex business transactions and Congress normally expects the IRS to fill in gaps with precise rules.

The business purpose requirement is such a gap filler. Section 355 provides that the nonrecognition provisions of the section apply only if the transaction is not a device for the bailout of the E&P of the distributing or controlled corporation. One of the best ways to prove that your transaction is not a device

---

55. *See e.g.*, Rev. Rul. 2003-74, 2003-29 I.R.B. 77; Rev. Rul. 2003-75, 2003-29 I.R.B. 79; Rev. Rul. 2003-110, 2003-46 I.R.B. 1083; and Rev. Rul. 2004-23, 2004-11 I.R.B. 585.

is to have a good business purpose. The rationale for the requirement of a business purpose (to be exact, a corporate business purpose) is that if a transaction is undertaken to achieve a business purpose of the corporation, then the transaction is likely not undertaken principally to bail out the E&P of the corporation.

Section 9.03(f)(1) Criteria for Business Purpose

The criteria for the business purpose requirement are found in regulation section 1.355-2(b). The section provides that a transaction is carried out for a corporate business purpose if it is motivated in whole or substantial part by one or more corporate business purposes. The section also provides that the principal reason for the business purpose requirement is to provide nonrecognition treatment only to distributions that are incident to readjustments of corporate structures required by business exigencies (the "exigency" requirement) and that affect only readjustments of continuing interests in property under corporate forms. Section 1.355-2(b)(2) provides that a purpose to reduce Federal taxes is not a valid business purpose. The section also provides that a shareholder purpose is not a valid business purpose unless it is so coextensive with the corporate business purpose as to preclude any distinction between the two. In such a case, the transaction is carried out for a valid business purpose. Section 1.355-2(b)(3) provides that if a corporate business purpose can be achieved through another transaction that does not involve the distribution of the controlled corporation and which is neither impractical nor unduly expensive, then the transaction is not carried out for a valid business purpose.

That was a mouthful! Is there any way to avoid this business purpose requirement? What if I can prove that the transaction involves no device whatsoever? The answer is no because section 1.355-2(b)(1) states that the business purpose requirement is independent of the other requirements under section 355.

Section 9.03(f)(2) Deciphering the Business Purpose

There are many ways to attack this business purpose requirement. Practicing attorneys in this area generally familiarize themselves with business purposes that have worked in the past (either through revenue or private letter rulings) and, we suspect, attempt to guide their client's cases toward these business purposes.[56] We discourage this approach because it may not be the

---

56. The IRS attempted to quash this type of business purpose shopping by requiring (when it was entertaining business purpose rulings in PLRs) that the taxpayer disclose all of its business purposes up front.

most ethical. In addition, unless you work extensively with section 355, this approach may not be worth the effort. Instead we recommend the following approach.

First, ascertain whether the transaction can be achieved by means other than a spin-off. You should start with this determination because it would be a waste of time to develop a great business purpose argument if the taxpayer's needs can be satisfied by means other than a section 355 transaction.

Example: Taxpayer Corporation conducts two businesses within the corporation. Over the years, Taxpayer has come to realize that the two businesses are not compatible and that each business needs to have its own team of managers focused on that business. After much study, Taxpayer submits a PLR request to the IRS. The IRS would likely make a determination whether the aims of the taxpayer can be achieved by the creation of a holding company structure—i.e., transfer of each of the two businesses to two separate corporations owned by Taxpayer. Because once the transfers are done, each corporation can have its independent team of managers, it is likely that the IRS would hold that the transaction does not have a valid business purpose.[57] This holding company structure argument is illustrated as follows:

Holding Company Option

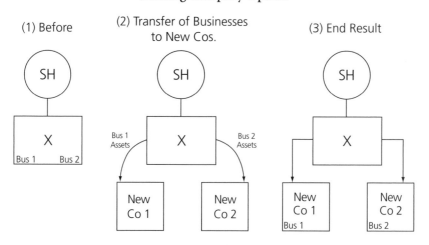

Even though the aim of the taxpayer can be achieved through a transaction other than a spin-off, you should still ascertain whether this other transaction will be too costly to your client (remember the holding company

---

57. *See* § 1.355-2(b)(5)(example 4) of the income tax regulations.

structure argument does not work for the IRS if it is too costly for your client).

Second, determine whether the business purpose is to benefit the corporation or the shareholders.

If the distributing corporation is a publicly traded corporation, this is generally not a problem unless the corporation has one or more significant shareholders (generally a shareholder who owns 5 percent or more of the corporation and is also an employee of the corporation). Enhancing shareholder value is an inherent purpose of publicly traded corporations. Therefore, any claim by a publicly traded distributing corporation that the purpose of a spin-off is to enhance shareholder value should work. If the corporation is not publicly traded, a shareholder business purpose may still work if it would ultimately help the corporation. The classic example is the warring shareholder groups: two groups of more or less equal shareholders are fighting it out and the corporation's business is being hurt as a result. Dividing the corporation would help both the shareholders and the corporation. Such a business purpose would be a valid corporate business purpose even though it is coextensive with a shareholder business purpose.[58]

Third, determine whether the business purpose is exigent. The exigency requirement contained in section 1.355(b)(1) provides in part that: "A transaction is carried out for a corporate business purpose if it is motivated, in whole or substantial part, by one or more corporate business purposes." Thus, if a taxpayer engages in a spin-off in order to satisfy a perceived business need, the transaction will likely meet the business purpose requirement. If on the other hand, the taxpayer's business purpose makes no sense, the transaction would not meet the business purpose requirement.

Section 9.04 Transactions Kicked out of Section 355

Section 9.04(a) In General

Both sections 355(d) and 355(e) deal with transactions that look like they qualify for tax-free treatment under section 355 but are nonetheless not given

---

58. For another example, see Rev. Rul. 2004-23, 2004-11 I.R.B. 585 (distribution expected to increase the aggregate value of the stock of the distributing and controlled corporations held a valid corporate business purpose even though the shareholder would also benefit).

complete tax-free treatment. Both sections were the subject of lively debate among practitioners, especially section 355(e). What's the big deal? The big deal is that following the repeal of the *General Utilities* doctrine, section 355 is essentially the only corporate Code section whereby corporations can distribute property tax-free to their shareholders. As such, this puts a lot of pressure on the section, and the Congress and the IRS have been policing the section ever since.

Briefly, the *General Utilities* doctrine was a threat to the double tax regime of corporations by providing that a corporation would recognize no gain on the distribution of appreciated stock of another corporation. From that doctrine grew a series of transactions under the so-called *Morris Trust* doctrine. The following is a typical *Morris Trust* transaction: distributing corporation is engaged in two businesses (banking and insurance). Distributing desired to merge with another bank but the bank was not interested in Distributing's insurance business. Consequently, Distributing transferred its unwanted insurance business to a newly-organized corporation and then spun-off the insurance company to its shareholders. Distributing was then free to merge with the bank. The *Morris Trust* transaction is illustrated as follows:

Morris Trust

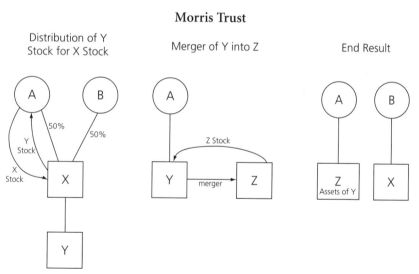

Morris Trust transactions were approved by the IRS in numerous rulings.[59] Over the years, several transactions that ultimately resemble cash sales but ap-

---

59. *See Commissioner v. W. Morris Trust*, 367 F.2d 794 (4th Cir. 1966). *See* Rev. Rul. 72-530, 1972-2 C.B. 212; Rev. Rul. 70-434, 1970-2 C.B. 83; Rev. Rul. 68-603, 1968-2 C.B. 148.

pear to qualify under section 355 as a *Morris Trust* transaction put a lot of pressure on the IRS and Congress to restrict such transactions. An example would be the declaration of a substantial dividend by a controlled corporation followed by the spin-off of the corporation and then the purchase of the corporation by another party or the merger of the corporation with another corporation. Under section 243, the dividend received by the distributing corporation would be tax-free. Additionally, the section 355 spin-off would be tax-free if it met all the requirements of the section. If the steps of the two transactions are collapsed, the transaction is essentially the sale of the controlled corporation by the distributing corporation in exchange for cash (the dividend paid by Controlled) and the stock or cash received by Distributing's shareholders. In response, Congress first enacted section 355(d) and later followed with section 355(e). The aim of these sections was to ensure that the goal of section 355 transactions—providing tax-free treatment only for divisions of a business among the shareholders of the same corporation[60]—would not be eroded.

Section 9.04(b) Section 355(d)—In General

As we have seen in several contexts, merely meeting the statutory scheme does not guarantee that taxpayers will enjoy the benefits of a particular Code section. Taxpayers should be prepared to establish that their transactions do not violate the policy behind that section. Section 355(d) is one section for which Congress provides guidance regarding transactions that should not qualify for benefits. In doing so, it appears to be using a substance over form analysis.

Sections 355(d)–(f) target transactions that may initially appear to qualify for tax-free treatment but are followed by other, disqualifying events.[61] We will discuss section 355(d) in this section and then move on to section 355(e) and (f) in the next two sections.

Section 355(d) generally provides that if a distributing corporation makes a disqualified distribution, such distribution will not be treated as a distribution of qualified property. Under section 355(c), only qualified property is permitted to be distributed tax-free. Hence, any distribution of property that is not qualified property will be taxed under section 355(c). This means that the distributing corporation will be treated as if it had sold stock of the controlled corporation at fair market value. Note, however, that running afoul of section 355(d) does not render the whole transaction taxable. The sharehold-

---

60. *See* H.R. Rep. No. 105-148, 105th Cong., 1st Sess. (1997); S. Rep. No. 105-33, 105th Cong., 1st Sess. (1997).

61. Section 351(e), discussed in Chapter 5, is another example of a statutory limitation.

ers of the distributing corporation that have received stock of the controlled corporation are not taxed on the transaction. The purpose of section 355(d) (and incidentally section 355(e)) is to prevent the distributing corporation from qualifying a disguised sale of the controlled corporation as tax-free.

Example: Distributing corporation owns all of the stock of controlled corporation, which represents 52 percent of the two corporations' combined value. Distributing wants to sell all its Controlled stock but does not want to recognize gain. What if Distributing takes the following steps? First, it sells 52 percent of its own stock to purchaser. Second, and shortly thereafter, Distributing transfers all its Controlled stock to purchaser in exchange for Purchaser's 52 percent stock in Distributing. Distributing argues that the sale to purchaser avoids recognition because of section 1032 and that section 355 makes the spin-off of Controlled a nonrecognition transaction. Unfortunately, for Distributing, section 355(d) applies and treats the spin-off as a sale of stock. The distribution to purchaser is a disqualified distribution.

Section 9.04(b)(1) Disqualified Distribution

What is a disqualified distribution? A disqualified distribution is any distribution, if immediately after the distribution any person holds disqualified stock in the distributing or controlled corporation (generally 50 percent or more of the stock of the corporation). What is disqualified stock? Disqualified stock is defined in section 355(d)(3) as any stock in the distributing and the controlled corporation acquired by "purchase" after October 9, 1990, and during the five-year period ending on the distribution date. What does this all mean? Congress, in enacting section 355(d) attempted to create a five-year holding requirement for stock in the controlled and distributing corporations. You will recall that section 355(b) generally imposes a five-year active trade or business requirement for the distributing and controlled corporations. In addition to conducting the business of Distributing and Controlled for five years or more, section 355(d) prevents Distributing from disposing of Controlled stock to shareholders who do not share a five-year history in either Distributing or Controlled.

Example: What if in the above example, the sale of Distributing stock was to two purchasers? Assume that the spin-off was pursuant to the same plan. Would this transaction escape taxation because under section 355(d)(2)(A), section 355(d) applies only if any "person" holds disqualified stock following the distribution?

It is not so easy to defeat section 355(d). Section 355(d)(7)(B) provides that if two or more persons act pursuant to a plan or arrangement with respect to acquisitions of stock, such persons shall be treated as one person for purposes of this subsection. If the persons are related (within the meaning of section 267(b) or 707(b)(1)), under section 355(d)(7)(A), they will be automatically treated as one person whether or not they have acquired the stock of Distributing or Controlled pursuant to a plan or arrangement.

Finally, section 355(d)(5) defines the term purchase as any acquisition if the basis of the property acquired is not determined in whole or in part by reference to the adjusted basis of such property in the hands of the person from whom acquired or under section 1014(a) and the property is not acquired in an exchange to which section 351, 354, 355 or 356 applies.

Section 9.04(c) Section 355(e)

Section 355(e) has gotten a lot of press and will continue to be closely monitored by the IRS and Treasury. The IRS has published, to date, a number of regulations[62] implementing the mandate of the section. In our opinion, the IRS and Treasury Department have been lenient on taxpayers and in the process may not have fully implemented congressional mandate.

Section 355(e) deals with what has been called the "*Morris Trust*" transactions (discussed above). Section 355(e)(1) provides for gain recognition by a distributing corporation if stock of its controlled corporation is distributed in a transaction to which the subsection applies. The subsection applies to any distribution to which section 355 applies and that is part of a plan pursuant to which one or more persons acquires directly or indirectly stock representing a 50 percent or greater interest (measured by vote or value) in either the distributing or the controlled corporation.

Example: Distributing distributes all of stock of controlled corporation which it owns to its shareholders. The transaction meets all the requirements of section 355 because both corporations have an actual trade or business both before and subsequent to the spin-off, there is a valid business purpose for the transaction and there is no device in the transaction. Following the spin-off of Controlled, an unrelated party acquires 60 percent of either Distributing or Controlled. Does this transaction violate section 355(e)?

---

62. *See* Prop. Reg. § 1.355-7, 64 Fed. Reg. 46155 (Aug. 24, 1999); Temporary regulations adopted by T.D. 8960, 66 Fed. Reg. 40590 (Aug. 3, 2001); Temporary regulations adopted by T.D. 8988, 67 Fed. Reg. 20632 (Apr. 26, 2002); final regulations adopted by T.D. 9198, 2005-18 I.R.B. 972, 70 Fed. Reg. 20279 (Apr. 19, 2005).

The transaction violates section 355(e) if the acquisition was part of a plan pursuant to which one or more persons acquire directly or indirectly the 60 percent stock interest.

Section 9.04(c)(1) Plan

What is a plan? section 355(e) provides some answers but leaves the bulk of the work to the IRS and Treasury to figure out. Section 355(e)(2)(B) presumes the existence of a plan if 50 percent or more of the stock of either distributing or controlled corporation is acquired during a four-year window period that begins two years before the date of the distribution and ends two years following the distribution. A taxpayer can rebut the presumption if it can prove that the acquisition is unconnected to the distribution of the controlled corporation. Before we delve into the definition of a plan, a few exceptions to section 355(e) need to be mentioned. Section 355(e)(2)(C) provides an exception to section 355(e), if following the completion of the plan, both the distributing and controlled corporations are part of the same affiliated group of corporations. This result makes sense because if the corporations are part of the same group, then essentially there is no escape from the double taxation regime, the essence of section 355(e).

The regulations are favorable to taxpayers and appear to have lessened the impact of section 355(e). The regulations, at first, provide a facts and circumstances test—meaning the existence or non-existence of a plan would be determined based on the ultimate facts and circumstances of a particular transaction. This initial rule is then subject to certain exceptions or safe harbor rules. If a taxpayer's transaction meets any of these safe harbor rules, the taxpayer will be deemed to not have a plan in contravention of section 355(e). With regard to acquisitions after a distribution, the regulations provide certain facts tending to show the existence of a plan; for example, in the case of an acquisition after a distribution, if the distributing or controlled corporation and the acquirer discussed the acquisition or a similar acquisition by a different person occurs after the distribution. Another example: in the case of an acquisition before a distribution (remember section 355(e) applies during a four-year period (two years before and two years after the acquisition)), if the distributing or controlled corporations and the acquirer discussed a distribution before the acquisition. The regulations provide that the weight to be accorded such discussion depends on the nature, extent, and timing of the discussions.

The regulations also provide certain facts tending to show that a plan does not exist. Not surprisingly, if there was no discussion between the distributing or controlled corporations and the acquirer, this would tend to show that a plan does not exist. Finally, the regulations provide certain safe harbor rules. For example, if an acquisition occurred more than six months after a section 355 distribution and the distribution was motivated by a corporate business purpose other than a business purpose to facilitate the acquisition, the transaction will be deemed not to be a part of a plan (or series of related transactions) pursuant to which one or more persons acquire directly or indirectly a 50-percent or greater interest in the distributing or controlled corporation.

The IRS continues to monitor this area very carefully. The regulations cited above are mostly temporary regulations. This means that after three years,[63] the IRS will either have to promulgate them as final regulations or sunset them.[64]

Section 9.04(d) Section 355(f)

Section 355(f) expands the reach of section 355(e) to transactions involving affiliated groups. Distributing corporations in these transactions will be taxed as if they had sold the controlled corporation. Because section 355(f) reaches transactions that would otherwise qualify for nonrecognition treatment under section 355, it appears to render section 243 inapplicable to such transfers. Perhaps taxpayers caught by section 355(f) will argue that section 355 does not apply at all to their transactions because of a lack of a business purpose or a technical violation of section 355.

The transactions prohibited by section 355(d), (e) and (f) are illustrated as follows:

---

63. *See* I.R.C. §7805(e)(2), which provides that temporary regulations are effective for only a period of three years.

64. It is unlikely that the IRS will allow the rules to sunset because they invested significant resources on developing the regulations. The key to the regulations is to remember that if there is no discussion between the acquirer and the distributing and controlled corporations, the transaction will pass muster.

Section 355(d) Transaction

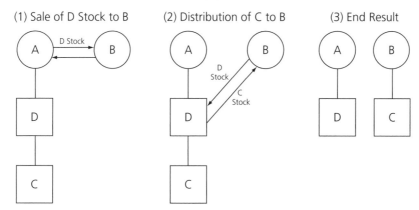

(1) Sale of D Stock to B

(2) Distribution of C to B

(3) End Result

D is taxable on distribution of C.
Result would be the same if:

  (a)   B purchased newly issued stock from D;
  (b)   B purchased D stock from public shareholders of D; or
  (c)   B purchased D stock and D split off C stock to A in exchange for D stock, leaving B in control of D.

Section 355(e) Transaction

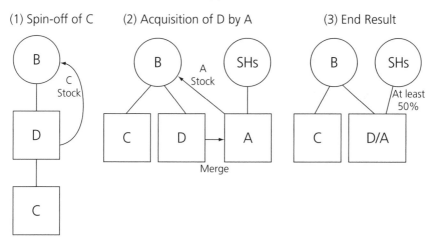

(1) Spin-off of C

(2) Acquisition of D by A

(3) End Result

D is taxable on spin-off of C if (1) and (2) were part of a "plan"; "plan" presumed to exist if (2) occurs within 2 years after (1).
Same result if, as part of spin-off plan:

  (a)   C is acquired after spin-off (rather than D);
  (b)   C or D issues at least 50 percent of (after-issuance) outstanding stock to new investor(s) after spin-off; or
  (c)   D merges with A prior to a spin-off of C by D/A (to all D/A shareholders, or to B only).

Basic Section 355(f) Transaction

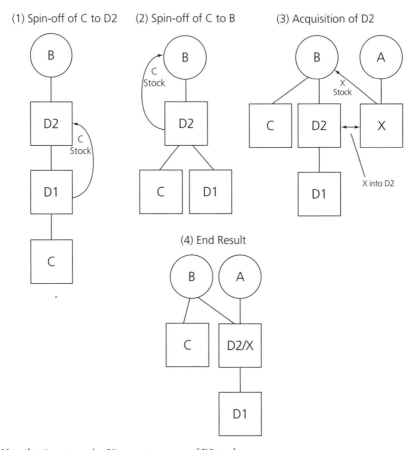

(1) Spin-off of C to D2   (2) Spin-off of C to B   (3) Acquisition of D2

(4) End Result

Note that A must receive 50 percent or more of D2 stock.

Before we embark on the tax consequences of a section 355 transaction, we need to remind you that sometimes a transaction may qualify for two or more nonrecognition sections. When that occurs, the Code may provide that one of the applicable sections prevails. For example, if a transaction qualifies both as a C and a D reorganization, it is treated as a D reorganization.[65] Sometimes the Code fails to provide a preference. In this case, both sections will apply to the transaction and the transaction will have to meet the requirements of both provisions. For example, a transaction qualifying as a D reorganization and under section 355 must satisfy the requirements of both sections.

---

65. *See* I.R.C. §368(a)(2)(A).

Section 9.05 Tax Consequences of Distributing Corporation

The distributing corporation's tax consequences may depend on whether the transaction includes a D reorganization (D/355 transaction). The discussion below treats D/355 transactions separately from other section 355 transactions.

Section 9.05(a) Gain or Loss

Section 355(c)(1) provides that the distributing corporation recognizes no gain or loss on any distribution to which section 355 applies. Section 355(c)(2) limits nonrecognition to distributions of "qualified property" (stock and securities of the controlled corporation). Property that is not qualified property is generally referred to as "boot." The distributing corporation recognizes gain if it distributes boot that is appreciated. It does not recognize loss.

Example: Distributing corporation distributes all of the stock of controlled corporation to its shareholders. Distributing also distributes appreciated intangible property that it held on behalf of controlled corporation. Distributing recognizes gain on the distribution of the intangible property.[66]

The distributing corporation generally computes its gain as the difference between its basis for the item of boot and the value of that item. Because losses are not deductible, it cannot aggregate gain and loss property and compute only a net gain.

If any of the boot is subject to a liability, gain will be computed using the liability amount if it exceeds the value of the property distributed.

Section 9.05(b) Liabilities Transfer—General Rule

Whenever you see liabilities transferred in a reorganization, you should think of section 357. Because significant property transfers can be achieved through the transfer of liabilities, Congress uses section 357 as a means of patrolling this area.

Section 357(a) applies if the liability of a taxpayer is assumed in a section 351 or section 361 transaction. It provides that the assumption is not treated as

---

66. Even if Distributing establishes that the distribution of the intangible property was not part of the section 355 distribution, it is still taxed on the gain because section 311 will apply.

money or other property received in the transaction. As a result, the assumption of liability is not treated as boot under section 356 and thus avoids taxation under that section. Section 357(a) also provides that the assumption of liability does not prevent the transaction from qualifying under section 351 or section 361.

Section 357(a) may initially appear over-generous because assumption of one's liability by another party should generally be treated as discharge of indebtedness. But its operation makes sense because it is assumed that the parties are entering into the reorganization transaction at arms' length. Hence, the assumption of one party's liabilities by another party would affect the price that the assuming party would pay in the transaction. In addition, nonrecognition facilitates transactions that occur for good business reasons.

Section 9.05(b)(1) Section 357(b) Exception

Section 357(b) provides an exception to the general rule. It applies if the principal purpose of the transfer of liabilities was the avoidance of federal income tax or if the purpose of the transfer was not a bona fide business purpose. If section 357(b) applies, the assumption of liability is treated as money received by the taxpayer. This money is taxed as boot under section 356. Depending on the circumstances, this assumption of liability may disqualify the transaction from nonrecognition of gain. Although its results are harsh, the threshold for applying section 357(b) is fairly high. It generally applies to clear and obvious attempts to take advantage of section 357.

Section 9.05(b)(2) Section 357(c) Exception

Planners are more likely to encounter section 357(c), which is also the more difficult provision to apply. Fortunately, its application is fairly limited. Section 357(c) applies only to section 351 transactions and to certain D reorganizations. In such cases, if the total amount of liabilities assumed exceeds the adjusted basis of the property transferred in the exchange, the excess liability amount is treated as gain from the sale or exchange of property. You should consider section 357(c) whenever liabilities are exchanged in a D/355 transaction.

Section 357(c) does not apply to liabilities whose payment would give rise to a deduction. Nor does it apply to liabilities described in section 736(a). Section 357(c), however, applies to the extent the incurrence of the liability results in the creation of, or an increase in, the basis of property. The regulations and revenue rulings provide additional guidance regarding section 357(c). We also discuss it in Chapter 5 in the context of corporation formations.

If contingent liabilities are transferred in the transaction, the viability of the transaction may hinge on their ultimate amount. Contingent liabilities are normally liabilities that have not yet arisen at the time of the transfer. To avoid section 357(c), contingent liabilities can be limited by contract. In some cases, an argument can be made that, at the time the liability was determined, it was actually a liability of the corporation that assumed it. And, as we saw above, if the liability would give rise to a deduction, it will not be subject to section 357(c). For example, the acquiring corporation may assume the acquired corporation's liability for retirement benefits. Their treatment by the acquiring corporation may depend on whether they had previously been deducted by the acquired corporation.

Section 9.05(b)(3) Changes to Section 357(c) Made in 2004

The American Jobs Creation Act of 2004 restricted the application of section 357(c) to divisive reorganizations. An acquisitive D reorganization is now treated like all other reorganizations in the sense that it is not subject to section 357(c). Section 357(c) now applies only to section 351 transactions and to D/355 transactions.

Section 9.05(c) Gain or Loss in D/355 Transactions

If the distributing corporation transfers assets before the section 355 transaction, the events may qualify as a D reorganization followed by a section 355 transfer. In such cases, section 361 grants nonrecognition to the distributing corporation. Section 361(b)(3) provides an added bonus. It exempts from tax money and property received in the transaction that would be subject to tax under section 357(c) if it were transferred to the distributing corporation's creditors.

Under prior law, if a distributing corporation transferred an asset with a basis of $10 and encumbered by a $50 note, it would report gain. If the controlled corporation borrowed $50 from a third party and distributed the money to the distributing corporation, which used the money to repay the $50 note, the transaction would be tax-free. The American Jobs Creation Act of 2004 ended this advantage. New section 361(b)(3) allows nonrecognition to the distributing corporation only up to the adjusted basis of the assets transferred in the transaction.

Section 9.05(d) Other Tax Consequences

The distributing corporation recognizes no gain or loss, and reports no other income, on the transfer of controlled corporation stock unless one of four factors applies:

(1) property other than stock or securities of the controlled corporation is transferred;

(2) liabilities in excess of basis are transferred or liabilities were transferred to the controlled corporation with a principal purpose of evading federal income tax or there was no business purpose for the transfer;

(3) there are investment credits subject to recapture; or

(4) The controlled corpoartion was part of a group filing consolidated returns, and the spin-off triggers certain gains to be recognized.

We discussed items (1) and (2) earlier in this chapter. This section introduces you to items (3) and (4).

The distributing corporation may have to recapture investment credit if, prior to the spin-off of Controlled, Distributing had transferred investment credit property to Controlled. Distributing would not be eligible for the exception provided in regulation section 1.47-3 because it would not have retained a substantial interest in the transferred property.[67] If Controlled was part of a group of corporations filing consolidated returns and was spun-off outside the group, the spin-off may cause the group (or certain of its members) to recognize certain types of gain. This rule generally applies to gains that have been deferred because the group was filing consolidated returns.[68] The filing of consolidated returns is addressed in Chapter 15.

Section 9.06 Shareholders' Tax Consequences

Section 9.06(a) Gain or Loss

As we saw earlier, section 355(a) provides that no gain or loss is recognized by a shareholder on the receipt of stock or securities in a transaction that qualifies for nonrecognition treatment under section 355. To qualify: (1) the transaction must not be a device for the distribution of the E&P of either corporation; (2) the transaction must have a valid business purpose; and (3) the distributing corporation must distribute at least 80 percent of the stock of the controlled corporation. The no gain or loss provision of section 355(a) addresses the shareholders' immediate concern—whether they owe tax because of the transaction.

While current tax liability is the immediate concern, shareholders must also ascertain their basis for any stock or securities received in the controlled cor-

---

67. We do not provide a detailed analysis of the recapture rules here. *See generally* Rev. Rul. 82-20, 1982-1 C.B. 6; Rev. Rul. 89-18, 1989-1 C.B. 14.

68. *See* Treas. Reg. §§ 1.1502-13(c)–(d) and 1.1502-19(b).

poration. Basis will be the most important factor in determining whether a selling shareholder owes taxes on a subsequent sale or exchange of that stock.[69] We will consider basis in section 9.06(b).

Section 9.06(a)(1) Section 355(a)

Section 355(a) establishes the general rule that no gain or loss is recognized by shareholders who receive stock or securities in a section 355 transaction.

Example: Distributing corporation distributed all of the stock of controlled corporation to its shareholders in a qualifying section 355 transaction. Shareholder A received twenty Controlled shares in the transaction. Shareholder A recognizes no gain or loss and reports no income on that receipt.

Section 9.06(a)(1)(A) Definition of Stock

Despite its apparent simplicity, section 355(a) leaves some questions unresolved. First, it does not define the term stock. Stock is generally defined as intangible property that has the following properties attached to it: (1) right to vote; (2) right to liquidation proceeds; and (3) right to participate in the earnings of the corporation. Clearly, if a person owns property that provides these three rights, that person owns stock. What if the property has only two of these rights? What if it has only one? When this issue arises, you should review the discussion of section 385 in Chapter 6.

Nonqualified preferred stock is treated as other property and not as stock if it is received in exchange for stock or securities of the distributing corporation.[70] This rule does not apply if the nonqualified preferred stock is received in exchange for other nonqualified preferred stock.

Section 351(g)(2) defines nonqualified preferred stock as preferred stock that has any of four characteristics: (1) it gives the holder the right to have the stock redeemed or purchased; (2) it obligates the issuer to redeem or purchase it; (3) it gives the issuer the right to redeem if, as of the issue date, such right is more likely than not to be exercised; or (4) the dividend rate varies based on interest rates, commodity prices, or similar indices. Because nonqualified

---

69. Because the sale may occur many years after the section 355 transaction, it is important to determine basis before records are lost or discarded. No seller wants to take the risk that the IRS will treat the basis as zero because the taxpayer has no evidence of a higher amount. *See, e.g.,* Rev. Proc. 81-70, 1981-2 C.B. 729.

70. I.R.C. §355(a)(3)(D). Stock that is precluded from qualifying if the transaction is tested under section 355 is not necessarily precluded from qualifying in another type of transaction. We discuss other possibilities in Chapter 10, which covers reorganizations.

preferred stock has a temporary nature, it is not treated as stock when received in exchange for distributing corporation stock in a section 355 transaction. Shareholders who relinquish a common stock interest and receive nonqualified preferred stock have altered their economic interests in the enterprise.

Section 9.06(a)(1)(B) Receipt of Boot

A second issue relates to section 355 restrictions on what a shareholder can receive. If the shareholder receives both qualified property (stock or securities permitted to be received in the transaction) and nonqualified property, the nonqualified property is treated as boot and subject to tax under section 356. Section 356 requires gain recognition, but it does not allow a loss deduction even if a loss occurred in the section 355 transaction.

Caveat: If too much boot is received, the entire transaction may fail to qualify for nonrecognition treatment.

In some instances, even stock in the controlled corporation will be treated as boot. Section 355(a)(3)(B) provides that stock of the controlled corporation that the distributing corporation acquired in a taxable transaction within five years of the distribution is treated as other property. Because it is treated as other property, the recipient has gain recognition with respect to that stock.

Example: Distributing corporation owned 80 percent of controlled corporation for ten years. It acquired the remaining 20 percent in a taxable transaction four years before the distribution. Distributing distributed all the Controlled stock to its shareholders. Shareholder A received 10 shares of Controlled. Because 20 percent of the Controlled shares were acquired in a taxable transaction, A must treat two shares of the Controlled stock as other property. As a result, A will be subject to tax. A's basis for those two shares will be their FMV.[71]

Section 9.06(a)(1)(C) Retained Stock

A third issue relates to retained stock. Section 355(a) permits the distributing corporation to retain some of its controlled corporation stock if there is a valid business purpose for such retention. For example, if stock is retained in order to pay debts of the controlled corporation or for any other reason approved by the IRS, such stock retention will not cause the shareholders to recognize gain. Generally, the IRS permits stock retention only if there is a plan to dispose of the stock within a reasonable time. If the stock is being retained

---

71. I.R.C. §358(a)(2). This rule reflects the general rule of section 1012, that the original basis of property is generally the cost to acquire it.

permanently, the IRS will normally treat such stock retention as a taxable retention of stock.

Section 9.06(a)(2) Receipt of Securities

If, in a section 355 transaction, a shareholder receives securities without exchanging securities or receives securities in excess of any securities exchanged, that part of the exchange will be taxable.[72] The rule applied to securities is stricter than the rule regarding issuance of nonqualified preferred stock. The rationale for this distinction may reflect the fact that securities are more liquid than preferred stock and can be more easily converted into cash.

Section 9.06(a)(3) Receipt of Property Attributable to Accrued Interest

Section 355(a)(3)(C) applies to stock, securities, or any other property received in exchange for accrued, but unpaid interest. It prevents recipients from receiving nonrecognition treatment for that part of the transaction. A taxpayer who receives property attributable to accrued interest on a security in a section 355 transaction must report the amount received as section 61 gross income.

Section 9.06(a)(4) Characterization of Boot Received

The character of income often affects the amount of taxes owed. There are two important distinctions in corporate taxation: (1) whether gain or loss is capital or ordinary; (2) whether other income is treated as a dividend. Because long-term capital gains and many dividends qualify for reduced tax rates, taxpayers normally prefer to have their income or gain characterized as one or the other. And, because they can offset basis against amount realized, they are likely to prefer capital gains to dividends.[73]

Section 356 governs the characterization of boot in a section 355 transaction. If shareholders in the distributing corporation exchange their stock for stock of the controlled corporation, there has been an exchange. Any boot received in that section 355 transaction is treated as gain from the sale or ex-

---

72. I.R.C. §355(a)(3)(A).

73. Corporate and individual shareholders have slightly different goals. Corporate shareholders qualify for a dividends received deduction, while individual shareholders qualify for a lower tax rate on dividend income. Dividends are discussed in greater detail in Chapter 7.

change of a capital asset.[74] If, however, there is a distribution of boot which has the effect of the distribution of a dividend, that boot distribution is treated as a section 301 dividend distribution.

Attribution rules apply in judging these transactions. Section 356(a)(2) provides that section 318 applies to the determination of dividend treatment. Even if a taxpayer appears to have no interest in either corporation following the exchange, section 318 may treat that taxpayer as having an interest in one or both corporations. In that case, the boot distributed may represent a dividend distribution.

Example: A and his son B each owned 50 percent of Distributing. Distributing held all the stock of Controlled. For a valid business purpose, Distributing distributed the stock of Controlled to A in exchange for A's shares of Distributing. As part of the transaction, Distributing also distributed $100 in cash to A. Assuming the transaction otherwise qualifies for nonrecognition treatment under section 355, the cash distribution is taxed as boot. Under section 356(a)(2), the $100 is taxed as a section 301 distribution because A is treated as continuing to own all of the stock of Distributing by attribution from Son.[75]

If the amount treated as a distribution exceeds the recipient's share of the corporation's E&P, the transaction is bifurcated. Section 356 limits the recipient's dividend treatment to the recipient's share of E&P. The remaining boot is treated as capital gain.

Section 9.06(b) Basis of Stock or Securities

Section 9.06(b)(1) Basis of Stock

Section 358 provides the relevant basis rules covering the controlled corporation stock and the remaining shares of the distributing corporation. The general scheme of section 358 is one of apportionment. The shareholder allocates the total basis of the distributing corporation's shares held prior to the transaction between the controlled corporation shares received in the transaction and any distributing corporation shares still held.

Example: Shareholder A had a basis of $100 in the distributing corporation's stock before a split-off. In the split-off, she exchanged all of those shares for shares in controlled corporation. Following the distribution, A has a basis of $100 in her controlled corporation shares.

---

74. *See* I.R.C. §356(a).
75. I.R.C. §318(a)(1)(A) (family attribution).

Example: Shareholder B had a basis of $100 in the distributing corporation's stock before a spin-off. In the spin-off, she received shares of controlled corporation. After the spin-off, B owned shares of both Distributing and Controlled. B's $100 basis will be allocated between the Distributing and Controlled shares based on their relative FMV. For purposes of computing basis, an actual exchange is not required.[76]

A shareholder who acquired stock in the distributing corporation in separate transactions probably owns stock with different per-share bases and holding periods. Proposed regulations section 1.358-2 provides for allocating basis in these circumstances. To the extent possible, shareholders are to allocate basis to the shares received in a manner that treats each such share as allocable to shares acquired on the same date and for the same price.

Example: Individual A acquired 100 shares of distributing corporation for $100 in Year 1 and 100 more shares for $120 in Year 2. In Year 10, distributing corporation transferred 50 shares of controlled corporation to A in exchange for all of A's shares of Distributing stock in a section 355 split-off. A takes a basis of $100 for 25 of the Controlled shares and a basis of $120 for the other 25.

Section 358(a) also covers situations involving boot and gain recognition. In computing the basis of any controlled stock received, the shareholder begins with his basis for the distributing corporation stock exchanged. That basis is reduced by any money received and by the fair market value of any other property received. It is also decreased by any loss recognized on the exchange. Finally, it is increased by any amount treated as a dividend and by any gain recognized.

Section 9.06(b)(2) Basis of Securities and Other Boot Received

If a shareholder receives securities and does not exchange any securities, the securities are treated as boot. Section 358(a)(2) gives them basis equal to their FMV. The same rule applies to any other boot received.

Section 9.06(c) Holding Period

If a shareholder's basis for property received in a section 355 transaction reflects her basis for stock that she has exchanged (or retained), the shareholder's holding period for the new property includes the holding period for the other property.[77] For all other property received, the shareholder's holding period starts with the property's acquisition.

---

76. I.R.C. § 358(c).
77. I.R.C. § 1223(1).

Section 9.07 Distributing Corporation's Tax Attributes[78]

This chapter focuses on corporate fission or division. If the distributing corporation does not already own subsidiary corporations, it may form such corporations and distribute some of its assets to them. Even if the subsidiaries already exist, the distributing corporation may transfer additional assets to them before the section 355 transaction.

If the distributing corporation remains in existence, the basis of its assets is divided between it and the controlled corporations based on the fair market value of the assets of each corporation. Hence, if the distributing corporation transfers 50 percent of its assets to the controlled corporation, the recipient's basis for these assets will be 50 percent of the distributing corporation's basis.

But what happens to the distributing corporation's remaining tax attributes, such as its E&P account? The treatment of E&P depends on whether the distribution was a D/355 transfer.

If the transaction qualifies as a D/355 transfer, the distributing corporation's E&P account is divided between it and the controlled corporation based on the FMV of each corporation.[79] However, if the distributing corporation had an E&P deficit, the controlled corporation cannot participate in that deficit.[80] In this sense, the controlled corporation is given a clean slate.

If the controlled corporation was formed and operating prior to the spin-off, or otherwise was not part of a D/355 transaction, then its E&P is determined under Treasury Regulations section 1.312-10(b). The distributing corporation's E&P are decreased by the lesser of: (1) the decrease that would have occurred if the stock had been transferred in the D reorganization; or (2) the amount by which the basis of the controlled corporation's assets (including cash) exceed its liabilities.

The controlled corporation's E&P is the greater of: (i) its E&P prior to the spin-off; or (ii) if it was part of a consolidated group, the amount of its former parent's decrease in E&P.

Tax attributes other than E&P remain with the distributing corporation. This is the general rule. The exceptions provided by section 381, which permit a number of tax attributes to be transferred among corporate taxpayers

---

78. We study tax attributes in Chapter 13.
79. I.R.C. §312(h); Treas. Reg. §1.312-10(a).
80. Treas. Reg. §1.312-10(c).

in certain transactions, are generally limited to reorganizations and transactions that qualify under section 351.

Section 9.08 Controlled Corporation's Tax Consequences

Section 9.08(a) In General

Controlled corporations are normally passive participants in section 355 transactions. The distributing corporation and its shareholders are the major parties to the transaction. Nevertheless, the controlled corporation does have tax consequences.

Section 9.08(b) Recognition of Gain or Loss

If the transaction is a D/355 transaction, the controlled corporation recognizes no gain or loss on receiving the distributing corporation's assets. That transfer qualifies for nonrecognition treatment under section 368(a)(1)(D), and the controlled corporation is a party to the reorganization.

What if the transaction is not preceded by a transfer of assets qualifying under section 368(a)(1)(D))? Or what if the distributing corporation's shareholders exchange some or all of their distributing corporation stock for stock of the controlled corporation, which subsequently transfers the stock to the distributing corporation? Section 1032 protects the controlled corporation from recognition in those cases. That section provides that a corporation recognizes no gain or loss on the receipt of money or property in exchange for its stock. Nonrecognition treatment makes sense because the recipient corporation is now under an obligation to provide some type of economic benefit to its shareholders. If it is successful, it will repay this "obligation" through dividends or increases in the value of its stock.

The section 1032 regulations provide broad nonrecognition language: "The disposition by a corporation of shares of its own stock (including treasury stock) for money or other property does not give rise to taxable gain or deductible loss to the corporation regardless of the nature of the transaction or the facts and circumstances involved."[81] The regulations also protect a disposing corporation when it transfers the stock of its parent corporation (controlling corporation) in exchange for property.

---

81. *See* Treas. Reg. §1.1032-1(a).

Example: Corporation X transfers 10 shares of Corporation Y, which owns all of Corporation X's stock, to individual C for $100. X recognizes no gain or loss in this transaction because it is treated as if, immediately before the transaction, it had purchased the Y stock for $100. Consequently, X is treated as having a basis of $100 in the stock sold to C.

The rationale for the result above is that the parties could have easily achieved the same outcome by having Y sell its shares to C and then transferring the cash received to X. Under section 1032, Y would have recognized no gain or loss in the sale. In addition, under section 351 neither X nor Y would recognize gain or loss on the transfer of cash to X.

Rev. Rul. 2002-1[82] extends the rationale of the regulations to a situation where, following a spin-off, restrictions on the distributing corporation stock received by the controlled corporation's shareholders lapse. The ruling also provides that the controlled corporation recognizes no gain or loss when its employees exercise options on the distributing corporation's stock. It gives the controlled corporation a deduction for the amount included in its employees' income as a result of exercising the option. This ruling illustrates that sometimes taxpayers are permitted to achieve a result by a direct route if the same result can be achieved through a convoluted set of transfers. Other times, however, doctrines discussed in Chapter 3 will be invoked and taxpayers will have to prove that a convoluted route is not an attempt to avoid the more direct route.

Section 9.08(c) Basis of Controlled Corporation's Assets

Obviously, the controlled corporation's basis in its assets held prior to the section 355 transaction, and not received as part of the transaction, will not change. With regard to basis of assets received from the distributing corporation, section 362 provides that such basis will be the same as it was in the hands of the distributing corporation, increased by any gain recognized by the distributing corporation. As we discussed earlier, the distributing corporation generally recognizes no gain or loss on the transfer of part of its assets in a section 355 transaction. It will have recognition if it receives property other than qualified property under section 356 or if there is debt relief under section 357.

Section 9.08(d) Transfer of Tax Attributes

We saw earlier that the distributing corporation retains most of its tax attributes in a section 355 transaction. Section 381, which provides for the transfer of

---

82. 2002-2 I.R.B. 268.

tax attributes, applies only to certain transactions, not including section 355. The only tax attribute generally permitted to be transferred to the controlled corporation in a section 355 transaction is part of the distributing corporation's E&P.

As we saw earlier, the distributing corporation's E&P is divided between it and the controlled corporation if the section 355 transaction is preceded by a section 368(a)(1)(D) transfer. If the section 355 distribution is not preceded by an asset transfer, there is no sharing of E&P. Each party retains its own E&P account.

If the parties were filing consolidated returns, some of the attributes that appeared on the parent's returns (such as NOLs) are transferred to the controlled corporation prior to the spin-off.[83] This is not a true transfer from the distributing to the controlled corporation. It is simply a "repayment" of the controlled corporation's contribution to its parent's NOLs.

Section 9.09 Tax Consequences of Taxable Spin-off

Section 9.09(a) Recognition of Gain or Loss

If the transaction does not meet the section 355 requirements for non-recognition, the transaction will be taxable. Although the distributing corporation and its shareholders will recognize gain or loss on the transaction, section 1032 will protect the controlled corporation from taxation. The controlled corporation will be treated as receiving property in exchange for its stock.

Interestingly enough, as the distributing corporation and its shareholders enjoy the most benefits from a tax-free section 355 transaction, they bear most of the burden from a taxable transaction. The distributing corporation will be taxed on the distribution of the controlled corporation stock if the stock is appreciated property in the hands of the distributing corporation.[84] The distributing corporation's shareholders will be treated as receiving a dividend distribution unless they exchange the distributing corporation's stock for the controlled corporation's stock. If they do make that exchange, they will be taxable under the redemption rules of section 302, which generally provide for capital gains treatment unless the redemption is essentially equivalent to a dividend.[85] Normally a redemption is essentially equivalent to a dividend if fol-

---

83. *See* Treas. Reg. § 1.1502-21(b).

84. *See* I.R.C. § 311. *See also South Tulsa Pathology Lab., Inc. v. Commissioner.*, 118 T.C. 84 (2002).

85. *See* I.R.C. § 302.

lowing the redemption, the interest of the redeemed shareholder has not significantly changed. Chapters 7 and 8 provide an in-depth discussion of corporate distributions and redemptions.

Section 9.09(b) Basis of Stock

If a spin-off is taxable, the section 1012 basis rules apply instead of the section 358 rules. Generally, under section 1012, the basis of property is its cost. As we have seen earlier, a taxable spin-off will be taxable either as a section 301 distribution or a section 302 redemption. In either case, the shareholder will report income based on the FMV of the stock distributed. Hence, the basis of controlled corporation stock received by the distributing corporation's shareholders will be the FMV of such stock.

With regard to both the distributing and controlled corporations, there will generally be no basis consequences on a taxable distribution. The one exception occurs if a section 338 election is made with respect to the controlled corporation on any of its stock that is deemed purchased. Generally, if a section 338 election is made, the corporation for which the election is made is treated as if it sold its assets prior to the sale of its stock. Hence, in such a case, the corporation will have a FMV basis in its stock. We will discuss section 338 in more detail in Chapter 12.

Section 9.09(c) Transfer of Tax Attributes

There are no transfers of tax attributes in a taxable transaction. Tax attributes are transferred in a nonrecognition transaction to preserve taxation for a later time. This is appropriate because the particular taxpayer involved has merely made a change in form and has retained the main features of his business. For example, a merger transaction is generally a mere combination of two or more corporations into one. Following the merger, the merged corporations continue their existences in the merged entity. Consequently, it is appropriate that their tax attributes survive. A taxable transaction has none of these features and hence, section 381 provides no survival of tax attributes in a taxable transaction.

Section 9.10 Review

Our treatment of section 355 has been lengthy because this is a very complex and important section. As we stated previously, section 355 may be the most important corporate section. Since the repeal of the *General Utilities* doctrine, section 355 may be the only mechanism for transferring corporate assets tax-free to non-corporate shareholders. As the large number of section 355 private letter rulings indicate, tax practitioners remain very interested in using section 355. Congress has also been active, enacting sections 355(d), (e), and (f) to close loopholes.[86]

Section 355 is very technical, and this book cannot make you an expert in all its facets. Nevertheless, you should be aware of its scope and of areas that attract the most interest from the IRS. One such area of interest is represented by section 355(e), the so called anti-*Morris Trust* rules. Although section 355(d) is similar in many respects to section 355(e), the IRS currently appears more interested in section 355(e). This may be because the section 355(d) regulations were more readily accepted by tax practitioners. The IRS has already made several changes to the section 355(e) regulations to satisfy practitioner concerns.

Currently, the section 355(e) regulations have no teeth. The only taxpayers who will be ensnared by them are those who do not have adequate counsel. In general, in order to avoid these regulations, a taxpayer only has to be aware that it should not enter into sales negotiations with a potential buyer prior to a section 355 transaction. Even if it engages in a section 355 transaction to make the controlled corporation stock more attractive to a potential buyer, the distributing corporation has not necessarily violated the section 355(e) regulations. These regulations contain several safe harbor rules that protect taxpayers from taxation, and some of the safe harbors have a time element to them. Hence, following a section 355 transaction, if a taxpayer waits for an adequate amount of time prior to selling the controlled corporation stock, its section 355 distribution will be safe.

Besides section 355(e), the most important rule regarding section 355 is the business purpose requirement. Prior to Revenue Procedure 2003-48, under which the IRS will no longer issue PLRs addressing this issue, business purpose was the issue the IRS spent the most time investigating in the processing of section 355 PLRs. Many practitioners believe that the IRS generally had accepted business purposes presented by taxpayers and that IRS personnel realized that challenging a business purpose in court would be fruitless. Under

---

86. With the possible exception of Treasury regulation § 1.1502-20 (the consolidated loss disallowance rules), no corporate tax provision has been the subject of so much recent congressional activity. Moreover, the attention given the loss disallowance rules is attributable to an unusual set of circumstances, including the invalidation of part of the regulation by the *Rite Aid* decision discussed in Chapter 15.

the regulations, a taxpayer only had to show that its transaction was motivated by a particular business purpose.[87]

Once you become aware of the technical aspects of section 355, you should concentrate on the tax consequences to the parties to a section 355 transaction. There are generally three parties in a section 355 transaction: the distributing corporation, the controlled corporation, and the shareholders of the distributing corporation. Tax consequences include recognition or nonrecognition of gain or loss, basis determination, and retention of tax attributes. Although corporate taxpayers may be subject to other Code sections (such as the section 1245 recapture rules), these three consequences are usually the most important tax aspects of section 355 transactions. As a result, you should always start your analysis with them.

Section 9.11 Conclusion

Every tax lawyer engaged in corporate transactions should be familiar with section 355. It provides a way out for shareholders who do not get along, and it also provides opportunities to rid a corporation of unwanted assets. Section 355 is also important in helping businesses achieve an important business objective: narrowing their focus by streamlining their businesses without prohibitive tax consequences. But taking advantage of its benefits requires that the lawyer carefully navigate the treacherous waters of section 355(d) and 355(e).

In addition to negative constraints, such as those found in section 355(d) & (e), the parties must meet numerous affirmative requirements. First, the distributing corporation is supposed to distribute all of its stock in the controlled corporation. If it retains stock of the controlled corporation, it must have a business reason to do so.

Second, the distribution must not be a device for the distribution of the E&P of either corporation. The IRS used to spend a significant amount of energy attempting to interpret this requirement, and its offshoot, the business purpose requirement. In light of recent changes made by the American Jobs Creation Act of 2004 and, more importantly, IRS difficulties in patrolling this area, it may be safe to assume that the IRS will spend less time making determinations of valid business purposes.

Third, both the distributing and controlled corporations must meet the active trade or business requirement.[88] This generally means that both corpora-

---

87. *See* Treas. Reg. § 1.355-2(b)(1).
88. *See* I.R.C. § 355(b).

tions must have conducted an active trade or business for at least five years prior to the distribution. For purposes of section 355, a corporation will be treated as engaged in an active trade or business if it is engaged, through its own employees, in active and substantial management and operational activities of the business.[89] If either the distributing or controlled corporation acquired a business less than five years prior to the distribution, that business could be used to meet the five-year requirement only if it was acquired in a non-taxable transaction.

Finally, if the transaction is preceded by a transfer of assets from the distributing corporation to the controlled corporation, the transaction must meet the requirements of section 368(a)(1)(D). If the preceding transfer of assets is taxable, the importance of qualifying under section 355 is greatly diminished because very little gain, if any, would be realized on the distribution of the controlled corporation's stock.

---

89. *See* Treas. Reg. § 1.355-3(b)(2)(iii).

CHAPTER 10

Corporate Reorganizations

Section 10.01 Introduction

Section 10.01(a) Origin of Reorganization Provisions

The first reorganization statute, enacted in 1918, provided that an exchange of stock or securities for other stock or securities was nontaxable if made in connection with a "reorganization, merger or consolidation."[1] Eight years later, the Revenue Act of 1926 defined a tax-free reorganization as a "merger or consolidation (including the acquisition by one corporation of at least a majority of the voting stock and at least a majority of the total number of shares of all other classes of stock of another corporation)."[2] The distinction between "A," "B," and "C" reorganizations was first made in 1932, when an "A" reorganization was defined as a "statutory merger or consolidation."[3]

Section 368 covers many types of reorganization, and this is a vibrant area of practice. Although large law firms and accounting firms are likely to handle reorganizations of publicly held companies, smaller corporations are likely to seek advice from smaller, more local firms. Even if you never plan to specialize in this area of taxation, you should understand the basic principles involved. To assist you in this endeavor, this chapter includes numerous diagrams. The diagrams help you follow complex transactions without losing track of asset transfers and stock exchanges.

Section 10.01(b) Defining Reorganization

The term reorganization has different meanings in different business settings. One of the definitions found in the dictionary is: "A thorough or dras-

---

1. Revenue Act of 1918, §202(b), 40 Stat. 1057, 1060 (1919).
2. Revenue Act of 1926, §203(b), 44 Stat. (Pt. 2) 9, 12 (1926).
3. Revenue Act of 1932, §112(i), 47 Stat. 169, 198 (1932).

tic reconstruction of a business organization."[4] Some of the reorganizations described in section 368 resemble the dictionary definition. Following the reorganization, a corporation may no longer exist, its assets may be substantially changed, or its ownership structure may be altered. Other reorganizations involve less drastic corporate reconstructions. One reorganization type involves a mere change of form, name or place of incorporation.[5]

Section 10.01(c) Significance of Attaining Reorganization Status

If a transaction qualifies as a section 368 reorganization, corporations and their shareholders may avoid gain recognition and be prevented from recognizing losses. In the reorganization setting, the transaction's form is significant. If a transaction does not fit within one of the statutory definitions, it will not qualify as a reorganization.[6]

Section 10.02 What Is a Reorganization?

Section 368(a)(1) lists seven types of transactions that qualify as reorganizations. The list below summarizes each reorganization. The discussion later in this chapter fleshes out the requirements for each type of reorganization. Each reorganization is referred to by the letter preceding its summary.

(A) a statutory merger or consolidation;
(B) the acquisition of control of another corporation, using the acquiring corporation's voting stock as sole consideration;
(C) the acquisition of substantially all of one corporation's assets, using the acquiring corporation's voting stock as sole consideration;
(D) a transfer of assets from one corporation to another corporation if immediately after the transfer the transferor, or one or more of its shareholders, controls the recipient corporation and the recipient's stock or securities are distributed as part of the transaction;
(E) a recapitalization;

---

4. *See* The Random House College Dictionary (rev. ed. 1975).
5. I.R.C. § 368(a)(1)(F).
6. You may be able to qualify some transactions for nonrecognition under Code sections discussed in other chapters. These include section 351 and section 1036.

(F) a mere change in a corporation's identity, form, or place of organization; or

(G) a transfer of assets from one corporation to another corporation in a
title 11 or similar case and a distribution of the recipient's stock or securities as part of the transaction.

Two other types of reorganizations are defined in section 368(a)(2)(D)) and
section 368(a)2)(E). They are known as triangular A reorganizations because
they involve three parties.

The diagrams below illustrate several of these reorganizations. The A reorganization is depicted by several diagrams to reflect transactions authorized
by the regulations under section 368(a). Additionally, the triangular mergers
also add flexibility to the A reorganization.

A Reorganizations

Basic Statutory Merger

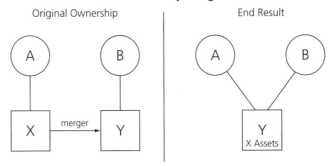

Forward Triangular Merger

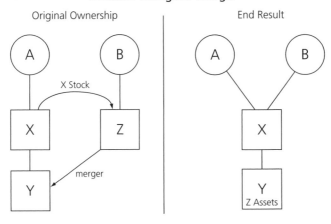

Reverse Triangular Merger

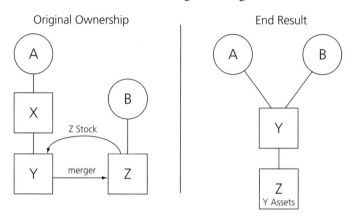

Merger under § 1.368-2T

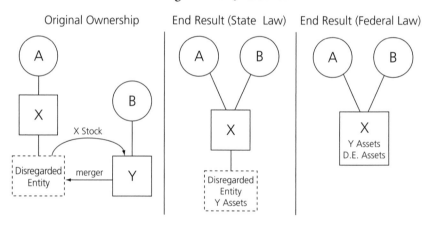

Consolidation

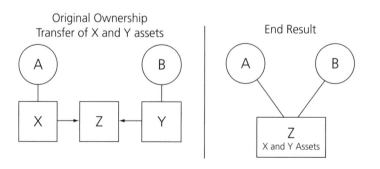

B Reorganization

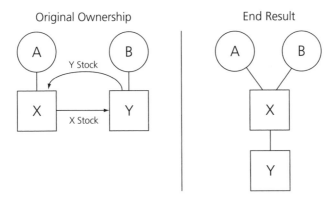

C Reorganization

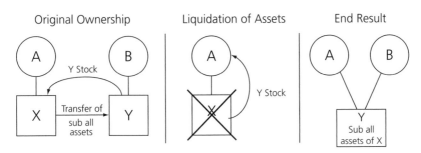

D Reorganization

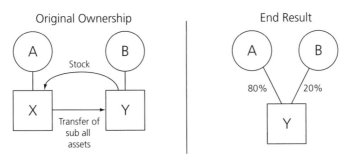

E Reorganization

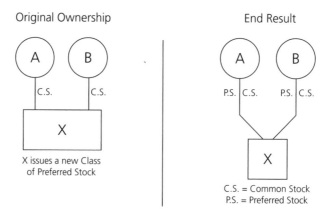

F Reorganization

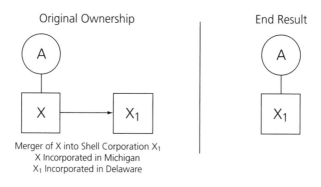

G Reorganization

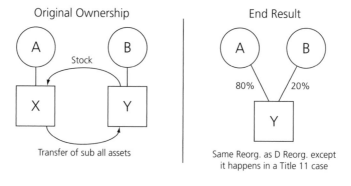

Section 10.03 Reorganization Terminology

E and F reorganizations involve internal restructuring of a corporation. The E reorganization is commonly referred to as an "E recap"; the F reorganization is called by its name. Most other types of reorganizations are either acquisitive or divisive reorganizations. The former involve one corporation acquiring the stock or assets of another corporation. They are the A (including the triangular reorganizations discussed above), B, and C reorganizations.[7] The D reorganization is often called a divisive reorganization because it is frequently combined with a section 355 spin-off, resulting in the division of a corporation into two entities. G reorganizations, which are used by corporations in financial distress, are also divisive in nature.

Two other terms are commonly used. Tax lawyers often refer to forward triangular mergers to describe section 368(a)(2)(D) mergers and to reverse triangular mergers to describe section 368(a)(2)(E) mergers.

Section 10.04 General Reorganization Requirements

Four judicially created tests apply to most reorganization types. Before we study the technical requirements applied to each reorganization type, and the tax consequences associated with reorganizations, we briefly consider those four tests, which now appear in the section 368 regulations: (1) business purpose; (2) continuity of interest; (3) continuity of business enterprise; and (4) step transaction.

Section 10.04(a) Business Purpose

Ever since *Gregory v. Helvering*,[8] courts require a business purpose for transactions claiming nonrecognition treatment under the reorganization provisions. They have held that meeting the technical requirements of a particular Code section is not sufficient if the transaction does not comport with the spirit of that section.[9]

---

7. Because it was enacted to permit mergers in states that severely restricted corporate mergers, the C reorganization is sometimes called a putative or virtual merger.

8. 293 U.S. 465 (1935).

9. Review section 3.03(b) to refresh your memory about Mrs. Gregory's transaction.

The regulations echo the *Gregory* requirement of a valid business purpose. They provide that the purpose of the reorganization provisions is to permit tax-free readjustments of corporate structure that "are required by business exigencies."[10] The regulations also require that taxpayers adopt a plan of reorganization.

Section 10.04(b) Continuity of Interest (COI)

This requirement was once referred to as the continuity of shareholder interest requirement. It is now referred to simply as COI because the reorganization provisions may apply in situations where there are no shareholders. For example, two non-stock corporations may merge.[11]

The purpose of COI is to ensure that the transaction is a mere readjustment of the structure of the corporations involved. It is designed to prevent transactions that technically meet the reorganization requirements but are really disguised sales from qualifying for nonrecognition treatment.[12] The IRS is likely to use the step transaction doctrine to determine whether the end result is a readjustment or a sale.

The COI regulations include an extensive set of examples. As written, they represent a major change in IRS thinking about sales or exchanges of stock received in a reorganization. At one time, a post-reorganization sale of stock or securities received could cause the transaction to fail the COI requirement. The current regulations have a different focus. Instead of focusing on what shareholders do with shares received, they focus on what the shareholders receive in the reorganization. If the shareholders of a target corporation receive stock in the issuing corporation reflecting a significant proprietary interest, COI is met even if they sell the stock received in the exchange.

The regulations cover when a proprietary interest is preserved and when it is not preserved.[13] That determination is made based on the facts and circumstances. The receipt by a shareholder of the target of a proprietary interest in the acquiring corporation is a positive factor. Consideration other than stock and redemptions after the stock exchange are potentially negative factors.

The regulations disregard pre-reorganization dispositions of stock in the target corporation if the new owners are unrelated to the target corporation and the issuing corporation. Regulations section 1.368-1(e)(3) defines related

---

10. Treas. Reg. §1.368-1(b).

11. *See* Rev. Rul. 69-3, 1969-1 C.B. 103 (merger of two nonstock savings and loans treated as a reorganization). *See also* Rev. Rul. 78-286, 1978-2 C.B. 145.

12. *See* Treas. Reg. §1.368-1(e).

13. Treas. Reg. §1.368-1(e)(1).

persons as corporations that are members of an affiliated group within the meaning of section 1504 or as corporations subject to the section 304(a)(2) redemption rules discussed in Chapter 8. As we will see in Chapter 14, two corporations are affiliated with each other if one owns 80 percent or more of the other's stock or if they are owned in this manner by a common parent or by another corporation that is a member of the group.

Section 10.04(c) Continuity of Business Enterprise (COBE)

COBE requires that the issuing corporation continue the historic business of the target corporation or use a significant portion of the target's assets in a business.[14] The regulations cover various aspects of this requirement. For example, if the target corporation has more than one line of business, then the acquiring corporation must continue a significant line of the target's business. A facts and circumstances test applies in determining whether a line of business is significant.[15] A facts and circumstances test also applies in determining if the acquiring corporation will use a significant portion of the target's historical business assets.[16]

The example below is derived from the COBE regulations.

Example: Target corporation conducts three lines of business that are of approximately equal value. On July 1, Year 1, Target sold two of those businesses for cash to an unrelated party. On December 1, Year 1, Target transferred its remaining assets to acquiring corporation in exchange solely for voting stock in Acquiring. If Acquiring continues Target's business, COBE is met.

Section 10.04(d) Step Transaction Doctrine

The step transaction doctrine pervades reorganization planning. When this doctrine applies, transactions that merely meet the technical requirements of the reorganization provisions may be precluded from claiming reorganization status. Transactions that purport to look like one type of reorganization may be collapsed and made to qualify as, or be tested as, another type of reorganization. A classic example involved the merger of a target corporation into the subsidiary of the acquiring corporation followed by the liquidation of the sub-

---

14. Treas. Reg. § 1.368-1(d)(1).
15. Treas. Reg. § 1.368-1(d)(2)(iv).
16. Treas. Reg . § 1.368-1(d)(3)(iii).

sidiary corporation into the parent corporation.[17] The revenue ruling describing that transaction is illustrated below.

Rev. Rul. 72-405

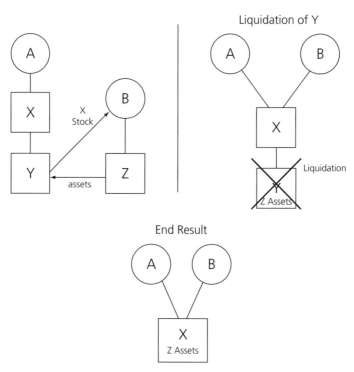

In the revenue ruling, the transaction was tested as a direct acquisition of Z assets:

Direct Acquisition of Z assets

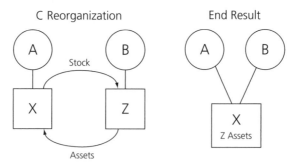

17. Rev. Rul. 72-405, 1972-2 C.B. 217.

The IRS concluded that the transaction still qualified for nonrecognition because it qualified as a C reorganization. This may not be the case for many transactions, because the "solely for voting stock requirement" requires a large amount of stock to be exchanged in the transaction.

The Service has invoked the step transaction doctrine in other rulings. In one ruling, it held that a transaction that failed to qualify as a B reorganization would qualify for tax-free treatment as a C reorganization.[18] It has since amplified that ruling and treated an acquisition merger of a target corporation followed by the liquidation of that corporation into the acquiring parent corporation as a straight merger of the target into the acquiring parent corporation.[19]

In Chapter 3, we discussed the application of the step transaction doctrine. As we indicated there, the IRS cannot assert application of the doctrine to create new steps in the transaction. The doctrine can only be applied to eliminate steps that have no economic significance in the transaction and are undertaken only to achieve a desired tax benefit. To protect themselves against application of the step transaction doctrine, taxpayers should ensure that each step of their transaction has economic substance.

Section 10.05 Technical Reorganization Requirements

Section 10.05(a) In General

Each section 368(a) reorganization type has its own set of requirements. If a transaction meets the qualifications of more than one provision, you should determine if section 368 provides which set of rules takes precedence. If section 368 is silent, both sections may be applicable to the transaction. The discussion below explains the technical requirements of each type of reorganization.

Section 10.05(b) Technical Requirements of A Reorganizations

There are two types of A reorganization, statutory mergers and consolidations. A statutory merger involves the transfer of all the assets of one corporation to another pursuant to state law or to federal or District of Columbia law. A consolidation involves the combination of two or more corporations

---

18. Rev. Rul. 67-274, 1967-2 C.B. 141.
19. Rev. Rul. 2001-46, 2001-2 C.B. 321.

into a newly-formed corporation. For example, Corporations X and Y combine to form new corporation Z. Because neither corporation survives, the consolidation may not be appropriate if one corporation has licenses, intellectual property, or goodwill that is associated with its name.[20]

State laws governing statutory mergers vary from state to state. Beginning in the 1980s, states started to compete with Delaware to be hospitable for incorporation purposes and as part of this competition reconsidered their merger statutes. Texas, for example, passed legislation permitting statutory mergers in which the merged corporation could survive. Texas also permitted a target corporation to merge into two or more corporations. The IRS issued a revenue ruling in response to these transactions.[21]

In the revenue ruling, the IRS outlined what it viewed as the elements of a statutory merger or consolidation. It indicated that mere compliance with a state statutory merger statute may not be sufficient. The COI and COBE requirements also apply, and the target corporation must cease to exist.

The IRS followed this ruling by issuing regulations. In addition to codifying its view of the statutory merger in a regulation, the IRS also addressed whether mergers involving disregarded entities (entities that are treated as non-existent for federal tax purposes) could qualify for tax-free treatment under section 368(a)(1)(A).

Section 10.05(b)(1) The Temporary Regulations

The regulations introduce the new concepts of combining entity and combining unit to the merger area. A combining entity is defined as a corporation. A combining unit is defined as a combining entity and all disregarded entities whose assets are treated as owned by the combining entity for federal tax purposes. The operative rule of the regulations is found in section 1.368-2T(b)(1)(C)(ii). The section provides that a statutory merger or consolidation is a transaction effected pursuant to domestic laws and in which all the assets and liabilities of each member of one or more combining units become the assets and liabilities of one or more members of another combining unit and the combining entity of each transferor unit ceases its separate legal existence for all purposes. This simply means that in a statutory merger all the assets of the merging corporation (including those of its disregarded entities) must be transferred to the acquiring corporation or its disregarded entities.

---

20. Treas. Reg. § 1.368-2T discusses consolidation but provides no consolidation examples.

21. Rev. Rul. 2000-5, 2000-1 C.B. 436.

The temporary regulations, made three important changes to the current law. First, they clearly state the federal requirements of a statutory merger. This means that in addition to meeting a particular state statute (or that of the District of Columbia), a statutory merger must meet the requirements outlined in the temporary regulations. Second, the regulations remove the "corporation law" requirements of the previous regulations. This means that a statutory merger does not have to be under the corporation law of a particular state. This is a recognition that many states now have merger statutes embedded in their LLC statutes. Finally, the regulations permit the merger of a corporation with and into a disregarded entity. It is interesting to note that although such a merger looks like a triangular merger, none of the requirements of the triangular merger need be met. Thus, the regulations provide maximum flexibility to taxpayers.

With regard to mergers involving foreign entities, the IRS and Treasury are in the process of determining whether such transactions should qualify for reorganization treatment. In the meantime, the temporary regulations provide that such transactions should not qualify for reorganization treatment. The IRS recently issued proposed regulations which would permit foreign statutory mergers to the extent that the same requirements for the domestic merger are met.[22] The proposed regulations also provide special basis rules and rules to preserve the E&P account of the merged entities. Commentators have said that the proposed regulations will be of little help because foreign countries' merger statutes will not mirror domestic law.

Section 10.05(b)(2) The Triangular A Reorganizations

The triangular A reorganizations were enacted to give greater flexibility to corporate taxpayers who wanted to obtain control over the assets of a target corporation but were not permitted to engage directly in merger transactions under state law. The triangular merger is also beneficial to taxpayers who want to acquire the assets of another corporation but who do not necessarily want to take over their liabilities. The triangular reorganizations also allowed taxpayers to use a currency (stock of corporation controlling acquiring corporation) that may be more attractive to the shareholders of the target corporation. The shareholders of a target corporation are important players in a merger transaction since they generally vote on the merger. Another advantage of the triangular merger is that the shareholders of the controlling corporation (which may be many) do not have to vote on the merger. Typically, the controlling corporation is the only shareholder of the acquiring corporation. Hence, it has full control of the transaction.

---

22. REG-117969-00, 70 Fed. Reg. 746 (Jan. 5, 2005).

There are, however, a few downsides to the triangular merger. Although at the time of its enactment, Congress wanted to ease the requirements of the A merger, over time, the requirements of the triangular reorganization have surpassed those of the straight merger.

Section 10.05(b)(2)(A) The Forward Triangular Merger

The first type of triangular merger is what practitioners call the forward triangular merger. Section 368(a)(2)(D) provides:

The acquisition by one corporation, in exchange for stock of a corporation (referred to in this subparagraph as "controlling corporation") which is in control of the acquiring corporation, of substantially all of the properties of another corporation shall not disqualify a transaction under paragraph (1)(A) or (1)(G) if—

(i)   no stock of the acquiring corporation is used in the transaction, and
(ii) in the case of a transaction under paragraph (1)(A), such transaction would have qualified under paragraph (1)(A) had the merger been into the controlling corporation.

The regulations concerning the forward triangular merger are contained in section 1.368-2(b)(2) and have the following requirements. First, the acquiring corporation must acquire substantially all the assets of the target corporation (the "sub all" requirement). For purposes of the regulations, sub all has the same meaning as given for purposes of section 368(a)(1)(C). As we have seen earlier, this means that transactions occurring before or after the triangular merger may come into play to cause the sub all requirement to fail. Next, the regulations require that the triangular merger qualifies for section 368(a)(1)(A) treatment only to the extent that it would have qualified as a merger had it been into the controlling corporation. The regulations explain that this does not mean that the transaction would have been permissible under state law, only that the transaction would have met the federal reorganization requirements (such as business purpose, continuity of interest and continuity of business enterprise) had the merger been into the controlling corporation.[23]

The regulations further provide that the only remaining restriction on the merger is that stock of the acquiring corporation cannot be used. Other property such as cash or securities of either the acquiring or the controlling cor-

---

23. *See* Treas. Reg. § 1.368-2(b)(2).

poration or both can be used in the transaction. Finally, the regulations provide that a transaction will qualify under section 368(a)(2)(D) whether or not the controlling or acquiring corporation was formed in anticipation of the transaction. The meaning of the preceding sentence is not clear except that it shows Congress' willingness to be flexible. The sentence more likely impacts the business purpose requirement. As we have stated before, the business purpose in the reorganization arena is not a high threshold. However, you need to be mindful that it is still a requirement that needs to be addressed.

Section 10.05(b)(2)(B) Liabilities of Disregarded Entities

As in the case of the straight A merger, we suspect that the use of the triangular merger is going to decrease dramatically because of the advent of disregarded entities and the temporary regulations that permit the merger of a corporation with and into a disregarded entity. As we stated above, the merger involving a disregarded entity presents all the conveniences of the triangular merger with none of the hurdles. There is no sub all requirement. There is also no need to test whether the transaction would have qualified as an A merger if the merger had been into the parent corporation. The only possible complication with a merger into a disregarded entity is with respect to liabilities assumed by the disregarded entity in the merger. Since the disregarded entity is treated as non-existing for federal income tax purposes, are the liabilities of the disregarded entity treated as being assumed by the owner of the disregarded entity? The answer to this question is not clear. On the one hand, the issue of liabilities is a state matter and is determined by state law. Under state law, the disregarded entity is respected as an entity and, thus, should be responsible for its own debts. On the other hand, section 301.7701-2(a) provides that all the assets, liabilities, and items of income or deduction of the disregarded entity are treated as those of its owner. It may be that section 301.7701-2(a) only applies for purposes of determining federal liabilities or the application of federal law. Thus, for purposes of section 357 and other federal income tax sections, the owner of the disregarded entity will be treated as assuming the debts of the disregarded entity. For purposes of determining other liabilities (e.g., collectors other than the federal government), the disregarded entity would be the debtor.

Once an entity becomes a disregarded entity, its assets, liabilities, and items of income and deduction become those of its owner. One issue that has arisen is whether the IRS can collect against the disregarded entity or should be able to collect only against the owner of the disregarded entity. The IRS recently promulgated final regulations that address the issue of tax liabilities of disregarded entities.[24] The regulations do not address liabilities other than Federal tax liabilities; hence, as to the issues not addressed by the regulations, it appears that state law would still control. The regulations apply to the three types of disregarded entity, the qualified REIT subsidiary, the QSub and the check-the-box disregarded entity. Reference to the disregarded entity is normally to all three types of entities. Hence, the regulations with regard to the three types of disregarded entity are identical and provide that an entity that is disregarded as separate from its owner will be regarded as an entity separate from its owner for purposes of

(1) Federal tax liabilities of the entity with respect to any taxable period for which the entity was not disregarded;
(2) Federal tax liabilities of any other entity for which the entity is liable; and
(3) Refunds or credits of Federal tax.

The regulations provide basic examples to illustrate the rules in the regulations. Most of the examples are straightforward except the examples under section 301.7701-2(c) appear to illustrate a bit more than can be gleaned from the language of the regulations. The examples are as follows:

Example 1. In 2001, X, a domestic corporation that reports its taxes on a calendar year basis, merges into Z, a domestic LLC wholly owned by Y that is disregarded as an entity separate from Y, in a state law merger. X was not a member of a consolidated group at any time during its taxable year ending in December 2000. Under the applicable state law, Z is the successor to X and is liable for all of X's debts. In 2004, the Internal Revenue Service ("IRS") seeks to extend the period of limitations on assessment for X's 2000 taxable year. Because Z is the successor to X and is liable for X's 2000 taxes that remain unpaid, Z is the proper party to sign the consent to extend the period of limitations.

Example 2. The facts are the same as in Example 1, except that in 2002, the IRS determines that X miscalculated and underreported its income tax liability for 2000. Because Z is the successor to X and is liable for X's 2000 taxes that remain unpaid, the deficiency may be assessed against Z and, in the event that Z fails to pay the liability after notice and demand, a general tax lien will arise against all of Z's property and rights to property.

Section 10.05(b)(2)(C) Basis in Triangular Reorganizations

You should be aware that there are special rules with respect to basis consequences following a triangular merger.[25] The purpose of these basis regula-

---

24. *See* Treas. Reg. §§ 1.1361-4 and 301.7701-2.
25. *See* Treas. Reg. § 1.358-6.

tions is to permit the controlling corporation to upgrade its basis in its subsidiary to reflect the merger transaction. The regulations apply to various types of triangular transactions, including triangular B and C reorganizations. These regulations permit corporations that do not file consolidated returns an increase in basis that corporations filing consolidated returns are normally permitted to obtain.

How do the regulations work? Generally, section 358 provides that in an exchange pursuant to a reorganization, the basis of the property received shall be the same as the basis of the property exchanged. In a simple two corporation merger (for example X merging into Y), the X shareholders are treated as exchanging their X stock for Y stock. The former X shareholders' basis in the Y stock received in the transaction would be the same as their basis in their X stock. What happens to the X stock? It disappears because X does not survive the transaction. Hence there is no basis issue with respect to X stock. The basis of the X assets in the hands of Y remains the same.

In a triangular transaction, the controlling corporation exchanges its own stock for stock in the target corporation. The assets of the target corporation are transferred to the acquiring corporation. If the basis of the stock of the subsidiary corporation in the hands of the controlling corporation is not adjusted, the controlling corporation will recognize excess gain on its disposition of the acquiring corporation stock. This excess gain is unwarranted. The regulations prevent the excess gain from being recognized by providing that the triangular transaction will be treated as the acquisition of the target corporation's assets by the controlling corporation as if basis was determined under section 362(b) (acquiring corporation takes over the basis of the target corporation in its assets) followed by the transfer of the target corporation assets to the subsidiary in a transaction in which the parent's basis in subsidiary stock is determined under section 358 (basis of stock is the same as basis of property transferred by parent). Fortunately, the regulations are not very complex and can be mastered quite easily. The regulations also contain a number of examples that are very helpful and easy to follow. A typical example is Example 1:

Example 1. Forward triangular merger.

(a) Facts. T has assets with an aggregate basis of $60 and fair market value of $100 and no liabilities. Pursuant to a plan, P forms S with $5 cash (which S retains), and T merges into S. In the merger, the T shareholders receive P stock worth $100 in exchange for their T stock. The transaction is a reorganization to which sections 368(a)(1)(A) and (a)(2)(D) apply.

(b) Basis adjustment. Under section 1.358-6(c)(1), P's $5 basis in its S stock is adjusted as if P acquired the T assets acquired by S in the reorganization directly from T in a transaction in which P's basis in the T assets was determined under section 362(b). Under section 362(b), P would have an aggregate basis of $60 in the T assets. P is then treated as if it transferred the T assets to S in a transaction in which P's basis in the S stock was determined under section 358. Under section 358, P's $5 basis in its S stock would be increased by the $60 basis in the T assets deemed transferred. Consequently, P has a $65 basis in its S stock as a result of the reorganization.

The regulations provide that it makes no difference whether S is newly-formed or whether it was a pre-existing corporation with assets. In either case, P's basis in its S stock is increased by the basis of the target corporation's basis in its assets. Part (c) of Example (1) illustrates this basic principle:

(c) Use of pre-existing S.

The facts are the same as paragraph (a) of this Example 1, except that S is an operating company with substantial assets that has been in existence for several years. P has a $110 basis in the S stock. Under section 1.358-6(c)(1), P's $110 basis in its S stock is increased by the $60 basis in the T assets deemed transferred. Consequently, P has a $170 basis in its S stock as a result of the reorganization.

Section 10.05(b)(2)(D) The Reverse Triangular Merger

The reverse triangular merger is the opposite of the forward triangular merger. Instead of the target corporation merging into the subsidiary of the controlling corporation, the subsidiary of the controlling corporation is merged with and into the target corporation. This transaction is defined in section 368(a)(2)(E) in the following manner:

A transaction otherwise qualifying under paragraph (1)(A) shall not be dis-qualified by reason of the fact that stock of a corporation (referred to in this subparagraph as the "controlling corporation") which before the merger was in control of the merged corporation is used in the transaction, if—

(i) after the transaction, the corporation surviving the merger holds sub-stantially all of its properties and of the properties of the merged cor-poration (other than stock of the controlling corporation distributed in the transaction); and

(ii) in the transaction, former shareholders of the surviving corporation exchanged, for an amount of voting stock of the controlling corpora-tion, an amount of stock in the surviving corporation which consti-tutes control of such corporation.

Congress permitted the reverse triangular merger because it saw no good reason why it should not be permitted and did not want the direction of a merger to decide whether a transaction would qualify as a reorganization or not.[26] The two mergers enjoy some things in common but also differ in important respects. In both mergers, there is a sub all requirement. In the forward triangular merger, the acquiring corporation must acquire substantially all the assets of the target corporation. In the reverse triangular merger, the surviving corporation must instead "hold" substantially all of its properties and the properties of the merged corporation. The meaning of hold has been subject to some controversy. A revenue ruling disposed of that controversy by stating that the word hold is used in the description of the reverse triangular merger because a surviving corporation cannot be said to have acquired its own properties in a merger.[27] As we have seen earlier, sub all has the same meaning in the reverse triangular as it has in the forward triangular merger.

The major difference between the forward triangular merger and the reverse triangular merger is that in the latter, the former shareholders of the surviving corporation must give up control of the surviving corporation. At least one commentator has been puzzled by this requirement stating that: "If Congress wanted to create reasonable parity between the two types of triangular transactions, these differences are hard to justify."[28] Upon closer scrutiny, the differing requirements make sense. If the former shareholders of the surviving corporation do not give up control of the surviving corporation, the transaction would look like a divisive transaction. This means that it would have to meet the requirements of section 355. Worse, it arguably looks like a stock swap—a transaction strictly prohibited by the section 355 regulations.[29] A stock swap is a transaction whereby shareholders of two corporations exchange stock of their corporations. A stock swap should not be confused with an exchange in the same corporation. If the exchange occurs with regard to stock of the same corporation, section 1036 provides that no gain or loss will be recognized.

Interestingly, section 368(a)(2)(E) begins with an assumption that the transaction would qualify as a merger under section 368(a)(1)(A) but for the fact that stock of the acquiring corporation is not used in the transaction. It is, thus, implied that continuity of interest, business purpose and continuity of business enterprise should be met. The reason why Congress seems less concerned about the reverse triangular merger transaction is that the transaction was not prohibited under state law.

---

26. *See* H.R. Rep. No. 91-1778, 91st Cong., 2d Sess. 2–3 (1970).

27. *See* Rev. Rul. 2001-25, 2001-1 C.B. 1291.

28. *See* Cheryl D. Block, Corporate Taxation 418 (Aspen Publishers, 3d ed. 2004).

29. *See* Treas. Reg. § 1.355-4.

Finally, like the forward triangular merger, the IRS has provided regulations to address the basis consequences of the controlling corporation following a reverse triangular merger. In providing these regulations, the IRS was addressing the same concerns found in the forward triangular merger. The IRS also used the same technique. In fact, section 1.358-6(c)(2) states that, for purposes of basis determination, the reverse triangular merger is treated like the forward triangular merger. Example (2) of the regulations provides a similar result with respect to basis computation in the reverse triangular merger:

Example 2. Reverse triangular merger.

(a) Facts. T has assets with an aggregate basis of $60 and a fair market value of $100 and no liabilities. P has a $110 basis in its S stock. Pursuant to a plan, S merges into T with T surviving. In the merger, the T shareholders receive $10 cash from P and P stock worth $90 in exchange for their T stock. The transaction is a reorganization to which sections 368(a)(1)(A) and (a)(2)(E) apply.

(b) Basis adjustment. Under section 1.358-6(c)(2)(i)(A), P's basis in the T stock acquired is P's $110 basis in its S stock before the transaction, adjusted as if T had merged into S in a forward triangular merger to which section 1.358-6(c)(1) applies. In such a case, P's $110 basis in its S stock before the transaction would have been increased by the $60 basis of the T assets deemed transferred. Consequently, P has a $170 basis in its T stock immediately after the transaction.

Section 10.05(c) Technical Requirements of the B Reorganization

The B reorganization is not a very popular reorganization because of its strict stock for stock exchange requirement. As we have seen earlier, a B reorganization occurs with the acquisition by one corporation, in exchange solely for all or a part of its voting stock (or in exchange solely for all or a part of the voting stock of a corporation which is in control of the acquiring corporation), of stock of another corporation if, immediately after the acquisition, the acquiring corporation has control of such other corporation (whether or not such acquiring corporation had control immediately before the acquisition). Under section 368(c), control is defined as stock possessing 80 percent of the combined voting power of all stock of the target corporation entitled to vote and 80 percent of the remaining stock of the target corporation not entitled to vote.

Section 10.05(c)(1) Creeping B Reorganizations

The definition contained above appears straightforward but many issues develop in interpreting the language. For example, when must the acquiring corporation acquire control of the target corporation? What if a transaction takes two or more years to complete? Would the series of acquisitions be considered as part of the overall transaction that gives control to the acquiring corporation? These sorts of acquisitions are called creeping reorganizations, as in a creeping B reorganization. Creeping acquisitions work because the statute only requires the acquiring corporation to have control of the target corporation following the acquisition.

Section 1.368-2(c) provides an example in which a corporation purchased 30 percent of the stock of a target corporation in 1939. Sixteen years later (in 1955), the acquiring corporation exchanged some of its stock in exchange for 60 percent of the stock of the target corporation. The regulation treats the acquisition of the 60 percent stock of the target corporation as a B reorganization. In fact, the regulation states that as long as an acquiring corporation acquires 80 percent of the stock of a target corporation, the exchange of stock in which it acquired control and any exchange thereafter will be tax-free. We caution you not to read too much into this. The regulation assumes that the step transaction doctrine would not collapse the two acquisitions. This is why the example in the regulation used a sixteen year gap between its two acquisitions.

In most corporate transactions, debt is usually assumed (either actual debt or contingent liability). Thus, to achieve a B reorganization, one would have to be extremely careful that no contingent liability is exchanged in the transaction. In addition, as we have seen above, the step transaction doctrine is always lurking in the background. For example, if a target corporation is merged with and into a newly-created subsidiary of the parent of the subsidiary (corporation owning the subsidiary) in exchange for stock of the parent company, the transaction will be tested as a B reorganization and not as a merger transaction.[30]

Given all these restrictions, why would a taxpayer engage in a B reorganization? Historically, there have been two reasons given but with the temporary merger regulations permitting mergers with disregarded entities, these two reasons should matter less. First, because the B reorganization does not involve a transfer of assets from the target corporation to the acquiring corporation, liabilities of the target corporation are not transferred to the acquiring corporation. In a merger with and into a disregarded entity, the liabilities of the target corporation are transferred to the disregarded entity, not the disregarded entity's parent. One's liabilities are determined under state law and since the disregarded entity is recognized for state law purposes, it would be treated as inheriting the liabilities of the target corporation.

---

30. *See* Rev. Rul. 56-613, 1956-2 C.B. 212; Rev. Rul. 67-448, 1967-2 C.B. 144.

The second reason is still somewhat more valid than the first one. Unlike the triangular mergers, there is no "sub all" requirement in the B reorganization. This provides flexibility for taxpayers to get rid of unwanted assets prior to a B reorganization. Following the B reorganization, a taxpayer will also have flexibility to transfer assets among its affiliates. Once again, if a taxpayer conducts its business through a number of disregarded entities, it will be able to transfer assets acquired in a merger among its disregarded entities without fear of taxation because such transfers will be ignored for tax purposes.

Section 10.05(c)(2) IRS Concerns

The IRS is mostly concerned with whether boot is transferred in a B reorganization. The exchanging parties in a B reorganization are the target corporation shareholders and the acquiring corporation. The IRS will scrutinize very closely what these parties receive.

Tax lawyers typically advise their clients that no consideration other than stock can be exchanged in a B reorganization even if 80 percent or more of the consideration is voting stock. Any advice to the contrary will certainly invite the scrutiny of the IRS and the IRS will litigate the case since this has been the IRS' litigating position for quite some time. In Rev. Rul. 75-123,[31] the IRS held that the acquisition of 80 percent of a target corporation stock for Acquirer stock did not qualify as a B reorganization where Acquirer purchased the 20 percent balance for cash. The IRS has the support of the courts on this.[32] However, the IRS is not totally unreasonable, it will permit some cash to be distributed in a B reorganization if the cash is transferred in lieu of fractional shares. This small amount of cash will, of course, be taxable but it will not cause the transaction to fail reorganization treatment.

Section 10.05(d) Technical Requirements of the C Reorganization

This reorganization is defined under section 368(a)(1)(C) as the acquisition by one corporation, in exchange solely for all or a part of its voting stock (or in exchange solely for all or a part of the voting stock of a corporation which is in control of the acquiring corporation), of substantially all of the properties of another corporation. The section further provides that

---

31. 1975-1 C.B. 115

32. *See Commissioner v. Turnbow*, 286 F.2d 669 (9th Cir. 1960), *aff'd on other issues*, 368 U.S. 337 (1961).

in determining whether the exchange is solely for stock the assumption by the acquiring corporation of a liability of the other, or the fact that property acquired is subject to a liability, shall be disregarded. The C reorganization has been called the virtual merger. This is because the C reorganization was introduced by Congress to allow corporations whose states did not permit them to engage in transactions similar to mergers.[33] The transfer of substantially all the assets of a corporation in exchange for stock of the acquiring corporation, while not a merger, looks like a merger because substantially all, in this context, means a transfer of almost all the assets of the target corporation.[34] In addition, as we will see later, under section 368(a)(2)(G), the target corporation is required to liquidate in a C reorganization.[35]

There are three major requirements to the C reorganization: (1) the acquisition of substantially all the assets of the target corporation must be solely for voting stock; (2) the target corporation must liquidate following the transfer of its assets; and (3) the target corporation must transfer substantially all of its assets to the acquiring corporation.

Section 10.05(d)(1) The Solely for Voting Stock Requirement

Unlike the B reorganization, the C reorganization is a bit less stringent in its requirement that only stock be transferred. Under the so-called boot relaxation rules of section 368(a)(2)(B), up to 20 percent non-stock consideration can be transferred in a C reorganization (cash or assumption of liabilities). But this is still small consolation for the potential of having your reorganization unravel right before your eyes. As we said above, the major danger involves contingent liabilities that may become due after the transaction and thus cause a change in the consideration exchanged in the transaction.

Example: Corporation X transfers some of its voting stock and cash to Corporation Y in exchange for substantially all of the assets of Corporation Y. At the time of the reorganization, the amount of cash represents 10 percent of the assets acquired by X and the voting stock transferred by X was transferred

---

33. *See* S. Rep. No. 73-558, 73d Cong., 2d Sess. 16–17 (1934).

34. For PLR purposes, see Rev. Proc. 86-42, 1986-2 C.B. 722.

35. Now that all states permit statutory mergers, the usefulness of the C reorganization may have run its course. In fact, most practitioners do not use the C reorganization because unknown liabilities could cause the reorganization to fail the solely for voting stock requirement. Nevertheless, the C reorganization is one of the enumerated reorganizations and it merits study.

for 90 percent of Y's assets. Thus, the transaction seemingly appears to qualify as a C reorganization. Shortly, following the reorganization, certain contingent liabilities of Y corporation become due and X pays off these liabilities using an amount equal to 15 percent of the Y assets acquired. Does this cause the transaction to fail reorganization status?

Yes, it does. The reason is that because the contingent liability is a liability of Y, X paying for it is treated as if X transferred an extra 15 percent cash in the transaction. Thus, the amount of cash or non-qualified property transferred in the transaction exceeds 20 percent and is not protected under the boot relaxation rules of section 368(a)(2)(B).

Section 10.05(d)(2) Creeping C Reorganizations

The issue of creeping C reorganizations existed for many years until promulgation of what has been called the *Bausch & Lomb*[36] regulations under section 1.368-2(d)(4). Prior to the regulations, prior ownership of stock in a C reorganization could potentially cause the C reorganization to fail because substantially all the assets of the target corporation were not acquired in the "C reorganization." The IRS' view was to strictly apply the C reorganization rules and require that in the C reorganization (defined as the transaction in which substantial all the assets of the target corporation are acquired) assets of the target corporation be acquired in exchange for stock of the acquiring corporation. Thus, if the acquiring corporation held stock of the target corporation prior to the C reorganization, the stock held prior to the asset acquisition could be used for purposes of determining whether the substantially all assets requirement is met.

The current regulations take another view. Under the regulations an old and cold (meaning prior) ownership of target stock by the acquiring corporation prior to the acquisition of the target assets in a potential C reorganization will not necessarily disqualify the transaction. Although not directly stated, the regulations apply a step transaction rationale to determine whether the potential reorganization will receive tax-free status. If the prior acquisition of stock would disqualify the transaction (i.e., the acquisition was for cash or property other than the acquiring corporation's stock) and is related to the subsequent acquisition, then the transaction would not qualify for C reorganization treatment even though it could qualify for tax-free treatment under another Code section. If the prior acquisition of stock was for stock of the acquiring corporation, then

---

36. See *Bausch & Lomb Optical Co. v. Commissioner*, 267 F.2d 75 (2d Cir. 1959), *cert. denied*, 361 U.S. 835 (1959).

this prior acquisition would not disqualify the transaction because the exchange in the prior acquisition would have been permissible under section 368(a)(1)(C).

Example: Corporation X acquires 60 percent of the stock of Corporation Y in exchange for X stock in Year 1. In Year 3, Y transfers all of its assets to X in exchange for additional X voting stock.

This transaction will qualify for C reorganization treatment whether the two separate acquisitions are related or not.

Example: Same facts as above, except that X acquired the original 60 percent of the stock of Corporation Y for cash.

Under the current regulations, the mere fact that X has a prior ownership in Y will not disqualify the transaction. However, if the prior acquisition of X stock is related to the acquisition of assets, the transaction will not qualify for C reorganization treatment because collapsing the two transactions would cause X to have acquired all the assets of Y in exchange for 60 percent cash and 40 percent voting stock, well outside the limits permitted by section 368(a)(2)(B).

Section 10.05(d)(3) The Liquidation Requirement

Under section 368(a)(2)(G)(i), a transaction will not qualify for C reorganization treatment unless the target corporation liquidates and transfers whatever remaining assets it has as well as the stock of the acquiring corporation that it has received to its shareholders. Under section 368(a)(2)(G)(ii), the Secretary may waive the liquidation requirements subject to any conditions that he imposes. What this generally means is that a target corporation in a C reorganization can remain in existence if it applies for a PLR. In these situations, the taxpayer must prove to the IRS that it has a very good reason to remain in existence. For example, it may be that the corporation needs to stay in existence to defend a lawsuit or to pay off creditors. The IRS may also permit a corporation to remain in existence if it has a valuable franchise that can only remain in existence if the corporation remains in existence.[37]

Section 10.05(d)(4) The Substantially All Requirement

Section 368 does not contain a definition for substantially all. The natural meaning of the words would lead one to assume that it has to be quite a bit of the assets of the target corporation. In fact, it is. For PLR purposes, the IRS requires that at least 70 percent of the gross assets (or 90 percent of the net

---

37. *See* S. Rep. No. 98-169, 98th Cong., 2d Sess. 204–06 (1984).

assets) of the target corporation be distributed in the transaction. These two alternative tests give some flexibility for taxpayers to meet the requirement.

Outside the PLR arena, the requirements are less stringent. Hence, if 70 percent of the operating assets of a target corporation are transferred in a C reorganization, the sub all requirement would be met.[38] Note that the revenue ruling focuses on the quality of the assets. In other words, the test is not a mere quantitative test, it requires operating assets of the corporation—assets without which the corporation cannot go on existing.

The challenge in determining whether sub all is met is with respect to the application of the step transaction doctrine. In other words, what happens if a target corporation gets rid of some assets prior to the acquisition? If the step transaction doctrine applies to the transaction, then the assets disposed of would be treated as part of the total assets of the target corporation. This may cause the transaction to fail the sub all requirement.

A note of caution: Not all dispositions would cause the transaction to fail sub all. For example Rev. Rul. 88-48[39] permits the sale of 50 percent of the assets of a corporation prior to a potential C reorganization to qualify as a C reorganization because the assets sold only changed the make-up of the corporation. The key to this ruling is that the cash received by the target corporation was transferred to the acquiring corporation. Hence, the target corporation did, in fact, transfer substantially all of its assets to the acquiring corporation.

On the other hand, if target assets are disposed of prior to a potential C reorganization and the disposal of the assets is related to the potential reorganization, the assets disposed of will count toward the total assets of the target corporation and may cause the transaction to fail. For example, Rev. Proc. 77-37[40] held that assets of a target corporation used to redeem dissenting shareholders were be treated as part of the total assets of the corporation for purposes of the sub all requirement. This result makes sense because if the target corporation did not engage in a reorganization, it would have no need to redeem dissenting shareholders.

Section 10.05(d)(5) Final Concerns

We have warned you about the application of the step transaction doctrine in the reorganization area. As you might suspect, the doctrine also af-

---

38. *See* Rev. Rul. 57-518, 1957-2 C.B. 253.
39. 1988-1 C.B. 117.
40. 1977-2 C.B. 568.

fects the C reorganization. In looking at a transaction, it may not neatly fit into the definition of the C reorganization except at the end of the transaction. For example a merger of a target corporation into a newly created subsidiary of an acquiring corporation in exchange for the acquiring corporation's voting stock followed by the merger of the subsidiary with and into its parent corporation will not be tested as a triangular A reorganization but will be tested as a C reorganization. This is because the transaction really is a transfer of all of the target corporation's assets to the acquiring corporation in exchange for voting stock of the acquiring corporation. This is important because if more than 20 percent non-qualified property is transferred in the transaction, it will fail C reorganization treatment and will be taxable. Meeting the A merger qualifications will not be helpful in this instance. Ultimately, you need to look at the structure of your corporations prior to your transaction and at the end of your transaction and determine what the transaction really looks like. In this sense, a merger followed by a liquidation of the acquiring corporation does not really look like a true merger but some other form of transaction. Also note that this is only true through the application of the step transaction doctrine. If the doctrine is not applicable, then the two steps of the transaction are not collapsed. Thus, you may actually have a merger followed by a liquidation.

The final concern that we want to apprise you of is possible overlap situations. A C reorganization may look like a D reorganization. Such a situation may occur in the following scenario: a target corporation transfers all of its assets to an acquiring corporation in exchange for acquiring corporation stock. Following the transfer, target shareholders receive control of acquiring corporation (note that under section 304, control is less than 80 percent; it is 50 percent). In this instance, the transaction would clearly qualify for C reorganization treatment because it is a transfer of substantially all the assets of a target corporation in exchange for voting stock of the acquiring corporation. The transaction would also qualify as a D reorganization because, as we will see later, it is a transfer of the assets of a corporation to an acquiring corporation and the target shareholders end up controlling the acquiring corporation. We saw above that if a transaction qualifies under two provisions granting tax-free treatment, both provisions potentially apply. In an overlap between a C reorganization and a D reorganization, Congress decided that the D reorganization provisions would take precedence.[41] This means that all of the tax consequences of the transaction would flow through its qualification as a D

---

41. *See* I.R.C. § 368(a)(2)(A).

reorganization. This may have important consequences because section 357(c) could potentially apply to the transaction now that it is a D reorganization but would otherwise not apply to the transaction. Similarly, a C reorganization may also qualify as a section 351 transfer. If this is the case, the same rule concerning section 357(c) would apply.

Section 10.05(e) Technical Requirements of the D Reorganization

A D reorganization is defined as a transfer by a corporation of all or a part of its assets to another corporation if immediately after the transfer, the transferor, or one or more of its shareholders (including persons who were shareholders immediately before the transfer), or any combination thereof, is in control of the corporation to which the assets are transferred—but only if, in pursuance of the plan, stock or securities of the corporation to which the assets are transferred are distributed in a transaction which qualifies under section 354, 355, or 356. The D reorganization can be a divisive reorganization in which case it has to meet the qualifications of section 355. In this case, the initial transfer of assets is only a small part of the transaction as the rigorous requirements of section 355 take precedence. Because we fully addressed the section 355 requirements in Chapter 9, we will now only address the technical requirements of the D reorganization in general and the requirements for the non-divisive D reorganization (a D not followed by a section 355 transaction).

There are three main requirements in a D reorganization. First, there must be a transfer of assets from one corporation to another. Second, the shareholders of the transferor corporation must control the transferee corporation. Finally, there must a distribution of the stock or securities received in the transaction.

Section 10.05(e)(1) Transfer of Assets

We start with some initial questions. How much of the assets must be transferred? Can it really be, as the statute says, only part of a corporation's assets? How does one define part? When the statute says part or "all," does it really mean all?

The answers to these questions are found in the distribution requirement— the part of the statute that says that the corporation receiving stock or securities in exchange for its assets must distribute such stock and securities in a transaction that qualifies under section 354, 355 or 356. In a transaction that qualifies under section 355, part of the assets of a corporation can be transferred. It could be 10 percent, 20 percent or 80 percent of the assets of the transferor corporation. So long as the transaction qualifies under section 355, it will qualify as a D reorganization. This is the classic corporate division scenario.

What if the transaction does not qualify under section 355? In this case, the transaction would have to qualify as a distribution under section 354. For this to occur, section 354(b) provides some restrictions. Namely, section 354(b) requires that to qualify as a D reorganization, the corporation to which the assets are transferred must acquire substantially all the assets of the transferor corporation (the sub all requirement). The section also requires that the transferor corporation distribute the stock and securities received in the exchange as well as the other properties of the transferor corporation in pursuance of the reorganization. Note that this a liquidation requirement but not necessarily a dissolution requirement. The corporation can remain in existence but it must be generally bare of assets. In most instances, however, this really means that the transferor corporation will go out of existence.

We have seen that, for purposes of the C reorganization, sub all essentially means that most of the operating assets of the corporation will be distributed in the transaction. The same analysis with regard to sub all in the C reorganization context applies to the sub all requirement mandated by section 354.

Section 10.05(e)(2) The Control Requirement

A transaction will qualify as a D reorganization only if the shareholders of the transferor corporation have control of the corporation to which the assets are transferred. Control is generally defined in section 368(c) as the acquisition of at least 80 percent of the total combined voting power of all classes of stock entitled to vote and 80 percent of the total number of shares of all other classes of stock of the corporation. This 80 percent control requirement applies only to transactions that qualify under section 355. Note, however, that under section 368(a)(2)(H)(ii), for transactions that qualify under section 355, the 80 percent control requirement will have to be met only immediately following the transaction. Section 368(a)(2)(H) provides that the fact that the shareholders who receive control dispose of their shares will have no impact on the control requirement. The fact that the controlled corporation (corporation that is controlled by the recipient shareholders) issues additional shares will also not be taken into consideration.

For D reorganizations that do not qualify under section 355 but that qualify under section 354, section 368(a)(2)(H)(i) provides that the control requirement is lowered to 50 percent. This a trap for the unwary! Thus, we caution you, as your tax professors have no doubt cautioned you to be very careful in reading the tax code. You must read a section in full even if the answer to your question appears to be answered in a particular subsection. There is a long history as to why Congress lowered the control requirements for the non-divisive D reorganization. This mainly deals with tax games that taxpayers used to engage in with regard to liquidation/reincorporation transactions.[42]

To complicate the trap, section 368(a)(2)(H)(i) does not simply lower the control requirement to 50 percent, it states that the term control shall be given such meaning as provided in section 304. This means that section 304 applies to a non-divisive D reorganization to the extent that the section defines control. Thus, you have to take a look at section 304. That section has complications. Section 304 indeed defines control as the acquisition of 50 percent or more of stock, but section 304(c)(3) states that for purposes of determining control, the constructive ownership rules of section 318 are applicable. Thus, once again, you must be wary of the constructive ownership rules of section 318 impacting this 50 percent requirement.

Finally, the control requirement has to be met immediately after the transfer of assets. This means that the control requirement has to be met in the transaction. Remember the discussion above regarding the *Bausch & Lomb* doctrine? This concern is not present here. Hence, the control requirement in a D reorganization will be met even if the shareholders of the transferor corporation owned 79 percent of the stock of the transferee corporation. Additionally, we note that there is not a solely for voting stock requirement for D reorganizations. Hence, taxpayers have a bit more flexibility. However, this flexibility is limited by the continuity of interest requirement.

What about the step transaction doctrine? Once again, the step transaction doctrine threatens to steal the show. Notwithstanding the requirement that control be determined immediately after the transfer of assets, if control is lost due to a transaction that, under the step transaction doctrine, is part of the reorganization transaction, control will not have been acquired. Thus, the transaction will not qualify as a D reorganization.

Section 10.05(e)(3) The Distribution Requirement

The language of the statute plainly requires that the stock or securities received as well as the other properties of the transferor corporation be distributed to its shareholders. Generally, if such stock or securities are not distributed the transaction will not qualify as a D reorganization. An exception exists if the transferor corporation transfers its assets to a related corporation. For

---

42. *See* Staff of Jt. Comm. on Tax'n, General Explanation of the Revenue Provisions of the Deficit Reduction Act of 1984, at 192–94 (1984).

example, Corporation X transfers all of its assets to Corporation Y and both corporations are owned by the same group of shareholders. No stock of Corporation Y is transferred in the transaction. Rev. Rul. 70-240[43] held that no actual distribution of stock is needed in such situations. The rationale for this ruling was to combat abuses in liquidation/reincorporation transactions that taxpayers argued did not qualify as a reorganization and hence permitted gain or loss to be recognized. The typical liquidation/reincorporation transaction preceded the repeal of the *General Utilities* doctrine and normally involved the transfer of assets of a corporation to the shareholders of the corporation in liquidation of the transferor corporation followed by the reincorporation of the corporation in a transfer usually qualifying under section 351. If there had been no exchange of the related corporation stock, the taxpayer would argue that the transaction was subject to taxation. Taxpayers that engaged in this type of transaction were normally attempting to recognize losses. The IRS used the D reorganization device to combat these transactions and disposed of the distribution requirement to ensure that these transactions would qualify as D reorganizations and that no gain or loss would be recognized.

If the taxpayer retains some of its properties, it runs the risk of disqualifying its transaction. Rev. Rul. 74-545[44] held that a transaction would fail D reorganization status if the taxpayer retained some of its assets in the transaction. There are exceptions, such as in the case of assets retained to pay off creditors, valuable charters that can be sold or continue in existence only if the corporation remains in existence.[45]

Section 10.05(f) Technical Requirements of the E Reorganization

With the E reorganization, we are back on more familiar ground because the IRS has published regulations on this type of reorganization. As you can tell by now, publication of regulations on a particular subject makes tax planning easier. Whether you like a particular set of regulations or not, it provides detailed explanation of the IRS's views on a subject. The regulations for the E reorganization (commonly called "E Recapitalization" or "E Recap") are contained in section 1.368-2(e).

---

43. 1970-1 C.B. 81.
44. 1974-2 C.B. 122.
45. *See* Rev. Proc. 89-50, 1989-2 C.B. 631, for the procedures to be followed in order to receive a PLR on this issue.

As usual, we begin our survey of the E reorganization by looking at the statute provided by Congress. Section 368(a)(1)(E) succinctly provides that a recapitalization will qualify as a reorganization. The word recapitalization contains the term capital. Thus, we know from this that the capital structure of the corporation is the item in play. Also from this language, we may deduce that this recapitalization generally involves a single corporation.

The regulations are somewhat helpful but could be better. They provide no definition of recapitalization and make no grand statement as to what a recapitalization should look like. They simply provide some examples of what they consider a recapitalization. For example, a recapitalization will occur if a corporation with $200,000 par value bonds outstanding, instead of paying them off in cash, discharges them by issuing preferred shares to the bondholders.[46] Another example would be an exchange of 25 percent of the corporation's preferred stock for common stock.[47] Three more examples would be (i) a corporation issuing preferred stock previously authorized but unissued, for outstanding common stock, (ii) an exchange of preferred stock, having certain priorities, for common stock having no such priority, and (iii) an exchange of an amount of preferred stock with dividends in arrears for other stock of the corporation.[48] This completes all the examples contained in the regulations.

By now, you understand that corporate tax laws, like the rest of the tax code are never that simple. You understand that issues lurk behind every tree, ready to jump at the unwary. So what are the issues that you should be concerned with respect to recapitalizations? There are really two main issues. The first issue involves the recognition of boot in the transaction. There is good news with respect to boot recognition. Since there is not a solely for voting stock requirement in the E reorganization, taxpayers have more flexibility. The second issue pertains to potential application of section 382. Briefly, section 382 is a loss limitation rule that curtails the use of losses by corporations that have undergone an ownership change. Section 382 is an attempt to limit loss trafficking and the application of the section is triggered when the ownership of the corporation has changed hands. The section contains many complicated rules which we will study in Chapter 13. But for now, keep in mind that if you have a corporation that is a "loss corporation" (generally a corporation that has a loss carryover) and it undergoes a recapitalization, it may be ripe for application of section 382.

---

46. *See* Treas. Reg. § 1.368-2(e)(1).
47. *See* Treas. Reg. § 1.368-2(e)(2).
48. *See* Treas. Reg. § 1.368-2(e)(3)–(5).

Section 10.05(f)(1) Boot Concerns

The regulations hint at the first concern by providing that if, in the exchange, certain shareholders received an increase in their proportionate interest in the assets or the E&P of the corporation, such shareholders may be taxed as receiving a dividend under section 301. Section 1.368-2(e) of the regulations does not completely address this concern and does not provide detailed examples of what the IRS would consider situations that should be taxed. What should concern you? In counseling your client, always keep the purpose of the reorganization provisions in mind. Section 1.368-1(b) provides that the "purpose of the reorganization provisions ... is to except from the general rule certain specifically described exchanges incident to such readjustments of corporate structures made in one of the particular ways specified in the Code, as are required by business exigencies and which effect only a readjustment of continuing interest in property under modified corporate forms." What is the general rule that the regulations are concerned with? The first sentence of the regulations provides the general rule that gain or loss must be accounted for if the new property differs materially from the property exchanged. Hence, as tax counsel, this is what you should look for—similar type property must be exchanged, for example, stock and securities for stock and securities, debt for the same quality debt. Any material change in the exchange should raise a red flag that this may potentially be considered a taxable exchange.

Section 10.05(f)(2) COI and COBE in Recapitalizations

What about the judicially created requirements of COI and COBE? Do they apply in an E recap? It appears that they would not be applicable under the language of the regulations because of the emphasis of the regulations on target corporation and acquiring corporation. Since E recaps involve a single entity, there is no target or acquiring corporation or, in other words, the same corporation is both the target and acquiring corporation. Due to this language, it would be hard for the IRS to argue that a change in the ownership structure of a corporation would fail E recap status because the continuity rules were not met. Nonetheless, the IRS made such arguments in several court cases.[49] The courts have ruled against the IRS and have held that the con-

---

49. *See, e.g., Commissioner v. Neustadt's Trust*, 131 F.2d 528 (2d Cir. 1942), *aff'g* 43 B.T.A. 848 (1941), *nonacq.*, 1941-1 C.B. 17, *nonacq. withdrawn, acq.*, 1951-1 C.B. 2.

tinuity of interest principle need not apply to recapitalizations under section 368(a)(1)(E) of the Code. This is because the considerations that make the continuity of interest requirement necessary in acquisitive reorganizations are not present in recapitalizations involving a single corporation.[50] The IRS agreed with the court decisions and held in Rev. Rul. 2003-48[51] that the COI requirement is not applicable to E recaps because the concern present in acquisitive reorganizations is not applicable to recapitalizations involving a single corporation. The IRS also relented with regard to the continuity of business enterprise. In Rev. Rul. 82-34,[52] it announced that continuity of business enterprise does not apply to E recaps.

The above rulings have recently been subsumed in final regulations which provide that the requirements of continuity of interest and continuity of business enterprise are not applicable to both the E and F reorganizations. The final regulations are applicable for transactions occurring on or after February 25, 2005. For transactions that occurred prior to that date, taxpayers may be able to rely on IRS revenue rulings that have been obsoleted by the final regulations.[53] Notwithstanding the regulations, you should keep in mind that the step transaction doctrine and other form over substance doctrines continue to apply to the E reorganization (but not the F). Consequently, a transaction that appears to qualify for E reorganization status may be disqualified as an E if it is part of a larger transaction.

Finally, note that the business purpose requirement continues to apply to the E recap. In the reorganization arena, this requirement is not used extensively to attack transactions. The good tax lawyer, however, will be mindful of this requirement. As we will examine later, there are certain paper requirements that taxpayers have to comply with under section 1.368-3. A description of the business purpose of the transaction in addition to any supporting paperwork (corporate minutes, statements of consultants etc.) normally suffices.

---

50. *See Hickok v. Commissioner*, 32 T.C. 80 (1959), *nonacq.*, 1959-2 C.B. 8, *nonacq. withdrawn*, 1977-2 C.B. 3; *Schoo v. Commissioner*, 47 B.T.A. 459 (1942), *nonacq.*, 1942-2 C.B. 31, *nonacq. withdrawn*, 1977-2 C.B. 3; *Berner v. United States*, 282 F.2d 720 (Ct. Cl. 1960); *Penfield v. Davis*, 105 F. Supp. 292 (N.D. Ala. 1952), *aff'd*, 205 F.2d 798 (5th Cir. 1953). The IRS eventually published Rev. Rul. 77-415, 1977-2 C.B. 311, and Rev. Rul. 2003-48, 2003-19 I.R.B. 863 (holding that the COI requirement does not apply to E recaps).

51. 2003-19 I.R.B. 863.

52. 1982-1 C.B. 59.

53. *See* Rev. Rul. 69-516, 1969-2 C.B. 56; Rev. Rul. 77-415, 1977-2 C.B. 311; Rev. Rul. 77-479, 1977-2 C.B. 119; Rev. Rul. 82-34, 1982-1 C.B. 59.

Section 10.05(g) Technical Requirements of the F Reorganization

Section 368(a)(1)(F) states that a mere change in identity, form, or place of organization of one corporation, however effected, is a reorganization. It is no accident that Congress uses the word "mere" to modify the type of change in identity or form, or place of organization that would qualify as an F reorganization. If a transaction involves more than a "mere" change, it will not qualify under section 368(a)(1)(F). Keep in mind, however, that, if the transaction does not qualify as a F reorganization, it may qualify as another type of reorganization.

Most F reorganizations are effected by the merger of one corporation into a newly-created shell corporation. For example, the reincorporation of an Indiana corporation in Delaware will generally be done by creating a Delaware corporation and then merging the Indiana corporation into the Delaware corporation. This transaction will not qualify as an A reorganization but will qualify as an F reorganization. What about the one corporation language in the F reorganization statute you might say? By one corporation, Congress really means one operating corporation. Hence, the merger of an operating corporation into a shell corporation qualifies as an F reorganization.[54]

Section 10.05(g)(1) Change of Tax Status

What if a corporation changes its tax status from taxable to tax-exempt? Would this be considered a mere change of form and thus able to qualify under section 368(a)(1)(F)? The answer is not clear. Such a transaction may, arguably, qualify under the definition of a F reorganization but would be hard pressed to meet the continuity of interest requirement since the former proprietors of the transferor corporation would probably lose all of their proprietary interest in the former corporation (especially if the tax-exempt organization receives its exemption under section 501(c)(3) of the Code). If somehow the transaction qualifies as a F reorganization, this would afford protection only to the shareholders of the transferor corporation. The transferor corporation would not receive protection under section 361 because application of the section would be overridden by section 1.337(d)-4 of the regulations. Under the regulations, a change in a corporation's status from taxable to tax-exempt status will be treated as a sale of the corporation's assets im-

---

54. *See* H.R. Rep. No. 97-760, 97th Cong., 2d Sess. 540–41 (1982).

mediately prior to the status change. Hence, gain or loss will be recognized in the exchange. The regulations were promulgated as part of the IRS' implementation of the repeal of the *General Utilities* doctrine. The rationale for this sale treatment is that this would be the last chance the government would have to impose taxation on the corporation.

Section 10.05(g)(2) Identification of Shareholders

Continuing our analysis of the "mere" change requirement of the F reorganization, the identity of the shareholders of the transferor corporation must be identical following such a reorganization. Why identical? Because the transaction must be a mere change of form, identity or place of incorporation. If the transaction results in a readjustment of the ownership of the corporation, then this would not be considered a mere change. Hence, even if the continuity of interest requirement is met, this will not suffice—all the prior shareholders of the transferor corporation must remain shareholders of the transferee corporation following the F reorganization. For PLR purposes, the IRS would allow a 1 percent change. Any change in ownership that exceeds 1 percent will cause problems. The only respite to this "identical shareholders" requirement is that the IRS has taken the view that for purposes of determining whether the ownership structure of the corporation has changed, an F reorganization is viewed separately even though it may be part of a larger transaction. Hence, the IRS will not apply the step transaction doctrine to a part of a transaction that is an F reorganization.

Why is the IRS so lenient? The IRS is lenient because in the 1980's it used the F reorganization to fight liquidation/reincorporation transactions that it considered abusive. The liquidation/reincorporation transaction was very popular prior to the repeal of the *General Utilities* doctrine since liquidations were not taxable. The liquidation/reincorporation scheme was a serious assault on the corporate income tax, as it permitted taxpayers to step up their basis in corporate assets without being subject to tax. To combat this scheme, the IRS treated certain liquidations/reincorporations as F reorganizations. Hence, no basis step up was permitted. What if the taxpayer argued that the F reorganization was a step in a larger transaction and that it should be integrated, hence destroying the F reorganization? The IRS would say that the F reorganization was viewed separately because of the uniqueness of the F reorganization and hence should not be included with the other steps of the transaction.[55] The IRS would normally win this no stepping argument because the

---

55. *See* Rev. Rul. 96-29, 1996-1 C.B. 50; Rev. Rul. 2003-48, 2003-19 I.R.B. 863.

step transaction doctrine cannot be used by taxpayers. Taxpayers are normally stuck with the form of their transaction.[56] This makes sense because permitting taxpayers to disavow the form that they chose for their transactions would be ceding too much control to taxpayers. Once the IRS took this position, it was hard to change it even after the repeal of *General Utilities* took hold and the F reorganization argument was no longer needed in this context.

Section 10.05(g)(3) Benefits of the F Reorganization

So what's the big deal about the F reorganization? The big deal is that since it is a mere change of one corporation, numerous limitations that are applicable to other types of reorganizations are not applicable to it. For example section 1.381(b)-1(a)(2) of the regulations provides that if a reorganization qualifies as an F reorganization, the acquiring corporation shall be treated (for purposes of section 381) just as the transferor corporation would have been treated if there had been no reorganization. Additionally, the section 382 limitations on losses would generally not apply to a corporation that underwent an F reorganization because, again, the corporation would be treated as remaining in existence. There are also other benefits, such as the taxable year of the corporation would not be closed by the F reorganization. This will save the corporation some money as it will not have to file a return for a short year.

A set of proposed regulations has recently been promulgated to address the F reorganization.[57] The regulations, not surprisingly, look like guidance that has been on the market for a while. There is a strict identity of shareholder requirement. The transferee corporation must not have any tax items before the transaction. These requirements are to ensure compliance with the one operating corporation principle. The transferor corporation must also completely liquidate. We expect these regulations to move smoothly through the process of becoming final and binding regulations because they are not controversial.

Section 10.05(h) G Reorganizations

G reorganizations, which apply to transfers in a title 11 or similar action, use the rules applied to D reorganizations. Corporations involved in bankruptcy often reorganize rather than liquidate. Taxing these reorganizations would be contrary to the goals of bankruptcy law. Thus, if a corporation undergoing bankruptcy transfers substantially all its assets in a transaction that,

---

56. For an example of a rare exception, see the Butterfly example in Chapter 3.

57. See Prop. Treas. Reg. § 1.368-2(m), 69 Fed. Reg. 49836 (2004).

but for the bankruptcy proceedings, would qualify as a D reorganization, it meets the requirements of section 368(a)(1)(G).

There are no regulations and relatively little other authority addressing G reorganizations. That is not a problem if you are familiar with the D reorganization rules. There are two additional rules to keep in mind. First, a G reorganization must be approved by the bankruptcy court.[58] Second, if a transaction qualifies as both a G reorganization and another type of reorganization, it will be taxed under the rules for G reorganizations.

Section 10.05(i) Drop Downs of Assets and Push Ups

The title of this part of the chapter is what corporate tax lawyers commonly use to refer to section 368(a)(2)(C). The section provides that in A, B, C, and some G reorganizations, the transaction shall not be disqualified by reason of the fact that part or all the assets or stock which were acquired in the transaction are transferred to a corporation controlled by the corporation acquiring such assets or stock. This section was enacted to repeal the remote continuity doctrine of *Helvering v. Bashford*.[59] Under the doctrine, transfers of assets following a reorganization were disqualified from reorganization treatment if the continuity requirements were not met. Additionally, under the step transaction doctrine, the subsidiary receiving the assets of the target corporation was treated as the purchaser of the target corporation. Section 368(a)(2)(C) only permits transfers to controlled corporations. A controlled corporation is generally a corporation that is owned 80 percent or more by another corporation. It makes sense that Congress would allow a drop down of assets after it expanded the definition of merger to permit triangular mergers. In fact, a drop down of assets after a merger looks very much like a triangular reorganization.

In a relatively recent revenue ruling, Rev. Rul. 2002-85,[60] the drop down rules have been extended to D reorganizations. The rationale for the extension was that section 368(a)(2)(C) was permissive and not exclusive or restrictive. Rev. Rul. 2001-24[61] held that section 368(a)(2)(C)'s drop down rule would also cover a transfer of stock of the subsidiary corporation that acquired the assets of a target corporation in a merger. It may be argued that the IRS and Treasury do not have the authority to extend statutory language to cover situations the statute was not intended to cover. Nevertheless, this is exactly

---

58. I.R.C. § 368(a)(3)(B).
59. 302 U.S. 454 (1938).
60. 2002-2 C.B. 986.
61. 2001-1 C.B. 1290.

what they have done in the revenue rulings cited above. The IRS generally argued that section 368(a)(2)(C) was permissive, not restrictive, hence permitting it to extend the rule to situations not enunciated in the statute.[62] It is very unlikely that these revenue rulings will be challenged because they are taxpayer favorable. A better argument may be that the reorganization statute is very formalistic and must be closely adhered to. In the case of the above revenue rulings, the IRS chose to read the statute broadly. The problem with this type of analysis is that the IRS leaves itself open to attacks if a taxpayer does not like the results of the revenue rulings discussed above.

This gets us to our next point about statutory reading: While the language of the Code is sometimes succinct, everything must come from the tax code. This means that any regulations, revenue rulings and other documents that purport to interpret the tax Code must not do violence to the language of the statute. Permitting a drop down following a D reorganization makes sense but is contrary to the formalistic nature of section 368. After all, a transaction that is "essentially" a merger will not qualify as a merger. It must meet all the requirements of the merger statute, section 368(a)(1)(A).

Section 10.05(i)(1) Push Ups of Assets

What about push ups of assets following a reorganization? There are no Code sections permitting a push up of assets. Tax lawyers have been trying for years to analogize push ups to drop downs. That is, if assets acquired at one level of a group of corporations are permitted to be pushed down to a lower level, as we have seen above, why not permit assets or stock acquired at a lower level to be sent up the organization chain?

Again, the same argument made above should apply to prevent analogizing a push up to a drop down and automatically grant tax-free treatment to the push up of assets. It is true that in some instances, the push up would not cause the transaction to be disqualified—for example, in a situation where the step transaction doctrine does not apply to collapse the push up with the prior reorganization. Clearly, in such a case you will have two separate transactions and they will be judged on their own merits. In a situation where the step transaction applies, it appears that a push up should not be permitted because it has to be assumed that Congress had either considered a push up and affirmatively decided against or had failed to consider it. It remains to be seen whether the IRS and Treasury will take on this legislative duty and permit push up of assets.

---

62. Id.

Section 10.06 Reorganizations Involving Investment Companies

Before we consider the tax consequences of a reorganization, we will take a brief detour and list some transactions that are specifically taken out of reorganization status even though they may be able to meet the statutory reorganization definitions. We took similar detours in Chapter 9 when we looked at sections 355(d) and 355(e), the exceptions to the general rule of section 355(a). We will now be looking at section 368(a)(2)(F), which provides that reorganizations involving investment companies will generally be denied reorganization treatment. The exceptions to this general rule are reorganizations involving RICS, REITS or corporations that meet the specific requirements of section 368(a)(2)(F)(ii).

Section 368(a)(2)(F) is a very interesting Code section to study and you should make note of it because it is a trap for the unwary. The purpose of section 368(a)(2)(F) is to prevent taxpayers from using the reorganization provisions to diversify their investment interests. The interesting part of section 368(a)(2)(F) is that it intersects with section 351 and section 721 (involving partnerships). You may recall that section 351 provides that no gain or loss will be recognized on the transfer of property to a corporation if the transferor or transferors have control of the corporation. An exception to the nonrecognition rule of section 351 is a transfer to an investment company under section 351(e). Section 721 applies similar rules regarding transfers to a partnership if the partnership would have been treated as an investment company had it been incorporated. Section 368(a)(2)(F) appears to be the reverse of section 351(e) but both sections were enacted to combat the same problem: tax-free diversifications of a taxpayer's investment portfolios.

The idea behind both sections is that taxpayers should recognize gain if they enter into transactions to diversify their portfolios. Section 351 takes a positive approach by providing in subsection (e) that any transfer to an investment company will be taxable. The regulations under section 351 provide that a transfer of property will be treated as a transfer to an investment company if (i) the transfer results in diversification of the transferor's interests and (ii) the transfer is to a RIC, a REIT or a corporation more than 80 percent of the value of whose assets are held for investment and are readily marketable. Section 368(a)(2)(F) takes a negative approach by providing that a merger between two or more investment companies will not qualify as a reorganization as to any of the investment companies unless it was a RIC, a REIT or a corporation which meets the diversification requirements of section 368(a)(2)(F)(ii).[63] Hence, section 368(a)(2)(F) permits corporations that are already well diversified to engage in a reorganization. If a corporation does not meet the requirements of section 368(a)(2)(F)(ii) and is an investment company, a reorganization involving this corporation will be taxable to the corporation and its shareholders. Note that the rule of section 368(a)(2)(F) does not apply to E reorganizations. The section is silent with regard to F reorganizations. This may be because the drafters of the legislation did not feel the need to address application of the F reorganization in section 368(a)(2)(F) since by definition the F reorganization involves only one corporation and, thus, is specifically excluded from the investment reorganization rule.

Section 368(a)(2)(F) provides detailed rules for the status of diversified corporation. The determination of RIC status is made under section 851 and the determination of REIT status is made under section 856. Section 368(a)(2)(F) also provides that its restrictions do not apply in a reorganization if the stock of the investment companies is substantially owned by the same persons in the same proportions.[64] This rule applies to investment companies that do not meet the diversification requirements outlined in the section. The rationale for this rule is that diversification is not achieved if the shareholders of two or more investment companies combine the two corporations because the investment interests of the owners remain the same. Hence, a reorganization involving these investment corporations would qualify for tax-free treatment.

Example: Corporations X and Y are investment companies; each is owned equally by the same four shareholders. More than 25 percent of the value of each corporation is invested in two publicly traded corporations that operate in the same industry. Corporations X and Y do not meet the section 368(a)(2)(F) diversification requirements. To save administrative expenses, X is merged into Y. The merger is not disqualified as a reorganization. Each investment company is owned substantially by the same persons. Diversification is not achieved in the transaction because shareholders' investment interests remain the same following the transaction.

Finally, section 368(a)(2)(F)(vi) provides that if an investment company which does not meet the special diversification requirements for investment companies acquires the assets or the stock of another corporation in a potential reorganization, the reorganization will be treated under section 1001 as a

---

63. Generally, this means that no more than 25 percent of the value of the total assets of the corporation is invested in the stock or securities of any one issuer and not more than 50 percent of the total assets of the corporation are invested in the stock of five or fewer issuers.

64. *See* I.R.C. § 368(a)(2)(F)(v).

sale or exchange of the stock or assets of the investment company. The investment company and its shareholders will recognize gain or loss on this deemed sale. Section 368(a)(2)(F)(vi) proves how serious Congress was in preventing diversification transactions from achieving tax-free status. The section is a recognition that diversification can be achieved by an acquisition of the investment company. The results may be harsh as they provide for sale or exchange treatment of all the assets or stock of the investment company no matter how small the acquisition in the potential reorganization. A better rule would have been to treat up to the value of the corporation acquired as sold or exchanged.

Section 368(a)(2)(F) is a trap for the unwary. Be careful of its application, especially if you are dealing with owners of non-operating companies.

Section 10.07 Tax Consequences to Shareholders

Section 10.07(a) In General

Before you can enjoy the benefits of a reorganization, your transaction must meet the definition of a reorganization and must meet the other requirements imposed by the Code and regulations. This is one area of the tax laws where form matters a great deal. Congress painstakingly defined a number of transactions that will qualify as reorganizations. If a transaction does not meet the definition contained in section 368(a)(1), it simply will not qualify as a reorganization. It will not be helpful to argue that the transaction is essentially a reorganization. You will have to look to another Code section for relief.

Section 10.07(b) Party to a Reorganization

The next part of the analysis toward tax-free nirvana is determining whether the reorganization involves a party to a reorganization. It should come as no surprise that tax-free consequences in a reorganization are tied with being a party to a reorganization. The major nonrecognition provisions, section 354 and section 361, grant nonrecognition treatment only if the stock, securities or property received in the exchange are received from a party to the reorganization.

So who can be a party to a reorganization? Obviously, the corporation or corporations engaged in a reorganization will qualify to be parties to the reorganization. Section 1.368-2(f) of the regulations provides the details regarding the definition of party to a reorganization. Because the regulations under section 1.368-2(f) are not very expansive, we replicate them here instead of paraphrasing them:

The term *a party to a reorganization* includes a corporation resulting from a reorganization, and both corporations, in a transaction qualifying as a reorganization where one corporation acquires stock or properties of another corporation. If a transaction otherwise qualifies as a reorganization, a corporation remains a party to the reorganization even though stock or assets acquired in the reorganization are transferred in a transaction described in paragraph (k) of this section. If a transaction otherwise qualifies as a reorganization, a corporation shall not cease to be a party to the reorganization solely by reason of the fact that part or all of the assets acquired in the reorganization are transferred to a partnership in which the transferor is a partner if the continuity of business enterprise requirement is satisfied. See § 1.368-1(d). The preceding three sentences apply to transactions occurring after January 28, 1998, except that they do not apply to any transaction occurring pursuant to a written agreement which is binding on January 28, 1998, and at all times thereafter. A corporation controlling an acquiring corporation is a party to the reorganization when the stock of such controlling corporation is used in the acquisition of properties. Both corporations are parties to the reorganization if, under statutory authority, Corporation A is merged into Corporation B. All three of the corporations are parties to the reorganization if, pursuant to statutory authority, Corporation C and Corporation D are consolidated into Corporation E. Both corporations are parties to the reorganization if Corporation F transfers substantially all its assets to Corporation G in exchange for all or a part of the voting stock of Corporation G. All three corporations are parties to the reorganization if Corporation H transfers substantially all its assets to Corporation K in exchange for all or a part of the voting stock of Corporation L, which is in control of Corporation K. Both corporations are parties to the reorganization if Corporation M transfers all or part of its assets to Corporation N in exchange for all or a part of the stock and securities of Corporation N, but only if (1) immediately after such transfer, Corporation M, or one or more of its shareholders (including persons who were shareholders immediately before such transfer), or any combination thereof, is in control of Corporation N, and (2) in pursuance of the plan, the stock and securities of Corporation N are transferred or distributed by Corporation M in a transaction in which gain or loss is not recognized under section 354 or 355, or is recognized only to the extent provided in section 356. Both Corporation O and Corporation P, but not Corporation S, are parties to the reorganization if Corporation O acquires stock of Corporation P from Corporation S in exchange solely for a part of the voting stock of Corporation O, if (1) the stock of Corporation P does not constitute substantially all of the assets of Corporation S, (2) Corporation S is not in control of Corporation O immediately after the acquisition, and (3) Corporation O is in control of Corporation P immediately after the acquisition.

Now that we know which corporations are parties to a reorganization, it is easier to determine the tax consequences of the reorganization. Following any tax transaction, the tax lawyer must determine the tax consequences of the transaction. In other words, who should be taxed in the transaction? Notwithstanding its complexities, the purpose of the Code is to raise revenues. Hence, the operative Code sections center around whether a transaction is taxable or not. The operative provisions of the reorganization sections are no different. In determining the tax consequences of a transaction, the tax lawyer is concerned about three issues: (1) gain or loss, (2) basis consequences, and (3) holding period. The first issue is the most important as it determines what is owed the IRS. Basis determination is also important but since the basis of property plays a central role only on the later sale or disposition of property, the importance of basis determination is delayed to a later date. In fact, in many occasions taxpayers do not have a good grasp of the basis of stock or assets received in a transaction. Fortunately, the IRS normally takes a sensitive stand and if a taxpayer shows that it has made a reasonable effort in ascertaining basis, the taxpayer's computation may be accepted. It may come as a shock to some that a taxpayer would not know its basis but such is the state of affairs sometimes. We will discuss basis shortly.

Section 10.07(c) Gain or Loss to Acquiring Shareholders

The acquiring corporation's shareholders are normally silent partners in a reorganization (except that they may vote on the reorganization depending on state law and the by-laws of the corporation). Hence, they generally have no tax consequences in the transaction. In some situations, an acquiring corporation's shareholder may redeem some of his shares prior to the reorganization so that the acquiring corporation will have enough shares to distribute to target corporation shareholders because some corporations have a limit on the number of shares that they can issue.

Section 10.07(d) Gain or Loss to Target Shareholders

The typical target corporation shareholder (especially a shareholder of a publicly held and widely traded corporation) normally hears about the merger of her corporation in the news. Next, the shareholder receives papers in the mail asking for her proxy. She promptly discards the proxy or signs it. After that, the shareholder receives a letter from her broker informing her that she now is the proud owner of 100 shares of XYZ corporation. Now does this sound as if our shareholder has made any money on the transaction? The answer is: it depends. If the attorneys involved in the merger are careful enough and the transaction qualifies as a reorganization, then the shareholders would generally recognize no gain or loss under section 354 on the receipt of stock and securities.

Is that all there is to section 354? Is that all there is to gain or loss recognition by Target shareholders? Hardly! Let's take a quick look at section 354. It provides a general rule in section 354(a) that no gain or loss will be recognized if stock or securities in a corporation a party to a reorganization are exchanged solely for stock or securities in another corporation also a party to a reorganization. What does this mean really? Are the target shareholders protected only to the extent that they exchange stock for stock or securities for securities? What if there is an exchange of stock for securities? For the answers, let's go to the regulations.

The regulations under section 354 are not voluminous but they provide some examples that clarify the issues. In example (1) of the regulations, the IRS provides that an exchange of common stock in the target corporation for common stock in the acquiring corporation will not be taxable. In example (2) the exchange of stock for stock and securities is held not to fall under section 354 but to fall under section 356. This sounds harsh at first, but looking at section 356 this means that the receipt of securities will be taxable. The receipt of stock will not be taxable.

Example: Corporation X merges into Corporation Y. A, a shareholder in X, receives stock of Y with a FMV of $60 and securities in Y with a FMV of $20 in exchange for his X stock worth $80 in which A had a basis of $60. Does A recognize any gain in the transaction? If so, how much gain does A recognize?

Pursuant to section 1.354-1 of the regulations, the transaction does not fall under section 354 but falls under section 356. Under section 356, the stock for stock exchange is protected from gain recognition. The receipt of securities, however, is taxable. Hence, A recognizes $20 of gain in the transaction.

This takes care of section 354(a)(1). Continuing our quest, let's move on to section 354(a)(2), which sets some limits on the exchange of securities. Target shareholders must receive the same principal amount of securities that they exchange in the transaction. If they receive more securities than they have exchanged, then the excess amount of securities received will be taxed under section 356 as boot. Section 356 would also apply if securities are received in the transaction and no securities are exchanged.

So far, we have essentially seen that to determine whether gain or loss is received in a reorganization, a taxpayer must compare property that she has given up to property that she has received. Generally, there must be a match in order for the exchange to be tax-free. If there is a mismatch, there is a likelihood that gain will have to be recognized in the transaction. We have also seen that receipt of stock in a reorganization is normally a good thing because it is generally not taxable. Section 354(a)(2)(B), however, provides an exception to this general rule for property received for interest accrued on securities. For purposes of this section, property means any type of property including stock or securities.

Example: Corporation X merges into Corporation Y. A, a shareholder of X, receives $60 worth of Corporation Y common stock in exchange for his Corporation X stock valued at $30 at the time of the exchange and in which A had a $60 basis, securities in X which A held valued at $25 at the time of the exchange and $5 in accrued interest on the securities. Does A recognize a gain in the transaction?

Even though A receives only common stock in the exchange, A recognizes income of $5 in the exchange. This is because A received the common stock as payment for accrued interest. The reason for the payment does not change because it was made in conjunction with the reorganization.

Section 10.07(d)(1) Nonqualified Preferred Stock

Next, section 354(a)(2)(C) provides that nonqualified preferred stock shall be treated as other property received in the transaction. This means that whenever that type of stock is received, it should be taxable—except where it is received in exchange for nonqualified preferred stock.[65] This fits in nicely with our matching principle discussed above. The section uses the same definition for nonqualified preferred stock as section 351 uses. Nonqualified preferred stock generally means preferred stock that is readily redeemable. The section provides a special exception in the case of an E recapitalization involving a family-owned corporation as defined therein.[66] This is in recognition that family businesses are often conducted based on special family connections and are not always at arms' length. The section also provides a somewhat extended statute of limitations in case the business no longer qualifies as a family-owned business.

Next, we look at section 354(b) which, at first, appears to be misplaced because it requires that a D or a G reorganization meet the sub all requirement.

---

65. You may recall that in the section 351 context, the receipt of nonqualified preferred stock is taxable even if it is received in exchange for nonqualified preferred stock.

66. *See* I.R.C. §354(a)(2)(C)(ii).

One would think that this requirement should have been included in section 368(a)(1)(D) or (G). Including this requirement in section 354(b), however, is appropriate because failing to meet sub all directly affects the exchange made by the target corporation shareholders. A typical merger (or reorganization, for that matter) involves the transfer of assets by a target corporation to the acquiring corporation followed by the transfer of stock of the acquiring corporation to the target corporation. The target corporation then transfers the acquiring stock received in the transaction to its shareholders in liquidation.

Section 10.07(d)(2) Transaction Involving Railroads

The last rule in section 354 is section 354(c) which provides a special exception for certain reorganizations involving railroads. The section provides that the reorganization provisions will apply to railroads "confirmed under section 1173 of title 11 of the United States Code, as being in the public interest." Section 354(c), as you might suspect, is rarely used. For our purposes, it will suffice to engrave somewhere in our memory that stock or securities received in a reorganization involving railroad companies are subject to a special rule under section 354.

Section 10.07(d)(3) Warrants

Finally, we note that the nonrecognition rules of section 354, in addition to applying to stock or securities, also apply to warrants. Warrants are simply options or rights to acquire stock or securities. Although the language of section 354 only mentions stock or securities, the regulations under section 354 and 356 have extended the scope of the section to cover receipt of warrants.[67] Prior to the promulgation of these regulations, issuance of warrants in a reorganization was treated as issuance of other property.

Section 10.07(e) Treatment of Boot

Once we have determined that a target corporation shareholder has received boot in the transaction, we know that this boot is taxable as gain in the exchange if there is gain. But we also know that gain may be taxable as capital or ordinary. As you may know, there is a continuing battle to give preference to capital gains. Sometimes the preference given capital gain is

---

67. *See* Treas. Reg. § 1.354-1(e).

significant. Because tax rates depend on whether gain is capital or not, it is important to determine the treatment of boot received in a reorganization. This is where section 356 comes into play.

First, you must determine the amount of gain that must be recognized in the transaction. Under section 1001, gain is the excess of the amount realized over the basis of property sold or exchanged. You must keep in mind that section 356 is concerned with other property received in a reorganization. Hence gain realized on the receipt of stock, which is not considered other property, will not be subject to section 356 and will not be taxable under section 354. Section 356(a)(1) provides that if money or other property is received, then gain to the recipient shall be recognized in an amount not in excess of the sum of such money and the fair market value of such property. What does this mean? Regulation section 1.356-1(c) illustrates this rule through an example which is partly reproduced below:

Example: A receives the following in exchange for a share of stock of Target in which A had a basis of $85:

One share of stock worth	$100
Cash	$25
Other property (FMV)	$50
Total Received	$175
Adjusted basis of Target stock	$85
Total realized gain	$90

How much gain is recognized?

In this example, the amount of gain to be recognized under section 356 is limited to the amount of cash and the FMV of the property received—$75.

The next question to be determined is whether this recognized gain is treated as capital gain or as a dividend. The answer depends on section 356(b). This section provides that an exchange that has the effect of a dividend (determined with the application of section 318(a)) will be treated as a dividend to the extent of the recipient's ratable share of the undistributed E&P of the corporation. Which corporation? The target corporation or the acquiring corporation? The acquiring corporation, because the target corporation may go out of existence. Additionally, the property received in the exchange is received from the acquiring corporation. Hence, in the above example, if A's ratable share of the E&P of the acquiring corporation is $30. A would be treated as receiving a dividend in the amount of $30 and a capital gain of $45.

If the amount of stock and property received by A amounted to $65, would A be able to recognize loss in the transaction? Section 356(c) provides that no loss will be recognized in section 356.

Section 10.07(f) Basis Consequences to Target Shareholders

The second issue that target corporation shareholders are concerned with (or should be concerned with) is the basis of property received in the reorganization. Basis issues are sometimes hard to deal with because taxpayers may not concern themselves with basis calculation at the time of a reorganization. It does not impact the current, more pressing, issue of gain or loss. Nevertheless, it is a mistake not to accurately determine your basis because such lack of basis determination may cause the IRS to impose a zero basis on a taxpayer's assets.[68] Additionally, the basis rules, as we saw above in the case of triangular mergers, can be quite interesting.

If the purpose of the reorganization provision is to "except from the general rule certain specifically described exchanges incident to such readjustments of corporate structures ... which effect only a readjustment of continuing interest in property under modified corporate forms," the basis of a taxpayer following a reorganization should be the same as the basis of property held prior to the reorganization. Section 358, in general, provides this result. Hence, the basis of property received in a reorganization will generally be the same basis as the property exchanged therefor.

Example: A has a basis of $30 in Target stock. Target merges into Acquiring with Acquiring surviving. A receives Acquiring stock worth $100. What is A's basis for the Acquiring stock?

Under section 358 and the regulations thereunder, A's basis in the Acquiring stock is $30. This is the answer that we anticipated and it makes sense because a reorganization should not cause a change in A's basis.

As we all know, life is never that simple. Often, shareholders receive more than Acquiring stock in exchange for their Target stock. Sometimes, shareholders receive cash or other property. Sometimes, debt is assumed in the reorganization. Sometimes, loss is realized in the transaction. How do you deal with all these contingencies?

At this point, as we tell our students, there are two ways to deal with the complexities of section 358 or any Code section for that matter. One way is to simply look at the Code section and meticulously decipher its meaning. A better way is to understand the economic rationale behind its language and then meticulously decipher its meaning. The regulations under section 358 provide examples that illustrate the workings of section 358.

---

68. *See, e.g.*, Rev. Proc. 81-70, 1981-2 C.B. 729.

Section 10.07(f)(1) Rationale of Section 358

Let's look at the rationale behind section 358. First, we start with section 1012, which states that the basis of property is its cost. If I purchase an item for $5, my basis in the item is $5. Similarly, if I receive a $5 item as compensation for services rendered, my basis in the item is also $5 because this would be deemed my cost in the item. The next concept we need to look at is the concept of gain/loss realization and recognition contained in section 1001. The section provides that gain/loss realized in a sale or other disposition of property is the difference between the amount realized and the basis of the property. Hence, if I sell an item for $10 and my basis in the item is $5, I realize a gain of $5. Implied in this gain concept is the notion that the first $5 received in the sale decreases my basis in the property to $0. Any excess amount received after basis is reduced to zero becomes the gain realized. Similarly, if I realize a loss in the sale or disposition, my basis in the property is reduced to zero due to the loss realized. Who cares about basis in property that is sold or disposed of, you might say? Since you disposed of the property, is not your basis necessarily zero? This is correct, BUT the purpose of the examples is to illustrate what really happens and why you have a zero basis. In a situation where you exchange property, as in a reorganization, it becomes crucial to know your basis increases and decreases.

How do we encounter these two concepts in section 358? Section 358(a)(1)(A) provides that basis of property received in a reorganization is the same basis as the property exchanged, decreased by the FMV of property or the amount of cash received in the transaction and the amount of loss recognized by the taxpayer. This decrease of basis serves two purposes. First, the property received must have a basis in the hands of the recipient. The decrease in the basis of the property exchanged becomes the basis of the property received. Second, the decrease in basis mirrors what happens under section 1001 in a sale or disposition of property. Section 358(a)(1)(B) then provides that the basis of property received in the exchange is increased by the amount of gain recognized and any amount that is treated as dividend. This section reflects the notion under section 1012 that the basis of property shall be its cost.

Example: In a merger of Corporation X into Corporation Y, A, a shareholder of X, receives stock valued at $80 and property valued at $20. A's basis in the X stock exchanged was $100 and the FMV of the X stock was the same, so A realizes no gain or loss. What is the basis of the stock and property received by A?

The basis of the stock and property received is the same as that of the X stock exchanged—$100. Under section 358(a)(1)(A), the basis of the property permitted to be received without gain (i.e., the Y Corporation stock) is $80—the original basis of the property exchanged $100 decreased by $20 (the FMV of other property permitted to be received). Under section 358(a)(2), the basis of the other property received will be $20, its FMV.

What if gain was recognized in the transaction or what if part of the gain was deemed to be a dividend? Would the answer above change? Yes, the answer would change. Under section 358(a)(1)(B), the basis of the Y stock would be increased by the amount of the gain or dividend recognized in the transaction.

Example: Same facts as the above example except that the basis of the X stock held by A was $80. What is the basis of the stock and property received by A?

Under section 358(a), the basis of the Y stock is $80—the original basis of the X stock ($80) decreased by the amount of other property received in the transaction ($20) and increased by the amount of gain recognized in the transaction ($20). The basis of the other property received in the transaction is its FMV—$20.

Section 358 contains some other interesting rules. For example, section 358(b)(1) provides that the basis determined under section 358(a) shall be allocated among the properties permitted to be received. Regulations implementing section 358(a)(1) generally provide that the basis determined under section 358(a) shall be allocated among the properties received based on the FMV of the property received. The regulations provide some examples that illustrate the allocation rules. The examples in this part of the regulations do a very good job of illustrating the workings of the Code section. Example (1) of the regulations is reproduced below:

Example 1: A, an individual, owns stock in Corporation X with an adjusted basis of $1,000. In a transaction qualifying under section 356 (so far as it relates to section 354), he exchanged this stock for 20 shares of stock of Corporation Y worth $1,200 and securities of Corporation Y worth $400. A realizes a gain of $600 of which $400 is recognized. The adjusted basis in A's hands of each share of the stock of Corporation Y is $50 determined by allocating the basis of the stock of Corporation X ratably to the stock of Corporation Y received in the exchange. The securities of Corporation Y have a basis in the hands of A of $400.

Continuing our study of section 358, we note that section 358(b) contains special rules for the allocation of basis in a section 355 transaction. While at the IRS, Professor Mombrun rewrote some of these rules to address certain gaps left in the regulations. His work culminated in proposed regulations sections 1.358-1(a), (c) and -2.[69] The proposed regulations address situations

---

69. *See* Prop. Treas. Reg. § 1.358-1.

where a target shareholder exchanges stock or securities that have the same FMV but different bases in exchange for stock or securities with the same FMV. Generally, the proposed regulations permit taxpayers to use the tracing method to the extent they can. This means that a taxpayer can claim that a specific share of acquiring stock was received for an identified share of stock of target stock. Hence, the basis of the share of stock of acquiring is traced to the basis of the target stock exchanged therefor.

Section 10.07(f)(2) Assumption of Liability

Section 358(d) provides that assumption of liability shall be treated as money received by the taxpayer in the transaction. As we have seen above, this money deemed received may cause a basis decrease. Section 358(d)(2) provides an exception for liabilities excluded under section 357(c)(3). Generally, these are liabilities for which the taxpayer will receive a deduction. Finally, the section contains other rules that are not relevant to our study of reorganizations.

Section 10.07(g) Holding Period of Acquiring Stock in the Hands of Target Shareholders

Determining one's holding period is necessary to ascertain whether gain or loss on property sold or exchanged will be long term or short term. This may not be crucial but it is still important because long term property is still given some preference in the tax Code. In a reorganization, the holding period of acquiring stock received by target shareholders will be determined under section 1223(1). It provides that if the basis of property received in a transaction is determined in whole or in part by reference to the basis of property exchanged, then the holding period of the property will include the holding period for which the property exchanged was held. In the above examples, this means that A's holding period in the Corporation Y stock received will include the holding period that A had in his Corporation X stock.

Section 10.08 Tax Consequences to the Acquiring Corporation

In a reorganization, there are three main consequences to the acquiring corporation: (1) recognition of gain or loss, (2) basis consequences, and (3) holding period. These are the same consequences that concern individual shareholders. Additionally, the acquiring corporation often takes over certain tax attributes of the target corporation under section 381. Tax attributes are items that may affect the tax treatment of certain transactions. Two prime examples of tax attributes are net operating losses (NOLs) and E&P.

Section 10.08(a) Gain/Loss

Unlike its shareholders, the acquiring corporation is actively involved in a reorganization and, thus, it must be concerned with the tax consequences flowing from the reorganization. Section 1032 provides nonrecognition to a corporation on the receipt of money or property for its stock. The rationale behind section 1032 is that sale of the stock of a corporation, unlike most other properties, carries with it the obligation of the corporation to ensure that the stock remains valuable in the hands of the shareholder. In this sense, it is as if the corporation has really incurred a debt. You may not approve of this rationale but the section nonetheless provides for nonrecognition. Under the section 1032 regulations, this nonrecognition treatment is extended to a subsidiary corporation that uses stock of its parent in a reorganization.[70] Under the regulations, the subsidiary corporation is treated in the same manner as if its parent had sold the stock. Note that this treatment applies only with respect to stock of the subsidiary's parent acquired for purpose of the reorganization. Stock of the subsidiary's parent acquired prior to the reorganization or in an unrelated transaction not in conjunction with the reorganization will be treated as other property exchanged in the reorganization.

The nonrecognition rule of section 1032 applies only for stock exchanged for property. If the acquiring corporation exchanges property other than its own stock (or stock of its parent as described above), the transaction would fall under section 1001.

Section 10.08(b) Basis Consequences to the Acquiring Corporation

Section 362 provides the basis consequences for the property received by the acquiring corporation in a reorganization. Its regulations are not very helpful. Thus, we must rely on our keen sense of statutory reading in deciphering section 362. Fortunately, section 362 is not very challenging. Section 362(b) provides that the basis of property received in a reorganization shall be the same as the basis of the transferor increased by the gain, if any, recog-

---

70. *See* Treas. Reg. § 1.1032-2(c).

nized by the transferor on the exchange. The basis scheme provided by section 362 is called carryover basis. This means that the basis of the property received in the exchange is carried over to the new owner of the property. By contrast, the basis rules under section 358 provided for an exchanged basis. This means that the basis of the property received is exchanged for the basis of the property exchanged therefor.

Although the basis rules provided in section 362(b) are straightforward, real life complicates matters. With regard to B reorganizations involving widely held corporations, it may not always be easy for the acquiring corporation to determine the basis of stock received in the transaction. Remember that section 362 provides that the acquiring corporation's basis in the stock of the target corporation received in the transaction will be the same as the basis of the stock in the hands of the target shareholders. In some cases, target shareholders may number in the thousands. Getting basis information from a great number of target shareholders may not be easy. The IRS recognized this difficulty and, in Rev. Proc. 81-70 permits taxpayers to use statistical methods to estimate the basis of target stock received in a B reorganization. The revenue procedure may be used where no information is received from the target shareholders or where target stock is widely held and it would be unduly expensive to get this information. Before he left the IRS, Professor Mombrun was supervising a project resulting in the publication of Notice 2004-44.[71] The notice requested comments from taxpayers regarding problems they may have encountered in complying with Rev. Proc. 81-70. This project may lead to changes to Rev. Proc. 81-70.

Section 10.08(c) Holding Period

The holding period of property received by the acquiring corporation is determined under section 1223(2) and includes the holding period of the assets in the hands of the transferor corporation.

Section 10.08(d) Carryover of Tax Items

Under section 381, if a transaction qualifies as a reorganization (except as a B reorganization), the acquiring corporation will succeed to and take into account certain tax attributes of the target corporation. Section 381(c) pro-

---

71. 2004-28 I.R.B. 32, regarding Rev. Proc. 81-70, 1981-2 C.B. 729.

vides a list of items that are subject to section 381, including NOLs and E&P. We study the carryover of tax attributes in more detail in Chapter 13.

Section 10.09 Tax Consequences to the Target Corporation

Section 10.09(a) Gain or Loss

Target corporations often disappear after a reorganization. Nonetheless, they may be subject to tax with respect to property received in connection with the reorganization. Section 361 recognizes that targets are often conduits for the transfer of property. Section 361(a) provides that no gain or loss will be recognized to a corporation if it exchanges property solely in exchange for stock or securities in another corporation. This rule avoids the harsh consequences of section 311. When section 311 applies to a corporate distribution, the corporation recognizes gain but does not recognize loss.

Section 361(a) applies only to distributions of stock and securities. Once again, we see the preference given stock and securities. Section 361(b)(1)(A) provides that if property other than stock or securities is received and such property is distributed by the corporation, the corporation will not be subject to taxation. If, however, the property is retained by the corporation, such retention of property will be taxed under section 361(b)(1)(B). In case receipt of other property would produce a loss, such loss cannot be recognized under section 361(b)(2).

Under section 361(b)(3), transfers of property to the creditors of the corporation are treated as distributions in pursuance to the reorganization. Generally, distributions pursuant to the reorganization are not taxable unless they involve distributions of appreciated property. In such cases, the distributing corporation will be taxed as if it had sold the property at its FMV.

Section 10.09(b) Basis and Holding Period of Property Received

Property received by the target corporation is normally distributed in connection with the reorganization to the shareholders or creditors of the corporation. If the target corporation retains property, it uses section 362(b) to ascertain that property's basis. The basis of property received is the basis of the property in the hands of the transferor. If the transferor recognized gain, the target increases its basis by the amount of gain recognized. Section 1223(2) provides that the target's holding period includes the transferor's holding period for the property.

Section 10.10 Reporting Requirements for Taxable Reorganizations Imposed by The American Jobs Creation Act of 2004

Obviously, if a reorganization does not meet the requirements of section 368(a), it will be taxable. Potentially, the transferor corporation and the shareholders of the target corporation will be taxed. The transferee corporation will be protected by section 1032 to the extent that it receives property in exchange for its stock.

The American Jobs Creation Act of 2004 adds section 6043A to the Code, imposing certain reporting requirements in the case of taxable transactions. The reporting requirements apply to transactions in which gain or loss is recognized on the acquisition of the stock or assets of one corporation by another. The acquiring corporation (or the acquired corporation) is required to provide: (a) a description of the transaction; (b) the name and address of each shareholder of the acquired corporation that recognizes a gain as a result of the transaction (or would recognize gain if there was built-in gain on the shareholder's shares); (c) the amount of money and the value of stock or other consideration paid to each shareholder described above; and (d) such other information as the Secretary may provide.

Chapter 11

Corporate Liquidations

Section 11.01 Introduction

When a corporation liquidates, its creditors have first call on corporate assets. The corporation then distributes any remaining assets to its shareholders. Shareholders who receive cash or marketable securities have relatively simple tax consequences. In most cases, they compute short-term or long-term capital gain or loss and report this on their tax return.

In some instances, liquidation does not end the business operations. A parent corporation may receive business assets from a subsidiary that is liquidating. The parent's tax consequences will reflect that business continuity in a manner similar to that used for the reorganizations described in Chapter 10.

Section 11.02 Relevant Code Sections

Section 11.02(a) Liquidations

The Code sections that apply to corporate liquidations depend on the type of liquidation. If the liquidating corporation is not a subsidiary of another corporation, its tax consequences will be determined under section 336. Its shareholders will use section 331 to compute gain or loss and section 334(a) to compute basis. These provisions are discussed in section 11.03.

If the liquidating corporation is owned at least 80 percent by another corporation, its tax consequences will be determined under section 337. Its "corporate parent" will use section 332 to compute gain or loss and section 334(b) to compute basis. Those provisions are discussed in section 11.04.

Section 346, which will be discussed where relevant, applies when the corporation makes a series of distributions rather than a single liquidating distribution.

Section 11.02(b) Section 338 Deemed Asset Purchases

Special rules found in section 338 apply to a corporation that undergoes a deemed sale and repurchase of its own assets. Those rules are discussed in Chapter 12.

Section 11.03 Liquidations of Corporations other than Subsidiaries

Section 11.03(a) Introduction

The rules described below apply to liquidations if none of the shareholders is a corporation. They also apply to any corporate shareholder that does not meet the ownership period and percent requirements imposed on an "80-percent distributee," referred to in this discussion as a "corporate parent."[1]

Section 11.03(b) Liquidating Corporation's Tax Consequences

Section 11.03(b)(1) General Rule

Section 336(a) provides that the liquidating corporation recognizes gain or loss on distributions to its shareholders as part of a complete liquidation. The corporation is treated as if it sold the corporate asset at its fair market value.

Example: Corporation X, which has no creditors, owns three assets. It owns its building (adjusted basis $60,000; fair market value $300,000), the land on which the building sits (adjusted basis $10,000; fair market value $50,000), and shares of stock in Corporation Z (adjusted basis $40,000; fair market value $25,000). X had purchased the Z shares as a temporary investment of surplus cash. X Corporation has three shareholders. All are individuals. Each is unrelated to the other shareholders.

If X sold its assets, it would realize and recognize a gain on the building and land and a loss on the Z stock. It would realize and recognize the exact same gain and loss if it instead distributed the property to its three shareholders.

---

1. *See* section 11.04 for the tax consequences of liquidations if there is a corporate parent.

Section 11.03(b)(2) Loss Disallowance Rules

Despite the general rule of section 336(a), the corporation may lose the ability to deduct losses realized on property it distributes in liquidation. The capital loss limitations discussed in section 11.03(b)(2)(A) are not unique to a liquidating distribution. Those limitations apply whenever a corporation has a net capital loss. The related party and plan of avoidance rules discussed in section 11.03(b)(2)(B) & (C) cover potential abuse situations.

Section 11.03(b)(2)(A) Capital Losses

Because X's investment in Z shares gave rise to a capital loss, we must consider whether section 1211(a) disallows that loss. In the original example, disallowance is unlikely. Because X's gains on the land and building are section 1231 gains, and there are no section 1231 losses, X will have sufficient capital gain to offset its capital loss.

Example: Corporation Y, which has no creditors, owns three assets. It owns its building (adjusted basis $600,000; fair market value $500,000), the land on which the building sits (adjusted basis $70,000; fair market value $50,000), and shares of stock in Corporation Z (adjusted basis $40,000; fair market value $25,000). Y had purchased the Z shares as a temporary investment of surplus cash. Y distributed its assets to its shareholders and liquidated.

Y realized a loss on all of its assets. It can deduct the losses on its land and building, because a net section 1231 loss is treated as ordinary and avoids the section 1211(a) limitations. Section 1211(a) precludes any current year deduction for the net capital loss of $15,000 on the Z shares. Unless Y realized capital gains in prior years, it cannot deduct any of that $15,000 loss.[2]

Section 11.03(b)(2)(B) Related Parties

If a corporation had only one shareholder, an individual, section 267 would normally disallow losses on sales or exchanges between them.[3] Fortunately, section 267(a)(1) provides that the loss disallowance rule does not automatically apply to distributions in complete liquidation.

---

2. Corporations can carry capital losses back three taxable years. I.R.C. § 1212(a).

3. Section 267 is not limited to a one-shareholder corporation. A shareholder and a corporation are related parties if the shareholder has actual or constructive ownership of more than 50 percent of the corporation's stock value. I.R.C. section 267(b) provides other examples of corporate-shareholder related party rules. In determining constructive ownership for this purpose, use section 267(c) and not section 318.

Section 336(d)(1) applies the related party loss disallowance rule in two situations. First, it applies if the distribution is not pro rata with respect to the shareholders. Unless each shareholder receives an interest in every item, both gain and loss property, the distribution is not pro rata.

Example: Corporation X owns two assets. Asset #1 has an adjusted basis of $150,000. Asset #2 has an adjusted basis of $25,000. Each asset has a fair market value of $120,000 and neither is "disqualified property." X has two equal shareholders, who are not related to each other. X can distribute Asset #1 to one shareholder and Asset #2 to the other. Because neither shareholder owns more than 50 percent of the X stock, neither is a related party. X can deduct the loss on Asset #1 no matter how it is distributed.

Example: Corporation Y owns two assets. Asset #1 has an adjusted basis of $150,000. Asset #2 has an adjusted basis of $25,000. Each asset has a fair market value of $120,000 and neither is "disqualified property." Y has two equal shareholders, who are brother and sister. Section 267 treats each shareholder as owning 100 percent of the Y stock. If Y distributes a one-half interest in each asset to each shareholder, it can deduct the loss on Asset #1. If it instead distributes Asset #1 to one shareholder and Asset #2 to the other, Y cannot deduct the loss on Asset #1.

The related party loss disallowance rule also applies to distributions of "disqualified property." Property is disqualified if the corporation acquired it in a section 351 transaction or as a contribution to capital during the five-year period ending on the date of distribution. If the corporation acquired substitute basis property in exchange for disqualified property, the substitute basis property inherits the original property's taint.[4]

Example: Corporation Z owns two assets. Asset #1 has an adjusted basis of $150,000. Asset #2 has an adjusted basis of $25,000. Each asset has a fair market value of $120,000. Z acquired both assets two years ago in a transaction governed by section 351. Z has two equal shareholders, who are brother and sister. Section 267 treats each shareholder as owning 100 percent of the Z stock. Even if Z makes a pro rata distribution, and each shareholder receives a one-half interest in each asset, it cannot deduct the loss on Asset #1. That asset was acquired within five years of the distribution in a section 351 transaction.

---

4. This rule and the rule applied in section 11.03(b)(2)(C) reflect that a section 351 transaction gives both shareholder and corporation a potential loss deduction with regard to the property contributed to the corporation. The corporation takes the shareholder's basis, and the shareholder's basis for the stock received is computed with reference to his basis for the property transferred. Section 351 transactions are discussed in detail in Chapter 5.

Example: With one exception, all facts are the same as in the preceding example. One year before liquidating, Z exchanged Asset #1 for Asset #3 in a section 1031 like-kind exchange. Because the basis for Asset #3 is computed with reference to the basis for Asset #1, Asset #3 is also disqualified property.

Section 11.03(b)(2)(C) Property Received in Nonrecognition Transactions

Section 336(d)(2) reduces the corporation's loss deduction when two conditions are satisfied. First, the corporation must have received the property in a section 351 transaction or as a contribution to capital. Second, the acquisition must have been part of a plan which had as a principal purpose the recognition of loss in connection with a liquidation. Section 336(d)(2)(B)(ii) provides a two-year look-back period. Property acquired after the date that is two years before the plan's adoption is treated as acquired pursuant to the proscribed plan unless the regulations provide a different treatment.

Section 336(d)(2)(B) does not completely disallow the loss. Instead, it taints only the amount by which the loss property's adjusted basis exceeds its value at the time the corporation acquired it. It accomplishes this result by reducing the corporation's basis at the time of the distribution by the excess amount.[5]

Caveat: Section 336(d)(2) applies even to losses that would not be disallowed by section 267.

Example: Corporation X was incorporated by four shareholders eighteen months ago. Three of the shareholders each transferred $250,000 in cash in exchange for 25 percent of the X shares. The fourth shareholder transferred land with a fair market value of $250,000 and an adjusted basis of $290,000 in exchange for 25 percent of the X shares. The shareholders planned to liquidate X. The land is currently worth $203,000. If X does not wait until the two-year look-back period has ended, it cannot deduct its full $87,000 loss. It must reduce its basis for the land by the $40,000 difference between the land's value at the time it was transferred to X and X's basis for it immediately following that transfer. Because the land's basis becomes $250,000, X's loss is reduced to $47,000.

If the corporation holds the property until the look-back period expires, it avoids automatic treatment as a plan to recognize the loss. The distribution may still be challenged based on facts and circumstances.

---

5. Basis will not be reduced below zero.

Caveat: Section 336(d)(2) taints both distributions to the shareholders and sales and exchanges that occur as part of the liquidation. The taint applies even to prior year sales if they are treated as part of the liquidation. Instead of loss disallowance for transactions in a prior year, the corporation can elect to increase its gross income by that amount in the year the plan of complete liquidation is adopted.

Section 11.03(b)(3) Effect of Liabilities

If the corporation distributed encumbered property or the shareholders assumed any other corporate liability, the liability may affect the corporation's computation of gain or loss on the liquidating distribution. Section 336(b) provides that the amount realized cannot be less than the amount of the liability even if the liability exceeds the property's value.

Example: Corporation X owns only one asset, a vacant lot. It has a basis of $15,000 and a fair market value of $100,000. The lot is subject to a mortgage of $62,000. If X distributes the lot, subject to the mortgage, its amount realized is $100,000 and its gain realized is $85,000.

Example: Corporation Y owns only one asset, a vacant lot. It has a basis of $15,000 and a fair market value of $100,000. The lot is subject to a mortgage of $102,000. If Y distributes the lot, subject to the mortgage, its amount realized is $102,000 and its gain realized is $87,000.

Section 11.03(b)(4) Earnings & Profits Account

The corporation's E&P account is extinguished after the liquidation. It does not carry over to its shareholders.

Section 11.03(c) Recipient Shareholder's Tax Consequences

Section 11.03(c)(1) Gains and Losses

Section 331(a) provides that amounts distributed in complete liquidation are treated as full payment in exchange for the shareholder's stock. The shareholder computes gain or loss realized by comparing the amount distributed to his adjusted basis. Section 301 does not apply to the amounts received.[6]

---

6. I.R.C. §331(b). An exception to this rule applies if the distributing corporation is a personal holding company. *See* I.R.C. §316(b)(2)(B).

The shareholder recognizes the gain or loss, which will generally be capital rather than ordinary. The shareholder can deduct any realized loss even if the corporation and shareholder are related parties.[7]

If the stock is section 1202 qualified small business stock, the shareholder excludes 50 percent of the realized gain.

Section 11.03(c)(2) Basis for Property Received

Section 334(a) provides that the shareholder's basis for property received is its fair market value at the time of distribution. Even if the shareholder assumes corporate debt as part of the liquidation, his basis cannot exceed the property's value.

Section 11.03(c)(3) Holding Period for Property Received

None of the section 1223 carryover basis rules apply to shareholders who are not corporate parents. If the shareholder will own the property as a capital asset or section 1231 asset, the holding period begins the day after it is received.[8] If the property is depreciable, depreciation begins when the shareholder is treated as placing it in service in a trade or business or an income-producing activity.[9]

Section 11.04 Liquidations of Corporate Subsidiaries

Section 11.04(a) Introduction

The rules described below apply if a shareholder is a corporation that meets both ownership and timing requirements, referred to here as a "corporate parent." If the liquidating corporation has both a corporate parent and other shareholders, there are two sets of tax consequences. One set applies to the corporate parent; the other applies to any additional shareholder. The liquidating corporation's tax consequences will likewise be bifurcated into those

---

7. I.R.C. § 267(a)(1).

8. *See* discussion in Rev. Rul. 70-598, 1970-2 C.B. 168.

9. The section 168(d) applicable convention rules (half-year, mid-quarter, and mid-month) apply.

that relate to distributions to the corporate parent and those that relate to other distributions.

Caveat: The rules described in these materials may not apply if the corporate parent is a tax-exempt entity. A discussion of the section 337(b)(2) rules is beyond the scope of this text.

Section 11.04(a)(1) Ownership Requirement

To be a corporate parent, the recipient corporation must own at least 80 percent of both the voting power and stock value of the corporation being liquidated.[10] This is the ownership requirement.

Example: Corporation X has one class of stock outstanding. Corporation Y owns 85 percent of these shares. Individual A, who is unrelated to Y, owns the other 15 percent. Y satisfies both the 80 percent voting power and 80 percent stock ownership requirement.

Example: Corporation X has two classes of stock outstanding. Corporation Y owns all of the X voting common stock. Individual B, who is unrelated to Y Corporation, owns all of the X nonvoting common stock. Y satisfies the 80 percent voting power requirement. We do not have enough information to determine if Y satisfies the 80 percent of value requirement.

Section 11.04(a)(2) Liquidation Completion Requirement

The corporate parent must meet the ownership requirement on the date the plan of liquidation is adopted. In addition, it must continue to meet that requirement until it receives the liquidating distribution.

Example: Corporation X has one class of stock outstanding. Corporation Y owns 72 percent of these shares. Individuals A and B, who are unrelated to Y, each own 9 percent. Six months after X adopts a plan of liquidation, Y buys A's shares and becomes an 81 percent owner. Y does not satisfy the ownership requirement.

Example: Corporation X has one class of stock outstanding. Corporation Y owns 85 percent of these shares. Individual A, who is unrelated to Y, owns the other 15 percent. Six months after X adopts a plan of liquidation, Y sells half of its X shares to B, an unrelated party. Y does not satisfy the ownership requirement.

---

10. This determination is made using the definition of I.R.C. § 1504(a)(2). Section 1504(a)(4) excludes preferred stock from the definition of stock if it meets four requirements. Such stock must not be entitled to vote, must be limited and preferred as to dividends, must have redemption and liquidation rights that do not exceed the issue price (other than reasonable premiums), and must not be convertible into another class of stock.

A second set of timing requirements apply to the adoption of the plan and the completion of the liquidation. Any distribution must meet one of two alternatives.

To meet the first alternative, the distribution must be in complete cancellation or redemption of the liquidating corporation's stock and the transfer of all its property must occur within the taxable year. If this requirement is met, section 332(b)(2) provides that the shareholder resolution authorizing the distribution is treated as a plan of liquidation even if the resolution fails to specify a completion date.

To meet the second alternative, the distribution must be one of a series of distributions pursuant to a plan of liquidation. Section 332(b)(3) requires that the plan must provide that the transfer of property under the liquidation will be completed within three years from the end of the taxable year in which the first distribution under the plan occurs.[11]

Example: Corporation X has one class of stock outstanding. Corporation Y owns 85 percent of these shares. Individual A, who is unrelated to Y, owns the other 15 percent. In Year 1, X adopts a plan of liquidation calling for the distribution of its property no later than three years from the close of the year in which the first distribution occurs. X makes its first distribution under the plan in Year 2. Distributions to Y qualify so long as all distributions are made by the end of Year 5, and Y continues to meet the 80 percent ownership requirement.

Example: If X does not complete the distributions above until Year 6, none of the distributions qualify. The prior distributions to Y are retroactively disqualified.

Example: If Y reduces its ownership below 80 percent before receiving its final distribution, none of the distributions qualify even if X completed the liquidation by the end of Year 5.

The corporation need not formally dissolve or distribute all of its assets to qualify the liquidation. The regulations allow it to retain a nominal amount of assets for the sole purpose of preserving its legal existence.[12]

Section 11.04(a)(3) Plan of Liquidation

Section 332 applies to distributions under a plan of liquidation. As noted in section 11.04(a)(2), a shareholder resolution will be treated as a plan if all

---

11. If the liquidation is not completed within a single taxable year, I.R.C. § 332(b) provides that the IRS can require the liquidating corporation to post a bond or file a waiver of the statute of limitations (or both). This protects the government's right to assess taxes if the liquidation ultimately fails to meet the section 332(b) requirements.

12. Treas. Reg. § 1.332-2(c).

distributions occur within a single taxable year. Even if the distributions take longer, and satisfy the three-year requirement, the plan need only meet the requirements of section 332(b). Distributions that satisfy section 332(b) qualify even if they are not so considered by the applicable state corporate law.[13]

Section 11.04(b) Liquidating Corporation's Tax Consequences

Section 11.04(b)(1) General Rule

Section 337 provides that the liquidating corporation recognizes no gain or loss on distributions to the corporate parent. Distributions to any other shareholder are governed by the rules discussed in section 11.03.

If the liquidating corporation is indebted to the corporate parent, it might transfer property other than cash to satisfy that debt. If the debt existed when the liquidation plan was adopted, gain or loss on those transfers is not recognized.

Example: Corporation Y owns 90 percent of the stock (by voting power and value) of Corporation X. X adopted a plan of liquidation in Year 1 and began winding down its operations. During Year 2, Y made a loan to X so that X could pay its rent. If X later distributes appreciated property to Y, X recognizes gain on that distribution. The debt to Y did not exist when the plan of liquidation was adopted.

Section 11.04(b)(2) Distributions to Minority Shareholders

Section 337 applies only to distributions to a qualifying corporate parent. It does not apply to distributions to any other shareholder. Those distributions are generally subject to section 336, discussed in section 11.03, which provides for gain or loss recognition.

Section 336(d)(3) limits a corporation's ability to profit by allocating loss property to minority shareholders and gain property to a corporate parent. That provision provides that losses are not recognized, even on property distributed to minority shareholders, if section 332 governs the liquidation.

Example: Corporation X has two shareholders. Corporation Y owns 90 percent of X's stock. Individual A, who is not related to Y, owns the remaining 10 percent. X owns two assets. Asset #1 has a basis of $10,000 and a fair market value of $15,000. Asset #2 has a basis of $160,000 and a fair market value of $135,000. If X distributes Asset #1 to A and Asset #2 to Y, it recognizes

---

13. I.R.C. § 332(b) (flush language); Treas. Reg. § 1.332-2(d).

$5,000 gain on Asset #1; it recognizes none of its $25,000 loss on Asset #2. section 336(a) applies to the distribution to A; section 337 applies to the distribution to Y.

Example: Corporation X has two shareholders. Corporation Y owns 90 percent of X's stock. Individual B, who is not related to Y, owns the remaining 10 percent. X owns two assets. Asset #1 has a basis of $10,000 and a fair market value of $15,000. Asset #2 has a basis of $160,000 and a fair market value of $135,000. If X distributes Asset #1 and Asset #2 pro rata to B and Y, it recognizes $500 gain on Asset #1 (10 percent of its gain); it recognizes none of its $25,000 loss on Asset #2. Section 336(a) applies to 10 percent of Asset #1; section 336(d)(3) applies to 10 percent of Asset #2; and section 337 applies to 90 percent of Assets #1 and #2.

Section 11.04(b)(3) Earnings & Profits Account and Other Tax Attributes

The liquidating corporation's E&P account is not extinguished by the liquidation. It is transferred to the corporate parent's account.[14] Under section 381, the corporate parent also receives other tax attributes of the liquidating corporation. We discuss corporate tax attributes in more detail in Chapter 13.

Section 11.04(c) Recipient Shareholders' Tax Consequences

Section 11.04(c)(1) Gains and Losses

Section 332(a) provides that the parent corporation recognizes no gain or loss when it receives a distribution in complete liquidation. This rule applies whether there is a single distribution or a series of distributions.[15]

Keep in mind two important limitations to section 332(a). First, it applies only to distributions made with respect to the parent's stock. It does not apply to distributions the parent receives in exchange for liabilities owed by the liqui-

---

14. I.R.C. §381; Treas. Reg. §1.312-11(a). If there are minority shareholders, distributions to them result in an appropriate reduction in E&P before this account is assumed by the parent corporation. Treas. Reg. §1.381(c)(2)-1(c).

15. Limited exceptions apply. I.R.C. §332(c) applies special rules to distributions from regulated investment companies and real estate investment trusts. I.R.C. §332(d) covers distributions by certain domestic holding companies to foreign parent corporations.

dating corporation.[16] Second, the rule does not apply if the corporate parent receives nothing at all because the stock is completely worthless. Instead of being subject to section 332, the parent deducts a loss from a worthless security.[17]

Section 11.04(c)(2) Basis for Property Received

The general rule of section 334(b)(1) is that the corporate parent takes the distributing corporation's basis for property it receives in the liquidation. This rule applies to property distributed in exchange for the parent's stock or in exchange for any indebtedness to the parent.[18]

As a consequence of the carryover basis rule, the corporate parent's basis for its investment disappears. Depending on which basis is higher, this rule may result in favorable or unfavorable tax consequences.

Example: Corporation X is at least 80 percent owned by Corporation Y. Y has a basis of $100,000 for its X shares. As part of a complete liquidation, X distributes property to Y. Neither X nor Y will recognize any gain or loss on this transaction. The tables below illustrate how differences between X's basis for the property, Y's basis for the stock, and the property's value affect tax consequences.

Situation	X's Basis	Property's Value	X's Unrecognized Gain/Loss
1	125,000	130,000	5,000
2	125,000	110,000	-15,000
3	125,000	92,000	-33,000
4	70,000	130,000	60,000
5	70,000	92,000	22,000
6	70,000	60,000	-10,000

16. Treas. Reg. § 1.332-7. Although the corporations are related, section 267(a) contains an exception for distributions in complete liquidation. Recognition applies only to the corporate parent. As noted in section 11.04(b)(1), the debtor corporation recognizes no gain or loss if it uses property other than cash to retire the debt.

17. I.R.C. § 165(g). If section 165(g)(3) applies, the loss will be ordinary rather than capital.

18. Section 334(b)(1) includes a reference to section 337(b)(1), which covers indebtedness to the corporate parent.

Situation	Y's Stock Basis	Property's Value	Y's Unrecognized Gain/Loss
1	100,000	130,000	30,000
2	100,000	110,000	10,000
3	100,000	92,000	-8,000
4	100,000	130,000	30,000
5	100,000	92,000	-8,000
6	100,000	60,000	-40,000

In Situation 1, X and Y had combined gain potential of $35,000. If Y sells the property, it will recognize X's $5,000 gain.

In Situation 2, X and Y had a net loss potential of $5,000. If Y sells the property, it will recognize X's $15,000 loss.

In Situation 3, X and Y had a combined loss potential of $41,000. If Y sells the property, it will recognize X's $33,000 loss.

In Situation 4, X and Y had a combined gain potential of $90,000. If Y sells the property, it will recognize X's $60,000 gain.

In Situation 5, X and Y had a net gain potential of $14,000. If Y sells the property, it will recognize X's $22,000 gain.

In Situation 6, X and Y had a combined loss potential of $50,000. If Y sells the property, it will recognize X's $10,000 loss.

Section 334(b)(1) provides two exceptions to this rule. If either applies, the corporation's basis for that property is its fair market value on the date of distribution. The first exception applies if the liquidating corporation recognizes gain or loss with respect to the property distributed.[19] The second exception applies if the liquidating corporation is a foreign corporation, the parent is a domestic corporation, and the aggregate basis of property described in section 362(e)(1)(B) exceeds its value.[20]

---

19. Gain or loss is recognized, for example, if the parent corporation is tax-exempt and won't be using the property in an unrelated business. I.R.C. § 337(b)(2).

20. Section 362(e)(1)(B) applies to property if gain or loss is not subject to tax while the transferor holds it and is subject to tax while the transferee holds it. This exception was enacted as part of the American Jobs Creation Act of 2004 and applies to transactions occurring after October 22, 2004.

Section 11.04(c)(3) Holding Period for Property Received

The corporate parent's holding period for property received in the liquidation includes the holding period of distributing corporation.[21] Section 1223(2) provides a carryover holding period when a taxpayer's basis for property is computed with reference to another taxpayer's basis. If one of the exceptions described in section 11.04(c)(2) applies, the recipient's holding period does not include the distributing corporation's holding period.

Section 11.04(c)(4) Earnings & Profits and Other Attributes

The corporate parent takes over the liquidating corporation's E&P and many of its other tax attributes.[22] If the distributing corporation had a positive E&P balance, it is added to the parent's E&P accumulated E&P account but does not affect the parent's current year E&P. If the distributing corporation had an E&P deficit, that deficit can offset the parent's post-distribution E&P. The deficit cannot offset parent E&P accumulated before the distribution.[23]

---

21. I.R.C. § 1223(2).

22. I.R.C. § 381. Other attributes covered by section 381 include net operating loss carryovers, capital loss carryovers, and depreciation methods. Section 381 also covers various accounting method requirements.

23. I.R.C. § 381(c)(2)(B); Treas. Reg. § 1.381(c)(2)-1.

CHAPTER 12

SECTION 338

Section 12.01 Introduction

Section 12.01(a) Significance of Section 338

This chapter discusses the situations in which section 338 treats stock purchases as if they were asset acquisitions. In studying section 338, you will note that it involves several terms that do not appear elsewhere in the Code. In addition, note that section 338(i) authorizes the IRS to issue legislative regulations to carry out the purposes of section 338. Because the regulations are to carry out the statute's purpose, it is possible they will actually appear to deviate from the statutory language.

When it applies, section 338 treats the target or purchased corporation as having sold all of its assets prior to the purchase. This means that, after the sale, the target corporation's basis for those assets will generally be fair market value. Gain on a future sale will thus be reduced. In addition, the assets will give rise to higher depreciation deductions.

Because the target corporation is taxed on its deemed-sale gain, there is a cost to obtaining the higher basis for its assets. That cost is reduced if the target corporation has offsetting losses. Even if the target has few losses to offset against its gains, the section 338 election may still be beneficial if the purchasing corporation intends to sell some of the target's assets soon after the purchase. In addition, as we will see later, an election under section 338(h)(10) provides some special benefits to the selling consolidated group.

Section 338 is important for at least two reasons. First, a section 338 election may be advantageous. Second, an election may be mandated by section 338(e), which provides for a deemed election under certain circumstances. Thus, an attorney must have a sound understanding of section 338 before advising corporate clients.

Section 12.01(b) Origins of Section 338

The history of section 338, which provides for liquidation treatment in situations that may not involve liquidations, can be traced to several judicial decisions and statutory provisions. As discussed in Chapter 9, the *General Utilities* doctrine stood for the proposition that no gain or loss was recognized on a distribution from a corporation to its shareholders in liquidation of the corporation. That doctrine, which was codified in section 336, was repealed in 1986.

Another judicial decision, *Kimbell-Diamond Milling Co. v. Commissioner*,[1] applied if a corporation acquired the stock of another corporation and liquidated the acquired corporation shortly thereafter. The *Kimbell-Diamond* doctrine treated the combined transaction as a direct purchase of the other corporation's assets, which resulted in a section 1012 cost basis for those assets. If *General Utilities* and *Kimbell-Diamond* both applied, one corporation could purchase the stock of a second corporation, liquidate it shortly thereafter, and take a fair market value basis in the liquidated corporation's assets. Neither corporation would pay tax on the pre-liquidation difference between those assets' basis and their FMV.

Because the *Kimbell-Diamond* doctrine involved the acquiring corporation's intent, taxpayers could claim they lacked the intent to purchase assets if direct purchase treatment did not provide tax advantages. This would be the case, for example, if those assets had a basis greater than their value. In that case, the acquiring corporation would prefer taking a carryover basis. To reduce taxpayers' ability to rely on intent, Congress enacted section 334(b)(2), which provided a bright-line test. If the liquidation of an 80 percent subsidiary occurred within a specified time after the acquisition, it was treated as an asset purchase. The acquiring corporation took a cost basis for the acquired corporation's assets.

Congress replaced section 334(b)(2) with section 338 in 1982. Section 338 replaced any nonstatutory treatment of a stock purchase as an asset purchase under the *Kimbell-Diamond* doctrine.[2] The *General Utilities* doctrine was effectively repealed by statutory changes in 1986. When section 338 applies under current law, the acquired corporation recognizes gain or loss on the deemed sale of its assets.

---

1. 14 T.C. 74 (1950), *aff'd per curiam*, 187 F.2d 718 (5th Cir. 1951), *cert. denied*, 342 U.S. 827 (1951).

2. *See* H.R. Rep. No. 97-760, 97th Cong., 2d Sess. 536 (1982), 1982-2 C.B. 600, 632.

Section 12.02 Section 338 Terminology

Section 338 focuses on a "purchasing corporation" and a "target corporation." Section 338(d) defines each of those terms with reference to yet another term. A purchasing corporation is one that makes a qualified stock purchase of another corporation; a target corporation is a corporation whose stock is acquired in a qualified stock purchase. The term "qualified stock purchase" involves definitions of "purchase," "acquisition date," and "acquisition period."

In applying section 338 to a target corporation's assets, we will differentiate between the "grossed-up basis" of "recently purchased stock" and the "basis" of "nonrecently purchased stock." Finally, we will encounter a so-called "consistency period," which may require a corporation to make a deemed section 338 election.

We discuss each of these terms at the appropriate point in this chapter.

Section 12.03 Qualifying for Section 338

Section 338 applies if a purchasing corporation that meets its requirements makes a timely election. It also applies if a corporation is required to make a section 338(e) deemed election. The discussion in this section covers situations where taxpayers qualify to make an election. Deemed elections are discussed in section 12.06.

A corporation can make a section 338 election if it qualifies as a purchasing corporation. To do so, it must make a qualified stock purchase. As the discussion below explains, a qualified stock purchase has two aspects. The purchasing corporation must obtain a sufficient amount of stock, and it must do so by purchase. The purchasing corporation must also concern itself with two time limits. One applies to the period in which it obtains the target corporation's stock; the other applies to making the section 338 election.

Although an individual cannot be a purchasing corporation, the regulations provide that an individual can form a corporation that qualifies to be a purchasing corporation. The new corporation will be allowed to make a section 338 election unless subsequent events indicate that such treatment would be inappropriate.[3] In other words, the step transaction doctrine may apply to prevent abuse.

---

3. Treas. Reg. § 1.338-3(b)(1) lists events, such as liquidating shortly after the purchase, that indicate the purchasing corporation did not make a purchase that qualifies for a section 338 election.

Section 12.03(a) Required Amount of Stock

The purchasing corporation cannot make a section 338 election unless the stock it acquires by purchase meets the requirements of section 1504(a)(2).[4] That section requires ownership of at least 80 percent of the target corporation's voting power and at least 80 percent of its stock value. Nonvoting stock with limited rights to share in corporate profits (generally, nonvoting preferred stock) is ignored in this computation.

Section 12.03(b) Purchase

Section 338(h)(3)(A) defines purchase in the negative. It is any stock acquisition other than one described in that paragraph. As a general rule, an acquisition is not a purchase if:[5]

(1) the basis of the stock in the hands of the purchasing corporation is determined in whole or in part by reference to the basis in the hands of the person from whom acquired or under section 1014 (property acquired from a decedent);

(2) the stock is acquired in an exchange covered by section 351, 354, 355 or 356 or other transaction that results in the transferor not fully recognizing realized gain or loss; or

(3) the stock is acquired from a person whose stock ownership would be attributed to the acquirer under section 318(a) other than through option attribution.

These exceptions should lead you to conclude that section 338(a) generally applies to situations in which the purchasing corporation takes a section 1012 cost basis for the stock acquired.

Section 12.03(c) Acquisition Period

To be treated as a qualified stock purchase, the stock acquired by purchase must be acquired during a 12-month acquisition period.[6] The purchasing

---

4. *See* Chapter 14 for a discussion of section 1504 in the context of affiliated corporations.

5. I.R.C. § 338(h)(3)(C) provides exceptions to these limitations for certain transactions between related corporations. *See also* Treas. Reg. § 1.338-3(b)(3).

6. I.R.C. § 338(d)(3).

corporation can acquire this stock in a single transaction or in a series of transactions.

Section 338(h)(1) generally defines the term 12-month acquisition period as the 12-month period beginning with the date of the first acquisition by purchase of stock included in a qualified stock purchase. Stock purchased before or after that period is generally excluded from this determination. In certain stock acquisitions from related persons, section 318 deemed ownership of stock may be taken into account.

Section 12.03(d) The Section 338 Election

Section 338(g) requires the purchasing corporation to make a section 338 election no later than the 15th day of the ninth month after the month in which the acquisition date occurs.[7] Section 338(g)(3) provides that the election is irrevocable.

Caveat: Terminology is important. The "acquisition date" is the date on which the requisite ownership is obtained. The 12-month acquisition period includes acquisitions by purchase leading up to the purchasing corporation actually obtaining 80 percent ownership.

Example: Corporation X makes the following purchases of Corporation Y's stock. X buys 10 percent on date 1, an additional 30 percent on date 2, 30 percent more on date 3, 20 percent more on date 4, and the remaining 10 percent on date 5. If all five purchases occurred during a twelve-month period, the "acquisition date" is date 4. That is the date on which X's total purchases equal at least 80 percent of Y's stock.

Section 12.04 Effect of Section 338 Election

If the purchasing corporation makes a section 338 election, the target corporation is treated as having sold all of its assets at the close of the acquisition date at FMV in a single transaction. It is then treated as a new corporation that purchased all of those assets as of the beginning of the next day. The target corporation recognizes gain or loss with respect to the assets it has "sold." On purchasing those assets from itself, it acquires a new basis and holding period.

---

7. Taxpayers may be eligible to make a late election under the section 301.9100 regulations.

Section 338(a)(2) treats the target corporation as a "new" corporation. As a result, its tax attributes are wiped out. Tax attributes are discussed in more detail in Chapter 13.

Section 12.05 Target Corporation's Tax Consequences

Section 12.05(a) Gain or Loss on Deemed Sale

Section 338 does not strictly follow the section 1001 gain or loss computation. The target corporation does not compare amount realized to adjusted basis; nor does it compare its assets' FMV to adjusted basis. Instead, it compares aggregate deemed sales price (ADSP) to adjusted basis. The formula for computing ADSP reflects the actual percentage of the stock that the purchasing corporation acquired. Instead of offsetting the deemed selling price, selling expenses are treated separately. This treatment has significance if the purchasing corporation does not purchase 100 percent of the target's stock during the 12-month period.

The computations below relate to ADSP for the assets as a group. Because assets may have different character, the corporation actually computes gain or loss with respect to individual assets. Those computations are described in section 12.05(c).

Section 12.05(a)(1) 100 percent of Target's Stock Acquired

Regulations section 1.338-4(b) defines ADSP as the sum of (1) the grossed-up amount realized on the sale to the purchasing corporation of the recently purchased target stock and (2) the target corporation's liabilities. If the purchasing corporation purchases 100 percent of the target's stock during the 12-month period, and the target has no liabilities, the grossed-up amount realized equals the purchase price.

Example: P Corporation purchased 100 percent of T Corporation's stock in a single transaction for $100. T had no liabilities at the time of the sale. Because T's unrealized gains and losses are equal, T would have no income tax liability if it actually sold those assets. ADSP in this case is $100.

We compute the target's liabilities on the day following the deemed asset sale. As a result, the target's liabilities can include its tax liability arising from that sale.

Example: Assume the same facts, except that T has liabilities of $2. ADSP is $102.

Example: In addition, T's unrealized gains slightly exceed its unrealized losses, giving rise to a potential $1 income tax liability. ADSP is $103.

Section 12.05(a)(2) Less Than 100 percent of Target's Stock Acquired

Regulations section 1.338-4(c) computes the grossed-up amount realized in three steps. First, divide the amount realized on the sale to the purchasing corporation by the percentage of target stock attributable to the recently purchased stock. The percentage computation takes stock value into account and ignores selling expenses. Second, subtract the selling expenses incurred by the selling shareholders. Third, add the target corporation's liabilities, including those arising as a result of the deemed sale.

If the purchasing corporation purchases all of the target's stock in the 12-month period, this formula will result in an ADSP equal to the amount realized minus selling expenses plus target liabilities. The examples below illustrate the ADSP computation when the purchasing corporation purchases a smaller amount of the target's stock.

Example: Corporation P purchased 90 percent of the stock of Corporation T for $90 in a single transaction; the selling shareholders incurred selling costs of $3. If the remaining 10 percent of T is worth $10 and there are no liabilities, the ADSP is $97. The $90 amount realized is divided by 90 percent, representing the percentage of recently acquired stock. From the $100 result, subtract the $3 selling expenses. T computes gain or loss by comparing its basis for its assets to the $97 ADSP.

Example: Assume the same facts, except that T has liabilities of $4. The ADSP is $101. The $4 liabilities are added in computing the grossed up amount realized.

Caveat: The value of all target stock, including preferred stock, is counted in computing the stock value percentage in the above computation.[8]

Section 12.05(b) Basis for Assets Deemed Purchased

When section 338 applies, we treat the target corporation as having sold its assets to itself. We must then compute the total basis for the assets it has "purchased" and allocate that basis among those assets.

---

8. *See* Treas. Reg. § 1.338-4(c)(2) (Example).

Section 12.05(b)(1) Total Basis

Just as section 338 modifies amount realized in computing the target's gain or loss, it also modifies basis concepts in determining the target's basis for assets it is treated as purchasing. Modification reflects two important aspects of the qualified stock acquisition. First, the purchasing corporation may have acquired less than 100 percent of the target's stock. Second, even if it acquired all of the target's stock, some of the purchases may have occurred outside the 12-month period.

Section 338(b)(1) computes basis with reference to two components: a grossed-up basis for recently purchased stock and a basis for nonrecently purchased stock. The computation also takes into account the target corporation's liabilities. Those three amounts constitute the adjusted grossed-up basis ("AGUB").

Section 12.05(b)(1)(A) Basis Attributable to Stock

Section 338(b)(6) defines both recently purchased and nonrecently purchased stock. Stock is recently purchased stock if the purchasing corporation (1) acquired it by purchase during the 12-month acquisition period and (2) held it on the acquisition date. Any other stock held by the purchasing corporation on the acquisition date is nonrecently purchased stock. Stock held by third parties falls into neither category.

To compute the basis allocable to recently purchased stock, multiply the purchasing corporation's basis for that stock by a fraction. The fraction's numerator is 100 percent minus the percentage of stock in the target corporation attributable to nonrecently purchased stock. The denominator is the percentage of stock in the target corporation attributable to recently purchased stock.[9] Both percentage computations are based on the stock's value.

The basis allocable to nonrecently purchased stock is the purchasing corporation's basis unless the purchasing corporation makes the election discussed in section 12.05(b)(1)(B).

The examples below illustrate the basis computation in a situation involving no liabilities.

Example: P Corporation purchased 100 percent of T Corporation in a single transaction for $200. All of the T stock is recently purchased stock. The fraction is 100/100. T's $200 asset basis is all attributable to recently purchased stock.

---

9. *See* Treas. Reg. § 1.338-5 for examples detailing the application of the regulation.

Example: P Corporation purchased 95 percent of T Corporation in a single transaction for $190. Five years previously P had purchased the other 5 percent of T Corporation for $4. That 5 percent is worth $10. Only the 95 percent is recently purchased stock. The fraction is 95/95. T's asset basis attributable to recently purchased stock is $190. T's asset basis attributable to nonrecently purchased stock is $4.

Example: P Corporation purchased 95 percent of T Corporation in a single transaction for $190. Third parties own the other 5 percent of T Corporation. Only the 95 percent is recently purchased stock. The fraction is 100/95. The 5 percent owned by third parties does not affect the denominator because it does not meet the definition of nonrecently purchased stock. T's asset basis attributable to recently purchased stock is $200 (100/95 multiplied by $190).

Section 12.05(b)(1)(B) Election for Nonrecently Purchased Stock

If the purchasing corporation is willing to recognize gain on its nonrecently purchased stock, it can elect a grossed-up basis for assets attributable to that stock.[10] The corporation is treated as selling this stock on the acquisition date for a so-called "basis amount." That amount is computed by multiplying the grossed-up basis for recently purchased stock by a fraction. The numerator is the percentage of the target's stock value attributable to nonrecently purchased stock. The denominator is 100 percent minus the numerator percentage. The example below illustrates this computation in a situation involving no target corporation liabilities.

Example: P Corporation purchased 95 percent of T Corporation in a single transaction for $190. Five years previously P had purchased the other 5 percent of T Corporation for $4. That 5 percent is worth $10. Only the 95 percent is recently purchased stock. The fraction is 95/95. T's asset basis attributable to recently purchased stock is $190. If P elects to recognize its $6 gain on the other 5 percent of T's stock, its basis for that stock will be $10. That amount equals the $190 grossed-up basis multiplied by 5/95.

Section 12.05(c) Allocation Rules

The section 338 deemed sale is not an asset by asset sale; it is the sale of an entire business. While some assets could have been sold separately, others—particularly goodwill and certain other intangibles—may have no value out-

---

10. I.R.C. §338(b)(3); Treas. Reg. §1.338-5(d). The purchasing corporation cannot use this election for recognizing loss on the target stock.

side the business. Because the target corporation is treated as two corporations, both a seller and a buyer, we must allocate the ADSP to each asset sold by the "old" corporation. We must also allocate the AGUB to the assets purchased by the "new" corporation. Section 338(b)(5) provides for an allocation based on the regulations.

Regulations section 1.338-6 allocates the ADSP and AGUB we computed in section 12.05(a) & (b). The regulation allocates these amounts to the target's assets using a seven-class asset ranking order:

Class 1: cash and bank accounts other than certificates of deposit;
Class 2: certain actively traded personal property and certificates of deposit;
Class 3: assets subject to mark to market rules and debt instruments;
Class 4: inventory assets;
Class 5: all assets not assigned to another class;
Class 6: Section 197 intangibles other than goodwill and going concern value;
Class 7: goodwill and going concern value.

The amount assigned to classes 1 through 6 cannot exceed the FMV of the assets in that class. The amount assigned to each class is allocated within the class based on relative FMV. If any amount is left after assigning ADSP and AGUB to classes 1 through 6, that amount is assigned to class 7 assets. The regulations provide several examples illustrating the application of these rules.

Section 12.05(d) Holding Period

If section 338 applies, the target corporation begins a new holding period for its assets. It no longer uses its original holding period.

Section 12.06 Asset and Stock Consistency Rules

Section 12.06(a) Statutory Provisions

Sections 338(e) and 338(f) provide so-called asset and stock consistency rules. These rules are designed to limit a corporation's ability to manipulate tax consequences by acquiring some stock or assets outside the 12-month acquisition period.

Section 338(e) treats a purchasing corporation as making a section 338 election if it acquires any asset of the target corporation at any time during a so-called "consistency period." Section 338(e)(2) provides several exceptions to the deemed election rules. The two most important exceptions are (1) acquisitions pursuant to a sale by the target corporation in the ordinary course of business; and (2) acquisitions in which the basis of the property acquired is determined wholly by reference to its basis in the hands of the person from whom acquired.[11]

Section 338(f) applies if the purchasing corporation makes qualified purchases of stock in both the target corporation and one or more target affiliates. If a section 338 election is made for the first qualified stock purchase, an election is also required for the other purchases. If no election is made for the first qualified stock purchase, no election can be made for the subsequent purchases.

The consistency period generally begins one year before the beginning of the 12-month acquisition period. It ends one year after the day following the acquisition date.[12] In other words, it spans a three-year period.

Section 12.06(b) Regulations

Section 1.338-8(a)(1) provides that no election is deemed made or required to be made with respect to the target corporation or any of its affiliates. If the consistency rules apply and no election is made, the person acquiring an asset will have a carryover basis in the asset.

Section 1.338-8(a)(2) provides that the asset consistency rules generally apply if the purchasing corporation acquires an asset directly from the target corporation when that target corporation is a subsidiary in a different consolidated group. Regulations section 1.338-8(a)(6) provides that the stock consistency rules apply when necessary to prevent avoidance of the asset consistency rule.

Example: Corporation P purchased an asset from Corporation T during the consistency period. At the time, T was a member of the Y consolidated group and was not a member of the P consolidated group. T recognized a gain of $30. P took a FMV basis for the asset. Under the section 1.1502-32 basis adjustment rules, T's gain was reflected in the basis of T stock held by Y. If P made a qualified stock purchase of the T stock, the consistency rules require P to take a carryover basis in the previously acquired asset unless P makes a section 338 election for the acquisition of T stock.

Unless the consistency rule applied, P would have a FMV basis in the acquired asset. On the sale of T stock to P, the Y consolidated group would not

---

11. Property acquired before September 1, 1982, is exempted. In addition, the IRS can issue regulations exempting other acquisitions.

12. I.R.C. §338(h)(4). Both section 338(e)(3) and 338(h)(4)(B) authorize the IRS to extend the reach of the deemed election rules.

recognize gain on part of the stock that reflected the sale of the asset. Because the consolidated return regulations should eliminate only one level of tax between members of the same consolidated group, the consistency rules require the P group to recognize gain on the T corporation asset that P purchased.

Section 12.07 Section 338(h)(10) Election

Section 12.07(a) In General

A section 338(h)(10) election is available when stock of a member of a consolidated group is purchased in a qualified stock purchase. The regulations also make this election available when S corporations are involved. The election must be made by both the purchasing corporation and the selling consolidated group (or the selling affiliate or the S corporation shareholders).

Section 338(h)(10) preserves the single tax regime available to these parties and reduces administrative burdens. The basis adjustments provided by section 1.1502-32 and the pass-through of gains and losses by S corporations result in consolidated groups and S corporation shareholders being taxed only once when corporations in which they hold stock sell assets. Because section 338(h)(10) taxes the target corporation on a deemed sale of its assets, the election exempts the selling group (or S shareholders) from tax on the sale of their stock.[13]

The regulations contain many examples detailing the tax consequences of a section 338(h)(10) election.[14] These examples apply to corporations that meet the definition of consolidated target, selling consolidated group, selling affiliate, and affiliated target. If an S corporation is involved, there will be an S corporation target and S corporation shareholders.

Section 12.07(b) Step Transaction Issues

As we discuss in Chapter 3, the step transaction doctrine may apply to separate transactions that are really parts of a single, integrated transaction. The tax consequences will be those of the single transaction.

One potential application of this doctrine involves the interplay between section 338 and the reorganization rules. Regulations section 1.338(h)(10)-

---

13. I.R.C. § 338(h)(13), as amended by the American Jobs Creation Act of 2004, takes the income tax attributable to the section 338(h)(10) deemed sale into account in determining an underpayment of corporate estimated tax liability.

14. *See* Treas. Reg. § 1.338(h)(10)-1.

1T, issued in 2003, applies to that interplay. These regulations apply if a corporation makes a qualified stock purchase of another corporation and later merges or liquidates the second corporation in a transaction that would qualify as a reorganization. The regulations allow the parties to make a section 338(h)(10) election with respect to the target corporation. If the election is made, the transaction is treated as a stock purchase. If the election is not made, the transaction is taxed under the reorganization rules.

Section 12.08 Section 1060

Section 12.08(a) Introduction

We have spent relatively little time discussing taxable acquisitions. Taxable acquisitions generally fall under the rules of sections 1001 and 1012 and are fairly straightforward. Gain or loss is the difference between the amount realized on the sale or exchange and the basis of the property sold or exchanged. The basis of property acquired in such sale or exchange is generally its cost.

The above rules generally apply when an asset is purchased alone. What if the purchase involves a group of assets, representing a trade or business? In that situation, section 1060 may apply.

Section 12.08(b) Applicable Asset Acquisition

Section 1060 applies to transactions that meet the definition of an applicable asset acquisition. That definition covers any transfer (whether directly or indirectly) of assets that constitute a trade or business if the transferee's basis is determined by reference to the consideration paid for such assets.[15] Because they use carryover basis, reorganizations, section 351 transfers, and section 355 transactions would not fall under section 1060.

The regulations issued for section 1060 have a corporate flavor. For example, Regulations section 1.1060-1(b)(2)(A) defines trade or business as the use of assets that would constitute an active trade or business under section 355.[16] The regulations also describe a trade or business as a group of assets to which goodwill or going concern value could attach.

The section 1060 regulations illustrate a topic we have referred to elsewhere in this book. Rules that are categorically stated at the beginning of a Code sec-

---

15. Section 1060(d) provides rules regarding certain partnership transactions.
16. *See* Chapter 9 for a discussion of section 355.

tion or regulation may be reversed in later sections. Section 1.1060-1(b)(1) provides that an asset acquisition is an applicable asset acquisition if the purchaser's basis in the transferred assets is determined wholly by reference to the purchaser's consideration. Although you might interpret that statement to mean that section 1060 applies only to transactions in which gain or loss is recognized, section 1.1060-1(b)(8) provides that a transfer may be an applicable assets acquisition even if no gain or loss is recognized with respect to a portion of the group of assets transferred. All of the assets transferred, including the nonrecognition assets, are taken into account in determining whether the assets constitute a trade or business.

Section 12.08(c) Asset Allocation Rules

Section 1060 involves the allocation concerns we discussed in section 12.05. In fact, section 1060(a)(flush language) provides for allocating the consideration received in the same manner as amounts are allocated to assets under section 338(b)(5).

Section 12.08(d) Holding Period

The holding period of assets acquired subject to 1060 is not determined under section 1223 because such property is acquired by sale or by deemed sale, and not by exchange. Hence, taxpayers who purchase business assets generally begin a new holding period. Because section 1.1060-1(b)(8) permits property to be acquired in an exchange in which gain or loss is not recognized, the holding period of any such property may be determined under section 1223.

CHAPTER 13

CARRYOVER OF TAX ATTRIBUTES

Section 13.01 Introduction

Although tax attributes may be less significant for smaller corporations than for large ones, every lawyer should understand their relevance. In the appropriate context, tax attributes may be as important as determining gain or loss, basis, or holding period.

Section 13.02 Relevant Code Sections

Section 381 is the primary Code section covering tax attributes. As we will see later, section 381 lists numerous tax items that may survive certain transactions listed in that section. Section 381 also provides conditions for and limitations on the use of those items. In addition to studying section 381, we will briefly consider its regulations.

One of the more important tax attributes a corporation can have is an NOL, which can be carried back and forward to shelter income. As we will see, section 382 and its regulations provide additional limits on the use of NOLs. We will conclude our discussion with overviews of sections 383 and 384, which apply additional limitations on attribute carryovers.

Section 13.03 Section 381

Section 13.03(a) Scope

Section 381 provides that an acquiring corporation carries over certain attributes that previously belonged to another corporation. Section 381 and its regulations indicate which types of acquisition are subject to these rules, define an acquiring corporation, list the affected attributes, and provide additional conditions and limitations. In the remainder of this section, we discuss acquisitions subject to section 381, acquiring corporations, and the affected attributes. We discuss general conditions, which the Code refers to as operating rules, in section 13.04. See section 13.05 for specific limitations on several of the most important tax attributes.

Section 13.03(b) Acquisitions Covered

Section 381 covers liquidations of a subsidiary that are governed by section 332, which we discussed in Chapter 11. It does not apply to partial liquidations.[1] Section 381 also covers transfers covered by five of the reorganization provisions we discussed in Chapter 10. The reorganizations subject to section 381 are the A, C, D, F, and G reorganizations. If the distributing corporation had remained in existence, it would have retained its tax attributes. To prevent their elimination, section 381 transfers those attributes to the acquiring corporation. Section 381 applies to both domestic and foreign corporations.[2]

B reorganizations are excluded from section 381 because they do not involve asset transfers; the acquired corporation remains in existence and continues to own its assets. E reorganizations are excluded because they represent a mere recapitalization of a single corporation. Corporations that undergo B and E reorganizations retain their tax attributes.

Additional rules apply to D and G reorganizations. Because those reorganizations can be divisive in nature, it may not be appropriate to transfer attributes to an acquiring corporation. D and G reorganizations are covered by section 381 only if the reorganization meets the requirements of section 354(b)(1). The transferee corporation must receive substantially all of the transferor corporation's assets. In addition, the transferor corporation must distribute the stock, securities, and other property received (and its remaining assets, if any) in pursuance of the reorganization plan.[3]

Section 13.03(c) Acquiring Corporation

Regulations section 1.381(a)-1(b)(2) defines acquiring corporation for purposes of section 381. It differentiates between liquidations described in sec-

---

1. Treas. Reg. §1.381(a)-1(b)(3).
2. Treas. Reg. §1.381(a)-1(c).
3. Those limitations prevent section 381 from applying to a divisive reorganization that meets the requirements of section 355. As we learned in Chapter 9, some tax attributes may be divided between the controlled corporation that is being distributed and the corporation that is making the distribution.

tion 381(a)(1) and reorganizations described in section 381(a)(2). A corporation that acquires its subsidiary's assets in a complete liquidation is the acquiring corporation. A corporation that ultimately acquires all the assets of a transferor corporation pursuant to a plan of reorganization is the acquiring corporation.

Only one corporation can be considered an acquiring corporation. If a transferor corporation's assets are ultimately split among several corporations, the regulations treat the corporation that directly acquired the assets as the acquiring corporation. It has this status even if it retains none of those assets itself.[4] The examples below illustrate this rule for a series of transfers made pursuant to a reorganization covered by section 381.

Example: Corporation X acquired all the assets of Corporation T in a reorganization in exchange for X stock. X is the acquiring corporation.

Example: After acquiring the T assets, X transferred all of them to a subsidiary, Corporation Y. Y is the acquiring corporation.

Example: X instead transferred 30 percent of the T assets to Y and retained the other 70 percent of those assets. X is the acquiring corporation.

Example: X instead transferred 70 percent of the T assets to Y and retained the other 30 percent. Even though Y received the majority of T assets, it did not receive all of those assets. Because X received those assets directly from T, X is the acquiring corporation.

Example: X instead transferred 50 percent of the T assets to Y and 50 percent to another subsidiary, Corporation Z. X is the acquiring corporation.

Caveat: If a corporation that is not the acquiring corporation receives assets, it is not governed by section 381. If it acquires any of the distributing corporation's attributes, the authority will not be section 381.[5]

Section 13.03(d) Attributes

Section 381(a) provides that the acquiring corporation takes the transferor corporation's tax attributes into account as of the close of the day of distribution or transfer. Although section 381(c) lists 26 attributes that carry over to the acquiring corporation, four of those have been repealed. As you can determine by reading that list, each of these items represents a potential tax benefit or detriment or other characteristic that can affect the computation of tax-

---

4. If a corporation is not an acquiring corporation, it is not subject to the section 381(c) rules even though it may receive possession of the transferor's assets. Treas. Reg. § 1.381(a)-1(b)(3).

5. Treas. Reg. § 1.381(a)-1(b)(3)(ii).

able income. These include NOL carryovers, E&P, capital loss carryovers, and accounting methods.

Section 381(c) provides operating rules for each of the attributes it covers, and the regulations expand on these rules. We address some of those rules in section 13.05.

Caveat: Do not apply section 381 to any attribute that is not listed in section 381(c). That attribute may be subject to carryover, but section 381 is not the provision that authorizes it.[6]

Section 13.04 Section 381(b) Operating Rules

Section 381(b) contains three operating rules that apply to transactions other than F reorganizations. These rules cover the taxable year, date of distribution or transfer, and treatment of certain NOL and capital loss carryovers. F reorganizations are exempted because they involve mere changes in form, name, or place of incorporation, that do not involve a meaningful transfer of assets from one corporation to another.

Section 13.04(a) End of Taxable Year

The taxable year of the distributor or transferor corporation ends on the date of the distribution or transfer. Regulations section 1.381(b)-1(c) requires it to file a short year income tax return for the period ending on the date of distribution or transfer. If it remains in existence after the date of distribution, it must file another short year tax return. That return covers the period beginning on the day following the date of distribution or transfer and ending on the date on which its taxable year would have ended if there had been no distribution or transfer.

Section 13.04(b) Date of Distribution or Transfer

The date of distribution or transfer is the day on which the distribution or transfer is completed. The section authorizes regulations that treat the date of distribution as occurring earlier. The regulations can use the date when substantially all of the transferor's property has been distributed or transferred if it has ceased all operating activities other than liquidating activities after such date.

---

6. Treas. Reg. § 1.381(a)-1(b)(3)(i).

The date of distribution is the date on which all the properties of the distributor or transferor corporation that should be distributed to the acquiring corporation are distributed. If the distribution or transfer takes more than one day, Regulations section 1.381(b)-1(b)(1) provides that the date of distribution is the day on which the distribution or transfer is completed.

Regulations section 1.381(b)-1(b)(2) provides for an alternate date of distribution. The taxpayer can elect to use the date on which substantially all the assets of the distributor or transferor corporation are transferred to the acquiring corporation and the distributor or transferor corporation has ceased all operations other than liquidating activities. Even in the absence of an election, the IRS can treat this day as the date of distribution if distribution of all the assets of the distributor or transferor corporation is unreasonably delayed. Because the regulations do not define "unreasonable delay," that determination will take into account the facts and circumstances behind the delay.

A corporation is considered to have distributed or transferred substantially all of its assets when it ceases to be a going concern. It is allowed to retain some assets to pay outstanding debts or to preserve its legal existence. Because the IRS recognizes that a corporate charter may be valuable, it allows a taxpayer to take advantage of section 381 even though it retains its corporate shell. The taxpayer may want to request a PLR to be assured this retention will not prevent it from using section 381.

The regulations address several procedural matters. If a distributor or transferor corporation elects to treat the date of transfer of substantially all of its assets as the date of distribution, its tax return must include information about the assets that were distributed and their dates of distribution, the assets not distributed and the purpose for retaining them, and the date on which the corporation ceased operations other than liquidating activities.[7]

Section 13.04(c) NOL and Capital Loss Carryovers

The acquiring corporation cannot carry back to a taxable year of the distributor or transferor corporation any NOL or a net capital loss for a taxable year ending after the date of distribution or transfer.

Example: Corporation X changed its place of incorporation by merging into newly created Corporation Y and then ceasing to exist. The transaction qualified as an F reorganization. In the year following the merger, Y had a

---

7. Treas. Reg. § 1.381(b)-1(b)(3).

$100 NOL. Because the transaction was an F reorganization, Y can carry that NOL back to use against X's taxable income from a pre-merger year.

Example: Corporation X merged into existing Corporation Y, which assumed all of the X assets and liabilities. X's shareholders received Y stock. The transaction qualified as an A reorganization. In the year following the merger, Y had a $100 NOL. Because the transaction was not an F reorganization, Y cannot carry that NOL back to use against X's taxable income from a pre-merger year.

Section 13.05 Tax Attributes Governed by Section 381

Section 13.05(a) Overview

As we indicated in section 13.03(d), the acquiring corporation inherits many of the transferor corporation's tax attributes. These include NOL carryovers, capital loss carryovers, E&P account balances, and accounting methods. These attributes largely fall into two general types: those that relate to a balance and those that relate to accounting methods. In sections 13.05(b) through 13.05(e), we discuss both types of tax attributes.

Section 13.05(b) NOL Carryovers

Section 172, which applies to corporate and noncorporate taxpayers, provides the NOL computation rules. The NOL computed using those rules has value only to the extent it can offset income of a non-loss year. If a transferor corporation ceases existence, its NOL has value only if the acquiring corporation can use it to offset its own income.

Each corporation's NOLs must be separately computed so that loss carrybacks offset only income of the corporation that had the loss.[8] Although section 381(c)(1) allows the distributing corporation to use the transferor's NOLS, it imposes limitations on that use. First, losses can be carried only to the acquiring corporation's taxable years that end after the distribution date. Second, in the first such year, a ratio applies to limit the amount of the acquiring corporation's income that can be offset. The numerator of that ratio is the number of days in the acquiring corporation's taxable year occurring after the transfer. The denominator is the total number of days in that taxable year.

---

8. Treas. Reg. § 1.381(c)(1)-1(a)(2).

Example: Corporation X acquired the assets of Corporation T in a C reorganization on April 30, Year 4. X's fiscal year ended on May 31, Year 4. T had an NOL of $50,000. X had taxable income of $300,000 per year in each of Years 1 through 3. X cannot use T's NOL to offset taxable income for Years 1 through 3, as those years ended before the transfer.

Example: Corporation X had taxable income of $200,000 in Year 4. There were 31 days in X's taxable year after X acquired the T assets. Because that represented 8.49 percent (31/365) of the taxable year, X can use the T NOL to offset $16,986 (8.49 percent) of its $200,000 Year 4 income.

The regulations for section 381(c)(1) address the sequencing of NOLs, the computation of carryovers and carrybacks when the date of distribution or transfer is not the last day of the acquiring corporation's taxable year, and successive acquiring corporations.[9] The regulations also include extensive examples.

Section 13.05(c) Capital Loss Carryovers

The rules applied to the transferor corporation's net capital losses are similar to those applied to its NOLs.[10] The ratio that limits the carryover to the acquiring corporation's first taxable year ending after the transfer is based on the acquiring corporation's net capital gain income, not on all its income. The capital loss that is carried to this and future years is treated as a short-term capital loss.

Section 13.05(d) E&P Carryovers

The acquiring corporation receives the transferor corporation's E&P at the close of the date on which the transfer occurs.[11] The acquiring corporation takes over the E&P account no matter whether it is positive or negative.

It is possible that the acquiring and transferor corporation will both have positive E&P accounts or E&P deficits. Likewise, one corporation may have a deficit while the other has a positive E&P balance. If either corporation has an E&P deficit, that deficit can offset only post-transfer E&P. A ratio similar to that discussed in section 13.05(b) is used to compute E&P that can be offset in the year of transfer.

---

9. Treas. Reg. §§ 1.381(c)(1)-1(e) through 1.381(c)(1)-1(g).
10. I.R.C. § 381(c)(3); Treas. Reg. § 1.381(c)(3)-1.
11. I.R.C. § 381(c)(2); Treas. Reg. § 1.381(c)(2)-1.

Section 13.05(e) Accounting Methods

The acquiring corporation takes over the transferor's accounting methods, including those used for inventory and depreciable property.[12] If the transferor's accounting methods, including those for inventory, differ from those used by the acquiring corporation, the regulations provide the appropriate accounting method rules. With respect to depreciable property received from the transferor, if the acquiring corporation's basis does not exceed that of the transferor, it uses the transferor's method of depreciating that basis. If the acquiring corporation's basis for the property exceeds the transferor's basis, the acquiring corporation depreciates that excess separately.

Section 13.06 Section 382

Section 13.06(a) Comparison to Section 381

Sections 381(c)(1) and 382 both limit the deduction for corporate NOLs, but they operate quite differently. Section 381 is essentially a timing provision. Preacquisition losses can be carried forward but not backward. Section 382 is essentially a disallowance provision; deductions attributable to preacquisition losses are reduced or disallowed altogether. Section 382 is an anti-abuse provision, which targets "trafficking" in NOLs.

The two sections also have different triggering events. Section 381 is triggered by corporate liquidations or reorganizations. One corporation is acquiring the assets of another corporation. Although these events may also trigger section 382, another trigger involves changes at the shareholder level without any change in the corporation itself.

Section 13.06(b) Section 382 Loss Limitation

Section 382(a) limits the amount of the taxable income of any "new loss corporation" for any "post-change year" that can be offset by "pre-change losses." The limitation is referred to as the "section 382 limitation." This limitation requires you to define the terms set off in quotation marks. In discussing post-change year, we encounter ownership and equity shifts. Each of those terms is defined below.

---

12. I.R.C. § 381(c)(4)-(6); Treas. Reg. §§ 1.381(c)(4)-1, 1.381(c)(5)-1 & 1.381(c)(6)-1.

Section 13.06(c) Section 382 Definitions

Section 13.06(c)(1) Loss Corporation

A new loss corporation is defined in section 382(k), which also defines "loss corporation" and "old loss corporation." A loss corporation is a corporation that has an NOL carryover or that has an NOL for the taxable year in which "the ownership change" occurs. The term also includes any corporation with a net unrealized built-in-loss.

A corporation is an old loss corporation if it was a loss corporation before an ownership change. A new loss corporation is a corporation that is a loss corporation after an ownership change. A single corporation can be both an old and a new loss corporation.

Section 13.06(c)(2) Ownership Change

Section 382(g) defines ownership change. An ownership change is deemed to occur if, immediately after an owner shift involving a 5-percent shareholder or an equity shift, the percentage of the loss corporation's stock owned by one or more 5-percent shareholders has increased by more than 50 percentage points over the lowest percentage of stock of the loss corporation (or any predecessor corporation) owned by such shareholder(s) at any time during the testing period.[13] A shareholder is considered if he owns stock before or after the change.

Example: Individual A owns 40 percent of the stock of Loss Corporation X. Individual B owns the remaining 60 percent. If B sells his shares to C, there has been an ownership shift. C's ownership increased from 0 percent to 60 percent.

Section 382(i) normally begins the testing period three years before the date of the ownership shift or equity structure shift. Shorter periods apply when there was a previous ownership shift or if the losses are all attributable to a period later than the beginning of the normal testing period.

Example: On Day 1, Year 1, Loss Corporation X is owned by four unrelated individuals, as follows: A, 15 percent: B, 15 percent; C, 25 percent; and D, 45 percent. On Day 1, Year 2, A purchased some of B's share. Immediately after that purchase, A owned 20 percent and B owned 10 percent. If no further changes occur, there has been no ownership shift.

Caveat: Do not confuse percentage increase with percentage point increase.

Example: A instead purchased all of B's shares. After the purchase, A owned 30 percent and B owned 0 percent. A's total ownership is 100 percent greater

---

13. Constructive ownership rules apply. I.R.C. § 382(l)(3).

than it was in Year 1, but this is not an ownership shift. An ownership shift requires that the ownership percentage itself increase by more than 50 percentage points. Because A began with 15 percent of the X stock, an ownership shift would occur only if she ended up with more than 65 percent of the X stock

Example: Assume instead that A's ownership percentage began at 15 percent on Day 1, Year 1 and changed on the first day of each year, as follows: Year 3, 25 percent; Year 4, 60 percent; Year 5, 66 percent. Although A's ownership increased by 50 percentage points or more, the increase occurred over more than three years. The requisite increase did not occur within the testing period.

Caveat: An ownership shift can be found based on changes in the ownership of more than one 5 percent shareholder. If one shareholder increases ownership from 10 percent to 40 percent, that is a 30 percentage point increase. If two shareholders both increase their ownership in this amount, the increase from 20 percent to 80 percent is a 60 percentage point shift.

Not every ownership shift is tainted. If it were, a loss corporation might be precluded from taking full advantage of an NOL merely because an owner died and bequeathed stock to a family member. Section 382(l)(3)(B) treats the new owner as if he were the old owner when stock is acquired because of death, inter vivos gift, or divorce.

The rules discussed above apply also to equity structure shifts. An equity structure shift is defined as any reorganization except divisive reorganizations and F reorganizations. Section 382 does not limit NOL carryovers unless the equity structure shift is accompanied by the more than 50 percentage point interest in stock ownership discussed above.

Section 13.06(d) Operation of Section 382

Section 382(b) limits NOL carryovers by a formula. Section 382(c) disallows them altogether. If section 382(b) applies, the maximum amount of NOL that can be used is the value of the old loss corporation multiplied by the long-term tax exempt rate.

Example: Corporation X became a new loss corporation on date 1. It had never earned income for which its NOLs could be used as a carryback. On date 1, X had a value of $100 and the long-term tax-exempt rate was 4 percent. New loss corporation X cannot deduct more than $4 of NOLs per year. Because the section 172 carryover period is 20 years, X will be unable to use its full NOL before the time period expires.

Section 382(l) prevents taxpayers from increasing the loss corporation's value, and thus increasing the allowable NOL deduction. Capital contributions are ignored if they are made pursuant to a plan a principal purpose of which is to avoid or increase any section 382 limitation. Unless the regulations provide otherwise, contributions within two years of the change date are considered part of such a plan.

Section 382(c) generally applies if the new loss corporation does not continue the business of the old loss corporation throughout the two-year period beginning on the change date. The change date is the date on which the ownership shift or reorganization causing an equity structure shift occurs.

Section 382 and its regulations contain numerous additional rules. These include rules governing built-in gains and losses and section 338 gains[14] and rules for capital contributions.[15] Study the Code and regulations carefully whenever you encounter a significant shift in a loss corporation's ownership structure.

Section 13.07 Section 383

Section 383 imposes similar limitations to those applied by section 382. If an ownership change, as defined in section 382 occurs, section 383 limits the post-acquisition use of net capital losses, section 39 general business credits, and section 53 minimum tax credits attributable to preacquisition years.

Section 13.08 Section 384

Sections 382 and 384 complement each other. Section 382 generally prohibits the use of NOLs following the acquisition of loss corporations. What if a loss corporation acquires a gain corporation? Section 384 restricts the use of losses following such purchases. Without section 384, a gain corporation could easily restructure its acquisition of a loss corporation and make the loss corporation the acquiring entity. The result would be the unrestricted use of NOLs of the loss corporation by the gain corporation since it is now under the umbrella of the loss corporation.

Section 384(a) applies if a corporation acquires control of another corporation or the assets of the corporation in an A, C or D reorganization.[16] If ei-

---

14. I.R.C. §382(h).

15. I.R.C. §382(l)(1).

16. The acquisition of control can be direct or done through one or more other corporations.

ther corporation is a gain corporation, income for any recognition period taxable year cannot be offset by any preacquisition loss (other than the loss of the gain corporation). The offset may be allowed if the two corporations were members of the same controlled group for at least five years.[17]

Section 384(c)(5) defines control using the tests in section 1504(a)(2), ownership of at least 80 percent of the voting power and stock value.

Example: Corporation L, a loss corporation, purchased all the stock of Corporation P for cash and did not make an election under section 338. Section 382 does not apply because there was no change in L's ownership. Because section 384 does apply, any gains realized by P within the five-year recognition period cannot be used in the L-P consolidated return to shelter L's pre-acquisition losses.

Example: Assume that L elected section 338 application with respect to P. In that case, section 384 would not apply, but P would be fully taxed on its recognized gains. Those gains could not be included in the L-P consolidated return under section 338.

---

17. I.R.C. §384(b). A shorter period is used if a corporation was not in existence for five years on the acquisition date.

Controlled Corporations, Affiliated Corporations, and Consolidated Returns

CHAPTER 14

CONTROLLED CORPORATIONS AND AFFILIATED CORPORATIONS

Section 14.01 Introduction

Part Five concerns issues that affect corporations under common control. We discuss controlled groups and affiliated corporations in this chapter and discuss consolidated returns in Chapter 15. Because an affiliated group is eligible to file consolidated tax returns, it is important to consider affiliation before discussing consolidated returns. If you are familiar with these concepts, you are more likely to spot the relevant issues when they arise.

Section 14.02 Controlled Corporations

Although this chapter primarily deals with affiliated corporations (a subset of controlled corporations), we begin with a short detour to discuss the broader concept of controlled corporations. This detour introduces restrictions imposed on controlled corporations and opportunities available to these corporations. Restrictions, such as those provided by section 1561, are generally designed to prevent these corporations from being treated separately and enjoying multiple tax benefits. A group does not necessarily avoid these restrictions by choosing not to file on a consolidated basis.

Section 14.02(a) In General

Section 1563 both defines controlled corporations and provides special rules for them. It lists four types of controlled corporations: (1) parent-subsidiary controlled group; (2) brother-sister controlled group; (3) combined group; and (4) insurance group. These rules cover only two or more corporations that are connected as determined under section 1563. A single, stand alone corporation does not fall under the definition of controlled corporation and is not subject to the restrictions imposed under section 1561.

Section 14.02(a)(1) Parent-Subsidiary Controlled Group

A parent-subsidiary controlled group exists if one or more chains of corporations are connected through stock ownership and have a common parent. There are two stock ownership tests involved. First, at least 80 percent of the total combined voting of all classes of stock entitled to vote or at least 80 percent of the value of all classes of stock of each of the corporations must be owned by one or more of the other corporations. Second, the common parent must directly own at least 80 percent of the total combined voting power or at least 80 percent of the stock value of at least one of the other corporations. An example of a parent-subsidiary controlled group is the following:

Parent-Sub Controlled Group

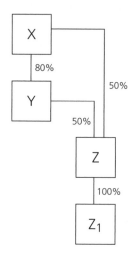

Section 14.02(a)(2) Brother-Sister Controlled Group

The brother-sister controlled group structure is more complicated than the parent-subsidiary structure. Section 1563(a)(2) covers two or more corporations with a particular minimum amount of common ownership. The identity of the owners, the computation of stock ownership, and the purpose for which the computation is made are subject to additional limitations.

The amount of ownership depends on which set of limitations apply. For purposes of the section 1561 limitations, the ownership requirement is that five or fewer shareholders must own more than 50 percent of the voting power or more than 50 percent of the stock value of each corporation.[1] This computation includes persons who are individuals, trusts, or estates. Both actual and constructive ownership, using section 1563(e) rules, is counted. However, a shareholder's stock ownership is counted only to the extent it is identical for each corporation.

The prior version of section 1563(a)(2), which remains applicable for purposes other than section 1561, also requires five or fewer owners who are individuals, trusts, or estates and ownership of more than 50 percent of the voting power or stock value. That version also requires those persons to own at least 80 percent of the total combined voting power of all classes of stock entitled to vote, or at least 80 percent of the total value of shares of all classes of stock, of each corporation. All ownership, not merely identical ownership, counts for purposes of the 80 percent computation.[2]

The illustration below is an example of a brother-sister controlled group under both the old and new versions of section 1563(a)(2). Corporations X and Y are owned equally by individuals A and B.

Brother-Sister Controlled Group

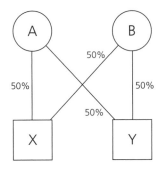

Because the Code imposes restrictions on controlled corporations, taxpayers prefer a narrow interpretation of controlled group. At one time, the regulations interpreted section 1563(a)(2) to count a person's ownership toward the 80 percent requirement even though the same person did not own stock in each of the brother-sister corporations. Those regulations were held invalid. The Supreme Court held that the statute applied only if each person whose stock is taken into account for purposes of the 80 percent requirement owns

---

1. This definition was added by the American Jobs Creation Act of 2004.
2. I.R.C. § 1563(f)(5).

stock in each corporation of the group.[3] Regulations section 1.1563-1(a)(3) now provides that owners are not taken into account for purposes of the 80 percent test unless they are also taken into account for purposes of the 50 percent test.

To count ownership, simply map out each shareholder's ownership in each corporation. Then, determine the shareholder's identical ownership in each corporation. This identical ownership is taken into account for purposes of the 50 percent test. If that test is satisfied, use those shareholders' total ownership to determine whether the 80 percent test is satisfied. Although they require some technical revisions to reflect the 2004 statutory changes, the regulations provide several examples that illustrate these computations.

Example: Unrelated individuals A and B each own 35 percent of Corporation X. A owns 60 percent of Corporation Y; B owns 20 percent of Y. No other person owns both X and Y stock. In computing common ownership, A is deemed to own 35 percent of each corporation; B is deemed to own 20 percent of each. X and Y are a brother-sister controlled group for purposes of the 50 percent test, because five or fewer shareholders own more than 50 percent of each corporation's stock. They do not satisfy the 80 percent test. For purposes of that test, A and B own 70 percent of X and 80 percent of Y.

Section 14.02(a)(3) Combined Group

Section 1563(a)(3) defines a combined group as three or more corporations that meet the following three requirements. Each corporation must be a member of a group of corporations described in a parent-subsidiary controlled or a brother-sister controlled group. One of these corporations must be a common parent corporation included in a parent-subsidiary controlled group of corporations. That corporation must also be included in a brother-sister controlled group. In other words, members of a combined group include members of a parent-subsidiary controlled group and of a brother-sister group.

The section 1561 restrictions discussed in this chapter apply to both sets of corporations as a group instead of applying separately to the brother-sister controlled group or parent-subsidiary controlled group. The illustration below reflects Regulations section 1.1563-1(a)(4)(Example 1). Individual A owns 80 percent of both Corporation X and Corporation Y.

---

3. *United States v. Vogel Fertilizer Co.,* 455 U.S. 16 (1982).

Combined Group of Corporations

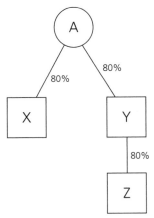

X, Y, and Z are members of a combined group

Section 14.02(a)(4) Insurance Group

The last controlled group covered by section 1563 is a group of two or more insurance companies subject to taxation under Code section 801. These insurance companies must be members of either a parent-subsidiary controlled group, a brother-sister controlled group, or a combined group. Insurance company taxation is a specialty that is beyond the scope of this book.

Section 14.03 Restrictions Applied to a Controlled Group

Section 1561 provides that the component members of a controlled group are subject to several restrictions. First, the combined amounts taxed in each taxable income bracket cannot exceed the maximum amount in each bracket available to a corporation that is not part of a controlled group. Second, they are limited to one $250,000 amount for purposes of computing the accumulated earnings credit under section 535(c)(2) & (c). That amount is reduced to $150,000 if any group member is a service corporation described in section 535(c)(2)(B). Third, they are limited to one $40,000 exemption amount for purposes of computing the minimum tax. Fourth, they are limited to one $2,000,000 exemption for purposes of computing the section 59A environmental tax. Thus, although dividing a business into separate corporations may be a good idea for liability purposes, it is unlikely to yield significant tax benefits.

Section 1561(a) generally provides that the amounts described above will be divided equally among the component members of the controlled group unless the members or the IRS allocates these amounts in a different fashion.

Section 14.04 Affiliated Groups

Section 14.04(a) In General

Affiliated corporations are a subset of controlled corporations. Because a group of corporations cannot file a consolidated return unless it meets the section 1504 affiliation requirements, the discussion of affiliated corporations and consolidated returns is intertwined. This chapter addresses the affiliation requirements. Chapter 15 covers selected issues pertaining to consolidated returns.

Section 14.04(b) Definition of Affiliated Group

Section 1504(a)(1) & (2) defines an affiliated group as one or more chains of includible corporations connected through stock ownership with a common parent corporation which is an includible corporation. The common parent must own directly 80 percent or more of the stock of at least one of the includible corporations. In addition, 80 percent or more of the stock of each includible corporation must be owned by one or more of the includible corporations. Although affiliated groups are likely to be owned 80 percent in a vertical line, other ownership structures can satisfy the statutory language. An example of an affiliated group is illustrated below.

Affiliated Group

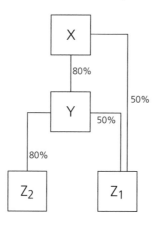

Section 14.04(c) The 80 Percent Test

Section 1504(a)(2) applies the 80 percent ownership requirement to both voting power and stock value. This requirement ensures that taxpayers have a significant economic interest in the corporations with which they are affiliated. In the absence of the voting power and value tests, corporations could affiliate with other corporations in which they have limited economic exposure. For example, a corporation could acquire 80 percent of the voting power of a corporation but only a small amount of the second corporation's stock value.[4] The corporations could then elect to file their returns on a consolidated basis, offsetting the income of one corporation by the losses of the other.

Because both voting power and stock value must meet the 80 percent tests, the acquiring corporation must make a significant investment in the acquired corporation. In addition, the consolidated return regulations contain significant restrictions on the use of losses of recently acquired corporations. Losses incurred following the acquisition can usually be taken into account in determining the group's consolidated income. But losses incurred before the acquisition are generally not available for use by the group.[5]

Section 14.04(d) Reconsolidation Following Disaffiliation

Section 1504(a)(3) generally provides that a corporation included or required to be included in a consolidated return that ceases to be a member of the group must wait five years before rejoining that group or joining another group headed by the same common parent or a successor of such common parent. This rule limits taxpayers' ability to enter and leave groups simply to exploit the use of tax losses or other benefits that might be used by the group. Section 1504(a)(3)(B) lets taxpayers rejoin their group sooner if they receive a waiver from the IRS.[6]

---

4. The second corporation might have two classes of stock. One class, consisting of relatively few shares, might have voting rights; a second class, representing the bulk of the shares, might be nonvoting.

5. *See* Treas. Reg. § 1.1502-21.

6. The Service provides for automatic waivers in Revenue Procedure 2002-32, 2002-1 C.B. 959. Corporations using the automatic procedure must include a statement that the disaffiliation and reconsolidation does not result in a tax benefit that would not have been available without those two events. Section 5.14 of the revenue procedure includes a list of tax attributes the statement must address.

A revenue ruling addresses whether section 1504(a)(3) prevents a corporation whose parent was acquired in a section 368(a)(1)(A) reorganization from being included in consolidated returns filed by the acquiring group.[7] The ruling was necessary because section 1504(a)(3) states that a corporation that ceases to be a member of an affiliated group cannot join a group with the same common parent or a successor of the common parent for five years. Section 1504(a)(3) does not define "successor." Arguably, a corporation that acquires the common parent of a disappearing group would be a successor to that common parent. If so, subsidiaries owned by the former common parent would not be allowed to join the new group unless they received a waiver from the IRS. The revenue ruling provides that section 1504(a)(3) was not intended to prevent such corporations from joining the new group. Following the acquisition of a common parent of a group in an asset reorganization, the subsidiaries of the former group must be included in the new group.

Section 14.04(e) Definition of Stock

Section 14.04(e)(1) Statutory Definition

Section 1504(a)(4) defines stock that is considered in the 80 percent tests discussed above. It provides that stock does not include stock which is not entitled to vote, is limited and preferred as to dividends and does not participate in corporate growth to any significant extent, has redemption and liquidation rights which do not exceed the issue price of such stock, and is not convertible into another class of stock. That definition excludes most types of preferred stock, which do not carry governance and corporate growth rights.

Section 1504(a)(5) gives the IRS authority to promulgate regulations implementing the purposes of section 1504(a). The provision indicates six actions the IRS can take but does not limit the Service to those actions:

(1) treat warrants, obligations convertible into stock, and other similar interests as stock (and treat stock as not stock);
(2) treat options to acquire or sell stock as having been exercised;
(3) provide that the requirements of section 1504(a)(2)(B) are treated as met if the group, in reliance on a good faith determination of value, treated such requirements as met;

---

7. Rev. Rul. 91-70, 1991-2 C.B. 361. This ruling also applies if the acquisition was a reverse acquisition described in Treas. Reg. § 1.1502-75(d)(3).

(4) disregard an inadvertent ceasing to meet the requirements of section 1504(a)(2)(B) by reason of changes in relative values of different classes of stock;

(5) provide that transfers of stock within the group shall not be taken into account in determining whether a corporation ceases to be a member of an affiliated group; and

(6) disregard changes in voting power to the extent such changes are disproportionate to related changes in value.

Section 14.04(e)(2) Regulations

The IRS has issued regulations covering the treatment of warrants, options, convertible obligations, or similar interests. Regulations section 1.1504-4(b)(1) provides that options are generally not treated as exercised. The major exception appears in section 1.1504-4(b)(2), which applies if the option is likely to be exercised and such exercise would cause the elimination of a substantial amount of federal income tax liability.

The purpose of these regulations was to prevent groups from retaining qualification under section 1504 while divesting their economic interest in a subsidiary. For example, a corporation might want to sell a subsidiary's stock but continue to include the subsidiary in its consolidated returns. In the absence of a contrary rule, the corporation could accomplish this result by selling options to acquire the subsidiary's stock. Until the options were actually exercised, the corporation could include the subsidiary in its consolidated returns and thus use the subsidiary's losses to shelter income of other group members. By treating such options as having been exercised, the regulations may cause deconsolidation before there is a change in actual stock ownership.

The regulations provide for judging the likelihood of exercise on a measurement date: a date on which an option is issued or transferred or on which the terms of an existing option or the underlying stock are adjusted.[8] There are safe harbor rules under which certain issuances or transfers will not be treated as measurement dates. These include transfers by gift, at death, or between spouses or former spouses under section 1041. The safe harbors also cover options issued or transferred between members of an affiliated group.

A facts and circumstances test applies in determining whether an option is reasonably likely to be exercised.[9] The regulation also provides safe harbor rules, which generally apply if the option exercise price is close to the stock's

---

8. Treas. Reg. § 1.1504-4(c)(4)

9. Treas. Reg. § 1.1504-4(g). The regulation includes a list of ten factors.

value. If one of the safe harbors applies, the option is not treated as exercised, and the group retains its affiliated status.

Section 1.1504-4(e) takes a broad approach to determining the elimination of federal income tax liability. It provides that the tax consequences to all involved parties must be examined. Using a deduction that otherwise would not be utilized or deferring gain recognition are examples of elimination of federal income tax liability. Obviously, if allowing affiliated status would cause no change in the group's income tax liability, there is little or no abuse potential. In that case, treating the options as exercised would be of little consequence.

The regulations contain several examples that illustrate application of these rules.

Section 14.04(e)(3) Notice 2004-37

Notice 2004-37 addresses both good faith reliance and inadvertently ceasing to meet the affiliation requirements.[10] The IRS will not challenge a group's affiliation if it is based on a good faith determination that the affiliation rules were met. The notice also discusses circumstances in which the IRS will not challenge a group's inadvertent disaffiliation.

This notice accomplished several goals. It provided guidance and requested taxpayer comments. These comments are likely to affect the regulations that are ultimately issued. Notice 2004-37 appears to give blanket protection to taxpayers who meet its guidelines. In reviewing this notice, you should pay particular attention to section 3.02 (good faith exception), section 3.03 (inadvertent disaffiliation), and 3.04 (designated events). Designated events include such activities as issuing stock to non-group members, redemptions from group members, and recapitalizations.

Section 14.04(f) Ineligible Corporations

Section 14.04(f)(1) General Rule

Section 1504(b) lists corporations that cannot be includible corporations. The following corporations cannot be part of an affiliated group: corporations exempt from taxation under section 501; insurance companies taxed under section 801; foreign corporations; corporations with respect to which a section 936[11] election has been made; RICs and REITs; domestic international sales

---

10. 2004-21 I.R.B. 947.

11. Section 936 provided tax incentives to corporations (especially manufacturers) operating in United States possessions, including Puerto Rico.

corporations; and S corporations. The special tax benefits these corporations enjoy make them inappropriate for inclusion in an affiliated group.

Section 14.04(f)(2) Exceptions

Sections 1504(c), (d), and (e) allow some otherwise excluded corporations to qualify for affiliation. Section 1504(c) permits two or more insurance companies subject to tax under section 801 to be treated as includible corporations for purposes of section 1504. It also lets the parent of an affiliated group treat these insurance companies as members of the group. These types of affiliated groups are called life/non-life groups. They can present interesting issues when a life company member of the group loses, and later regains, its life insurance status. If the corporation that lost its status and then regained it was a member of an affiliated group during this sequence, it is subject to the section 1504(a)(3) five-year rule.

Section 1504(d) permits domestic corporations to treat certain foreign corporations as includible corporations. To qualify for includible status, the foreign corporation must meet three requirements. First, the domestic parent must own 100 percent of the foreign corporation's capital stock (except directors' qualifying shares). Second, the foreign corporation must be organized under the laws of a contiguous country (Mexico or Canada). Third, the foreign corporation must be organized solely for the purpose of complying with the laws of the other country as to title and operation of property. If these requirements are met, the domestic parent may elect to treat the foreign corporation as a domestic corporation.[12]

The IRS narrowly construes section 1504(d), allowing these elections only if they are made solely for purposes of ownership and operation of property. In one ruling, it held that the purposes of section 1504(d) were not met when a domestic corporation formed a Canadian corporation solely for purposes of applying for a grant program operated by the Canadian government.[13]

Courts may not interpret a statute this narrowly. *U. S. Padding Corp. v. Commissioner,*[14] although arguably decided on different grounds, nevertheless represents a departure from that IRS ruling. That decision involved a domestic corporation that bought a manufacturing business in Canada. Canadian law permitted the purchase or establishment of a business in Canada if this

---

12. Rev. Rul. 69-182, 1969-1 C.B. 218, permitted a section 1504(d) election to be made with regard to a corporation organized under the laws of Mexico to conduct an advertising business. Mexican laws imposed restrictions on foreigners conducting such business.

13. Rev. Rul. 71-523, 1971-2 C.B. 326.

14. 88 T.C. 177 (1987), *aff'd,* 865 F.2d 750 (6th Cir. 1989).

would provide significant benefits to Canada. The government agency that determined "significant benefits" looked favorably upon businesses that were incorporated even though incorporation was not required under Canadian law. The domestic corporation followed advice of Canadian counsel and incorporated the business. The court concluded that section 1504(d) was designed to address any existing practice or policy of a contiguous foreign country that results in a domestic corporation finding it necessary to maintain its foreign business and properties as a foreign corporation in order to operate in that country.

In another case, the Federal Circuit interpreted section 1504(d) more narrowly. It held that a domestic group could not include its Canadian subsidiary in its consolidated returns because it would derive a benefit not contemplated by section 1504(d).[15] The domestic taxpayer was advised by its Canadian counsel to incorporate. Upon incorporation, it would also become eligible to apply for a Canadian grant.

The North American Free Trade Agreement (NAFTA) and other changes in Mexican and Canadian law may affect the application of section 1504(d).[16] For example, in 1996 Mexico removed many restrictions on foreigners owning real estate. In 2001, the IRS declared obsolete a 1970 ruling that permitted consolidated returns to include Mexican corporations that were incorporated for the purpose of holding real estate in Mexico.[17] Changes in Canadian banking laws permitting foreign banks to function directly in Canada led to Notice 2000-7, providing that section 1504(d) would no longer apply to domestic corporations that incorporated a corporation in Canada in order to engage in the banking business in Canada.[18] Section 1504(d) relief is unnecessary if domestic corporations can engage in activities directly.

Notwithstanding the *U.S. Padding Corp.* opinion, taxpayers should still be concerned about section 269, which applies to acquisitions made to evade taxes. If that section applies, the IRS can deny the benefit of a deduction, credit or other allowance which should not have been taken. Because section 269 requires that the "principal purpose" of the acquisition be evasion or avoidance of income tax, the IRS may have difficulty convincing a court of its application. The Service can also attempt to deny section 1504(d) status using

---

15. *Kohler Co. v. United States*, 124 F.3d 1451 (Fed. Cir. 1997).

16. The North American Free Trade Agreement between United States, Mexico, and Canada entered into force in January 1994.

17. Rev. Rul. 70-379, 1970-2 C.B. 179, *obsoleted by* Rev. Rul. 2001-39, 2001-2 C.B. 125.

18. 2000-1 C.B. 419.

substance over form arguments or other technical arguments. It might, for instance, argue that the transaction has no significant business purpose.

Section 1504(e) allows a group of tax-exempt corporations to form an affiliated group and thereby become eligible to elect to file their returns on a consolidated basis.

Chapter 15

Consolidated Returns

Section 15.01 Introduction

In Chapter 14, we discussed the concept of affiliated corporations. Unless corporations are affiliated, they cannot elect to file their returns on a consolidated basis. This chapter provides an overview of consolidated returns and highlights selected areas that are potential pitfalls.

Code section 1501 indicates that affiliated groups of corporations have the "privilege" of filing a consolidated income tax return. Because the section grants a privilege, it is not surprising that section 1501 also includes certain requirements. The most important is that of consent. Section 1501 requires that all members of the affiliated group consent to the section 1502 regulations, which are discussed below.[1] Unless the parent receives an extension, the consolidated return is to be filed by the due date for its return.

Section 1501 also addresses the treatment of any corporation that is part of the group for only a portion of the year. The consolidated return includes that corporation's income only for the part of the year during which it was a group member.

Section 1502, which authorizes the Secretary to prescribe consolidated return regulations, is a far more important Code provision. It authorizes regulations covering time periods before, during, and after the affiliation period. The regulations aim to accomplish the congressional purposes of having a

---

1. The corporate parent indicates that a consolidated return is being filed by checking a box on Form 1120, the U.S. Corporation Income Tax return. It attaches Form 851 to identify the common parent and each group member and provide other information about group members. Each subsidiary completes a Form 1122 to indicate its consent to being included in the consolidated return (and future consolidated returns if it remains eligible). The parent attaches the Forms 1122 to the consolidated tax return. Section 1501 also provides that the making of a consolidated return is treated as consent to make such a return.

clear reflection of income tax liability and preventing the avoidance of that liability. Because of the specific authorizing language in section 1502, its regulations are legislative regulations. As we discussed in section 1.02(c), legislative regulations receive more deference than interpretative regulations, which are issued pursuant to section 7805.

Section 15.02 Consolidated Return Issues

Section 15.02(a) In General

In thinking about consolidated returns, keep one important fact in mind. Corporations filing consolidated returns engage in the same transactions that stand alone corporations engage in. Corporations must consider both the rules applicable to stand alone corporations and consolidated corporations in determining how to report a transaction. For example, if a corporation that is included in a consolidated return engages in a reorganization, it must satisfy the rules governing reorganizations. Consolidated return rules, such as those dealing with intercompany transactions and basis adjustments, will also apply to the transaction.

Section 15.02(b) Deciding to File Consolidated Returns

Consolidated returns have both advantages and disadvantages. Advantages relate to sharing profits and losses on a single tax return. If one member's profits can be reduced by another member's losses, the profitable member's income may be taxed less heavily; the loss member may be able to avoid the section 172 NOL carryover limitations. Because group members may deal with each other as they do with others, they can avoid paying taxes on gains from transactions within the group. They can also receive tax-free dividend distributions from other group members.

There are also disadvantages associated with filing consolidated returns. Group members may have fewer options for using accounting methods and periods because of a need to conform to the group. There are a variety of loss deduction limitations and loss deferral rules applied to group members.

Generally, consolidated returns are filed by large groups of corporations that conduct diverse businesses. A small group will seldom find that the benefits of filing consolidated returns outweigh the costs of tracking the complex regulations involved. Simplification is not achieved by substituting a single consolidated return for several separate returns. Because the consolidated return rules are not easy to comprehend, and the election is generally binding in the absence of IRS permission to deconsolidate, taxpayers should carefully assess both advantages and disadvantages of this election.

Section 15.03 Consent to File Consolidated Returns

Consent by all group members is necessary in order for the group to file its returns on a consolidated basis. If a group member fails to sign Form 1122, it may still be considered part of the group based on the facts and circumstances. Relevant factors include whether its income and deductions were included in the consolidated return, whether it filed a separate return for that taxable year, and whether it was included in the affiliation schedule, Form 851.[2]

Generally, if a group member fails to consent to the filing of a consolidated return, each corporation's tax liability is determined on a separate basis unless the IRS is satisfied that the failure was due to a mistake. The parent can apply for relief by requesting a PLR. If the time for filing a consolidated return has expired, taxpayers can apply for relief under regulation sections 301.9100-1 through 301.9100-3.

Caveat: The IRS does not treat such relief as merely a procedural undertaking. A taxpayer that would not substantively be eligible for relief under the underlying Code provision will not receive relief.

Section 15.04 Difficulty in Deconsolidating

After corporations elect to file consolidated returns, their decision is difficult to undo. The election is, in many ways, a permanent one. The operative rules are found in Regulations section 1.1502-75. Section 1.1502-75(a) provides for an election to file consolidated returns in lieu of separate returns when all the corporations in the group consent to such filing. Section 1.1502-75(a)(2) provides that a group which filed or was required to file a consolidated return for the immediately preceding year must file a consolidated return for the current year unless it has an election to discontinue filing under section 1.1502-75(c).

Section 1.1502-75(c)(1) authorizes the IRS, for good cause shown, to grant permission to discontinue filing a consolidated return. This provision is a trap

---

2. Treas. Reg. § 1.1502-75(b)(2).

for the unwary. The Service has not granted such relief in decades, and revenue rulings pertaining to this regulation are all negative. For example, Revenue Ruling 74-378 held that saving on taxes imposed by a state on out of state subsidiaries was not good cause.[3] Revenue Ruling 74-91 held similarly in the context of achieving international tax savings.[4] The revenue ruling stated that events, activities, and economic conditions affecting individual members of a group are not considered material insofar as the inter-relationships of the group members are concerned. Such circumstances, including the shifting from a consolidated return basis to a separate return basis in order to achieve temporary tax reductions or advantages, are not good cause.

There are limited methods for achieving deconsolidation. Obviously, if a corporation no longer meets the ownership threshold necessary for affiliation (80 percent vote and value), it will become a disaffiliated member and will not be eligible for inclusion on the consolidated return. This can be a high price to achieve deconsolidation, but it may be the only one available to most taxpayers. The only other way to deconsolidate is to obtain permission based on Regulations section 1.1502-75(c)(1)(ii) and (iii). Permission will be granted only if there is a change in the law that causes detriment to a consolidated group or that would prevent a consolidated group from continuing filing consolidated returns.

A few PLRs have permitted groups to deconsolidate under section 1.1502-75(c) because of changed circumstances. A closer look at these PLRs reveals that the applicable rationale should really have been disaffiliation under section 1504. For example, in two rulings, the IRS found good cause for deconsolidation when the parent corporation was no longer in existence under state law.[5] As proof of its reluctance to allow deconsolidation, the IRS denied deconsolidation when a group member was in bankruptcy and the trustee did not file the necessary consent.[6]

The IRS appears to consider only changes that it makes to the consolidated return regulations as qualifying taxpayers for deconsolidation. In these circumstances, it generally issues a blanket permission-granting document based on Regulations section 1.1502-75(c)(2) rather than forcing taxpayers to request PLRs.[7] Taxpayers who deconsolidate under these blanket permission

---

3. 1974-2 C.B. 287.

4. 1974-1 C.B. 252.

5. PLR 9048003 (Aug. 22, 1990); PLR 9048004 (Aug. 22, 1990).

6. *See* Revenue Ruling 63-104, 1963-1 C.B. 172.

7. *See, e.g.,* Rev. Proc. 91-11, 1991-1 C.B. 470 (promulgated in response to the section 1.1502-20 loss disallowance regulations); Rev. Proc. 95-11, 1995-1 C.B. 505 (promulgated in response to changes to the consolidated basis investment rules of section 1.1502-32);

procedures must enter into a closing agreement with the IRS. Such agreements, when properly drafted, are not subject to court challenges. They effectively seal the tax results provided in the agreement.

Section 15.05 Group Remaining in Existence

The life of a consolidated group is not static. New members join the group, and other members leave. Regulations section 1.1502-75(d) provides rules for determining when a group remains in existence.

A group remains in existence for a tax year if the common parent remains as the group's parent and at least one subsidiary that was affiliated with it at the end of the prior year remains affiliated with it at the beginning of the tax year. This rule applies whether or not one or more subsidiaries ceased to be subsidiaries at any time after the group was formed. So long as the parent of the group has at least one member that is continuously affiliated with it, the group will be treated as continuing in existence. The example below is based on those regulations.

Example: Corporation P acquired 100 percent of the stock of Corporation S on January 1, Year 1, and P and S filed a consolidated return for that calendar year. On May 1, Year 2, P acquired 100 percent of the stock of S-1, and on July 1, Year 2, P sold the stock of S. The group (consisting originally of P and S) remains in existence in Year 2. P has remained as the common parent and at least one subsidiary (now S-1) remains affiliated with it.

In some instances, even the disappearance of the group's common parent will not cause deconsolidation. Regulations section 1.1502-75(d)(2)(i) treats the group as remaining in existence if the parent engages in an F reorganization. Because an F reorganization is a mere change in form rather than one in substance, this rule makes sense. A group's existence will also continue if the parent disappears but the other members become the owners of substantially all the former parent's assets and there remain one or more chains of includible corporations.

Regulations section 1.1502-75(d)(3) contains some interesting rules relating to the merger of two or more groups. If Group A's parent merges with and into Group B's parent, which group survives and must continue to file its returns on a consolidated basis? Does the merger cause both groups to cease existence and hence cause deconsolidation for both groups? The regulations pro-

---

Rev. Proc. 95-39, 1995-2 C.B. 399 (promulgated in response to changes made under the intercompany rules of section 1.1502-13).

vide that the larger group is treated as the survivor. In determining size, the regulations look to the percentage of stock received by the shareholders of the merged group.

Example: Consolidated Group A merges with consolidated Group B. The shareholders of Group A receive more than 50 percent of the stock of the parent of Group B. Group A will be treated as surviving and must continue filing its consolidated returns with the parent of Group B as its new common parent.

The IRS went to great lengths to write rules that conserve the filing of consolidated returns in almost all situations. Allowing taxpayers to deconsolidate and reconsolidate at will could lead to abuses in the computation of corporate tax liability. Regulations section 1.1502-75(e) provides that the failure to include an affiliated member in the group's consolidated return will not invalidate the consolidated return to the extent a consolidated return is required. The taxes, if any, paid on a separate basis will be treated as paid on a consolidated basis. Similarly, under section 1.1502-75(f), including a non-includible corporation in the consolidated return does not invalidate that return. Instead, the tax liability of those corporations will be computed as if separate returns were filed.

Section 15.06 Computation of Income and Liability for Tax

Computing the group's taxable income is challenging. The consolidated return regulations sometimes take a single entity approach (items are calculated on a separate corporation basis) and sometimes take an aggregate approach (items are calculated on an aggregate basis). The general rules for calculating consolidated taxable income are found in Regulations sections 1.1502-11 and 1.1502-12. Their complexity is increased by the impact of other provisions, especially sections 1.1502-13, 1.1502-20, and 1.1502-32, which are discussed in sections 15.07 through 15.09.

After calculating the group's consolidated tax liability, the group's parent normally pays tax on behalf of the group. If the parent fails to pay, the IRS can pursue the entire group or it can attempt to collect from any group member. Regulations section 1.1502-6(a) makes each group member severally liable for the entire tax owed by the group. Regulations section 1.1502-6(c) provides that agreements between group members or any other person regarding apportionment of tax liability do not affect the tax liability imposed by the section. Regulations section 1.1502-6(b) lets the IRS limit the potential liability of a group member that has been sold before the assessment of a deficiency against the group. If the IRS believes that the recovery of the deficiency will not be jeopardized, it can decide to collect from the former member only an amount attributable to it.

Section 15.07 Intercompany Transaction Rules

Section 15.07(a) In General

The intercompany transaction rules are an important aspect of consolidated returns. The regulations contain specific rules for specific transactions. When encountering an intercompany transaction, you should first determine whether a specific rule is applicable. If you find no specific rule applicable, use the regulation's general rules to determine the outcome. This section provides a short overview of those rules.

Section 1.1502-13(a)(1) provides that the purpose of the intercompany transaction rules is to clearly reflect the taxable income of the group. The rules operate to prevent transactions between group members from "creating, accelerating, avoiding, or deferring consolidated taxable income (or consolidated tax liability)." Section 1.1502-13(a)(2) is especially important. It provides that group members are treated as separate for some purposes and as divisions of a single corporation for other purposes. When one group member sells to another, this regulation affects the buyer and seller corporations. It treats the two corporations as separate entities with respect to the amount and location of the intercompany item. It treats them as divisions of a single entity with respect to timing, character, source, and attributes. As a general rule, the selling member will maintain an account for gain realized on a sale within the group. It will defer recognizing that gain until the property is sold outside the group. An example of these transactions appears in section 15.07(c).

Section 15.07(b) What Is an Intercompany Transaction?

Section 1.1502-13(b)(1)(i) defines an intercompany transaction as "a transaction between corporations that are members of the same consolidated group immediately after the transaction." Examples of intercompany transactions include sale or exchange of property between members of the group, performance of services by one member to another and the accounting for such services by the recipient member, and distributions of cash or property from one member to another. Virtually every economic transaction between group members is an intercompany transaction and is subject to the section 1.1502-

13 intercompany rules. The technical rules that apply are the section 1.1502-13(c) matching rules and the section 1.1502-13(d) acceleration rules.

Section 15.07(c) Matching and Acceleration Rules

The matching rule ensures that gains or losses are appropriately assigned to group members. The regulations use several formulas to achieve this result. These formulas involve so-called intercompany items, corresponding items, and recomputed corresponding items.

If one group member sells to another, the seller's income, gain, deduction, and loss attributable to the transaction are the intercompany items. The buyer's income, gain, deduction, and loss are the corresponding items. The recomputed corresponding items reflect the amounts that would be reported if the two corporations were part of a single entity rather than separate corporations. These concepts are illustrated by the example below, which is based on example (1) of Regulations section 1.1502-13(c)(7).

Example: In Year 1, S (selling member of consolidated group) sold land to B (buying member) for $100. S's basis for the land was $70. B later sold the land to a nonmember for $110. S and B each held the land for investment and each held it more than one year. The intercompany item is S's $30 gain on the sale to B. The corresponding item is B's $10 gain on the property, and the recomputed corresponding item is the $40 gain on the sale to the nonmember. When the land left the group, the group recognized a $40 long-term capital gain, allocable $30 to S and $10 to B.

The acceleration rule applies when treating the corporations as divisions of a single entity is no longer achievable. Generally, this occurs when one of those corporations leaves the group or is otherwise no longer affiliated with it. In that instance, the acceleration rules cause the group to recognize income and treat the deferred intercompany transaction as a sale or exchange to a nonmember.

Example: Assume the same facts as above, except that S was sold outside the group. Because the land was not sold to a nonmember before S was deconsolidated, the intercompany item is $30, the corresponding item is $0 and the recomputed corresponding item is $0. Because S was sold, the matching rule is no longer applicable. S was required to take its intercompany gain into account immediately before becoming a nonmember. The group recognized and reported a $30 gain on the sale of the S stock.

The intercompany transaction rules contain many specific rules that apply to particular situations. These include rules for intercompany debt, transactions involving member stock, boot in intercompany transactions, and inter-company to non-intercompany status shifts. You should study the particular rules that apply to your transaction in addition to considering the general concepts applied to intercompany transactions. The regulations' preambles provide good foundational materials.

Note that Regulations section 1.1502-13(h) provides anti-avoidance rules. This section is reminiscent of section 269, as it provides that if a transaction is structured with a principal purpose to avoid the purposes of the intercompany transaction regulations, then adjustments must be made to carry out those purposes.

Section 15.08 The Basis Investment Adjustment Rules

Section 15.08(a) Introduction

The underlying concept of the basis investment adjustment rules in Regulations section 1.1502-32 is quite simple: a subsidiary's outside or stock basis should be adjusted to reflect changes in its inside basis. If that outside basis is not adjusted, economic distortions will occur. The basis investment rules ensure that the basis one group member has in another member's stock reflects the fluctuating investment of that member.

Example: P transferred $100 to S, a newly-created corporation, in exchange for all the S stock. The transaction qualified under section 351, and the two corporations elected to file a consolidated return. P's original basis in its S stock is $100. During the first year of consolidation, S earned $100, which was included in the group's consolidated taxable income. P then sold its S stock for its $200 value. Unless P is allowed to adjust its basis in the S stock to include the income recognized by S, P will recognize a gain of $100 on its sale of S stock. As a result, the S income would be taxed twice.

P could avoid double taxation by having S distribute a $100 dividend, which will reduce the S stock value and eliminate P's gain. Section 243 would give P a 100 percent dividends received deduction. The basis investment rules give the same result without requiring S to distribute assets. P increases its basis in S stock to $200 to reflect the S income. P then recognizes no gain on its sale of S stock.

The basis adjustment rules also work in reverse by requiring P to reduce its basis if S recognizes a loss. Otherwise, P could receive a double deduction.

Section 15.08(b) Adjustments to Basis

Before 1994, the basis investment rules were keyed to the subsidiary's E&P. In 1994, the regulations were changed to de-link subsidiary basis adjustments from E&P because the prior linkage did not produce the desired results. The current regulations provide for adjusting the subsidiary's basis with respect to four items: (1) taxable income or loss; (2) tax-exempt income; (3) noncapital, nondeductible expenses; and (4) distributions with respect to the subsidiary's stock.[8]

When a parent corporation receives a tax benefit attributable to its ownership of subsidiary stock, its basis should generally be decreased. Noncapital, nondeductible expenses represent a decline in the subsidiary's wealth. The regulations increase the parent corporation's basis by the amount of these disallowed expenses. This taxpayer-favorable rule effectively provides backdoor deductibility of those expenses. A similar rule applies to tax-exempt income. When a subsidiary receives tax-exempt income, the basis of the subsidiary stock should generally be increased.

Example: P created S with a $100 investment. S earned $100 in tax-exempt income, which increased its value to $200. P is allowed to increase its basis in S stock to $200. Unless P was permitted to make this adjustment, it could be taxed P on S's tax-exempt income.[9]

The regulations provide for a basis decrease for distributions made by the subsidiary. As was discussed in Chapter 7, section 243 provides a 100 percent deduction for dividends received from an affiliated subsidiary. A distribution that reduces the subsidiary's wealth increases the wealth of the parent corporation. The parent's basis for the subsidiary stock is decreased to reflect this nontaxable accession of wealth. Without this adjustment, the parent would be able to shelter gain or recognize loss when it sold the subsidiary's stock.

Example: P formed S with $100 in contributions. S earned $100 in the year of its formation, which resulted in P's basis increasing to $200. S then distributed $100 to P (nontaxable under section 243). P must decrease its basis in the S stock to $100, as it has effectively received that amount tax-free. Otherwise, P would be able to recognize a noneconomic loss of $100 when it sells the S stock.

Section 15.09 Loss Disallowance Regulations

Regulations section 1.1502-20 was promulgated to prevented a so-called duplicate loss deduction. It prevented a parent from deducting a loss when it

---

8. Treas. Reg. § 1.1502-32(b)(2).
9. Treas. Reg. § 1.1502-32(b)(5) (Example 3).

deconsolidated a subsidiary. In 2001, the Federal Circuit invalidated the regulations as being outside the scope of section 1502.[10]

In the American Jobs Creation Act of 2004, Congress responded by amending the underlying statute. Section 1502 now includes the following language: "In carrying out the preceding sentence, the Secretary may prescribe rules that are different from the provisions of chapter 1 that would apply if such corporations filed separate returns." The term "preceding sentence" refers to the broad authority granted the IRS and Treasury to promulgate legislation under section 1502.

---

10. *See Rite Aid Corp. v. United States*, 255 F.3d 1357 (Fed. Cir. 2001), *citing Schuler Industries, Inc. v. United States*, 109 F.3d 753 (Fed. Cir. 1997). For a discussion of the *Rite Aid* case, see Mombrun & Johnson, *Loss Disallowance Post-*Rite Aid: *The IRS and Treasury Revisit the Treatment of Subsidiary Stock Losses*, Taxes, May 2003, at 21.

TABLE OF CASES

Baan v. Commissioner, 45 T.C. 71 (1965), 147

Commissioner v. Baan, 382 F.2d 485 (9th Cir. 1967), 147

American Bantam Car Co. v. Commissioner, 11 T.C. 397 (1948), aff'd per curiam, 177 F.2d 513 (3rd Cir. 1949), cert denied, 399 U.S. 920 (1950), 20

Helvering v. Bashford, 302 U.S. 454 (1938), 232

Bausch & Lomb Optical Co. v. CIR, 267 F.2d 75 (2d Cir. 1959), cert. denied, 361 US 835 (1959), 218, 244

Berner v. United States, 282 F.2d 720 (Ct. Cl. 1960), 228

Cerone v. Commissioner, 87 T.C. 1 (1986), 98

Culligan Water Conditioning of Tri-Cities v. United States, 567 F.2d 867 (9th Cir. 1978), 44

United States v. Davis, 397 U.S. 301 (1970), 115

Dillard v. Commissioner, 20 T.C.M. 137 (1961), 37

E.I. Dupont de Nemours and Co. v. United States, 471 F.2d 1211 (Ct. Cl. 1973), 38

Eisner v. Macomber, 252 U.S. 189 (1920), 91, 92

Esmark, Inc. v. Commissioner, 90 T.C. 171 (1988), 44

Fin Hay Realty Co. v. United States, 398 F.2d 694 (3d Cir. 1968), 66

General Utilities & Operating Co. v. Helvering, 296 U.S. 200 (1935), 139, 169, 191, 225, 230, 231, 266

Commissioner v. Gordon, 391 U.S. 83 (1968), 47

Gregory v. Helvering, 293 U.S. 465 (1935), 18, 19, 147, 201

Halliburton v. Commissioner, 78 F.2d 265 (9th Cir. 1935), 37

Hanson v. U.S., 338 F. Supp. 602 (D. Mont. 1971), 159

Hickok v. Commissioner, 32 T.C. 80 (1959), 228

Holstein v. Commissioner, 23 T.C. 923 (1955), 37

Hurst v. Commissioner, 124 T.C. 16 (2005), 110

Intermountain Lumber Co. v. Commissioner, 65 T.C. 1025 (1976), 21

James Armour, Inc. v. Commissioner, 43 T.C. 295 (1964), 81

John Kelley Co. v. Commissioner, 326 U.S. 521 (1946), 66

Kimbell-Diamond Milling Co. v. Commissioner, 14 T.C. 74 (1950), aff'd per curiam, 187 F.2d 718 (5th Cir. 1951), cert. den. 342 U.S. 827 (1951), 266

King Enterprises, Inc. v. United States, 418 F.2d 511 (Ct. Cl. 1969), 20

Kohler Co. v. United States, 124 F.3d 1451 (Fed. Cir. 1997), 304

Lessinger v. Commissioner, 872 F.2d 519 (2d Cir. 1989), 50

Metzger Trust v. Commissioner, 76 T.C. 42 (1981), aff'd, 693 F.2d 459 (5th Cir. 1982), cert. denied, 463 U.S. 1207 (1983), 98

Commissioner v. Neustadt's Trust, 131 F.2d 528 (2d Cir. 1942), 227

Penfield v. Davis, 105 F. Supp. 292 (N.D. Ala. 1952), aff'd, 205 F.2d 798 (5th Cir. 1953), 228

Peracchi v. Commissioner, 143 F.3d 487 (9th Cir. 1998), 50

Portland Oil Co. v. Commissioner, 109 F.2d 479 (1st Cir.), cert. den., 310 U.S. 650 (1940), 37

Pulliam v. Commissioner. 73 T.C.M. (CCH) 3052 (1997), 150

Rite Aid Corp. v. United States, 255 F.3d 1357 (Fed. Cir. 2001), 191, 317

Schoo v. Commissioner, 47 B.T.A. 459 (1942), 228

Schuler Industries, Inc. v. United States, 109 F.3d 753 (Fed. Cir. 1997), 317

Superior Oil Co. v. Mississippi, 280 U.S. 390 (1930), 19

South Tulsa Pathology Lab. v. Commissioner, 118 T.C. 84 (2002), 189

Commissioner v. Turnbow, 286 F.2d 669 (9th Cir. 1960), aff'd on other issues, 368 U.S. 337 (1961), 216

U. S. Padding Corp. v. Commissioner, 88 T.C. 177 (1987), aff'd, 865 F.2d 750 (6th Cir. 1989), 303, 304

United States v. Vogel Fertilizer Co., 455 U.S. 16 (1982), 296

West Coast Marketing Corp. v. Commissioner, 46 T.C. 32 (1966), 60

Table of Revenue Rulings

Rev. Rul. 55-36, 1955-1 C.B. 340, 60
Rev. Rul. 56-117, 1956-1 C.B. 180, 146
Rev. Rul. 56-613, 1956-2 C.B. 212, 215
Rev. Rul. 57-126, 1957-1 C.B. 123, 163
Rev. Rul. 57-464, 1957-2 C.B. 244, 157
Rev. Rul. 57-492, 1957-2 C.B. 247, 157
Rev. Rul. 57-518, 1957-2 C.B. 253, 220
Rev. Rul. 59-197, 1959-1 C.B. 77, 150
Rev. Rul. 59-259, 1959-2 C.B. 115, 43
Rev. Rul. 63-104, 1963-1 C.B. 172, 310
Rev. Rul. 63-260, 1963-2 C.B. 147, 146
Rev. Rul. 64-56, 1964-1 C.B. 133, 37
Rev. Rul. 66-204, 1966-2 C.B. 113, 158
Rev. Rul. 66-365, 1966-2 C.B. 116, 156
Rev. Rul. 67-274, 1967-2 C.B. 141, 205
Rev. Rul. 67-448, 1967-2 C.B. 144, 215
Rev. Rul. 68-55, 1968-1 C.B. 140, 52
Rev. Rul. 68-603, 1968-2 C.B. 148, 169
Rev. Rul. 68-629, 1968-2 C.B. 154, 50
Rev. Rul. 69-3, 1969-1 C.B. 103, 37, 202
Rev. Rul. 69-156, 1969-1 C.B. 101, 38
Rev. Rul. 69-182, 1969-1 C.B. 218, 303
Rev. Rul. 69-357, 1969-1 C.B. 101, 37
Rev. Rul. 69-516, 1969-2 C.B. 56, 228
Rev. Rul. 69-608, 1969-2 C.B. 42, 135
Rev. Rul. 70-18, 1970-1 C.B. 74, 146
Rev. Rul. 70-240, 1970-1 C.B. 81, 225
Rev. Rul. 70-379, 1970-2 C.B. 179, 304
Rev. Rul. 70-434, 1970-2 C.B. 83, 169
Rev. Rul. 70-598, 1970-2 C.B. 168, 257
Rev. Rul. 71-523, 1971-2 C.B. 326, 303
Rev. Rul. 71-383, 1971-2 C.B. 180, 148
Rev. Rul. 71-593, 1971-2 C.B. 181, 146
Rev. Rul. 72-405, 1972-2 C.B. 217, 204
Rev. Rul. 73-234, 1973 C.B. 180, 158
Rev. Rul. 73-237, 1973-1 C.B. 184, 159

Rev. Rul. 74-91, 1974-1 C.B. 252, 310
Rev. Rul. 74-378, 1974-2 C.B. 287, 310
Rev. Rul. 74-545, 1974-2 C.B. 122, 225
Rev. Rul. 76-385, 1976-2 C.B. 92, 116
Rev. Rul. 77-415, 1977-2 C.B. 311, 228
Rev. Rul. 77-479, 1977-2 C.B. 119, 228
Rev. Rul. 78-286, 1978-2 C.B. 145, 202
Rev. Rul. 78-383, 1978-2 C.B. 142, 151
Rev. Rul. 79-394, 1979-2 C.B. 141, 159, 160
Rev. Rul. 80-181, 1980-2 C.B. 121, 159–160
Rev. Rul. 82-20, 1982-1 C.B. 6, 180
Rev. Rul. 82-34, 1982-1 C.B. 59, 228
Rev. Rul. 82-219, 1982-2 C.B. 82, 163
Rev. Rul. 84-44, 1984-1 C.B. 105, 38
Rev. Rul. 85-164, 1985-2 C.B. 117, 52
Rev. Rul. 86-4, 1986-1 C.B. 174, 151
Rev. Rul. 86-126, 1986-2 C.B. 58, 159
Rev. Rul. 88-48, 1988-1 C.B. 117, 220
Rev. Rul. 89-18, 1989-1 C.B. 14, 180
Rev. Rul. 89-27, 1989-1 C.B. 106, 159
Rev. Rul. 89-57, 1989-1 C.B. 90, 120
Rev. Rul. 91-70, 1991-2 C.B. 361, 300
Rev. Rul. 92-17, 1992-1 C.B. 142, 160, 161
Rev. Rul. 96-29, 1996-1 C.B. 50, 230
Rev. Rul. 2000-5, 2000-1 C.B. 436, 206
Rev. Rul. 2001-24, 2001-1 C.B. 1290, 232
Rev. Rul. 2001-25, 2001-1 C.B. 1291, 213
Rev. Rul. 2001-39, 2001-2 C.B. 125, 304
Rev. Rul. 2001-46, 2001-2 C.B. 321, 205
Rev. Rul. 2002-1, 2002-2 I.R.B. 268, 299, 188, 323
Rev. Rul. 2002-49, 2002-2 C.B. 288, 161
Rev. Rul. 2002-85, 2002-2 C.B. 986, 232

Rev. Rul. 2003-48, 2003-19 I.R.B. 863,
323, 154, 155, 165, 191, 228, 230
Rev. Rul. 2003-74, 2003-29 I.R.B. 77, 165
Rev. Rul. 2003-75, 2003-29 I.R.B. 79, 165

Rev. Rev. Rul. 2003-110, 2003-46 I.R.B.
1083, 165
Rev. Rul. 2004-23, 2004-11 I.R.B. 585,
168

TABLE OF REVENUE PROCEDURES

Rev. Proc. 77-37, 1977-2 C.B. 568, 220

Rev. Proc. 81-70, 1981-2 C.B. 729, 243, 248

Rev. Proc. 83-59, 1983-2 C.B. 575, 39

Rev. Proc. 86-42, 1986-2 C.B. 722, 217

Rev. Proc. 89-50, 1989-2 C.B. 631, 225

Rev. Proc. 91-11, 1991-1 C.B. 470, 310

Rev. Proc. 95-11, 1995-1 C.B. 505, 310

Rev. Proc. 95-39, 1995-2 C.B. 399, 311

Rev. Proc. 96-30, 1996-1 C.B. 696, 160, 164

Rev. Proc. 2002-32, 2002-1 C.B. 959, 299

Rev. Proc. 2003-48, 2003-29 I.R.B. 86,
154, 155, 165, 191, 228, 230, 322

Rev. Proc. 2005-1, 2005-1 I.R.B. 1, 9, 10

Rev. Proc. 2005-3, 2005-1 I.R.B. 118, 10

Rev. Proc. 2006-1, 2006-1 I.R.B. 1, 9

INDEX

accounting methods, 28, 92–93, 264, 282, 284, 286, 308
acquiring corporation, 122, 124, 131, 133, 164, 179, 196, 201–203, 205–209, 211, 213–221, 227, 231–232, 237–239, 241–242, 246–248, 250, 266, 279–281, 283–286, 299
acquisition period, 267, 269, 272, 274–275
active trade or business, 151, 156–164, 171, 192–193, 277
affiliated group, 79, 173, 203, 293, 298, 300–303, 305, 307
Association, 39–40
assumption of liabilities, 48, 53, 178, 217
attribution rules, 96–98, 100–103, 105, 110, 112–113, 115–116, 121, 123, 131–134, 184
  family attribution, 96–98, 104–105, 110, 112–113, 184
  attribution from entities, 98, 101
    estates, 98, 101
    Partnerships, 99,
    S corporations 102, 113, 122, 205, 211
    Trusts, 99–100,
    C corporations, 100
  attribution to entities, 101
    estates, 98
    Partnerships, 101
    S corporations, 101
    Trusts, 99–100, 102
    C corporations, 102
  option attributions 103
basis, 6, 14, 33–35, 39, 44, 47–57, 61, 71, 73–74, 76–77, 79–88, 91, 93–94, 125, 127–134, 142–143, 154, 172, 177–186, 188, 190, 192, 207, 210–212, 214, 230, 238–240, 242–249, 251–257, 260–273, 275–279, 286
binding commitment test, 20–21, 44
Boot, 14, 47, 145, 155, 177–178, 182–185, 218, 226–227, 241, 314
business purpose, 18–20, 60, 149–150, 152–155, 165–168, 172, 174, 178, 180, 182, 184,
191, 201–202, 208–209, 213, 228
capital loss, 183, 253, 257, 264, 282–285
carryover of tax items, 248
check-the-box regulations, 31
combined group, 293, 296–297
consistency period, 267, 274–275
consolidated returns, 9, 27, 53, 180, 189, 211, 293, 298–301, 304–305, 307
constructive ownership, 97–98, 105–109, 121, 224, 253, 287, 295
continuity of business enterprise, 14, 164, 201, 203, 208, 213, 228, 237
continuity of interest, 14, 60, 143, 164, 201–202, 208, 213, 224, 228–230
control group issues, 45
controlled corporation, 140, 143–153, 155, 160–163, 165–166, 170–174, 177, 179–193, 223, 232, 280, 294, 296–297
corporate business purpose, 149, 152–153, 166, 168, 174
corporate deductions, 28–29, 139
corporate formation, 33
corporate taxable year, 30
debt-equity, 65
deemed asset purchase 252
device, 143, 147–156, 158–159, 165–166, 172, 180, 192
  device factors, 148, 152–153
  non-device factors, 148, 152
disaffiliation, 299, 302, 310
disproportionate distribution, 88, 90
disregarded entity, 31, 206–207, 209–210, 215
distributing corporation, 72, 78, 140, 143–155, 160–161, 165, 168–174, 177, 189–193, 249, 256, 264
double tax regime, 17, 25–26, 78, 148, 150–151, 169
drop downs, 232–233
economic rationale, 15, 243
end result test, 20, 44
E&P, 14, 25, 51, 61, 64, 71–77, 80–84, 87, 91–94, 124–135, 147–150, 152–156, 158,

165–166, 180, 184, 186, 189, 192, 207, 227, 242, 247, 249, 256, 261, 264, 282, 284–285, 315–316
accumulated, 74–77, 81, 93, 153, 264,
current, 74, 81, 93, 125, 153–154, 264, 316
financial accounting, 92
general counsel memorandum (GCM), 10
General Utilities, 139, 169, 191, 225, 230–231, 266
holding period, 34, 54, 57, 71, 73, 78–80, 86, 91, 142, 185, 238, 246, 248–250, 257, 264, 269, 274, 278–279
hybrid instruments, 67
independent contractors, 157–159
individual deductions, 28
insurance group, 293, 297, 302–303
intercompany transactions, 308, 313–315
investment company, 57–59, 79, 156, 158, 234–236
Kimbell-diamond, 266
loss corporation, 226, 286, 287–290
loss disallowance rule, 253–254
loss limitation, 286
method of accounting, 30–31, 92
Morris Trust, 169–170, 172
mutual interdependence, 20, 44
NOL carryover, 282, 284, 287–288, 308
non-qualified preferred stock, 40–43
non-recently purchased stock, 273
recently purchased stock, 267, 273
non-Redemption dispositions, 128
Options, 147, 188, 300–302, 308
ownership change, 226, 287, 289–290
party to a reorganization, 236–237, 239
person, 28, 36, 39, 41–42, 46, 97, 103, 110, 121, 129, 143, 171–173
personal holding company, 256
plan of reorganization, 18, 280–281
preferred stock, 40–43, 47, 51–52, 79, 89–91, 121, 124–127, 129, 144, 146, 181-183, 226, 240
private letter rulings (PLRs), 9–10, 14, 154–158, 160, 162, 165, 167, 191, 217, 219–220, 225, 230, 283, 309–310
property, 14, 17, 33–61, 66, 71–74, 78–84, 86–89, 91–93, 95–96, 118, 120, 122–126, 130–133, 135, 139–140, 145, 154, 158–159, 163, 169–170, 172, 177–183, 185, 187–190, 206, 208, 210–211, 217–218, 221, 227, 234, 236, 238–250, 252–257, 259–260, 262–264, 268, 274–275, 277–278, 280, 282, 286, 303, 313–314
publicly traded, 26, 95, 116, 153, 168, 235,

push ups, 232–233
qualified distribution, 114
recapitalization, 146, 196, 225–226, 240, 280
reconsolidation, 299
redeeming corporation, 129–130
redemption, 40, 42, 71, 74, 90, 95–135, 148, 155, 189–190, 203, 258–259, 300
related party, 253–254
remote continuity, 232
reorganization, 18, 20, 39, 60–61, 71, 115, 125, 142, 149–150, 164, 176–179, 186–187, 195–197, 203, 205, 207–209, 211, 244, 246–250, 276–277, 280–281, 283–285, 288–289, 300, 308, 311
A reorganization, 195, 205, 289,
B reorganization, 195, 199, 201, 205, 214–217, 248, 280
C reorganization, 176, 195–196, 199, 201, 205, 216–223, 280, 285, 289
D reorganization, 142, 176–177, 179, 186, 199, 201, 221–225, 232–233, 240, 289
E reorganization, 200–201, 228,
F reorganization, 200–201, 228–231, 283–284,
G reorganization, 200, 231–232, 240, 280
Triangular A reorganization, 201, 221,
Forward triangular merger, 208, 211–214
Reverse triangular merger, 212–214
section 306 stock, 108, 124–129, 131–132
solely for voting stock requirement, 156, 205, 217, 224, 226
spin-off, 140, 144, 146, 149–152, 160, 163–164, 167–168, 170–172, 175, 180, 185–186, 188–190, 201
split-off, 140, 184–185
split-up, 140
step transaction, 16, 18, 20, 43–45, 146, 201–203, 205, 215, 218, 220–221, 224, 233, 267, 276
substance over form, 16–18, 20, 45, 146, 170, 228, 305
substantially all requirement, 208, 218–219, 223
tax attributes, 61, 93, 186, 188–190, 192, 246–249, 261, 264, 270, 279–290, 299
tax doctrines, 15
tax policy, 15, 25
tax rates, 25, 29–30, 127, 148, 156, 183, 242
technical advice memorandum (TAM), 10
The American Jobs Creation Act of 2004, 5, 40, 50, 55, 61, 179, 192, 250, 263, 276, 295, 317
title, 11, 59, 197, 231, 241
warrants, 147, 241, 300–301
widely held, 153, 238, 248